FORMAL MODELS AND PRACTICAL TOOLS FOR INFORMATION SYSTEMS DESIGN

IFIP Working Conference on
Formal Models and Practical Tools
for Information Systems Design
Oxford, U.K., April 17-20, 1979

organized by
IFIP Technical Committee 8,
Information Systems
International Federation for Information Processing

NORTH-HOLLAND PUBLISHING COMPANY
AMSTERDAM • NEW YORK • OXFORD

FORMAL MODELS AND PRACTICAL TOOLS FOR INFORMATION SYSTEMS DESIGN

Proceedings of the IFIP TC-8 Working Conference on
Formal Models and Practical Tools for Information Systems Design
Oxford, U.K., April 17-20, 1979

edited by

Hans-Jochen SCHNEIDER
Technische Universität Berlin
F.R.G.

1979

NORTH-HOLLAND PUBLISHING COMPANY
AMSTERDAM • NEW YORK • OXFORD

ISBN: 0 444 85394 4

Published by:
NORTH-HOLLAND PUBLISHING COMPANY – AMSTERDAM • NEW YORK • OXFORD

Sole distributors for the U.S.A. and Canada
ELSEVIER NORTH-HOLLAND, INC.
52 Vanderbilt Avenue
New York, N.Y. 10017

Library of Congress Cataloging in Publication Data

IFIP TC-8 Working Conference on Formal Models and
Practical Tools for Information Systems Design,
Oxford, Eng., 1979.
Formal models and practical tools for information
symtems design.

"Organized by IFIP Technical Committee 8, Informations
Systems, International Federation for Information Processing."
1. Information storage and retrieval systems--
Congresses. 2. Formal languages--Congresses. 3. Electronic digital computers--Programming--Congresses.
I. Schneider, Hans-Jochen. II. International Federation
for Information Processing. Committee on Information
Systems. III. Title.

Z699.A1I16 1979 029 79-19860

PRINTED IN THE NETHERLANDS

TABLE OF CONTENTS

PREFACE

In 1975, the general assembly of IFIP (International Federation of Information Processing) initiated a new Technical Committee TC 8 with the name "Information Systems". In 1976, the Working Group WG 8.1 on "Design and Evaluation of Information Systems" started work and established the following scope and aims

Scope

The scope of the working group is the development of approaches for the analysis, design, specification and evaluation of computer-assisted information systems.

Aims

The aims of the working group are:

1) to identify concepts and to develop theories relevant to the design of information systems;
2) to develop methods and tools for applying these theories to the design process;
3) to develop methods for the specification of information needs within an enterprise, with emphasis on interface aspects;
4) to develop methodologies for evaluating proposals for information systems;
5) to develop methodologies for evaluating the operational effectiveness of information systems.

In 1977 the Working Group WG 8.2 on "The Interaction of Information Systems and the Organization" was officially approved.

In Oxford in April 1979, WG 8.1 held his first Working Conference. The title of this conference was "Formal models and practical tools for information systems design". The aim was to address special research and development problems within the scope and aims of the Working Group WG 8.1.

The conference concerned itself specifically with that branch of information systems which deals with the development of formal models and practical tools for information systems analysis, design, realization and evaluation. Emphasis was placed on

Requirement Definition

- Involving the end-user in the requirement definition.
- Formal models and formal languages for stating requirements.
- Transparency of the requirement specification. Documentation and representation problems.
- Tools for analysis and evaluation of requirement specifications.
- Methods for handling systems complexity in information systems analysis and design.
- The role of data semantics in requirement definition.

- Methods for integrating different users views of the information system.
- The use of system prototypes, based on simplifying assumptions about the system, for development of precise requirement specifications.
- (Any) special problems in modelling highly interactive systems?
- The role of requirement specifications in making decisions on the structure of the application environment.
- Involving the end-user in the development of priorities and planning horizons of the information system development project.

Requirements and Software Systems

- Comprehensive methodology for information system design, development and operation.
- Methods for controlling that a proposed software system design meets the stated requirements.
- (How) should changes in the software system be reflected in the requirement specification during debugging and maintenance?
- Methods for utilizing requirement specifications in software systems design, e.g. for software production, consistency testing.
- Methods for testing that software system changes are consistent with the stated requirements.
- Methods for controlling evolution in the requirement specifications and the corresponding implementation of software extensions and software changes, i.e. methods for enhancing systems flexibility.
- Automatic software generation based on direct use of the requirement specifications.

Experimental Evaluation of Methods and Tools of the Systems Analyst and Designer

- Comparative studies of methods and tools. Studies concerning method proposals and studies concerning well established methods and tools are of equal importance.
- The relative importance of new methods and tools on the overall economy of the development, operation and maintenance of an information system.

Computer-assisted information systems, and their components, are becoming of ever increasing interest in our society. The data processing community has evolved towards a recognition of the importance of tools for handling large masses of data. However, the introduction and utilization of such tools for building information systems is not the end of the story. Users are now realising a need for tools which support the complete problem definition and solution process. Specifically such tools are needed when designing and installing information systems in industry, civil service, and in all other environments where such systems are used.

The fourteen papers presented represent a significant contribution to the scope and aims of WG 8.1 as listed above. Some ninety top-ranking professionals from 15 countries and from various groups such as industry, computer manufacturers, research institutes and universities were invited to participate in the conference. Presentations were given by well-known experts from main organizations and Universities in Europe and America.

The 36 papers submitted were reviewed by the Program Committee members

Chairman	A. Sølvberg	Norway
Members	F. Bodart	Belgium
	G. Bracchi	Italy
	M. Klein	France
	P. Kovaćs	Hungary
	F.F. Land	U.K.
	C. McGowan	U.S.A.
	H.-J. Schneider	Fed.Rep.Germany
	H.G. Sol	Holland
	F.Stella de R. Germano	Brazil
	A.I. Wasserman	U.S.A.

who together with the Organizing Committee members

Chairman	R.K. Stamper	U.K.
Members	P. Atkinson	U.K.
	H. Ellis	U.K.
	C. Marks	U.K.
	W. Olle	U.K.

prepared the conference with the general chairmanship of Prof. A.S. Douglas. We are also indebted to the Principal and Fellows of St. Edmond Hall for their hospitality and to the London School of Economics for its valuable contribution. The greatest part of the administrative load was taken by Mary Eades and Buffy Gibons.

The help of a member of very well-known specialist provided the basis for the success of this conference. I would like to thank all of them very much for their contributions.

I hope that this book provides a challenge to the information system community and a stimulus to researchers, implementers and users.

June 1979

Hans-Jochen Schneider

Technische Universität Berlin

Formal Models and Practical Tools for Information Systems Design
H.-J. Schneider, Editor
North-Holland Publishing Company

TOOLS FOR INFORMATION SYSTEM DESIGN AND REALIZATION

B.E.Meyer, H.-J. Schneider

Institut für Angewandte Informatik, Fachbereich Informatik,
Technische Universität Berlin, Otto-Suhr-Allee 18/20
D-1000 Berlin 10

The paper is concerned with requirements for an information system in a multi-user environment of an industrial or administrational institution and with an approach to meet these requirements by a method and model base system called BOSS. The system presented consists of the following basic components: a method base system, a model base system, a data base system, interfaces to modules of a program library and to external programs, a dialog system as a very comfortable user interface, and a monitor system for the control and communication between these components.

1. INTRODUCTION

Today we can recognize two essential trends of information system developments: The so-called application based information systems and the generalized information systems. The application based systems disclaim universality, they are systems for specific areas, e.g. medicine, building industry, jurisprudence, special branch systems, etc. As a part of generalized information systems the data base systems are well established today, but the development of methodologies and concepts for method or model base systems is just at the beginning. This paper will deal with the latter systems.

Data processing in the past was determined by the fact that different programs written in different programming languages had been developed for one application environment (e.g. an industry firm or an administrational institution) and that within one computer system different data bases, model bases or method bases together with specific user interfaces had been established. Therefore the need for so-called 'integrated solutions', i.e. the creation of generalized information systems, is recognized. In this context tools have to be provided to support the integration and to unify the handling of the different system components.

Looking some years ahead one can have complete problem solution support systems (PSSS) which are tools supporting the whole problem solution process just from the beginning. First you will define your terminology precisely, then you will fix which words in your application field are of interest and which are not (semi-automatic thesaurus construction). After this you will define the important relations in your problem area. Which relations should be activities and which informations, personal, material is needed to run an activity and which information, material is produced by an activity (precedence structure). This will be described on several levels, the problem will be broken down to a program-specification level. Now you will be able to define for restricted problem classes all informations you need to specify what a program has to do. You do not have to say how this has to be done, you can remain on a non-procedural or descriptive level. Generator programs create the source code in a procedural language (such as ALGOL, BASIC, COBOL, FORTRAN, PL/1, RPG II) and on this level special supplements can be made in a computer-assisted manner.

With such systems the whole problem solution process is computer-assisted and documented. You will have simultaneously interfaces generated to file or data base systems, to data base design aid systems and data dictionaries. The organization, the project-management and the data processing tasks are described in a common language, those will be no problem in the communications of data processing and application people. Consistency checks on each level of refinement will provide a faster and better problem solution.

The terms model and method base are used in the literature more and more frequently. (cf. [4], [10], [11], [12], [21]). There are many definitions of these two concepts. As we are in a very new research field it is very difficult to define these concepts precisely. Nevertheless we will try to give a short description: A method and model base system is a system which enables the casual user (cf. chapter 3) in a multi-user environment to solve his problems easily and fast with a minimum of programming efforts and a maximum of system support.

The terms method and model have a very general meaning, therefore it is not possible to define these terms in such a manner that all meanings are covered. We will use the term method in the sense of basic algorithms and procedures which are utilized in interdisciplinary subject areas. Examples of such methods are basic algorithms in statistics, mathematics, economy. Models we will use in the sence of mappings of the real world which can be described by equations (linear, non-linear equations, difference and differential equations) or graphs for example.

This paper is concerned with the requirements for such generalized systems within an industrial or administrational institution and with an approach to meet these requirements by the method and model base system BOSS (Berlin method and mOdel baSe System). The design concepts and the realization are discussed.

First we will give a historical overview to the way of development starting with classical data processing via file processing up to data base, method and model base processing. The method and model base system presented consists of the following components: a method base, a model base, a data base, interfaces to a program library and to external program, a user interface and a monitor system for the control and communication between these components. The requirements for such a system with respect to different user groups (e.g. method and model base administrator, application programmer or the casual user) are discussed (cf. chapter 3), the system architecture, the concepts and properties of single components are presented (cf. chapter 4). How to meet user requirements for very comfortable dialog systems with respect to method and model base systems and to different user classes is shown by the realization of our dialog interface (cf. chapter 5).

2. REMARKS ON THE HISTORY OF THE DEVELOPMENT OF DATA BASE, METHOD BASE AND MODEL BASE SYSTEMS

The following pictures represent only very rough the functional interrelationship between the corresponding components. In figure 1 the situation at the beginning of data processing in the mid-fifties is shown. Data descriptions, methods and eventually models were all integrated in the user program. The number of data was very limited, each user program was running seperately. The data were used for one user and one program at a time.

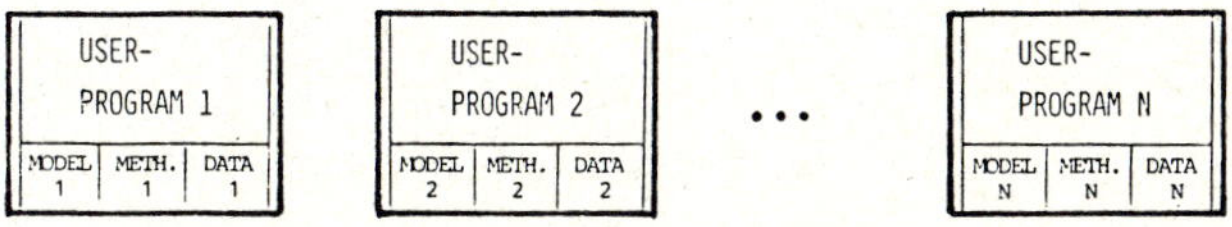

Fig. 1: Classical data processing

Then, in the beginning of the sixties, when monitor systems were first installed, user programs could be run with several data sets. The data were separated from the program but the physical data description remained in the program.

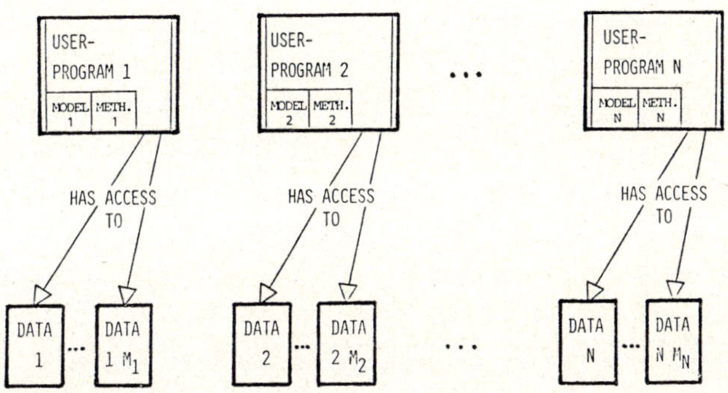

Fig. 2: Data processing with monitor systems

The number of persons engaged in data processing grew fast. The amount of data stored in the computer was increasing super-exponentially. Consequently data could not be used economically by one person alone. Data were used simultaneously by several users. To be able to handle these kinds of problems file management systems were introduced. The system architecture is described in figure 3. Several users are sharing the different data files. The physical data record description is still needed in the user programs.

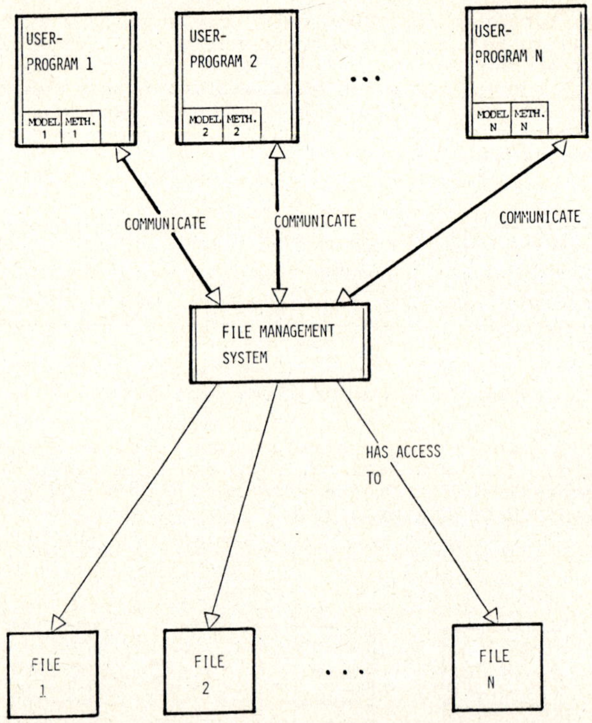

Fig. 3: File management system

A disadvantage of file management systems is on the one hand the redundancy and on the other - and this is more serious - the inconsistency of data, i.e. there is no support to keep the data consistent. By updating, the updating status of duplicates may be divergent. To guarantee the semantic consistency of data, data base systems were introduced (see figure 4). Same as in file management systems the user has no direct access to data, he has to communicate with the data base system which then delivers data to him or makes the required updates. The data base system is fully responsible for the consistency of the data base. In data base systems one gains the so-called data independence which means that user programs contain only the logical description of data structures and the corresponding operations running on these data structures. Only the data base system knows the physical description of the data structures and the corresponding access methods. The data base can be re-structured without influencing the user programs.

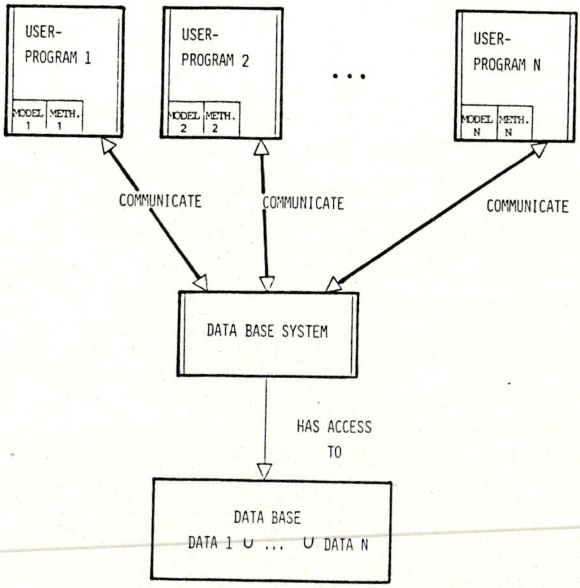

Fig. 4: Data base system architecture

The data base systems have helped us to get support in getting data independence which is very important in developing organisations. In addition to this data dictionaries within data base systems help us to understand the data base schema and the operations allowed.

With method base systems we will get support in handling methods consistently in a multi-user environment. The user will be guided by the system to his problem solution. The user need not have expert knowledge in every subject field. A rough description of the structure of method bases is given in figure 5.

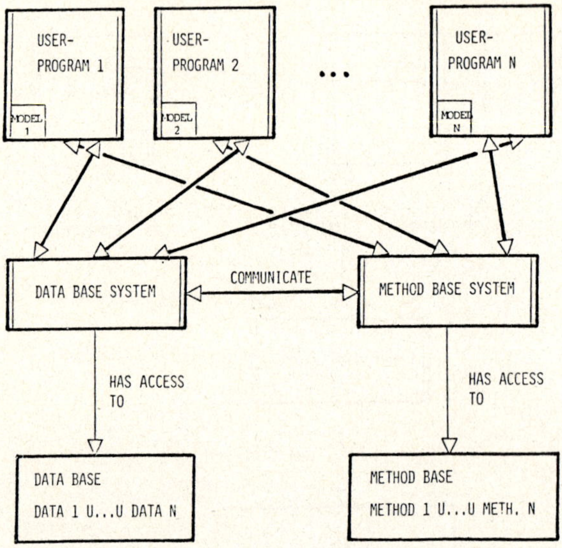

Fig. 5: Method base system architecture

The next step could be foreseen now. The programs will be independent of special models in a method and model base system environment.

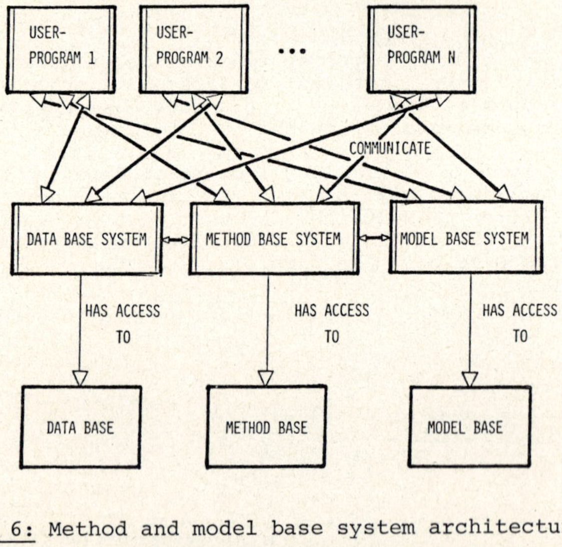

Fig. 6: Method and model base system architecture

We have gained independence, flexibility and multi-user access to data, method and model bases on the one hand, but on the other hand it is obvious that such software systems are very complex and difficult to handle. This complexity is the reason for the development of new ideas and methods for the planning and realization of such systems. To shorten the mass of concepts, of functions and the mass of software systems, it is necessary to come to an integration of these systems on the following levels:

- on the functional level,
- on a language level and
- on a system architecture level.

The following approach can be viewed as an attempt to satisfy the corresponding requirements and to solve the problems mentioned. Further possibilities to handle such complex systems are given in chapter 4.

3. REQUIREMENTS FOR A METHOD AND MODEL BASE SYSTEM

The necessity for a method and model base system is easily made plausible by means of a specific application example. If we constitute e.g. an information system for planning reasons within an operational environment of an industrial firm and if we want to run this system in the daily operation, we have to provide - among other things - tools for input, for validation, for manipulating the data of the firm etc. (cf. for example BLUMENTHAL [2]).

If we want to establish organizational models for planning we have to make available within the system mathematical methods, software-engineering instruments, simulation methods, possibilities for the verification, calibration, sensitivity analysis and validation of these models. Further tools are necessary which help to design and to maintain the layout of reports, and which generate reports automatically. To compare the real data with the planned data we need statistical methods, comparison measures etc.

Many authors have been concerned with the definition of requirements for such method and model base systems and with the motivation for these systems (cf. [4], [10],[11], [12], [18], [21]). In many papers these problems have been discussed very generally. We will focus on - in our opinion - most important requirements and we will try to show how to meet these requirements by practical tools.

The treatment of method and model base systems could not be performed without looking at the user who handles and utilizes these systems.

For the following we will distinguish between 3 user classes

1. the method and model base administrator,
2. the application programmer and system specialist,
3. the expert with respect to various application fields (e.g. the statistician, the manager, the engineer etc.) whom we will call the 'casual user'.

All these user classes are concerned with the system in some way and for all these users tools have to make available which allows these users to handle the system in an user-oriented and adequate way with respect to their knowledge.

In particular we would like to deal with the last-mentioned user class, the casual user, not only because this is the biggest user group, but also because the motivation for the establishment of method and model base systems is derived from this user environment. This user class within a multi-user environment should have the possibility to solve problems by a minimum expenditure of time and money and by a maximum system support in a very quick and easy way.

This user is not at the same time a specialist in matrices, in statistics, in investment models and data base systems, but he is a user who has heard about these things during his education and wants to have an adequate expert support by the system. The main task of these users is not the development of large programs but the solution of problems. This problem solving support should be guaranteed in an interactive way. A very important tool in this context is a comfortable dialog instrument. In addition this instrument can help the user in structuring his problems and generating models (see chapter 5).

These method and model base systems in particular are adequate tools for the analyst, the system designer, the planner, the scientist, the manager, the man of practice, the application-oriented man, the system trainer, the system evaluator.

Some years ago the development of data base systems was characterized by the fruitless discussion which system is the most user-friendly and best. After these discussions the data base people agreed upon what they called the 'coexistence view' (cf. [1], [15]). The essential point of this view is the attempt to have for the user views as much freedom as possible. Our opinion is that we should transfer these ideas also to method and model base systems, i.e. we should try to give this freedom to the user. Therefore we need methods for integrating different user views of information systems. We should diminish the conceptual distance between the user views and system's view.

This idea fits some of the requirements of WILL (cf.[21]) who stated that models should easily be adaptable to the changing needs of the users and that these models must reflect their problem view. In addition the method and model base system should provide the various users with the possibility for applying and creating models with respect to their tasks and their knowledge.

Further requirements to such systems are derived from the need to be supported by the system to come to a better problem solution. This could be satisfied by

- concepts and language elements which are easy to learn,
- comfortable fault detecting routines,
- comfortable consistency checks,
- improvement of the communication interface between user and machine and
- improved graphical interfaces.

If we look at the industry or the administration of the past, a lot of different information systems for analysis, decision or planning reasons had been developed. In various departments independent solutions by means of specific tailored models and methods had been produced. The interfaces to other departments or to other problem areas had not been realized. In addition these program packages have been written on the base of different methodologies and in different programming languages. Therefore the need to integrate such models and methods in an overall system and to realize the interfaces between single problem areas is obvious. By means of the last point the interrelations between different parts are considered to map real industrial or administrational processes in a more problem-adequate way. For this it is necessary to make software-technical support available by the system which allows the communication between different programs written in different languages. This communication (i. e. the realization of the interfaces) must be controlled by the system.

Beside the requirements of MERTENS (cf.[12]), namely for providing an extensive collection of methods, to support the user in selecting methods, to combine methods and models, to supply the models with the right parameters and data, to interprete and to document the results, it is necessary to give to the system the central control of the models and methods and the data base (see chapter 5). By means of this the consistency of the method and model applications is guaranteed.

The system has to take over the main part of the responsibility, so that the user is supported by the system in selecting, applying and manipulating methods which are necessary regarding specific problem solutions. For specific problem classes structured problem solving paths can be delivered by the computer, data and method dictionaries will inform the user about all available tools and possibilities of the system. The information in the dictionaries has to be installed by the specialists for the different subject areas.

The handling of models and methods should be accomplished in a uniform and consistent way. The independence and the flexibility of models and methods and their applications should be guaranteed.

With respect to models and methods we will formulate further requirements:

- models and methods of different programming languages should be inserted without the need of changes

- the model base should have the capability to integrate the so-called 'stand-alone-models' as well as 'interrelated' models (cf. chapter 4.2)

- models and methods should be self-descriptive, if they are not self-descriptive they should be completed by corresponding informations (s. chapter 4.2 and 5).

- models and methods should be easy to handle, to change, to insert etc.

Requirements for the system which should be really a matter of course are e.g.

. the transparency and structuredness of the system

. the system must be safe and robust

. the system must be easily changeable, evolvable and extensible.

Similar to the developments within the data base area where result-oriented and non-procedural data base languages have been developed, it is necessary for method and model base systems, to provide the user by powerful language tools. In the past the development of such languages had been neglected. It is true that we have some knowledge about the handling of method and model base systems today, we have obtained some insights into the functions of such systems, but we have not developed such integrated languages in practice.

There are functions and methods built in some programming languages and methods and models are used as procedure or function calls, but real integrated method and model base system languages are research matter of today.

The power of the tools in general allows the simple establishment of alternative solutions. The user has the possibility to control the solution process less or more depending on his wishes and needs.

Further the system should support the documentation, the user-oriented consistency checks and fault diagnosis during the problem solving processes.

4. SYSTEM ARCHITECTURE OF BOSS

4.1 Components of the system

Regarding the requirements for a method and model base system it is essential that the architecture of the system mentioned (cf.chapter 2) be modified. If we look at the model base system, the method base system and the data base system as self-contained and independent components, the interfaces between each other for communication and the corresponding processing and controlling structure has to be realized. For this reason we have developed a system monitor which performs and controls this communication between model, method and data base system on the one hand and the user on the other. In addition the interfaces to modules of the program library and to external programs has been established, also under the control of the monitor (cf. figure 7 and chapter 4.5).

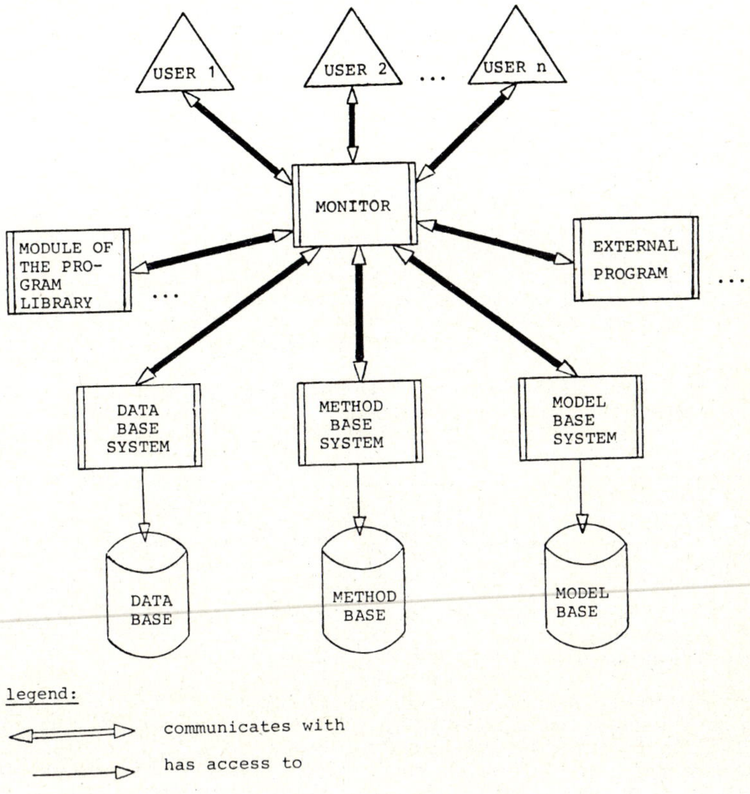

Fig. 7: System architecture of BOSS

Looking at the realization of interfaces between models itself it is possible to control and perform the communication by the monitor system also among different models written in different languages as parts of the model base (cf. chapter 4.6).

The monitor system of BOSS is also responsible for the control and processing of the user interfaces, i.e. the different dialog and language components with respect to different user views and user classes (cf. chapter 5).

The system has to ensure that any model, method or data can be added, changed or deleted, where - as mentioned above - models and methods can be written in different programming languages.

The cooperation of different types of models, e.g. a planning model for the marketing area or an actual control model on the one hand, a production or financial model on the other is made possible in a very flexible way. Methods and models can be handled in a very consistent and uniform way. Independence and flexibility of models and methods and their applications are guaranteed. The system implemented ensures a safe and robust development and handling of any model configuration.

With respect to the results of the dialog the monitor of BOSS performs all underlying instructions automatically or semi-automatically, i.e. applies a specific calibration method to a model, supplies the corresponding model with the correct data from the data base, produces specific outputs with results eventually dependent on specific user options.

Therefore the monitor system is not only responsible for all control and performing functions between models but also has the complete overall control and performing function, i.e. it is responsible for all system components, for the communication between these components, the user interfaces included. With respect to the different requirements for a method and model base system and with respect to different user groups (cf. chapter 3) there is a strong need for supporting the different kinds of users by the system.

This support is accomplished by information dectionaries integrated in the different components where the user can be informed - by order or if it is necessary automatically - of all functions of the dialog system, of available models, methods and data and the information dictionaries itself. These information dictionaries have been established with regard to the casual user who is able to 'learn' during dialog sessions by means of this feature.

4.2 Model base

As this system is installed in an university environment for research and teaching purposes different application areas are covered by models which are stored in the model base.

One of the main applications is the simulation of socio-economical processes within enterprises. There are some co-called '<u>stand-alone-models</u>' which describe and simulate a specific application field. These models are written in simulation languages like CSMP, DYNAMO, or SIMULA. For these self-contained models the interface to the data base, method base and to the user is realized by the monitor system.

One of these models is the IFICUS-System (cf. [19]) which simulates the operational processes within an enterprise by means of FORRESTER's continuous simulation methodology of SYSTEM DYNAMICS (cf. [5]). IFICUS can be viewed as a decision and forecast model for the top-management and middle-management level. It is available in a CSMP as well as in a DYNAMO version (testing reasons). The top-management-level describes the physical oriented cycle of goods and materials and the financial model which is represented by the balance facts. The interrelation between these two areas is given by the so-called 'function-area model' which combines the more physical oriented areas like marketing, management, production etc. by means of a budget on the one hand and the financial area by means of expenditures on the other. Decision rules and hypotheses are represented in the system, data, i.e. initial values, parameters and constants, are delivered by the corresponding data base (cf. chapter 4.4). The model becomes a very powerful prognosis instrument by observing the cause and effect relations also regarding future developments. Questions like "What happens with... (e.g. the liquidity), if ... (e.g. the budget for advertisments raises 10%)?" can be answered (cf.[19]). The aggregated top-management level consists of 34 level equations.

An extract of the IFICUS model (production part) is shown in figure 8.

```
        PRODUKTION


PBUD=INTGRL(PBUDAN,(PBUZU-PBUAB))                                         100 L
PBUDAN=500000                                                           100. 0 N
   PBUD   PRODUCTION BUDGET (DM)
   PBUDAN INITIAL VALUE OF PRODUCTION BUDGET (DM)
   PBUZU  INFLUX PRODUCTION BUDGET (DM)
   PBUAB  OUTFLUX OF PRODUCTION BUDGET (DM/WEEK)

PBUZU=PVARZU+PFIXZU                                                     100. 1 R
   PBUZU  INFLUX PRODUCTION BUDGET (DM)
   PVARZU VARIABLE PERCENTAGE OF INFLUX TO PRODUCTION BUDGET (DIMLES)
   PFIXZU FIXED PART OF INFLUX TO PRODUCTION BUDGET (DIMLES)

PBUAB=(FL+FM+FGV)*PR+FGKF                                               100. 2 R
FL=12.                                                                  100. 3 C
FM=80.                                                                  100. 4 C
FGV=10                                                                  100. 5 C
   PBUAB  OUTFLUX OF PRODUCTION BUDGET (DM/WEEK)
   FL     PRODUCTION WAGE (DM/PIECE)
   FM     STANDARD COSTS OF PRODUCTION MATERIAL (DM/PIECE)
   FGV    VARIABLE COMMON COSTS IN PRODUCTION (DM/WEEK)
   PR     PRODUCTION RATE (PIECE/WEEK)
   FGKF   FIXED COMMON COSTS IN PRODUCTION (DM)

PFIXZU=PPR*STHK*FIXTEL                                                    101 A
FIXTEL=0,6                                                              101. 0 C
   PFIXZU FIXED PART OF INFLUX TO PRODUCTION BUDGET (DIMLES)
   PPR    PLANNED PRODUCTION RATE (PIECE/WEEK)
   STHK   STANDARD COSTS OF MANUFACTURING (DM/PIECE).
   FIXTEL FIXED PERCENTAGE OF PRODUCTION BUDGET (DIMLES)

PAS=PPR/(PMABAN*ARANZ*PF)                                                 102 A
ARANZ=100                                                               102. 0 C
PF=0.115E-06                                                            102. 1 C
   PAS    PLANNED CAPACITY (HOURS/WEEK)
   PPR    PLANNED PRODUCTION RATE (PIECE/WEEK)
   PMABAN
   ARANZ  NUMBER OF WORKERS IN THE PRODUCTION PROCESS (MAN)
   PF     PRODUCTION FACTOR (PIECE/(DM*MAN*HOUR))

STHK=FM+FL+FGK                                                            103 A
FM=80.                                                                  103. 0 C
FL=12.                                                                  103. 1 C
   STHK   STANDARD COSTS OF MANUFACTURING (DM/PIECE)
   FM     STANDARD COSTS OF PRODUCTION MATERIAL (DM/PIECE)
   FL     PRODUCTION WAGE (DM/PIECE)
   FGK    COMMON COSTS IN PRODUCTION (DM/WEEK)

PVARZU=AR*STHK*VARTEL                                                     104 A
VARTEL=.4                                                               104. 0 C
   PVARZU VARIABLE PERCENTAGE OF INFLUX TO PRODUCTION BUDGET (DIMLES)
   AR
   STHK   STANDARD COSTS OF MANUFACTURING (DM/PIECE)
   VARTEL VARIABLE PART OF PRODUCTION BUDGET (DIMLES)

FGKF=PROFIX*ARANZ+MAFIX*PMABA+GHATEL*ARANZ/SPOC                           105 A
PROFIX=400                                                              105. 0 C
ARANZ=100                                                               105. 1 C
MAFIX=0.416                                                             105. 2 C
GHATEL=970                                                              105. 3 C
ARANZ=100                                                               105. 4 C
SPOC=7.5                                                                105. 5 C
   FGKF   FIXED COMMON COSTS IN PRODUCTION (DM)
   PROFIX FIXED PERCENTAGE OF LABOUR OVERHEAD RATE (DIMLES)
   ARANZ  NUMBER OF WORKERS IN THE PRODUCTION PROCESS (MAN)
   MAFIX  FIXED PART OF MATERIAL COSTS (DM)
   PMABA  PRODUCTION ASSETS (DM)
   GHATEL SALARY PERCENTAGE OF THE PRODUCTION COSTS (DIMLES)
   SPOC   SPAN OF CONTROL (MAN)

FGK=FGV+FGKF/EAR                                                          106 A
FGV=10                                                                  106. 0 C
   FGK    COMMON COSTS IN PRODUCTION (DM/WEEK)
   FGV    VARIABLE COMMON COSTS IN PRODUCTION (DM/WEEK)
   FGKF   FIXED COMMON COSTS IN PRODUCTION (DM)
   EAR    EXPECTED ORDER INPUT RATE (PIECE/WEEK)
```

Fig. 8: Extract of the IFICUS model

Within the cycle of goods and materials only the production of one product is modelled. Regarding real facts within enterprises, it was necessary to take into account different product types. This leads to the higher structured level of the production sub-system where on the disaggregated level of the middle-management more detailed questions can be answered and detailed decision provings can be applied. This disaggregated sub-model contains more than 200 level equations.

Other application areas have been modelled and integrated in the model base, e.g. function net models which describe and simulate production processes (cf. [8]). These function nets are based on abstracted and timed Petri nets and represent a new simulation methodology. The programming languages used for implementing function nets are PL/1 and SIMULA.

Beside these stand-alone models we have implemented so-called <u>interrelated models</u>. As an application example the process system of TRIER (cf. [20]) is integrated. For planning reasons within an enterprise environment different models, written in different simulation languages, which describe various areas of this enterprise are coupled. Mainly structural reasons within organizations or programming language barriers had prevented in the past, that interrelations between parts of these organizations could have been realized by means of software technical tools.

The communication between the following models is implemented:

1. the IFICUS top-management model of STÜBEL (CSMP, cf. [19]),
2. the model of FRÖHLICH for financial planning (FORTRAN, cf.[6]),
3. the model UNISIM for production planning (FORTRAN, cf. [9]),
4. the model EOQ as a process of the order policy (FORTRAN, cf.[9]), and
5. the model FUTURE as a prognosis instrument for the marketing (FORTRAN, cf. [9]).

The following picture shows these interrelations

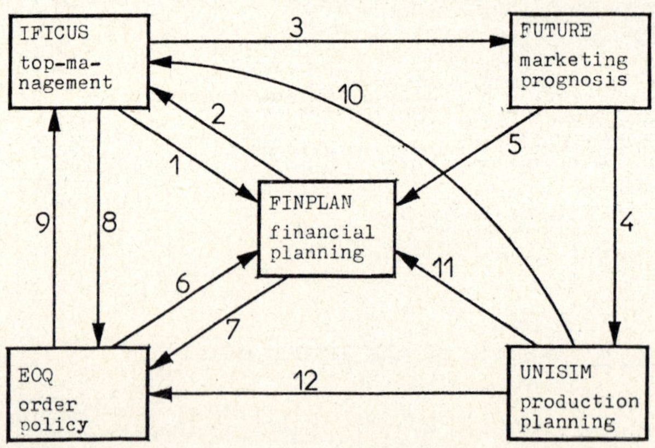

<u>Fig. 9:</u> The model of TRIER

IFICUS gives all initial values for the financial planning to FINPLAN (1) which calculates the prospecting financial difference; this difference goes back to IFICUS (2) as needed credit. FUTURE is provided by IFICUS (3) with the history data of the order rate, which is needed by UNISIM extrapolated for the production planning (4) and by FINPLAN for the financial planning (5). EOQ coordinates the order policy with FINPLAN (6,7), receives the effective inventory from IFICUS (8) and gives back the order quantity (9). UNISIM supplies IFICUS with the production plan (10), FINPLAN with the planned costs per production unit (11) and EOQ with the planned production rate (12).

The control of these communication processes is performed by a monitor system (cf. chapter 4.6). The interactive creation, manipulation and evaluation of all kinds of models is discussed in chapter 5.

4.3 Method base

In the past great parts of software applications in industry and administration had been collected in program libraries and had been - dependent on the need - integrated by the development of new programs. These libraries contain in general programs representing methods in linear algebra, statistics, operations research, differential equation systems etc. These methods have been supplemented by methods from application-oriented areas. Therefore it was necessary to standardize these programs and to integrate them in a large method base system. Now it is much easier to program problem solutions which occur in the daily industrial and administrational environment.

According to the realization of our method base system we have integrated methods for the validation of simulation models and other statistical methods. Their usage is controlled and performed by the monitor system and assisted by the interactive dialog system (cf. chapter 5).

The creation of models is only a very short step on the way to mapping parts of reality into a model. It is evident that this creation of simulation models cannot be viewed seperately from methods for proving the validity of these models (cf. [19], [16]). One step towards this validity is to compare the real system behaviour with the behaviour of the model (e.g. to compare corresponding time series). Verification, calibration, sensitivity analysis and validation are important tools for supporting this process. Most of them are based on statistical methods which are integrated components of the method base, e.g. THEIL.test, regression analysis, smoothing methods, different distributions, gradient methods etc.

Because of the complexity and quantity it is obvious that application of all these methods 'by hand' is as difficult as unreasonable. Therefore we have implemented methods to support the calibration and sensitivity analysis automatically. In particular a method to find those parameters which lead to the smallest difference between the real system and the model results should be mentioned. An example in applying this statistical method base interactively is given in chapter 5.

4.4. Data base

The data base component used as a part of our method and model base system is the WELL system. This data base system is based on the WEB model by MUNZ (cf. [14]), a binary data model in which entities and their relationships are described by graph-like data structures with labelled nodes and edges. These data structures are called WEBS.

Relationships between entities or between entities and values are represented by directed arcs. These data structures together with a changeable schema provide a high degree of data independence, flexibility and evolvability. A powerful graph-pattern matching technique is used for accessing and manipulating the data base. These operations are performed by means of the WEB-model-language (WELL) which

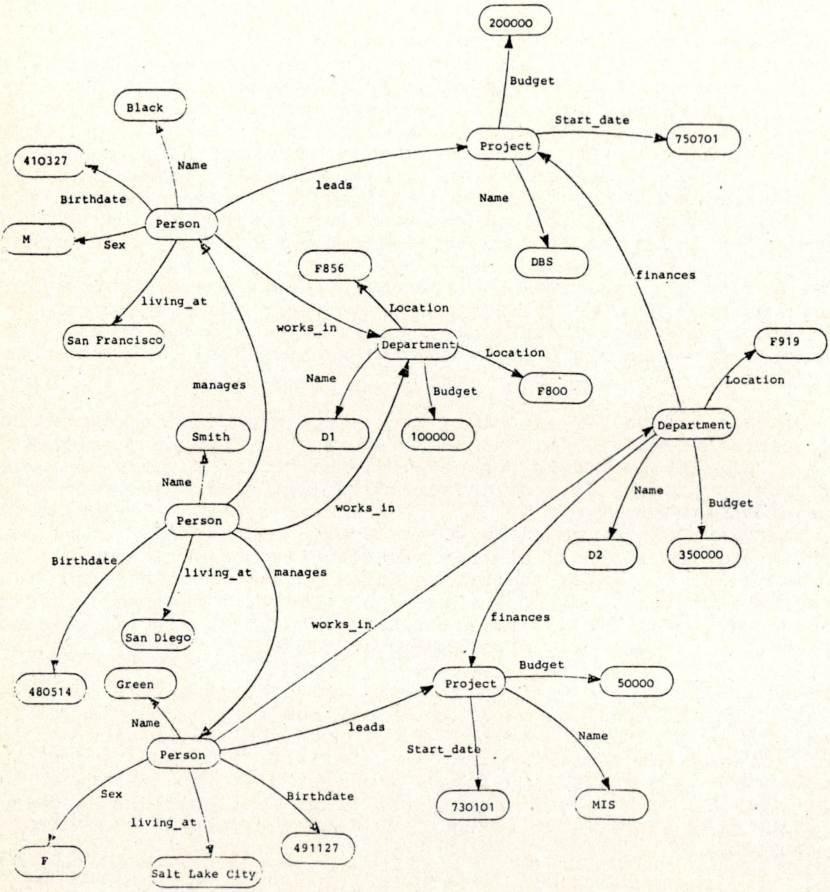

Fig. 10: Example of a data base WEB

uses an associative, content-addressing method. Parts of the data base which should be accessed or manipulated could be viewed as subwebs. To describe the structure and parts of the content of a searched subweb, another subweb is used in which certain node labels have a particular meaning. These subwebs serve as patterns for the associative addressing and select those parts of a WEB with which they match. The WELL language is used to formulate such patterns.

In our system there are two possibilities of using the data base:

1. with respect to the user dialog (s.chapter 5) the accesss to the data base is performed automatically, e.g. if the user wants to run a specific model or method, the corresponding data are provided from the data base automatically via the monitor system by translating monitor language statements into WELL statements.

2. users with more practice (e.g. specialists, system programmers, the system administrator) have direct access to the data base by WELL which can be used as a command like language during the various dialog versions or independently of the dialogs.

4.5 Modules of the program library and external programs

Beside the methods discussed with respect to the method base (cf. chapter 4.3) programs which are operating, manipulating and assisting the evaluation processes are integrated in the program library.

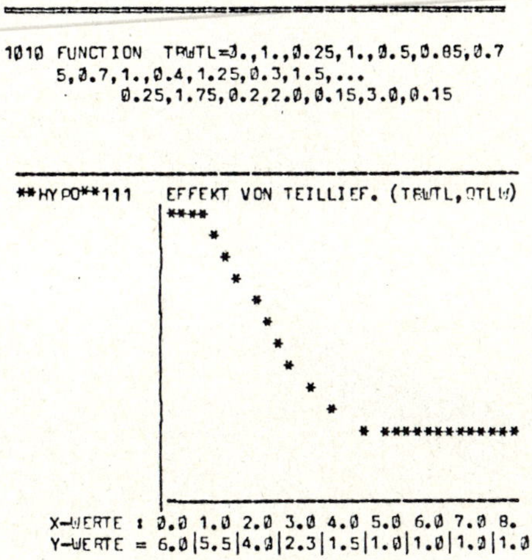

Fig. 11: Display of hypothesis (the effect of short deliveries)

The hypothesis and decision rule base was established with respect to different simulation models, where the mapping of real system behaviour demands could only be made by means of assumptions, or where this behaviour must be determined by specific decisions. To examine the model and system behaviour the change of such hypothesis and decision rules must be easily accomplished. Therefore we have implemented a tool that provides the user with the possibility for creating and changing hypotheses and decision rules interactively and for combining the changed versions directly with the corresponding models. This interactive process has graphical support (cf. figure 11).

As stated above some simulation models are based on the methodology of feedback loops. To examine the structure of systems, of complex systems in particular, we have established a specific utility program which is able to detect these feedback loops in systems.

To make models and methods more readable and to support the understanding of these models and methods another utility tool was generated: By means of a definition dectionary where the names of variables, parameters etc. are stored it is possible to explain programs in different languages automatically.

Other utility programs consist of tools for supporting different output forms, e.g. the plot interface. Dependent on the variation of parameters of simulation models it is possible to constitute a 3-dimensional result graph, where additional system's evaluations can be made by detecting relative minima or maxima (cf.figure 12).

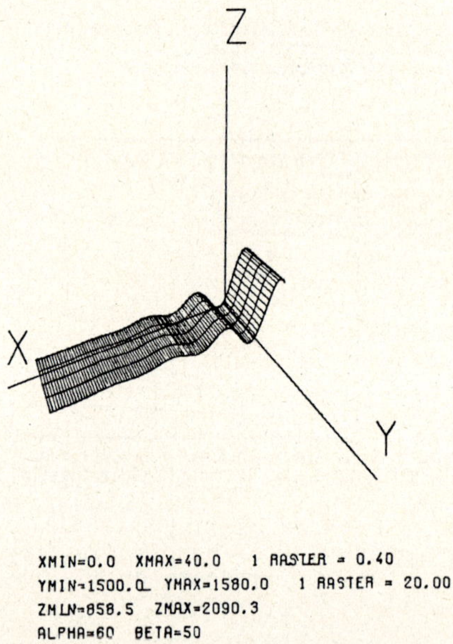

Fig. 12: 3-dimensional simulation output

Further methods for the aggregation of data, clustering analysis methods, automatic methods - which are based on Petrinets - for other examinations of the system's structure (like deadlock properties) will be added to the system.

One application example for the interface to external programs is the coupling of the FAKIR-System which is an information retrieval system (cf. [3]). This system has been conceived to assist lecturing, to be a helpful tool for the documentation of the administration and for research reasons (e.g. experimental proving of hypothesis).

4.6 Monitor system

The monitor controls and performs the communication between the system components discussed and the user interface. The realization of the user interface monitor functions has been assisted by the generalized interactive system GIAS (cf.[13]and chapter 5).

The system handling by different user classes is controlled by the monitor. Depending on the user demands or commands which occur within the dialog, the monitor provides the desired models, methods and data. For single model runs the monitor supports these models by the needed initial values and parameters, he loads corresponding methods to these models and performs these methods on the models themselves or on the resulting data.

Dependent on the different answer forms within the dialog system the monitor performs the desired tasks in different ways:

1. answers which occur as a reaction of a 'menu'- or an open question ('yes/no', cf. chapter 5) are translated into the monitor- (or dialog-) language and the corresponding action is performed.

2. commands and options during the dialog versions are stated in the monitor language and can directly be executed. There is also an option to use the available programming languages for method and model base handling and for access to the data base the corresponding data base language WELL, in this cases the monitor takes over only the control and provides the corresponding execution.

To realize the communication between models, i.e. to realize the temporal synchronisation of models (processes) on sequential machines we have integrated into the monitor the system of TRIER (cf. [20]) which allows the communication of programs written in different programming languages. He has developed language tools for this communication of processes. By means of this language a process is able

1. to <u>receive</u> and to <u>send</u> information,
2. to <u>wait</u> for information, where the process may interrupt its activity at any real time point, or to <u>become informed</u> about messages.

The corresponding language statements are: RECEIVE, SEND, WAIT and INFORM. The overall model consists of a set of orders where orders can contain several processes. The processes are defined independently of any host-language, the syntax of processes is shown in figure 13 .

```
<process>               ::=  PROCESS[:<name>](<host language>)<program>
                             [ENDOFPROCESS[:<name>]]
<program>               ::=  {<command>} ...
<command>               ::=  <host language command>|<communication>|
                             <real-time process>
<host language>         ::=  FORTRAN|CSMP| ...
<communication>         ::=  RECEIVE<arguments>|SEND<arguments>|
                             WAIT|INFORM
<arguments>             ::=  <channel>[,<deposit instruction>]
<deposit instruction>   ::=  {<name>[(<begin>[,<number>])]} ...
<real-time process>     ::=  TIME:=<arithmetic expression in host language>
<name>                  ::=  <name of variable in host language>
<channel>               ::=  1|2|3|...|9999
<begin>                 ::=  <position in a 1-dimensional array to which
                              resp. from which information should be
                              transferred>
<number>                ::=  <number of arrays to be transferred>
```

Fig. 13: The syntax of processes (modified BNF-notation)

5. USER INTERFACE

Everyone who is concerned with big and complex systems in industry or administration will agree that the interactive way of retrieving and manipulating information and of programming in general becomes more and more important. This experience is e.g. based on extensive user interviews within various application areas (cf. [7]). The need for powerful tools for supporting the user in his problem solving processes was mentioned above.

In addition it should be mentioned that up to today most of the planners or specialists on the different decision levels of industry or administration have some prejudice regarding modern simulation techniques, the corresponding models and methods are viewed as too complicated and difficult (cf. [17]), there is a psychological barrier to use such systems, therefore it is obviously necessary to persuade those people by means of an user-oriented implementation.

There exist some very useful investigations in the area of user requirements for dialog systems (see e.g. [7]). We will not repeat these requirements, but we will show how the dialog interface of the BOSS system meets most of these requirements stated there.

This chapter is concerned with the concept of the dialog interface of BOSS, which we have implemented on the one hand and which we are going to realize on the other. The user interface of BOSS is established by means of the Generalized InterActive System GIAS (cf.[13]). GIAS can be viewed as an instrument for the specification and automatic generation of dialog programs which is used for the control and processing of model base systems. By means of only a few descriptive commands and functions it is possible to establish the corresponding interfaces and to construct complex dialog structures needed for the applications. All dialog components, the control and processing properties are generated by means of a screen-controlled dialog.

With respect to the concept of this generalized interactive system we mainly distinguish two user classes: The designer of a dialog program whom we call the dialog program author who handles the GIAS-generator for establishing dialog programs interactively and the user of the correspondent dialog programs, whom we call the dialog system user, the casual user in general who executes the generated dialog programs and handles by means of this program corresponding modules, the model base, the method base, the data base etc. Figure 14 roughly shows typical processes working interactively with a model base system. We have chosen such a system concept that - if desired - the user has the possibility to influence the way of his problem solving.

If the user has no knowledge of the system he first can have all informations about the system by means of the underlying information dictionaries (the first module). The user is supported by module 2 in selecting models and in creating new ones. The selection of methods from the method base for problem solving and the establishing of new methods together with the storing of these new methods into the method base is performed in module 3. This selection may be dependent on the selection of a specific model.

Module 4 provides the data for the corresponding models and methods. For statistical reasons we will develop aggregation features on the data. In module 5 models, methods and data will be combined to a program, a protocol of the selected components and their interrelations is generated in module 6.

If we try to run simulation models the selection of parameters is very important. By means of an interactive process these parameters are established in a calibration phase and are eventually changed in a validation phase. These automatic calibration and validation processes are already implemented and we are just concerned with their integration in BOSS. Modules 8 to 11 can be viewed as one single unit, they have to be passed through several times until satisfying solutions are produced.

In module 8 the actual program execution happens. The user has the possibility to decide which partial results he wants to have generated : a protocol or a report. In future method and model base systems automatic report-generator-components should be provided. The user has to decide in module 9 the output facilities, e.g. tables or graphical output on a display or plotter.

In module 10 the analysis and interpretation of results and the validation tests are performed. This is a very important part of the system where powerful statistical methods, the sensibility analysis and data preparation methods will be used. The problem solving process ends if the results are satisfying. Otherwise further iteration steps have to be performed by e.g. changing parameters, data, methods or models.

Regarding the various user classes and the different application areas we have realized various dialog features. Corresponding to

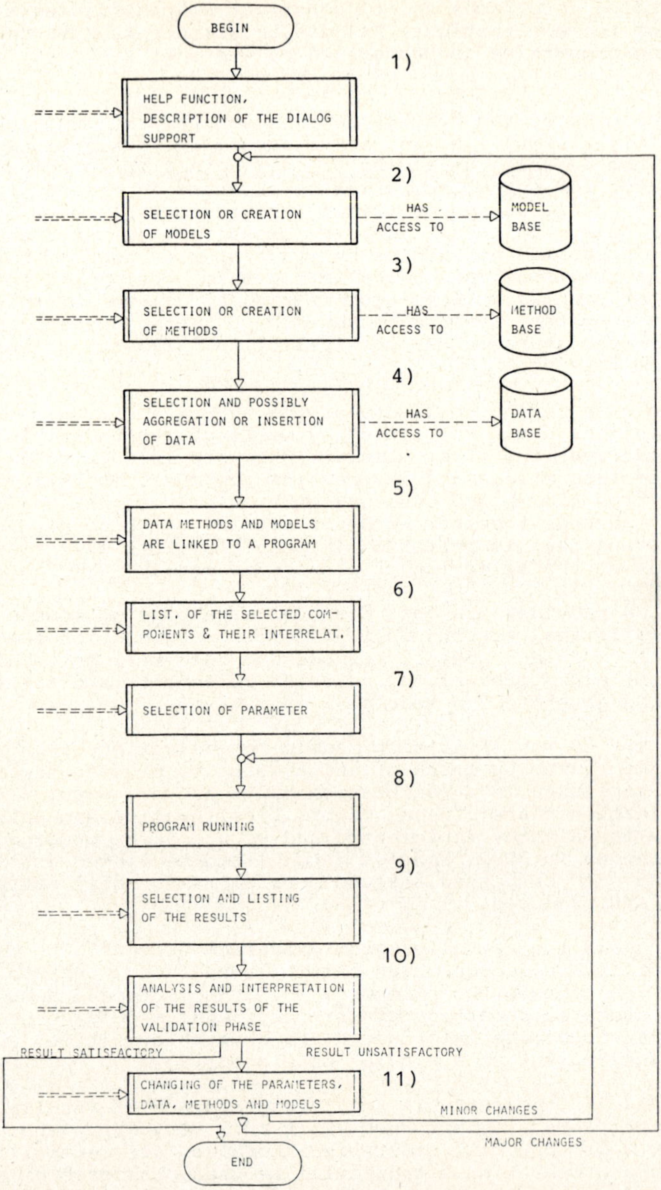

Fig. 14: Interactive method and model base system processes

different applications and different models and methods, the user is provided by different dialog versions, i.e. for example that we have different dialog versions for handling DYNAMO models, CSMP models, SIMULA models etc. Dependent on the choice of a model the dialog passes through different branches of the dialog tree. These branches are structured tree-like or sometimes sequentially. Figure 15 shows the standard version of the CSMP dialog, where the automatic validation features are not regarded. Corresponding to the knowledge of users we established different kinds of dialogs, simple ones or more advanced ones.

The input facilities depend on the user's knowledge, e.g. users who are trained can have different input features than users who are inexperienced. The user is provided with aids which can be delivered from information dictionaries. Dialog input and answers are not bound to formats. The dialog system provides powerful fault detection routines. The quality and quantity of fault messages depend also on the user's knowledge, i.e. for example an untrained user is provided by detailed explanations together with correction hints. The user has the possibility for interrupting these messages and others if desired.

Our dialog system is a teaching system. The user without any knowledge of the system or of the dialog is guided by the system in such a way that he learns to handle the system. In this context it is reasonable to use mnemonic names for functions and commands, to make these concepts more easily readable and understandable. Initial system and administration tasks are performed automatically by the dialog system. The user only has to specify what he wants, e.g. what model, what method he needs. The dialog system as a part of the monitor system checks the corresponding input and e.g. stores the desired model or method in the temporary storage.

The user has three specification (answering) possibilities

1. The menu-technique.

   By means of this technique the user can e.g. specify the model or method he wants to work with or that he wants to use the data base system directly; typical questions or commands are:

   SPECIFY THE MODEL YOU WANT TO WORK WITH
   SPECITY THE METHOD YOU WANT TO WORK WITH
   WHAT IS THE FORMAT OF YOUR PLOT-OUTPUT?

2. The yes/no form for the performing of specific tasks, e.g. for output facilities, protocols, documentation.

   Typical questions are:

   DO YOU LIKE TO HAVE A PROTOCOL?
   WOULD YOU LIKE TO SEE THE XY-MODEL?
   DO YOU WANT TO CHANGE THE XY-MODEL?
   DO YOU WANT TO APPLY ANOTHER METHOD?
   DO YOU WANT TO CHANGE THE PARAMETERS?
   DO YOU WANT TO ESTABLISH FURTHER PLOTS?
   DO YOU WANT TO MAKE A NEW SIMULATION RUN?
   DO YOU WANT TO HAVE ANOTHER MODEL?

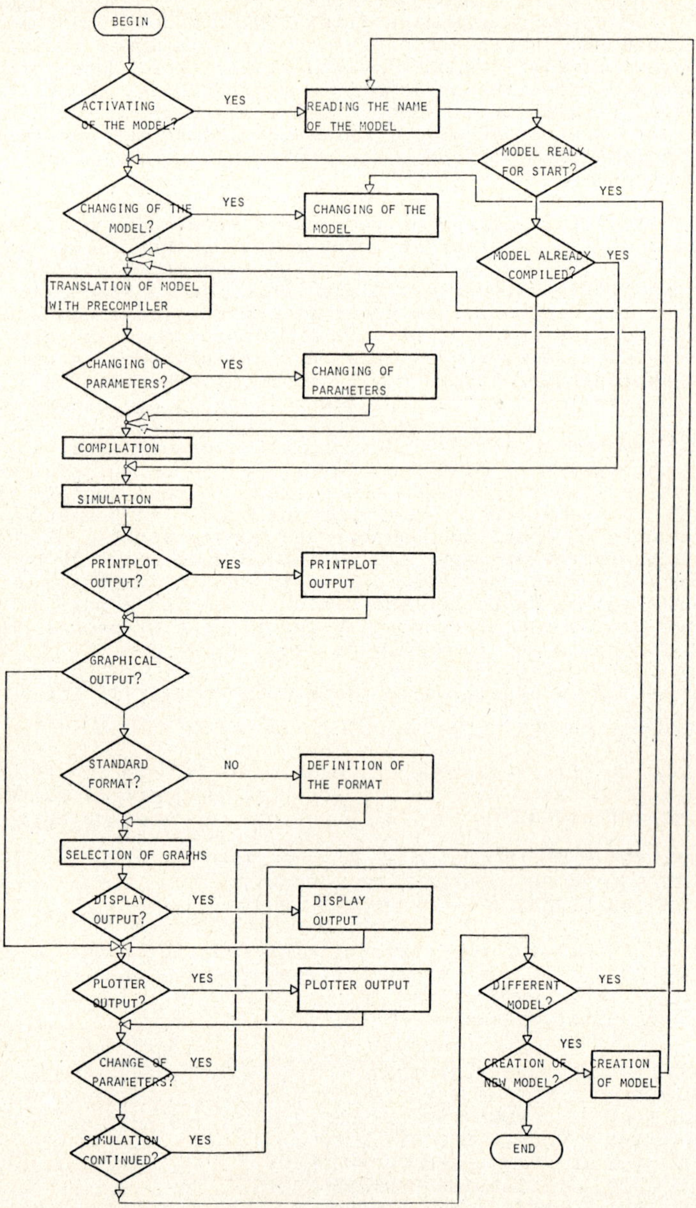

Fig. 15: Standard CSMP-dialog

3. Direct access to all components and direct control of the dialog by means of a dialog language.

Within the dialog it is possible for the expert user (e.g. the system programmer) to formulate his problems via programming languages (e.g. with respect to models and methods) or via the data base language.

The heart of the system's guide is the information dictionary. At any time the user, if he desires, must be provided with information about the dialog system with all its components, operations and languages. This tool supports the learning process. On the other hand this information can be given automatically if the system observes that information is needed.

By means of the statement '?' or 'HELP' the user is provided by global information (global with respect to the actual branching structure, local with respect to the overall system). Local information regarding specific subsystems can be obtained by adding '?' to specific key words of the dialog language.

The user can be supplied with information about

. the dialog system itself
. specific simulation dialogs
. the different specifications (techniques)
. input-specifications
. treatment of faults
. systems control
. the individual components of the system
. the dialog language
. specific models and methods, the usage and the meaning of which are described in the information dictionaries.

The dialog control is also guaranteed by the dialog language, e.g. the following tasks can be performed

. jump to the begin of the dialog
. jump to the end of the dialog
. showing the model and method base library on the display
. jump to the entry for changing models, methods or parameters
. jump to the entry for the simulation of models
. jump to the documentation, plot modules
. one step for- and backward in the dialog
. repetition of specific questions
. options to quicken the dialog.

Further the user can specify the usage of the definition dictionary for automatic documentation. He is forced to define the variables and constants of models by names or statements for explanation purposes. During dialog sessions the user may be asked if he wants to have programs documented. In this case the monitor provides the programs with respective definitions. This is a very important tool for better readability and understandability of methods and models.

All relevant functions with respect to the model base system are realized directly via the dialog or by means of commands in the dialog language, e.g. printing functions, editor functions, debugging

```
************************************************************
*                                                          *
* WHICH PART OF THE STATISTICAL METHOD BASE DC YOU WANT ? *
*                                                          *
* 1 curve presentations (smoothing algorithms)             *
* 2 calculation of elementary statistical values           *
* 3 statistical tests and analysis                         *
*                                                          *
************************************************************

3

************************************************************
*                                                          *
* WHAT SHOULD BE TESTED OR ANALYZED ?                      *
*                                                          *
* 31 variances and averages of normal distributions data   *
*    (parameter tests)                                     *
* 32 the destination of a distribution                     *
*    (goodness of fit test)                                *
* 33 dependencies between m values (correlation)           *
* 34 influence of m values to a result (distribution       *
*    independent tests, variances analysis)                *
*                                                          *
************************************************************

31

************************************************************
*                                                          *
* SHOULD THE VARIANCES OF THE AVERAGES OF PCPULATIONS      *
* BE COMPARED, TESTED RESPECTIVELY ?                       *
*                                                          *
************************************************************

variances

************************************************************
*                                                          *
* SHOULD THE VARIANCES OF TWO POPULATIONS (YCU HAVE        *
* 2 SAMPLES)                                               *
* OR OF MORE POPULATIONS (YOU HAVE MORE THEN 2 SAMPLES)    *
* BE COMPARED ?                                            *
*                                                          *
************************************************************

more

************************************************************
*                                                          *
* BARTLETT TEST                                            *
*                                                          *
************************************************************
```

Fig. 16: Dialog example

and testing tools, various I/O facilities like the plot interface or the graphic display interface, automatic documentation facilities.

The way to problem solving by means of the dialog system by using the method base is shown in figure 16. To assist the way of problem solving and to improve the knowledge of the user with respect to the various problem solving paths and the available methods an interactive graphic interface is provided where the user can be guided through the problem solving tree.

The interrelations between problem solving, methods and the corresponding programs are described by means of a so-called information graph where nodes without predecessor contain information about the application areas which are represented in the method base. Nodes with predecessors contain detailed information about parts of the predecessor information. Going through this graph means to limit the corresponding problem. This leads to the description of a specific problem solving method and to the documentation of the programs which can also be started.

6. CONCLUSIONS

This paper was concerned with the requirements for an information system in a multi-user environment of industrial applications and with an approach to meet these requirements by a method and model base system. The properties of the end-user interfaces with respect to this method and model base system, the dialog facilities regarding different user classes, i.e. the integration of different user views of information systems, were discussed.

By means of this method and model base systems we are able to handle models and methods of many different users in an uniform and consistent way. Supported by the monitor system we have gained independence, flexibility and multi-user access regarding the different components of the system.

The system introduced can be seen as a powerful tool for the analysis design and realization of information systems and for the interactive problem solving by different user classes.

Looking at the current information systems development and regarding the software-technical view it is clear that these systems are hard to improve and to maintain. New ideas of planning, realizing and handling such systems have to be produced. A lot of research will be concentrated on the development of better languages and dialog interfaces for method and model base systems. Much more support by the system for problem solving processes is necessary. These method and model base systems can be a base for decision support and for analysis and design support systems.

One possibility to gain better handling of such systems is also to concentrate research in particular on so-called 'growing' systems and on distributed method and model base systems.

7. REFERENCES

[1] ANSI/X3/SPARC study group on data base management systems, Interim Report, ACM SIGMOD Newsletters EDT 7,2, (1975).

[2] Blumenthal, S.C.: Management Information Systems: A Framework for Planning and Development (Prentice Hall, Inc., Englewood Cliffs, 1969).

[3] Bollmann, P.; Konrad, E.; Schneider, H.-J.; Zuse, H.: Das FAKYR- Projekt 1972-78, Fachbereich Informatik, Technische Universität Berlin (1978).

[4] Esprester, A.C.: Datenbank und Methodenbank, data report 9, Heft 3 und 4 (1974).

[5] Forrester, J.W.: Principles of Systems (Wright/Allan Press, Cambridge, Mass., 1971).

[6] Fröhlich, H.J.: Ansätze zur Ermittlung des Finanzbedarfs einer wachsenden Unternehmung,Dissertation (Ph.D. Thesis), Göttingen (1968).

[7] Dzida, W.; Herda, S.; Itzfeld, W.: GMD-Factors of User-Perceived-Quality of Interactive Systems, Gesellschaft für Mathematik und Datenverarbeitung, Schloss Birlinghoven (1978).

[8] Godbersen, H.; Meyer, B.E.: Function Nets as a Tool for the Simulation of Information Systems, in: Proc. of the 1978 Summer Computer Simulation Conference, Newport/California (1978).

[9] Harris, R.D.; Maggard, M.J.: Computer Models in Operations Management (New York, Evanston, San Francisco, London, 1972).

[10] Keppel, E.; Kogon, R.; Kropp, D.: Interactive Programming by Endusers - general information -, IBM Germany, TR 75.12.008.

[11] Klein, M.; Tixier, V.: Scarabee: A Data and Model Bank for Financial Engineering and Research, IFIP Congress (1971).

[12] Mertens, P.; Neuwirth, W.; Schmitt, W.: Verknüpfung von Daten- und Methodenbanken, dargestellt am Beispiel der Analyse von Marktforschungsdaten, Wirtschafts-Informatik Symposium, IBM, (1976).

[13] Meyer, B.E.; Pflugbeil, G.; Schneider, H.-J.: A Generalized Interactive System for Automatic Generation of Dialog Programs, Internal CIS-report 11/78, Institut für Angewandte Informatik, Technische Universität Berlin (1978).

[14] Munz, R.: The WELL-System: A Multi-User Database System Based on Binary Relationships and Graph-Pattern-Matching, Information Systems, Vol. 3, No. 2 (1978) pp. 99-116.

[15] Nijssen, G.M.: A Gross Architecture for Next Generation DBMS, in: Modeling in Data Base Management Systems (Ed. by G.M. Nijssen, North Holland, Amsterdam, 1976).

[16] Nolan, R.L.: Verification/Validation of Computer Simulation Models in: Proc. of the 1972 Summer Computer Simulation Conference, San Diego (1972).

[17] Prautsch, W.; Riethmüller, Ch.: A Pragmatic Attempt of Supporting the Process of Developing Dynamic Models, in: Proc. of the 1978 Summer Computer Simulation Conference, Newport/California (1978).

[18] Schneider, H.-J.: Möglichkeiten und Grenzen normativer Ansätze für die Gestaltung von Informationssystemen, in: Entwicklungstendenzen der Systemanalyse, Lectures and Tutorials, Band 6, H.R. Hansen (ed.),R. Oldenbourg, München, Wien (1978).

[19] Stübel, G.: Methodologische und Software-engineering-orientierte Untersuchungen für ein Unternehmensmodell verschiedener Strukturiertheitsgrade, Diss.(Ph.D.Thesis), Universität Stuttgart (1975).

[20] Trier, B.: Die Theorie der parallelen Prozesse als Instrument zur Modellierung und Simulation sozio-technischer Systeme, Dissertation (Ph.D.Thesis),Universität Stuttgart (1977).

[21] Will, H.: Model Management Systems, in: Grochla, E./Szyperski, N., Information Systems and Organizational Structure (De Gruyter, Berlin - New York, 1975).

Formal Models and Practical Tools for Information Systems Design
H.-J. Schneider, Editor
North-Holland Publishing Company

USE: a Methodology for the Design and Development of Interactive Information Systems

Anthony I. Wasserman

Medical Information Science
University of California, San Francisco
San Francisco, CA 94143 USA

USE (User Software Engineering) is an approach to the specification, design, and implementation of interactive information systems. The project is based on a philosophy combining principles of user-centered design with those of software engineering. The goal is to provide the designer of information systems with a powerful set of tools that can make it possible to achieve the essential requirements of software reliability and usability.

USE attempts to span the software development life cycle, giving attention to various aspects of the system creation activity. Initial efforts have focused on design and implementation of the programming language PLAIN, a Pascal-like language addressed to goals of systematic programming and needs of interactive programs. More recent activities have dwelled on the development of specification techniques for the class of programs for which PLAIN was designed. Finally, a Module Control System (MCS) is being created as a tool for linking together the various modules of a software system in such a way as to support their systematic, but independent, development.

Design Goals for Interactive Information Systems

Information systems are a rapidly growing aspect of computing, spanning a broad range of applications. There is every indication that this area will continue to grow for the foreseeable future, fueled by both the increasing volume of information in modern societies and by the sharply reduced costs associated with most computing equipment.

Within this field, interactive information systems (IIS), involving conversational access to data bases by computer naive users, are experiencing especially rapid growth. Such systems, exemplified by airline reservation systems and hospital information systems, permit users to access and modify data stored on a secondary storage device by means of a command language, a database query language, natural language-like dialogue, multiple choice (menu selection), or a similar method.

These users view the computer simply as a tool and are willing to use that tool only if it is easy to use and if it simplifies their work. Accordingly, the designers and implementors of these interactive information systems must provide programs that are satisfactory to these users in terms of ease of use and reliability. A number of desirable characteristics can be enumerated for these programs, including reliability, simplicity, invisibility of underlying system software, user-friendliness, learnability, usability, economy, maintainability, security, flexibility, and portability.

It is difficult to quarrel with these objectives. Unfortunately, however, many existing interactive information systems are extremely rigid in their requirements upon the user and fail to exhibit these characteristics.

User Software Engineering

The development of high quality systems requires that attention be given both to the needs of the interactive user and to the process of software development. The term 'user software engineering' will be used to refer to the colection of principles and practices that support the systematic creation of these conversational programs. User software engineering is a combination of software engineering principles with human factors considerations aimed at producing satisfactory human/computer environments. In this context, software engineering may be defined as the collection of tools associated with the specification, design, implementation, management, testing, and maintenance of software construction.

User software engineering requires a broad range of considerations by system designers throughout the system creation process, beginning with requirements definition. It is essential to provide system designers and programmers with a set of tools that permits effective design and development of these systems.

Our focus, then, is on the practical tools being provided for the information system development environment. In succeeding sections of this paper, we shall described the system environment in more detail, then describe several components of the environment: the IIS specification technique, the programming language PLAIN, and the Module Control System (MCS) to support the construction and integration of the IIS.

The IIS Environment

As noted in a previous paper [1], the design and implementation of reliable, user-centered IIS's requires the *harmonious* cooperation of the language system, the operating system, and the support system(s) for secondary storage (file system and/or data base system). These systems would be part of a unified system environment, as shown in Figure 1.

This environment supports four classes of users: information system developers, information system users (parametric users), nonprogrammers, and a database administrator. A fifth class of users, termed programming environmment developers, provides the facilities to be used by the information system developers and the database administrator. The programming environment developers are responsible for the development and maintenance of the software systems enclosed within the large box in Figure 1.

The tools available within the programming environment go a long way toward determining the nature of the IIS that will eventually be provided to the end user, who will potentially work within the same environment, albeit with a different set of permissible operations.

From Figure 1, it is apparent that the programming environment contains "languages" for software specification, design, and implementation, as well as libraries of software modules and assorted other tools. We shall now examine this programming environment in more detail.

A critical consideration is to provide the IIS designer/developer with facilities to manage the complexity inherent in the problem being programmed. Failure to understand user requirements fully, failure to perceive subtle interactions among system components, and failure to take all cases into consideration are all results of the limited amount of processing capability of the human mind. Techniques for problem decomposition and modularization, such as top down design and stepwise refinement, can be combined with automated tools to provide assistance in this area.

A well-disciplined approach to software development involves the production of a complete specification, a complete problem solution, and program design prior to the inception of actual coding [2]. In practice, this approach requires the production of a nonprocedural system specification and a design representation showing program structure and logical data structures with the action of each module specified in some "program design language" [3]. A disciplined approach to software development, then, requires both a *design stage* and a *construction stage*. In this way, then, the completed design can be verified (formally or informally) against the original specifications and the "software blueprints" can provide the basis for implementation (or redesign). Similarly, the specification can provide the basis for acceptance testing.

It thereby follows that different notations are applicable for the different stages of the IIS development. In [1], these were termed the specification language, the design language, and the implementation language. All of these languages support the way that information system designers *approach* problem solutions.

Specifying Interactive Information Systems

As the first detailed statement of system function, specifications play a critical role in the development activity, providing a foundation for future work and a link between the user's concept of the system and its actual implementation. The specification must perform four different functions: precisely stating the system requirements, providing insight into the problem as a way of helping the designer structure the system, providing the basis for testing and verification activities, and serving as a baseline for modifications and enhancements.

In addition, a good specification must be complete, unambiguous, writeable, consistent, testable, implementable, modifiable, and comprehensible to the persons who must use the specification. Furthermore, it must be traceable, so that the specification can be validated against user requirements.

Achievement of these diverse goals is difficult, since some of them, particularly testability, consistency, and unambiguity, entail a greater degree of formalism than is present in most specifications, while the formalism of tools such as algebraic specifications may not be adequate for comprehensibility by end users. Accordingly, some blending of formal and informal specification techniques is necessary.

From a specification standpoint, an IIS may be seen as consisting of three major components: the user interface, the operations upon the data objects, and the data base (or files). In the succeeding sections, we will present the USE specification method for such programs. We shall begin by discussing the nature of a specification in more detail, then proceed to the specifics of our method.

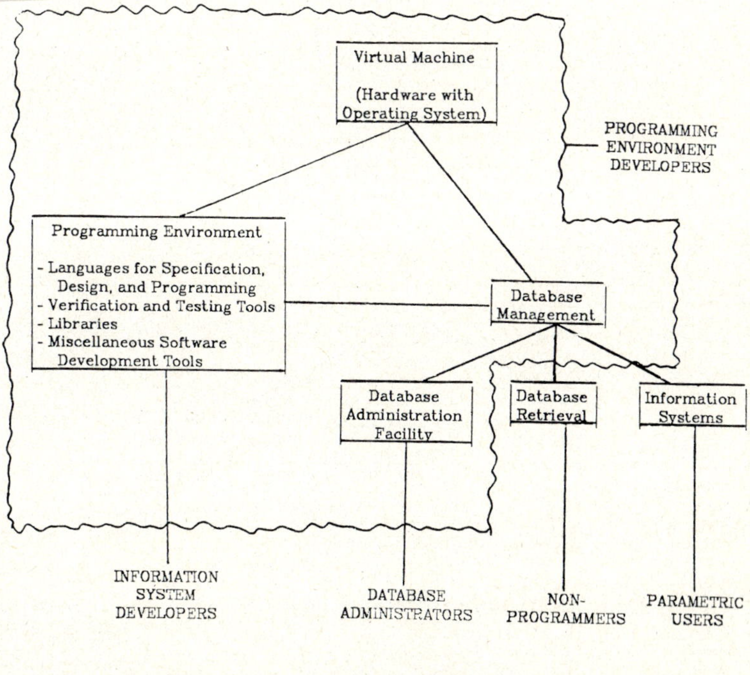

Figure 1 -- Unified System Environment

Three Views of a Specification

Our approach to specification consists of three logical parts: an end user view, a design view, and a verification view. Each of these views accommodates at least one of the functions of the specifications, and is intended to address one or more of the goals for specifications listed above. The model, depicted in Figure 2, emphasizes that all of these functions must be addressed early in the software development process.

The *user view* specification is based upon the requirements definition and is a detailed, but informal, description of the system function formulated by the developer working closely with the end user. This informal description can serve as a contract between developer and user, and can also serve as the starting point for more formal specifications. It is often the case that more than one class of users will have access to a given information system, frequently with different privileges and operations. In such a case, it would be necessary to specify a separate view for each user class.

The user view specification is aimed at meeting the specification goals of comprehensibility for the reader and completeness of the system description. It is written using the terminology of the task environment, reflecting the user's view of the problem. Hence, it provides external documentation for the system. This system model is intended for a user who is knowledgeable concerning the proposed system function, but is not familiar with the technical aspects of designing and programming it. (It should be noted that this characterization fits the large majority of end users and persons who contract for software development; not many are familiar with computer terminology, specification languages, or related topics.)

Historically, specifications (if they were written at all) were limited to this user view. However, the multiple uses of a specification require other views as well.

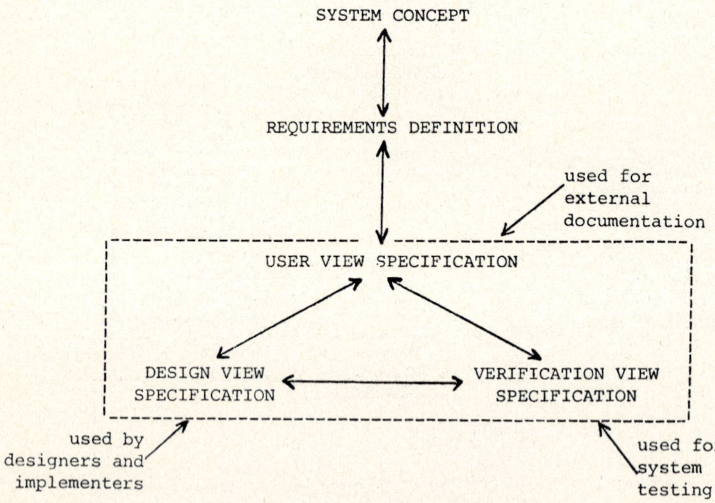

Figure 2 -- Specification Model

The *design view* specification serves as the link between the specification and design stages of the development life cycle, and may be considered as a form of architectural design. This view defines a high level program structure, identifies program modules to the greatest extent possible, and shows the logical data flow between the modules.

The design view specification is used to aid the software designer in implementing the system, easing the transition between the specification and design phases of the software life cycle. Typically, the functions of the module will be described in behavioral, i.e., non-procedural, terms; the detailed design stage will then evaluate and produce a procedural (algorithmic) version that can be shown to be equivalent to the specification. Similarly, data design will be at the logical level rather than at the physical level, except insofar as outside constraints or interfaces require the binding of low-level representational information. The design view primarily addresses the specification goals of implementability and consistency.

Finally, the *verification view* specification concentrates on correctness issues of the specification, making it possible to establish testing and verification procedures for the implemented system. Accordingly, this view treats the specification goals of unambiguity, testability, and consistency. The verification view uses a formal notation and defines the conditions that must be met by the implementation. Some of the recent work in specification languages [4,5,6] seeks to provide a single tool that can serve both the design view and the verification view of a specification.

The formal notations used for the design and verification views make it possible to utilize machine aids for consistency checking. Names, value ranges, and module interfaces can all be checked from such a specification approach.

Although we have identified three views of a specification, our method combines the design view and the verification view into a single unit, with the end result being an informal specification (user view) and a formalizable specification (information system engineering view). This simplification reduces the potential difficulties of writing three different specifications and then needing to demonstrate their equivalence. In this approach, we will adopt two notations, one corresponding to the user view and another corresponding to the information system engineering view. The first notation will be informal natural language, while the second will be more formal. Although the informal notation of the user view will preclude a formal proof of equivalence between the two views, it will be possible to link them explicitly and to demonstrate their equivalence informally.

The User Interface

The IIS user interface provides the user with a language for communicating with the system. As noted earlier, the interface can take many forms. In all cases, however, the normal action of the program is determined by user input, and the program may respond in a variety of ways, including results, requests for additional input, error messages, or assistance in the use of the IIS.

The critical observation, though, is that the semantics of the IIS, i.e., its actions, are driven by raw or transformed user input. As with programming languages, the user language in its runtime context determines the semantic actions to be performed; the resemblance between such a user language and an interpreted programming language is quite strong.

Accordingly, an effective specification technique for programming languages can be used effectively for specifying user interfaces. In our method, we use transition diagrams [7], as used in the definition of American National Standard MUMPS [8]. Such an approach has also been suggested by Parnas [9].

A transition diagram is a network of nodes and directed paths. Each path may contain a token, corresponding to a character string in the primitive alphabet (such as ASCII), or the name of another diagram. If the path is blank, it will be traversed as a default case, i.e., if all other paths leaving a given node fail. Scanning of the diagram begins at a designated entry point and proceeds until reaching an exit node or a dead end (no successful match on the paths from a given node). A semantic action may be associated with any path; traversal of the path causes the action to occur.

As a simple example, consider the transition diagram shown in Figure 3. The entry point is shown by the node labeled E, the exit point is shown by the node labeled X, subconversations, i.e., other diagrams, are shown within boxes along a traversed path, and output message names are shown within nodes. Thus, the input string 'HOP' would result in the semantic action 1 and the output message MSG; the input string 'SKIP' would initiate the subconversation named HOWFAR (another diagram). An illegal input would cause the diagram to fail to reach an exit point; we shall take up this matter in more detail in the longer example below.

Data Base Definition

The next aspect of the specification is to define the data base, since IIS operations are generally tied to the logical structure of the data base. We follow the ANSI/SPARC framework [10], focusing primarily upon the external model(s), defined in relations [11]. We design a separate external model for each user class, thereby providing a separate view of the data base, typically determined by a different set of operations, thereby producing a number of user view specifications.

The first necessary step is to identify the data elements and, to the largest extent possible at an early stage, to specify constraints (as a limited form of semantics) upon the data items, forming a conceptual model. Various kinds of constraints include the following:

1 a data type in the programming language sense, such as integer or string

2 a range for acceptable values of that object, possibly a numeric subrange or a number of characters

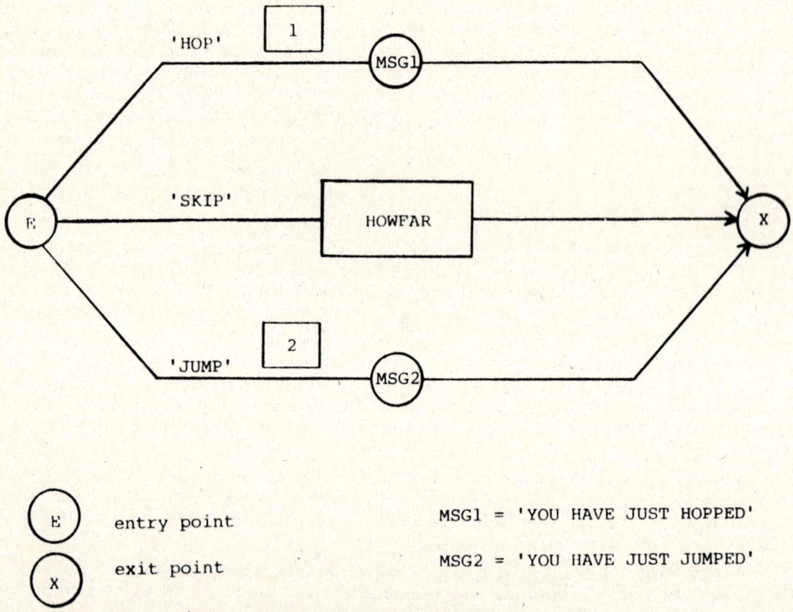

Figure 3 -- Sample transition diagram; Message names shown in circles; Semantic actions are numbers in small rectangles; Subconversations are names in boxes

3 access rights for the object, designating which classes of users may access and/or modify that object

4 relationships among the data objects, e.g., that one value must always exceed another value or that a change in one item necessitates a change in another item

We then produce external models using the relational model of data, analyzing the data elements to define, for ech external model, a set of relations that are normalized to eliminate dependencies among attributes within a relation and hence to prevent various anomalies from occurring within the data base.

We are continuing to investigate several other data models that provide better support at the conceptual level and that incorporate more semantics into the database design. For the present, though, the relational model has several significant advantages, especially the support for relational data base management provided by PLAIN.

Operations

It is now apparent that the structure of an IIS is based upon user input causing various operations to be carried out. Some of the operations may involve conversational access to the data base, while others, such as online assistance, may not. Operations upon the data base are organized by user class, achieving the mapping from a conceptual model to the relational database organization defined by the database specification phase.

It is important to distinguish between the user view of an operation and the internal view of an operation. A user operation typically results in a number of system-level operations. We will use the term "structured operation" to refer to the user's view of an operation; this notion encompasses the idea of a "transaction" upon a data base, as well as other logical operations requested by the user of an IIS [12].

In early stages of the specification, one can be less precise about the data base operation, tightening the specification when the database design is determined. In this way, there is an iteration between pure specification and architectural design, as well as between process and data specification.

For a given IIS, if we specify the actions for each of the structured operations, the result is a complete specification of the operations. In combination with the data base specification and the user interface definition, the product is a complete specification of the IIS, our desired goal.

The definition of the structured operations forms the link between the user interface and the data base. It is necessary to define the semantic actions, i.e., the structured operations, where they are designated on the transition diagrams. The specification of the actions contains the operations on the data base, using a relational algebra or calculus-like notation to define formally the retrieval or update operation(s). Any relationally complete language can be used effectively in this role. For continuity, we have used PLAIN in the example below; SEQUEL2 [13] embedded in a programming language could have been used alternatively.

The entire process of specifying these structured operations can rely heavily upon notions of data abstraction, as applied to data base management [14,15,16,17], extending the work on algebraic specification of data types [18,19]. From the user perspective, the logical operation to be performed as a result of the user input is independent of both the representational detail of the data (physical level) and the data base organization (logical level). In other words, what appears to be a transaction to the user is mapped into a set of lower-level operations, the details of which are hidden from the user. Furthermore, different data abstractions can be developed for different user classes, providing each class with a different "view" of the system, corresponding very closely to the ANSI/SPARC notion of multiple external models.

There are a number of advantages to using the data abstraction approach to the design of operations. First, as noted above, it is possible to achieve a high degree of data independence, since information about data base organization may be effectively hidden from large parts of the IIS. Second, necessary checks on data validity and semantic integrity [20] can be incorporated within each operation, thereby gaining additional control over correctness. Third, restrictions of access may be achieved by limiting the set of abstract operations available to a given user class, thereby offering some protection against malicious users.

It is important to note here that this approach to operations definition is workable for those systems where a large percentage of the operations upon the data can be determined in advance. Such is the case for most IIS's used by computer-naive users. In general, however, it is also necessary to provide an alternative mechanism for retrieval from the data base, e.g., a query language, to handle special "one-time" user requests. Our specification methodology concentrates on the routine structured operations with relatively little consideration given to the unstructured special requests.

PLAIN -- the IIS Implementation Language

Certain characteristics of programming languages were seen as essential for the construction of an IIS, including:

1 features for string handling

2 features to support user/program dialogue, including input/output operations and a rudimentary pattern specification and pattern matching capability to control input and to format output

3 features for data base, as well as file, management

4 features for trapping and handling exceptional conditions during program execution, typically caused by user input errors

5 facilities for data declarations, including both program variables and persistent objects (files and data bases), along with the ability to define new objects and operations upon them

6 features that support a systematic approach to coding, providing restricted control structures and effective modularization of program units

A study of numerous existing programming languages revealed that no language provided all of these important features. The general tendency was for languages supporting systematic programming practices to be weak on features for input/output and data management, while those languages heavily used for interactive programs were equally weak in their support for systematic programming.

The implication of this discovery was that one could have an elegant design or a precise specification and would then be unable to realize them in any available programming language. The resulting IIS would then fall short of meeting the desires of the users or the designers.

As a result, the programming language PLAIN (Programming LAnguage for INteraction) was designed [21]. PLAIN is primarily derived from Pascal [22], with features added to address the needs of IIS implementers and with some modifications to strengthen the support for modularity and abstraction. These features for systematic programming, described at length in [23], add facilities for data abstraction and enhance the visibility of data flow within programs.

A key difference between PLAIN and many other programming languages is that PLAIN *integrates* the notions of programming languages and data base management, rather than simply providing an interface. This is achieved in several ways:

1 PLAIN supports two types of data base type declarations: **relation** and **marking**. A relation has the property that all tuples are unique, with the persistence of the relation independent of program execution. A marking is used for intermediate results during operations on relations; their persistence is determined by the lexical scope of their declarations. A marking may or may not have duplicate tuples.

Attributes of markings and relations are declared to be of a given type so that type checking may be carried out on database objects in the same way that one performs type checking on program variables.

2 At the lowest level of relation access and manipulation, it is possible to name a tuple of a relation and to name individual tuples within the relation. If a relation of degree N has M key fields, where $M <= N$, the specification of the values for the M key fields designates a unique tuple of the relation (or no tuple at all).

Consider the following relation declaration:

```
var j: relation [key jnum] of
        jnum: char [2];
        jname: string;
        city: string
    end j;
```

If we then write j['j2'], that designates at most one tuple of the relation j. Given that specification, it is then possible to specify attributes within that tuple, such as

j['j2'].city

This use provides an *associative* addressing mechanism for the data base for those cases where all the values for the key attributes are known.

This attribute designator may appear within any expression in the program, thereby achieving a tight mesh between program variables and database entries within a PLAIN program. Furthermore, an attribute designator may appear on the left-hand-side of an assignment statement as one way of updating the data base.

3 The **assert** statement of PLAIN can be used for database objects, thereby providing a rudimentary facility for checking database integrity.

4 The iterative features of the language, including the **foreach** clause and the **loop-repeat** construct, provide for tuple-by-tuple processing where appropriate.

In summary, these facilities, combined with the high level operations on relations -- selection, projection, join, union, intersection, and difference -- and the aggregation functions -- count, sum, avg, min, and max -- help to achieve a highly effective integration of the necessary data management features.

Another important feature of PLAIN for the construction of interactive information systems is the exception-handling mechanism. This mechanism, described at greater length in [24], seeks to provide a well-structured flow of control following the occurrence of an exceptional condition. Such a situation is quite common in IIS usage, mainly due to input errors by users. Consider, as an example, the following statement in a (generic) high level language:

READ (fmt) A(I)

where fmt is a programmer-defined format or picture, A is an array of real (floating-point) numbers, and I is an integer subscript. The READ statement will read input from a user terminal. The following (incomplete) list shows some of the difficulties that can occur in the *execution* of this statement:

1 the value of I may be outside the valid bounds for the array A

2 the input may be non-numeric when a numeric value was expected

3 there may be a physical input/output error during the READ

4 the value input may cause arithmetic overflow or underflow on the host computer

5 the user may type some unusual character, such as a break, an escape, or a rubout

6 the user may type nothing at all for an indefinite period or time or may forget to transmit what has been typed.

In short, every effort should be made to check for these possibilities and to prevent them from affecting the end user adversely.

In PLAIN, the programmer may create a **handler procedure** that can be associated with the occurrence of a specific exception at a specific program location. In addition to the builtin exceptions, including those for arithmetic underflow and overflow, division by zero, subscript index, undefined values, input/output errors, and character conversion errors, the programmer may define new exceptions and handle them as well.

When an exception is raised, either through the **signal** statement or through an automatic mechanism in the language processor, the handler procedure can carry out any required actions, potentially clear the offending exception, and then return control to normal program flow, to the beginning of the statement in which the exception occurred (**retry**), or to the invocation point of the procedure in which the exception occurred. In this way, exceptions can be passed through succeeding levels of invocation with any necessary actions being taken at each level.

Since exception-handling is done with procedures, it is possible to pass parameters from the environment of the exception to the handler procedure, following the normal rules for scoping of declarations. At any point, the active exception may be cleared by the handler for that level so that normal program operation may continue.

Taken together, these features provide a powerful facility for trapping and handling exceptional conditions, especially those resulting from user errors. Furthermore, it is relatively easy to program the handlers for the various exceptions, so that the information system developer is not discouraged from incorporating the necessary provisions for imparting the desired robustness to the system and protecting the users against the potentially catastrophic consequences of their own errors.

The third important group of features in PLAIN provides for the specification of patterns, along with some elementary facilities for matching these patterns against strings. Patterns in PLAIN serve multiple purposes, including:

1 a basis for verifying the presence of a string or string class within another string

2 a means to specify the required format for input

3 a means for formatting user output

All of these capabilities are important for interactive programs. However, the first use is the most critical and serves several functions. First, it is possible to determine that a given string meets certain requirements, such as containing a key word out of a class of key words or that the object character string contains only digits. Next, it is possible to apply these checks against data in the data base as a partial solution to problems of semantic integrity. Finally, it is possible to group patterns into pattern sets, determine which element of the set (if any) is matched by a given string, and then branch accordingly.

The pattern declaration facility consists of patterns, comprised of string literals, pattern codes, repetition codes, other pattern names, or pattern sets, which consist of one or more patterns or pattern sets.

The pattern codes designate commonly used groupings of characters, such as alphabetic characters (A), digits (N), or graphics (G). These pattern codes may be grouped together, so that LU (designating upper and lower case characters) is equivalent to A and NPC includes all non-alphabetic characters (digits, punctuation, and control characters). Each pattern code, grouping of pattern codes, or pattern unit (a subpattern) is preceded by a repetition designator, which may be definite (an integer) or indefinite, either zero or more (*) or one or more (.). Thus, *G refers to a pattern of any length (possibly null) of printing characters, and 12N refers to a pattern of 12 digits.

The pattern contains oprerator (?) and the pattern equality operator (?=) are used for comparing strings with patterns and return a boolean result. The built in functions contains and match are used for comparing strings with pattern sets and either return the name of a pattern (the first match found) or a nomatch indication. Additional facilities exist for splitting a string into parts according to a pattern specification and for combining variables and literals into a string according to a pattern. These capabilities are especially useful for decomposing input strings and forming output strings.

The pattern-matching facility used with the variable string length mechanism greatly simplifies the task of writing the inneractive dialogue, since many of the detailed character-by-character checking previously required can now be performed with the pattern matching facilities.

When these diverse features are combined, it becomes apparent that the problems of writing code for some common classes of IIS's are sharply reduced. Consider an interactive program in which the user is expected to type in commands and where certain operations are then carried out on the basis of the given command. Then, each legal command can be specified in a pattern, all of the commands can be grouped into a pattern set, and the program can continuously execute a loop in which an input string is read and compared against the pattern set, with the resulting match determining the operation to be performed. If the match is successful, the operation (typically a procedure) can perform further analysis on the string or can request additional input, possibly conforming to a different set of patterns. An unsuccessful operation may result in the signalling of an exceptional condition. If the pattern match is unsuccessful, a diagnostic can be provided. If the user wishes to quit, the loop can be exited.

These operations, invoked from the main program loop, correspond to "high-level" data base operations, since the IIS usually involves access to, addition to, or modification of a data base. In short, then, the facilities described here are central to the construction of many IIS's. These features, missing from other programming languages, suggest the need for PLAIN as a tool for IIS construction.

An Example

In this section, we will present an application of the specification technique described here. Space limitations prohibit a complete specification; thus, we show just enough to give the flavor of the method and to convince the reader of its practicality in serving the needs of the three different views of the specification.

Requirements Definition

An on-line computer system is needed to improve the speed and accuracy of the tellers' transactions with bank customers. It must allow the teller to carry out the routine transactions of opening, closing, crediting and debiting accounts, and determining account balances easily and quickly. All transactions involving changes to an account must be recorded on a transaction log.

At the time that an account is opened, each authorized signer for that account must supply a signature for a signature card. The type of account (personal checking, Key Account, commercial checking, limited service, student account, senior citizen account) must be selected and checks must be ordered. Each cosigner on an account must provide name, address, telephone number, and mother's maiden name. One of the cosigners is designated as the primary account holder for the purpose of mailing statements and other documents.

The system maintains an account record for each account that contains an account number, the account type, identifying information for the primary account holder, a list of transactions, and a current balance. For each transaction, an identification number, the account number, a date, a transaction type, and an amount must be recorded on a transaction log.

The system must provide prompt and reliable responses to all interactions. The system shall be capable of interfacing with a system that will print regularly scheduled statements for customers.

User View Specification

System Commands

Each of the system's commands and their operations are defined in this section. The proper usage of each command is defined by means of a simple notation. Uppercase letters are used to denote the actual command entry while lowercase letters indicate that the user should substitute a value of the type listed. For example, the general structure of the credit command is defined as:

CR accountnumber dollaramount

This command can be used to credit $25.00 to account number 1234567 by entering:

CR 1234567 25.00

The definition is followed by the sequence of steps that are performed when the command is given. In addition, the system checks that the account number is valid and that all dollar amounts typed in are positive amounts containing a decimal point and two places after the decimal point.

CREDIT: CR accountnumber dollaramount

Operations:
- Add 'dollaramount' to current balance of 'accountnumber'
- Enter transaction on transaction log
- Display 'accountnumber', transaction type, 'dollaramount', and new balance for teller verification

DEBIT: DB accountnumber dollaramount

Operations:
- Check 'accountnumber' for sufficient funds
- Subtract 'dollaramount' from current balance in 'accountnumber'
- Enter transaction on transaction log
- Display 'accountnumber', transaction type, 'dollaramount', and new balance for teller verification

BALANCE: BAL accountnumber

Operations:
- Display 'accountnumber' and current balance for 'accountnumber'

NEW: NEW

Operations:
- System prompts teller to
    - enter name, address, telephone number and mother's maiden name for each cosigner
    - select type of account
    - order checks for printing
- Generate new account number for chosen account type
- Display customer identification and account type for teller verification
- Enter account information into set of account records

CLOSE: CLOSE accountnumber

Operations:
- If account type of 'accountnumber' is Key Account and balance is negative, collect funds owed (manual operation)
- Request closing statement for 'accountnumber' (manual operation)
- Remove account and associated information from system

HELP: HELP

Operations:
- Display message listing all legal commands and a summary of their function and use

QUIT: QUIT

Operations:
- Display signoff message
- Log user (teller) off system

System Data Base

The data items included in the data base are described in Table 1, showing their domains and the constraints upon their values.

(Additional user view specification is omitted here.)

Design/Verification View Specification

The transition diagram for the user interface to the banking system is shown in Figure 4. The relational data base organization is shown in Figure 5; key attributes are underlined in each relation. The diagram provides for subconversations for five of the operations, those requiring more than one item of input. Figure 6 shows the subconversation for the 'CR' command. ACCTNO and AMOUNT are of the form (7N) and (*N,'.',2N), respectively, using the PLAIN pattern notation; ACCTNO and AMOUNT may be represented by diagrams also. The semantic actions for the 'CR' command are shown in Figure 7; action 1 relies upon the data base design of Figure 5.

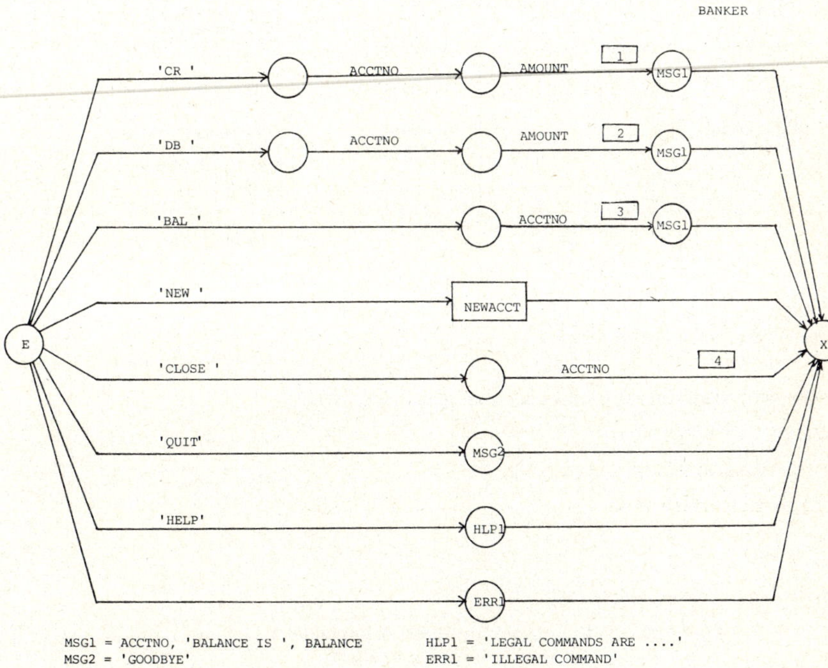

Figure 4.– Transition Diagram for Simple Banking System Version 1

Table 1. Data Items for Teller Information System Example

User Name	System Name	Domain	Constraints
Account Number	ACCT	Integer	7 digits; first digit matches account type
Name	NAME	String	
Address	ADDRESS	String	
Telephone Number	PHONE	String	7 to 10 numerics
Mother's Maiden Name	MMNAME	String	
Account Type	ACCTTYPE	1..6	1=personal checking; 2=commercial checking; 3=student account; 4=senior citizen account; 5=Key Account; 6=limited
Primary Signer	PRIMARY	Boolean	
Transaction Number	IDENT	0..9999	
Transaction Date	DATE	Char[6]	6 numerics; format YYMMDD
Transaction Type	TTYPE	1..4	1=check; 2=deposit; 3=service charge; 4=loan payment
Transaction Amount	AMT	0..999999.99	2 digits after decimal
Current Balance	BALANCE	0..999999.99	2 digits after decimal
Next Account Number	NUM	Integer Array	1 element per account type; values are 7 digits; first digit matches account type

INFO (**ACCT**, NAME, ADDRESS, PHONE, MMNAME, PRIMARY, ACCTTYPE)

CHECK (**ACCT**, BALANCE)

CHECKTRANS (**ACCT**, **IDENT**, DATE, TTYPE, AMT)

NEXTNUM (**ACCTTYPE**, NUM)

Figure 5 -- Relational database organization for simple banking system

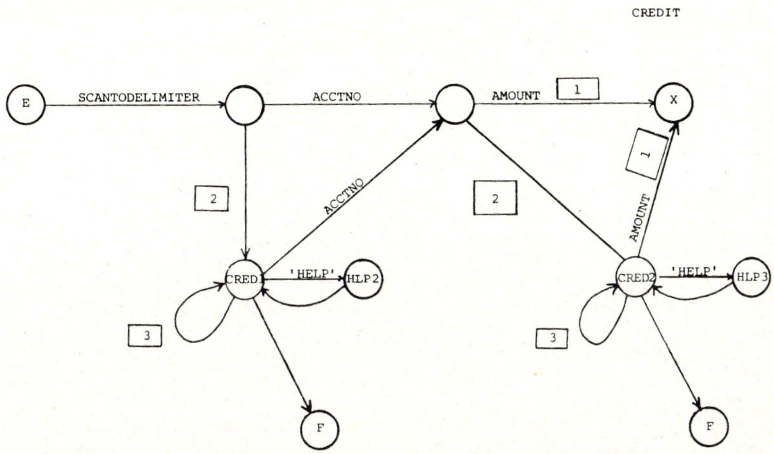


```
CRED1 = 'ACCOUNT NUMBER:    '
CRED2 =          'AMOUNT:    '

HLP2 = 'ACCOUNT NUMBER IS 7 DIGITS'
HLP3 = 'AMOUNT IN DOLLARS AND CENTS,
        SUCH AS 874.23'
```

Figure 6 -- Transition diagram for Credit command subconversation of Simple Banking System

```
[1]
    exception badacct;
    imports CHECK, CHECKTRANS: modified

    if exists (CHECK [acctno])
    then
        CHECK% := CHECK [acctno];
        CHECK%.BALANCE := CHECK%.BALANCE + dollaramount;
        CHECKTRANS :+ [ <acctno, id, today, 2, dollaramount> ];
        write acctno, ' credit $', dollaramount, \n,
            'new balance $', CHECK%.BALANCE

[2]
    errcount := 1

[3]
    if errcount ≥ 3
    then
        {fail}
    else
        errcount := errcount + 1
```

Figure 7 -- Semantic actions in PLAIN for transition diagram of Figure 6

Specification into Implementation

The transition diagrams, the data base design, and the description of the operations provide a specification, which must eventually lead to an executable PLAIN program. This can be seen most clearly by comparing the PLAIN code of Figure 8 with the transition diagram of Figure 4 and the database design of Figure 5. The transformation is quite straightforward, with paths on the diagram mapping into patterns or pattern sets, subconversations into procedures with the input line passed as parameters, and the database design directly encoded. Similarly, the subconversation CURRBAL is shown in Figure 9. Note that it imports the relation checkrec and makes an associative reference to the appropriate tuple. (This code has been simplified for illustrative purposes, eliminating the algorithm to count repetitions in the event of improper input along with the associated exception.)

Nonetheless, it can be seen that the transition between the specification and PLAIN is not highly complicated and that the design of the data base and the data manipulation suffices for many of the design activities. Furthermore, the transition diagram approach decomposes the operations into relatively small steps, leading to small system modules, a desirable goal.

The specification technique and the PLAIN language, combined with the mapping between them, is at the heart of the USE methodology and constitutes that part of the methodology that has been worked out carefully to this point. Ongoing work is concentrating on design analysis and evaluation of design alternatives, along with strategies for testing and verification of the PLAIN program against the specification.

The Module Control System

Another activity in creation of the USE environment is design of the Module Control System (MCS), a tool intended to help manage the specification, design, and program text for all of the different system modules, along with the supporting documentation. In the design and development of a medium-to-large information system, a large number of module descriptions are produced. In addition to overall system documentation, such as system requirements, there is information concerning each of the system modules. Thus, one would have a behavioral (non-procedural) description of the module as a specification, a program design language version of the algorithm, one or more versions of the code (perhaps source and object), and description of the test cases and results. This documentation would be supplemented by user documentation, data directories/dictionaries, and information for linking the code together into an executable unit. Some machine assistance is essential for managing all of these different pieces of text and for managing the software development activity that has produced them.

Considerable attention has been given to this and to related problems. Baker and Mills, in their formulation of the Chief Programmer Team approach to management of software development, have identified the librarian as a key member of the team and have made the librarian responsible for the Program Production Library (PPL) [25], including most of the items listed above. Our objective may be viewed as providing automated assistance to the librarian.

The developers of the Programmers' Workbench have created the Source Code Control System (SCCS) [26] and Make [27], tools that also address this problem, but are directed to the various pieces of code, rather than to all of the different forms of documentation surrounding a system. One important feature of SCCS, though, is its ability to handle multiple versions of a system and to configure the system as it existed at a given time.

The goal of MCS is to combine these capabilities, providing a means for handling all of the required documentation and linking together all of the documents related at both the system level *and* the module level. Thus, for any given module, one could examine the specification, design, code, and test data. Furthermore, the MCS could require the specification for the module to be produced prior to the code for that module.

```
program banker;
{this program provides the operations available to a teller using the banking system}
type money = 0..999999.99;
     inforec = record
                    acct: integer;
                    name: string;
                    address: string;
                    phone: char [10];
                    mmnname: string;
                    accttype: 1..6;
                    primary: boolean
               end inforec;
     checktransrec =  record
                          acct: integer;
                          ident: 0..9999;
                          date: integer;
                          ttype: 1..4;
                          amt: money
                      end checktransrec;
     checkrec =  record
                     acct: integer;
                     balance: money
                 end checkrec;
     nextnumrec =  record
                       accttype: 1..6;
                       num: integer
                   end nextnumrec;
var info: relation [key acct, name] of inforec;
               {info stores information on account holders}
    checktrans: relation [key acct, ident] of checktransrec;
               {checktrans stores information on all transactions for all accounts}
    checkrec: relation [key acct] of checkrec;
               {checkrec holds current balance for all accounts}
    nextnum: relation [key accttype] of nextnumrec;
               {nextnum stores next available account number for each
                account type to be given to new accounts}
    inline: string; {holds the current input line}
patset commands [cr, deb, bal, newa, closea, help, quit];
               {set of legal commands}
pattern cr ('cr', *G);            {the credit command}
        deb ('db', *G);           {the debit command}
        bal ('bal', *G);          {the balance command}
        newa ('new', *G);         {the new account command}
        closea ('close', *G);     {the close account command}
        help ('help');            {the help command}
        quit ('quit');            {the quit command}
handler procedure trouble;
begin
    write 'fatal input/output error in reading command';
    signal fail  {terminates program in event of terminal I/O error}
end trouble;
{begin main program here
**********BANKER**********}
begin
    loop
        read inline ![ioerr: trouble];
        case match (inline, commands) of
            when cr: credit (inline)
            when deb: debit (inline)
            when bal: currbal
            when newa: newacct (inline)
            when closea: closeacct (inline)
            when help: write 'legal commands are ....' {full text omitted}
            when quit: exit
            else write 'illegal command'
        end case
    repeat;
    write 'goodbye'
end banker.
```

Figure 8 -- PLAIN main program for Simple Banking System

```
procedure currbal;
imports inline, checkrec: readonly;
pattern bal2 ('bal', *A, .X, 7N);
var acctno: integer;
begin
    {this procedure finds the current balance for a given account}
    if inline ?= bal2   {search inline for pattern bal2}
    then
        split (inline, bal2 → $,$,$,acctno);
        checkrec% := checkrec [acctno];  {set current tuple indicator}
        if checkrec% = nil
        then
            write 'nonexistent account number'
        else
            write acctno, 'balance is ', checkrec%.balance
        end if
    else
        write 'proper command format is bal, followed by a space', \n,
    end if
end currbal;
```

Figure 9 -- PLAIN code for currbal operation

Thus, while PLAIN and the specification technique are intended to support the technical activities of IIS development, MCS is aimed more directly at the managerial and organizational issues in software construction. Information concerning the status of every module can be maintained online and thus makes it possible to monitor progress and identify problems. Furthermore, the various members of a project team have access to the information, so that some of the traditional communication and interface problems between members of a group and their subsystems can be overcome.

Conclusion

The aim of the USE project is to devise techniques and automated tools that can lead to a systematization of the IIS development process and to the straightforward creation of reliable, economical, user-centered information systems.

The environment is being created at the University of California, San Francisco, using the UNIX operating system [28] on the PDP-11 computer. Work is progressing on both the implementation of a PLAIN interpreter and a transition diagram processor; it is expected that both of these tools will be operational by the end of 1979.

The work described here leads in several directions. First, the implementation of the language and the specification method only provide a small set of the tools that can truly be useful in the software development process. While many other useful tools exist in the UNIX environment, it will be necessary to integrate some of the other tools as well as to design and build additional tools before having a sufficiently powerful environment for IIS development.

There is also an evaluation component to be addressed. Experience with these software engineering techniques and languages is still very limited and it will be necessary to gain more knowledge about the relative strengths and weaknesses of each. Furthermore, it will be helpful to evaluate the software systems produced using this methodology and set of tools to determine the extent to which the systems or the IIS developers benefited from their use.

The effectiveness cannot be ultimately determined until several systems have been specified, implemented, and tested using the methodology in the USE environment. In the final analysis, though, we hope to show that these tools are of considerable assistance to the IIS developer and that they provide greater support for this class of programs than other extant methods.

Acknowledgments

This work was supported in part by the National Library of Medicine (LM 00153). Computing support was provided by the National Institutes of Health grant RR-1081 to the UCSF Computer Graphics Laboratory, Principal Investigator: Robert Langridge. The comments of Peter Freeman, Susan Stinson, and the referees on an earlier draft of this paper are greatly appreciated.

References

[1] Wasserman, A.I. and C.J. Prenner, "Toward a Unified View of Database Management, Programming Languages, and Operating Systems," *Information Systems*, vol. 4, no. 2 (June, 1979), in press.

[2] Wasserman, A.I., "On the Meaning of Discipline in Software Design and Development," in *Software Engineering Techniques*, ed. D. Bates. Maidenhead: Infotech International, 1977, vol. 2, pp. 343-359.

[3] Caine, S.H. and E.K. Gordon, "PDL -- a Tool for Software Design," *Proc. AFIPS 1975 NCC*, vol. 44, pp. 271-276.

[4] Roubine, O. and L. Robinson, "SPECIAL Reference Manual," SRI International, Technical Report CSG-45, Menlo Park, CA, 1976.

[5] Austin, S.L., B.P. Buckles, and J.P. Ryan, "SSL -- a Software Specification Language," Science Applications Inc., Report SAI-77-537-HU, Huntsville, AL, 1976.

[6] Hamilton, M. and S. Zeldin, "AXES Syntax Description," Technical Report TR-4, Higher Order Software, Cambridge, MA, 1976.

[7] Conway, M.E., "Design of a Separable Transition-Diagram Compiler," *Comm. ACM*, vol. 6, no. 7 (July, 1963), pp. 396-408.

[8] MUMPS Development Committee, *American National Standard MUMPS Language Standard*. ANSI X11.1-1977.

[9] Parnas, D.L., "On the Use of Transition Diagrams in the Design of a User Interface for an Interactive Computer System," *Proc. 24th National ACM Conference*, 1969, pp. 379-385.

[10] ANSI/X3/SPARC Study Group on Data Base Management Systems: Interim Report 75-02-08, *FDT*, vol. 7, no. 2 (1975).

[11] Codd, E.F., "A Relational Model of Data for Shared Data Banks," *Comm. ACM*, vol. 13, no. 6 (June, 1970), pp. 377-387.

[12] Gray, J., "Notes on Data Base Operating Systems," IBM San Jose Research Laboratory, Research Report RJ2188, February, 1978.

[13] Chamberlin, D.D. *et al.*, "SEQUEL2: a Unified Approach to Data Definition, Manipulation, and Control," *IBM Journal of Research and Development*, vol. 20, no. 6 (November, 1976), pp. 560-575.

[14] Weber, H., "A Software Engineering View of Data Base Systems," *Proc. 4th Int'l Conf. on Very Large Data Bases*, 1978, pp. 36-51.

[15] Smith, J.M. and D.C.P. Smith, "Database Abstractions: Aggregation and Generalization," *ACM Transactions on Database Systems*, vol. 2, no. 2 (June, 1977), pp. 105-133.

[16] Lockemann, P. *et al.*, "Data Abstractions for Database Systems," *Transactions on Database Systems*, vol. 4, no. 1 (March, 1979), pp. 60-75.

[17] Wasserman, A.I., "The Extension of Abstract Data Types to Data Base Management," in preparation, 1979.

[18] Guttag, J.V., "Abstract Data Types and the Development of Data Structures," *Comm. ACM*, vol. 20, no. 6 (June, 1977), pp. 396-404.

[19] Liskov, B. and S.N. Zilles, "Specification Techniques for Data Abstractions," *IEEE Transactions on Software Engineering*, vol. SE-1, no. 1 (March, 1975), pp. 7-19.

[20] Brodie, M.L., "Specification and Verification of Data Base Semantic Integrity," University of Toronto, Computer Systems Research Group, Technical Report CSRG-91, April, 1978. (Ph.D. dissertation)

[21] Wasserman, A.I., D.D. Sherertz, and E.F. Handa, "Report on the Programming Language PLAIN," University of California San Francisco, Laboratory of Medical Information Science, Technical Report No. 34, 1978.

[22] Wirth, N., "The Programming Language Pascal," *Acta Informatica*, vol. 1, no. 1 (1971), pp. 35-63.

[23] Wasserman, A.I., "The Design of PLAIN -- Support for Systematic Programming," submitted for publication, 1979.

[24] Wasserman, A.I., "Design and Evaluation of a Procedure-Oriented Exception-Handling Mechanism," in preparation, 1979.

[25] Baker, F.T., "Chief Programmer Team Management of Production Programming," *IBM Systems Journal*, vol. 11, no. 1 (1972), pp. 56-73.

[26] Rochkind, M.J., "The Source Code Control System," *IEEE Transactions on Software Engineering*, vol. SE-1, no. 4 (December, 1975), pp. 364-369.

[27] Feldman, S.J., "Make -- A Program for Maintaining Computer Programs," *Software -- Practice and Experience*, vol. 9, no. 4 (April, 1979), pp. 255-265.

[28] Ritchie, D.M. and K. Thompson, "The Unix Time Sharing System," *Comm. ACM*, vol. 17, no. 7 (July, 1974), pp. 365-375.

Formal Models and Practical Tools for Information Systems Design
H.-J. Schneider, Editor
North-Holland Publishing Company

PROPERTIES OF USER REQUIREMENTS

M. Hamilton & S. Zeldin

Higher Order Software, Inc.
806 Massachusetts Avenue
Cambridge, Massachusetts 02139

The concept of a user is discussed here in terms of a systematic point of view. Just as with any system there are certain properties that are generic to all users, as well as with systems, in general. The major difference between defining a system as a user or defining a system as something else, say a developer, is simply one of viewpoint. Such a viewpoint is discussed in terms of three basic types of objects used to define any system and the integrated control relationships of these objects which determine a control hierarchy for a user and its subusers. Although there are many kinds of users, both human and otherwise, we chose to concentrate here on that user who is able to make use of the properties of a system definition in order to know how to develop a system. In particular we show an example of a definition with methodology dependent properties where a user is able to determine from this definition how to resource allocate his system. In this example, we show a possible relationship between one user and another user within a dynamic multiprocessor environment.

1. INTRODUCTION

More often than not, the user is the one who makes the decision as to what is technology and what is not. More often than not, the user is the one who decides whether or not a particular technology is part of, or is responsible for, a revolution or an evolution. A potential technology could conceivably be the greatest invention of all times; yet, if there is no one to use it, is that "technology" indeed a technology?

Technologists often refer to the potential users of their technology as "naive" users. The users, on the other hand, view these same technologists as being presumptuous to think they have answers to problems they don't understand. We believe that there are some very simple measures that can be taken to alleviate a communication gap that often appears to be much larger than it really is. These measures include a means of establishing a basic set of common meanings (or semantics) between the user and the technologist. These meanings should be able to be communicated as simply as possible and there must be room for flexibility in the ways that these meanings can be expressed. That is, there must be an opportunity to discuss more complex concepts in terms of primitive basic meanings as well as a means of changing requirements as more is understood about a particular system environment. There must also be a means to separate the what in a meaning from the how in a meaning with respect to a particular viewpoint; for a what to one user is a how to another user. We have found in our own experience that once a successful communication link is established between users and technologists in a particular project, that the differences in viewpoint can no longer be categorized with respect to whether someone is a user or a technologist; but rather these differences show up much more often with respect to those who want or are able to accept change versus those who do not want or are not able to accept change within their own environment. And, major changes are usually more successful when both users and technologists, who are ready for change in their respective environments, work out the requirements for those changes together.

More often than not, the most successful venture is one where the user and the technologist continuously exchange functions, and where it is impossible to tell who is the user and who is the technologist, for both, after all, are ultimately users as well as technologists.

We have also found that no matter who or what the user is that there are some very basic properties that are generic to all users. We believe that once these generic properties are better understood by both the user and the technologist that both the user and the technologist will be able to support more successfully the needs of a particular user and similarly, therefore, the needs of a corresponding technologist.

2. WHAT IS A USER?

In Webster's dictionary a user is one who or that which uses. Use on the other hand, is an act of employing anything. In a generic sense, these definitions are quite appropriate. In various environments, however, "user" often conveys more specific meanings. In fact, these meanings vary with respect to various viewpoints (or axes) within a particular environment. A user, for example, could be (1) a set of organizations, an organization, or a person; (2) a higher level or a lower level entity; (3) an automated or a manual process; (4) a synchronous or an asynchronous process; (5) an object consisting of hardware, software, humanware, firmware or a combination thereof; (6) a receiver of the final output on a particular project (e. g., from a manufacturing process) or a receiver of an intermediate result from one of the tools within that project that are used to deliver that final output (e. g., from a simulation of a manufacturing process); (7) an "operating system" within a system (such as software) or merely a CALLer of a particular subroutine within that system; (8) a static or a dynamic process; (9) a human being or a simulated human being; (10) something or someone which interacts or (11) only a human being.

3. THE USERS IN A SYSTEM DEVELOPMENT PROCESS

The type of users we have had most experience with in our own work has been that set of users who have been involved in developing systems, of which software is usually a part. In order to understand such users, we attempt to define each type of user in terms of a user model. The system development process can also be viewed as a user model where each instance is continuously receiving user requirements for a particular target system as inputs and producing specifications as outputs[1]. In such a model requirements are those items which are desired or needed by a user and specifications are the results which realize those requirements. One user's requirements could, of course, be another user's specifications. In such a case, each user is relating to the same development process, but each relates with a different emphasis. Each instance of output from a development process is a particular target system which is developed for a user of that target system. Within a development process, there are several types of users.

A manager, as a user, would view the development process, as a user model, with respect to properties of control.

A designer, as a user, would view the development process, as a user model, with respect to properties of definition.

A documentor, as a user, would view the development process, as a user model, with respect to properties of description.

A resource allocator, as a user, would view the development process, as a user model, with respect to properties of implementation.

A verifier, as a user, would view the development process, as a user model, with respect to properties of execution.

The user of each target system resulting from the development process, as a user model, will, of course, be concerned with all aspects of the development process, since a successful execution of the target system is directly dependent on a successful execution of the development process.

4. GENERIC PROPERTIES OF AN INTEGRATED USER

The generic properties of a user are defined in terms of an integrated point of view. That is, not every user behaves the way we'd like him to, but we are setting up an ideal set of behavior patterns in order to compare users with respect to "goodness" and "badness" traits. We define the user as a controller [3], and therefore (in our terms) as an integrator of all aspects of control. This means that a user is in control of the functions to be performed, input and output of these functions, where its functions receive their inputs, where its functions place their outputs, how these functions handle errors and the ordering, including relative importance of these functions, with respect to each other.

An integrated user, even though explicitly defined, with respect to being in control, can allow varying degrees of flexibility with respect to satisfying that user's needs.

A user, for example, could be specified to control, directly, each individual input and output for that user's functions to be performed or the same user could specify a set of functions which could perform on one of a possible set of inputs to produce a corresponding output, or a set of functional relationships could be specified which could perform on one of a possible set of functions which in turn performs on one of a possible set of inputs. Similarly, the user could be specified with even a more abstract environment by controlling a set of relationships which control relationships. Ultimately, however, the user's needs are performed when all relationahips, all functions and all inputs and outputs under his control are determined. In this respect, a user system can be defined in terms of a function, since the "bottom line" is when that system is being performed.

5. UNDERSTANDING A PARTICULAR USER

There are several steps to perform in understanding a particular user's needs. First, we narrow down the problem. This is done by collecting information such as the user's greatest problems, wish lists, desired properties currently existing in that user's system, manual processes of the user and interfaces of that user [2]. From such information, we attempt to group certain types of data into categories as well as to prioritize those categories which appear to be the most practical ones to tackle first. Once such a process has been completed, usually after several iterations between users and technologists, we attempt to key in on a particularly important area and define a user model, as it currently exists, in terms of the specification language, AXES [4]. Such a technique has helped us in the area of asking questions that might never have been asked and of accelerating the asking of questions that would eventually have been asked [5]. It also ensures that the user model definition is consistent and logically complete.

A user model can be represented as a system in terms of a hierarchy. In these terms we use AXES for decomposing a system throughout it's various levels of definition. Although other methodologies such as [6], [7], [8] and [9] define systems which adhere to hierarchical treelike definition, there are a collection of properties in systems defined with AXES which make them behave quite differently than other systems. Some interesting ones, from a user point of view, are summarized here. A more complete and detailed discussion of these and other properties can be found in [10]. We use this set of properties as a model against which we analyze a particular methodology for its areas of effectiveness.

In an AXES decomposition, there is an explicit set of rules that must be followed in order to proceed from one level of decomposition to another. By following these rules, one is able to determine if a function has properly been decomposed with respect to complete replacement, no more, no less. By following these rules, one is able to specify a system without data conflicts or timing conflicts.

AXES systems can be defined in terms of three primitive control structures. They can be either used directly to define systems or used to define mechanisms which are used to define systems.

Rather than key in on a best or only way to define a syntax (including graphics) to describe a system, AXES allows for alternative methods of description. For example, the user can define his own syntax providing that all syntax is backed up by semantic definitions, that such use is consistent with AXES standards and that the user describes everything that is necessary and sufficient.

At any node in an AXES hierarchy a user is able to identify any object with respect to an integrated set of aspects of control (see Section 4) which inherently incorporates types of models and viewpoints. That is, every node on an AXES hierarchy represents a controller (the definition of which, in terms of structures, is the user model) that relates functions (the definitions of which, in terms of operations, is a functional model). Those functions in turn relate input to output (the definition of which, in terms of data types, is an informational model). And, every node on an AXES hierarchy is expressed in terms of all of its viewpoints (i.e., definition, description, implementation and execution). The fact that all aspects of control, all types of models and all viewpoints are inherently integrated with respect to each other at a given node significantly simplifies any given system definition. And, every user in a development process of an AXES system is able to relate to every node in his own unique way (e. g., the manager with respect to control). We have found that these are the properties that should be integrated in a system definition and not artificially decoupled for the sake of "modularity"; for such a separation has often resulted in enhancing the errors in a system. On any AXES hierarchy, one knows when a system definition is complete, because the bottom nodes are represented by primitive operations or previously defined structures and operations [10].

An AXES definition can be viewed as a specification which can be directly implemented in terms of a distributed processing environment. Other types of implementations (e. g., multi-programming and single CPU processing) are special cases of a distributed processing environment.

6. IMPLEMENTATION OF A USER MODEL

Once a user model has been defined in terms of an AXES specification the information about the what of that user is known. This includes his structures, functions, and data types. Performance constraints are inherently part of such a specification. The next process shows how that particular user is to be implemented. Whereas the what of a function runs in one user model, the how of a function runs on another user model. A description is one of the inputs to the implementation process. A resource allocated architecture, which includes a representation (or simulation) of the specification, is one of the outputs of this process. Often, designers skip the definition of the what and jump immediately to the how before they begin to build their systems. Such a process is not only error prone, but it also often locks developers in unnecessarily, by including constraints which are only relevant to a particular implementation environment. (It is reminiscent of the times when several of our higher order language programmers received "high level" specifications to the level of detail of assembly language, when an assembly language was no longer being used, only because the specification engineers had "grown-up" in such an environment prior to the use of a new language. These specifications not only slowed down the programmers but they also forced things like special bit manipulations that would no longer have been necessary.)

A particular resource allocation process is able to make use of an AXES description in order to determine what procedures and data are to be implemented, what their properties are (with respect to aspects such as ordering, (including time), scope, access rights, priority and data flow), what can be done in common, what can be done to safely implement them and what can be done to most efficiently implement them. These relationships between a specification and its possible set of implementations are discussed in [10]. Such a process can be performed by a human being or eventually by a machine.

7. SUPPORT OF A USER

There are many ways to support a user's needs. One way is to let a user go along and essentially perform the same function, but to help speed-up those functions with more standardization or automated tools which support already existing support aids. Another way is to provide additional information at certain checkpoints which help to make better decisions faster or which prevent the making of errors, or which recover from errors already made. Ultimately, one would like to help a user make the best decision at the latest time possible, which in turn is basically the only way to make the very best decision. Such a decision support tool is of course dynamic, as opposed to static. The aim of interactive information systems is to be able to support such a concept. Emphasis on the user, in this respect, is discussed in [11]. Another way is to help the user by replacing entirely some of the user functions. Another way is to change the user model so that the user has a whole new set of functions. And, of course, there could be some combination of all of these methods.

The advantage of defining the users own user model first is to help determine which of these ways make most sense, considering a balance between the ideal and the practical.

8. THE PROCESS OF DEFINING A USER MODEL

We consider two major aspects in defining a user model. The first, is the user modelling technique itself, as a user model. The second is the proper use of that technique. We use the AXES technique of defining a STRUCTURE as the technique of defining a user model (Appendix 1). Instances of a particular structure can themselves be user models, as well. In the end the final "plugged-in" instances represent a particular scenario (or combinations of scenarios) of a well defined user model. Such a user model can represent a large set of user scenarios and thus there is no need to define each one on an individual by individual basis.

Defining user models in the beginning of a project (or projects) is harder than later on. For, once a few generic ones are defined, they are saved in a user model library and can be used to build others. Often, one user on a project defines user models that several users within that project can use. Projects also can share user models, as well.

The way in which one goes about defining user models can vary depending on who's doing it. We have found that an effective way of speeding-up the process is to come up with a representative set of scenarios for a particular user environment. Aspects of those scenarios are then classified. (For example, an astronaut in an astronaut user model would point a spacecraft. An instance of such a model would be pointing a spacecraft at a star. An instance of that model would be the pointing of a spacecraft at a particular star.) These more composite scenario aspects are then defined as STRUCTURES, or STRUCTURES of STRUCTURES, etc. Then actual scenarios are used as instances of the models and a user verifies that these models do or do not represent his point of view.

9. VARIOUS VIEWPOINTS OF AN INTEGRATED USER

We are only concerned with the relationships of any user with respect to those functions he controls. From a practical standpoint this means that the integrated user is not concerned with who is controlling him and he has a minimum number of interfaces to contend with. He merely knows what he is to do for whomever his controller is. A user of a user model can relate to that model from several points of view.

In Figure 1, in order to define A, the definitions of B and C are needed and in order to define B, the definitions of D and E are needed. A, B and C are related by a JOIN structure where B depends on C; and B, D and E are related by an OR structure where D or E is to be performed [4]. Both the definition of A and the definition of B are user models. But A is a user with respect to B and C as user models, and B is a user with respect to D and one of the N configurations (or reconfigurations) of E as user models. These relationships are in terms of a <u>definitional</u> point of view. A definition of a master sequencer of two routines in a software system is an example of a user relating to definitions of user models. The <u>description</u> of A is

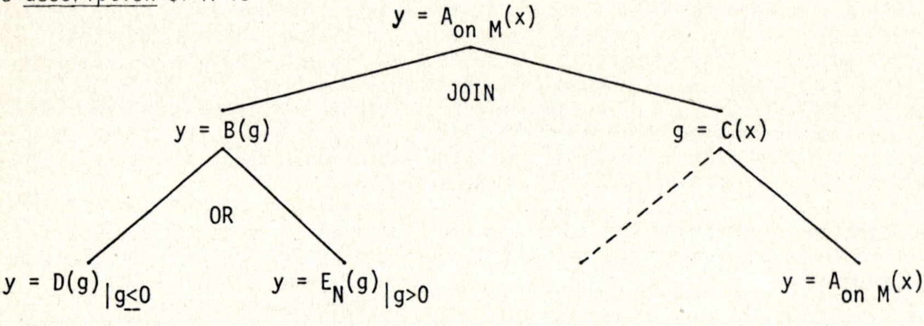

FIGURE 1: <u>The Definition of A</u>

realized by the evidence of Figure 1's existence (i.e., its "pencil" marks). These relationships can of course be more complicated. If, for example, in system A, x is a member of data type "description of user model," A, as a user, could relate to x as a particular description of its own user model (e.g., a description of part of B might be given to B by C in order to show how to schedule B). That description could be in English, FORTRAN, AXES or whatever means is available to convey what that particular model does. A compiler or an analyzer is an example of a tool that relates to a description of a user model (usually before execution begins) and an operating system is an example of a tool that relates to a description of a user model (as well as its definition) after execution begins.

Again, if user A is considered with respect to a machine (in this case M) user A is considered from the viewpoint of a user with respect to its own implementation. An example is A being prepared to run on a particular type of computer. In this case, the description of A would be included as part of M's input since A runs on the M structure. That is, whereas a lower definition level of A relates to A, as an object, a lower implementation layer of A relates to "A," as an object (i.e., the description of A).

If A is considered with respect to its execution, then A is considered from the point of view of an instance being completed for all of A. An example is pushing the "on" button on a computer which resulted in the invocation of A.

The user (or controller) of A is a different one, depending on which viewpoint of A it is that is to be employed, or used. And, when A, itself, is being discussed, it is important to distinguish between its viewpoints (or development layers). Thus, for example, whereas A refers to A's definition, "A" refers to A's description,

$A_{on\ M}$ refers to A's implementation and $[A_{on\ M}]$

refers to A's execution. A, as a user model itself, refers to its' own definition. But unfortunately, a user of A is often meant to imply not only a user of A but also one if its many viewpoints. The ability to differentiate between a user, as a user model, and a user with respect to another user model, and the ability to determine the various viewpoints (often there are more than one of each viewpoint) of a user with respect to the various viewpoints of a user model is the key towards successfully defining the requirements of a particular user. Otherwise, we could define the wrong requirements for a user, or requirements for a wrong user.

10. EXAMPLE OF A PARTICULAR USER

Once a user has defined what he wants to do, he is in a position to ask how best to do it. If a user is interested in how best to use the resources that are available, he can identify, for example, a resource allocation algorithm which uses as input the description of the definition he has created, the resources that are available and time estimates for the functions to be performed (Figure 2). The resource allocation algorithm is, of course, just another user's problem definition.

Assume a user who wants to know "What is the best way to organize time to perform work?" To help such a user get the information he wants, the user is prompted to supply the function to be performed, including its inputs and outputs:

$$(y_i, y_j, y_g) = F_0(x_a, x_b, x_c)$$

The function definition for F_0 may already exist or it may have to be created. In the event the function definition has yet to be created, the user is prompted to select a control structure (Appendix 1) and to assign particular functions and variables as appropriate.

Suppose the user response is:

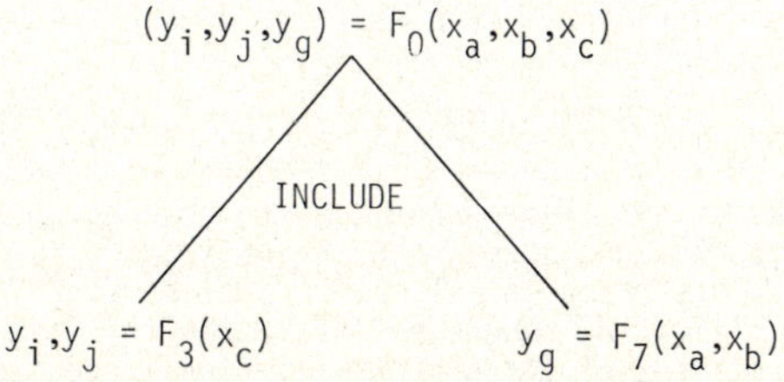

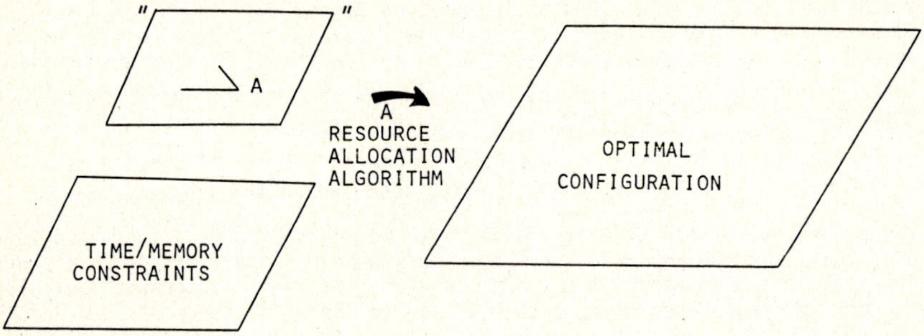

TIME OPTIMAL:	ASSUME UNCONSTRAINED NUMBER OF PROCESSING UNITS UNLIMITED MEMORY
MEMORY OPTIMAL:	ASSUME SINGLE PROCESSING UNIT UNLIMITED EXECUTION TIME
OPTIMAL CONFIGURATION:	COST (TIME OPTIMAL ("A"), MEMORY OPTIMAL ("A"), TIME/MEMORY CONSTRAINTS))

Figure 2: <u>A Resource Allocation Algorithm</u>

The user response is verified by checking the structure definition in the library with the use of the structure. For example, access to variable names are traced according to the rules of the INCLUDE structure (the INCLUDE is used to define independent functions), function F_7 and F_3 are checked to see if they have been previously defined, variables are checked to see if they are associated with defined data types, and the collective use of F_3 and F_7 are checked to see if the level logically replaces function F_0.

In the case where F_3 and F_7 are not previously defined, the user is prompted to repeat the same process of creating levels of decomposition for both F_3 and F_7 until the point at which a previously defined operation is reached. An example of a logically complete decomposition for function F_0 is shown in Figure 3. At this step, the user has defined what he wants to do and the user's responses can be verified for logical consistency.

Some properties of the user's requirements are inherently a part of the definition itself while others can be implied from the foundations upon which the definition is based. We can make use of these properties to respond to specific user needs. With respect to the foundations upon which the definition is based, each primitive control structure has resource allocation implications, as shown in Figure 4. In the case of a repetitive, or recursive, system definition we cannot statically determine how <u>many</u> instances of the system will finally be executed. But, here, we can <u>use</u> the recursive property with respect to a particular definition to

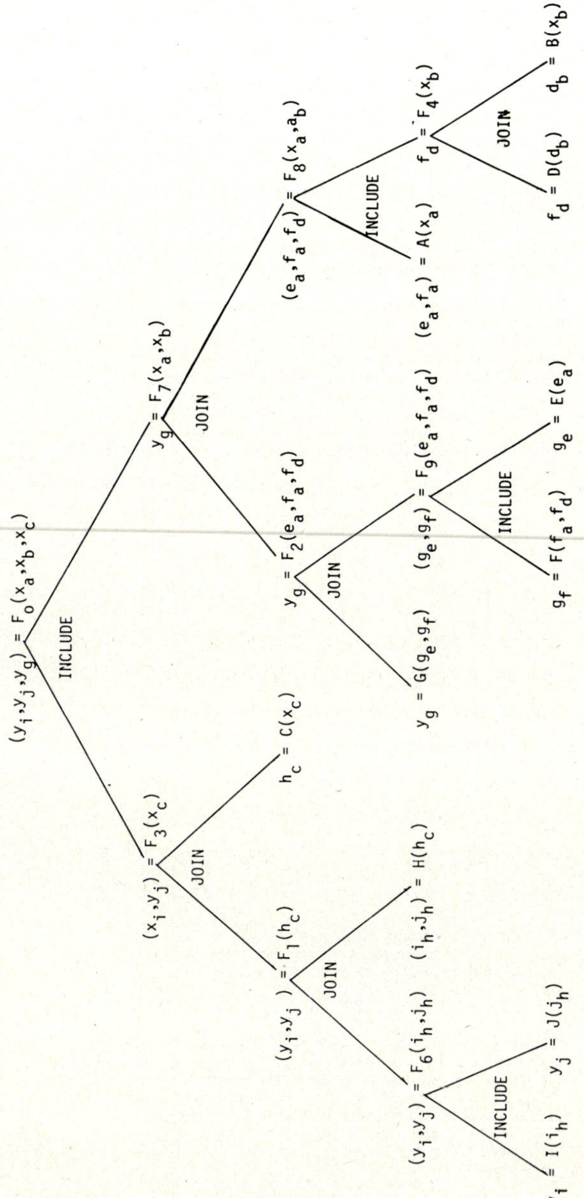

FIGURE 3: The Decomposition of F_o in Terms of Previously Defined Operations A, B, C, D, E, F, G, H, I, J

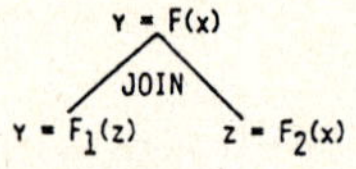

Z EXEMPLIFIES THE GENERATION OF DATA THAT IS LOCAL TO A MODULE. STORAGE SPACE FOR Z DOES NOT NEED TO BE ALLOCATED UNTIL F_2 HAS GENERATED ITS VALUE. WHEN F_1 HAS COMPLETED ITS REFERENCES TO Z, THE STORAGE FOR Z MAY BE RELEASED.

THE STORAGE FOR Y NEED NOT BE ALLOCATED UNTIL ITS VALUE IS GENERATED BY F_1.

BECAUSE F_2 IS NOT NEEDED AFTER Z IS DEFINED, THE STORAGE FOR ITS INSTRUCTIONS MAY BE RELEASED WHEN Z IS DEFINED.

SIMILARLY, THE STORAGE FOR F_1'S INSTRUCTIONS NEED NOT BE ALLOCATED UNTIL Z IS DEFINED.

BECAUSE THE DATA DEPENDENCY OF F_2 AND F_1 IMPLY A SEQUENTIAL EXECUTION, F_1 AND F_2 MIGHT BEST BE PERFORMED WITHIN A SINGLE PROCESSOR TO MINIMIZE THE OVERHEAD OF TRANSFERS. HOWEVER, IF IT CAN BE ASSUMED THAT F_1 WILL BE ABLE TO BEGIN EXECUTION BEFORE ALL OF F_2 IS COMPLETED, IT MIGHT BE ADVANTAGEOUS TO EXECUTE THESE FUNCTIONS ON DIFFERENT PROCESSORS.

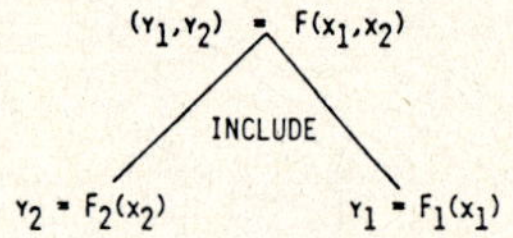

FUNCTIONS F_1 AND F_2 ARE STRICTLY INDEPENDENT AND MAY BE EXECUTED ON DIFFERENT PROCESSORS PROVIDED THE EXTRA OVERLOAD IS JUSTIFIED.

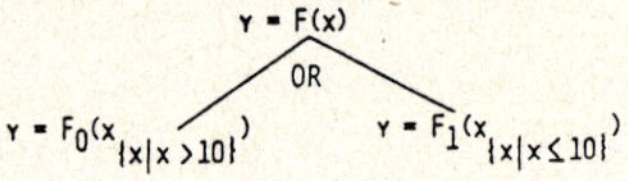

ONLY ONE OF THE FUNCTIONS F_1 OR F_0 IS PERFORMED FOR ANY GIVEN INVOCATION OF THE MODULE. CONSEQUENTLY, THE DECISION TO EXECUTE F_0 OR F_1 CANNOT BE MADE UNTIL THE VALUE OF X HAS BEEN DETERMINED.

BECAUSE NEITHER THE OUTPUT OF F_0 OR F_1 CAN BE PRODUCED BEFORE THE VALUE OF X IS DETERMINED, IT MIGHT BE DESIRABLE TO POSTPONE LOADING INSTRUCTIONS FOR F_0 OR F_1 UNTIL THAT TIME. HOWEVER, IT IS ALSO POSSIBLE THAT THE TIME OVERHEAD OF LOADING F_0 OR F_1 DYNAMICALLY MAY BE MORE EXPENSIVE THAN LOADING BOTH F_0 AND F_1 INTO STORAGE BEFORE THE VALUE OF X IS DETERMINED.

FIGURE 4: Allocation Implications of the Primitive Control Structures

identify data rates. In the case of a system definition that includes the selection of one function or another based on particular properties of the input we cannot statically determine which function will be selected. But, here, we can <u>use</u> the particular specification with respect to selection properties to identify decision points. In the case of a variable system definition we cannot statically determine the particular system that will finally be executed. But we can <u>use</u> the variable property with respect to a particular structure definition to identify reconfiguration points. As a specific example, examine the definition of F_0 in Figure 3. The particular precedence constraints for each task to be performed are inherent in the definition while the fact that precedence constraints <u>must</u> exist unambiguously is implicit in every definition (function x is a predecessor of function y if x must be completed before y can be started; such a relation is called a precedence constraint). By tracing the data access (assuming that, as soon as a function completes, its outputs are available to start the function that requires that output as input and that we have available to us an unlimited number of processors) the precedence constraints among the "bottom" functions (Figure 5 in terms of a conventional precedence graph) can be derived from the

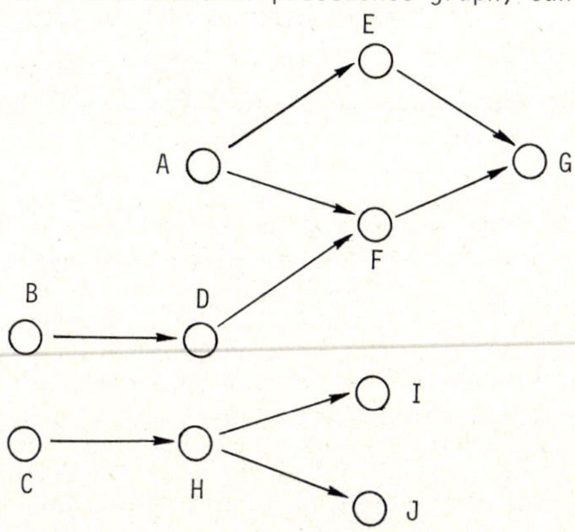

FIGURE 5: <u>Prcedence Constraints</u>

definition shown in Figure 3. In Figure 6, the user has provided time estimates for each defined function (e.g., function G is estimated to take 17 time units from start to finish, function I is estimated to take 7 time units to execute, and so on). Figure 6 also shows the data flow derived from the definition.

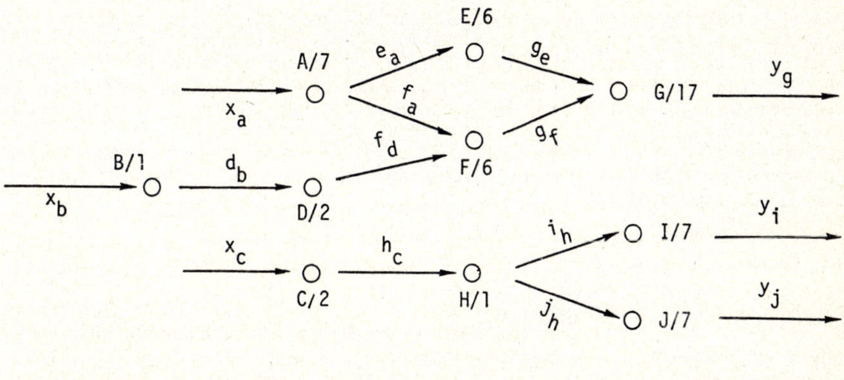

FIGURE 6: <u>Precedence Contraints and Data Flow</u>

Table 1, which shows the order of execution and the processor assignments for the unlimited processor case, was derived from the precedence constraints of the definition and the user supplied execution times for "bottom" functions.

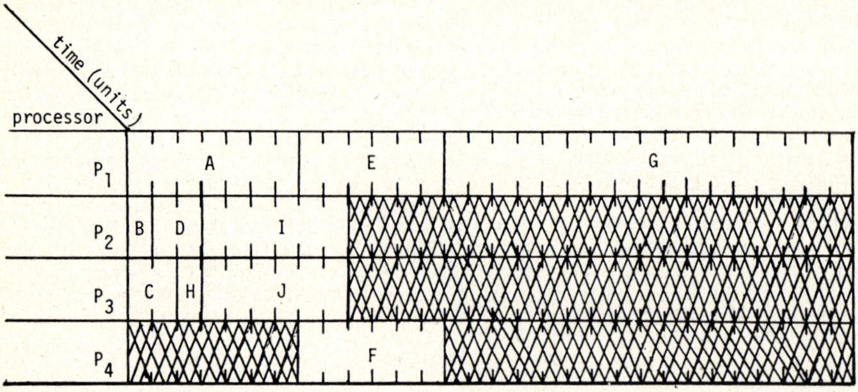

TABLE 1: Precedence Constraints for Unlimited Processor Case for Function F_0

Table 1 shows the implementation of a scheduling algorithm (i.e., a set of rules by which tasks are assigned to processors) in which once a ready task is located it is always assigned to the available processor, P_i, with the lowest index, i. Accordingly, functions A, B and C can start immediately since data x_a, x_b, and x_c are input to F_0. Since our processing power is unlimited, the importance (or priority) of A with respect to B and C is irrelevant for this particular case. Function D can begin as soon as B is complete since D requires B's output as input. Similarly H can begin as soon as C is complete. I and J depend on the completion of function H while function F and E must wait for A to complete. Function G can begin only when E and F have completed. The shaded areas of Table 1 indicate time in which a processor is idle. Therefore, the minimum number of processors needed is 4. These processors can, of course, represent computers, people, assembly lines or other "machine" devices. Processor assignments can thus be made automatically and indicated to the user.

It is also interesting to note here, that in the case of limited resources and particular scheduling algorithms the intuitive notion that the more processors one has available the less time it will take to perform all functions is not always true [12]. In the limited resource case, we again use the system definition for F_0 (of Figure 3) to obtain precedence constraints; but, in addition, we use the definition to obtain priority, or importance, constraints as well. If storage requirements are also limited we make use of other properties of our definition (e.g., once function B is complete, space set aside for data x_b can be reallocated since x_b is never used again) to respond to user queries such as "How much material do I need?".

With limited resources, it is especially important to be as flexible as possible in assigning resources to particular functions. If allocations are initially assigned, we need a mechanism to reevaluate these assignments after each function is complete so that our system can respond dynamically to a changing environment in case our estimates are not precisely known in advance (i.e., a closed loop, or feedback system, is desirable rather than an open loop system).

Suppose the user has only two processors available to perform function F_0. In this case, more than one function will be ready to execute at the same time and when this occurs, a priority relation must exist so that the most important task can be completed first. Our definition of F_0 can help limit the combinations of choices available because it restricts the number of priority relations to control. We could statically select which functions would be more important than others or we can use the property of the definition that each function must be ordered with respect to the others but assign that priority based on some criteria to suit our specific needs. The particular example, here, is based on a static selection of priorities.

F_0 is the most important function and is assigned the highest priority. In this example, the priority of F_3 is lower than the priority of F_7. Since the priority of F_7 is higher than the priority of F_3, then all the offspring functions of F_7 are more important than all the offspring of F_3. Since F_1 depends on information from C, C is more important than F_1. Similarly, H is more important than F_6.

Both I and J are less important than H since F_6 depends on the results of H to get started. Using the same criteria, the relative importance of the offspring of F_7 can be determined. In the case of a dynamic selection of priorities, the number of priority relations are less restrictive as shown in Table 2.

A	B	D	F	E	G	C	H	I	J
A	B	D	E	F	G	C	H	I	J
B	D	A	E	F	G	C	H	I	J
B	D	A	F	E	G	C	H	I	J
A	B	D	F	E	G	C	H	J	I
A	B	D	E	F	G	C	H	J	I
B	D	A	E	F	G	C	H	J	I
B	D	A	F	E	G	C	H	J	I
C	H	I	J	A	B	D	F	E	G
C	H	I	J	A	B	D	E	F	G
C	H	I	J	B	D	A	E	F	G
C	H	I	J	B	D	A	F	E	G
C	H	J	I	A	B	D	F	E	G
C	H	J	I	A	B	D	E	F	G
C	H	J	I	B	D	A	E	F	G
C	H	J	I	B	D	A	F	E	G

highest priority → lowest priority

TABLE 2: Restricted Combinations of Priority Relations From F_0 Definition

Using the criteria, or performance constraint, that we want to complete the work in the minimum time using only two processors, we observe an interesting phenomenon: it is not always optimal to begin to execute a function immediately if one is ready to execute. Table 3 shows the results of selecting the best combination of Table 2 (i.e., combination 2) assuming no idle processing time.

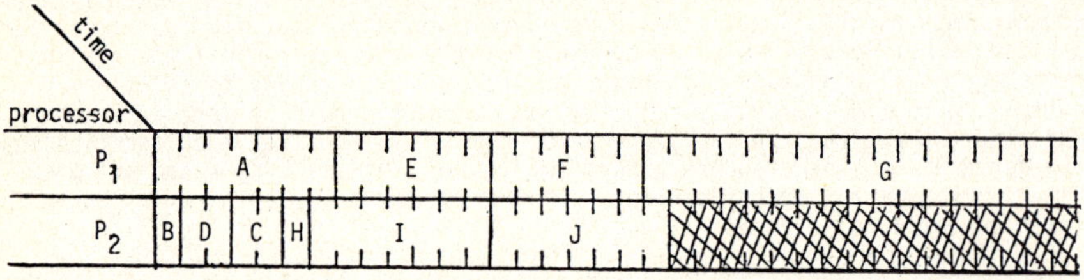

TABLE 3: Best Limited Processor Scheduling Assuming No Idle Processor Time (Total Execution Time = 35 Units).

Table 4 shows the results of incorporating a check to see if the next ready task completes before a higher priority task can begin to be executed. If it does complete, then the function is executed, otherwise the processing waits for the higher priority function to be ready. In this case, we end up with the same total execution time result as we did in the unlimited case. (A manager could make use of this result. For example, if two people were assigned all of the work, it would be better to schedule a vacation for the person associated with P_2 during the course of the work than to work continuously.)

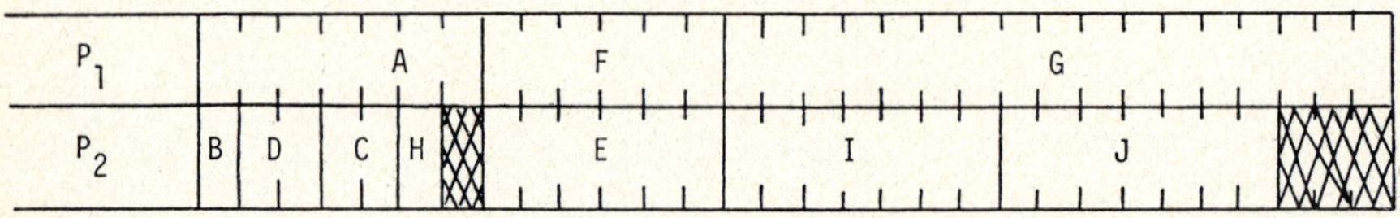

TABLE 4: Allowing Idle Processor Time Sometimes Gives More Optimal Results (Total Execution Time = 30 Units)

The previous example concentrated on how a user could create a function and how, once created, precedence constraints, priority relations and storage, or volume requirements could be determined from the definition. Thus, the definition of the system itself can be used in order to identify characteristics and criteria for an effective execution model of that system.

11. SUMMARY

We have found that it is helpful to know the generic set of properties which exist in the definition process and the definition of any model. Any model can always be viewed as a user model with respect to a user. That user, in turn, can also be viewed as a user model. By viewing any model in this way, the same basic techniques that are used for defining a target system can also be used to define the system for developing that system as well as the different types of users developing that system or receiving the final outputs of the development process of the target system itself.

Such a technique is helpful in the manufacturing of any type of product. It could be an airplane, a computer, a communications system, or a software program.

In every one of these environments, there are three basic aspects that must be considered: the data, the functions and the relationships between functions. If these aspects can be properly integrated in any given system, that system definition and the process for defining that system can both be made much more simple and much more reliable. We described here a user model in terms of our own concepts for defining systems in general since our primary interest is to attempt to relate to as many users as possible. And we too are after all users.

FOOTNOTES

1. A detailed discussion of the system development process as a system can be found in [1] and [2].

REFERENCES

[1] Hamilton, M. and Zeldin, S., Integrated Software Development System/Higher Order Software Conceptual Description, HOS, Inc. Technical Report 3, Higher Order Software, Inc., Cambridge, Massachusetts (November 1976).

[2] Hamilton, M. and Zeldin, S., The Manager As An Abstract Systems Engineer, in: Digest Of Papers Fall COMPCON 77 (Washington, D.C.), IEEE Computer Society, Catelogue No. 77CH1258-3C (September 6-9, 1977).

[3] Hamilton, M and Zeldin, S., Higher Order Software - A Methodology For Defining Software, in: IEEE Transactions On Software Engineering, Volume SE-2 No. 1 (September 1975).

[4] Hamilton, M. and Zeldin, S., AXES Syntax Description, HOS, Inc. Technical Report 4, Higher Order Software, Inc., Cambridge, Massachusetts (December 1976).

[5] The Application Of HOS To PLRS, HOS, Inc. Technical Report 12, Higher Order Software, Inc., Cambridge, Massachusetts (November 1977).

[6] Davis, C.G. and Vick, C.R., The Software Development System, in: Proceedings 2nd International Conference On Software Engineering (October 1976).

[7] 1975 IR & D Structured Design Methodology Volume II: Structured Design, Hughes Aircraft Company, Fullerton, California, FR 76-17-289 (1975).

[8] Ross, D., Structured Analysis (SA): A Language For Communicating Ideas, in: IEEE Transactions On Software Engineering, Volume SE-3 No. 1 (January 1977).

[9] Robinson, L. and Holt, R.C., Formal Specifications For Solutions To Synchronization Problems, Computer Science Group, Stanford Research Institute, Stanford, California (1975).

[10] Hamilton, M., and Zeldin, S., The Relationship Between Design And Verification, Journal Of Systems And Software, Volume 1 No.1 (1978).

[11] Wasserman, A.I. and Stinson, S.K., A Specification Method For Interactive Information Systems, in: Proceedings Specifications For Reliable Software, IEEE Computer Society (April 1979).

[12] Graham, R.L., The Combinatorial Mathematics Of Scheduling, Scientific American (March 1978).

[13] Hamilton, M. and Zeldin, S., The Foundations For AXES: A Specification Language Based On Completeness Of Control, Revised Document R-964, The Charles Stark Draper Laboratory, Inc., Cambridge, Massachusetts (March 1976).

APPENDIX 1

A SUMMARY OF AXES

AXES is a formal notation for writing definitions of systems. Although it is not a programming language, AXES is a complete and well-defined language capable of being analyzed by a computer. AXES [4] and [10] provides mechanisms to define data types (in order to identify objects); functions (in order to relate objects of types); and structures (in order to relate functions). AXES is the vehicle to define a system so that we can automatically check interface specifications statically. The foundations of AXES are based on a set of control axioms derived from empirical data of large systems [3]. (Figure 1 illustrates this evolvement by the connecting dashed lines.) Each axiom describes a relation of immediate domination with respect to a functional system. We call the union of these relations control. From these axioms, a set of three primitive control structures have been derived [13]. These three control structures identify control schemas on sets of objects. From the assumption that we can identify an object or a set of objects, a mechanism for defining an algebra for each distinct set of objects is provided in AXES. Each algebra takes the form of a set of axioms that relate operations applied to objects of a type.

To form a system, control structures are defined in terms of the primitive structures; operations are defined implicitly by deriving them mathematically from the axioms on a type or explicitly in terms of control structures using already defined operations on a type. When an operation is defined both implicitly and explicitly, we can cross-check the intent of the specification for correctness (Figure A-1).

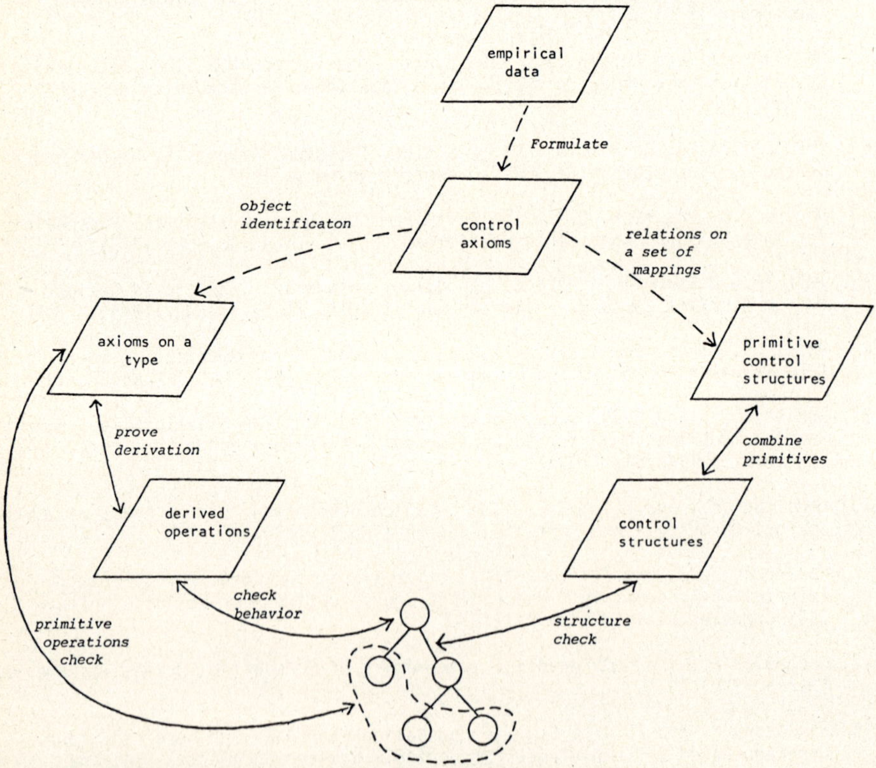

FIGURE A-1: AXES Relationships

Formal Models and Practical Tools for Information Systems Design
H.-J. Schneider, Editor
North-Holland Publishing Company

LOGICAL AND SEMANTICAL PROPERTIES OF ENVIRONMENTAL SITUATIONS FOR STATING INFORMATION REQUIREMENTS

Hannu KANGASSALO

Department of Mathematical Sciences, Computer Science,
University of Tampere, P.O. BOX 607, SF-33101 Tampere 10, Finland

In this paper the concept of information, the problem of stating information requirements and a classification of different situations for stating information requirements are defined and analysed from the point of view of data base management. The basic primitives used in this paper are the notion of concept and the notion of fact construct. Using these primitives the concept of knowledge and the concept of information are defined. An information requirement definition is a set of sentences which describes the information needed in a certain environment. A classification of different situations for stating information requirements is developed and some examples of different situations are given.

1. INTRODUCTION

All models for information systems design process contain a phase of work for the explicit definition of information requirements which the user of the system regards as necessary for performing his task. For some examples, see [3,4,14,24]. An information requirement definition is a set of sentences which describes the information needed in a certain environment. Information requirement definitions are used as a basis for the subsequent phases of the design work. The semantical content of all data items in the system is derived using these requirements. The information requirement definition is the basic construct on which the whole data processing system will be built. However, very little attention has been paid to logical and semantical aspects of the notion of information as well as to the consequences of these aspects in the environmental situation where information requirements are stated.

Information requirements are always defined in order to accomplish a given task which can be described by stating the goal to be reached. Besides the explicit state of affairs to be reached a definition of the goal may also express the direction of development without defining any exact figures. Hence the information requirement definition is always related with the definition of the goal. On the other hand, because it must be possible to conclude that the goal can be reached from the actual situation where information is needed, the information requirement definition is always related with the description of the present state of affairs, too.

The description of the present state of affairs at the time when information is needed, and the description of the goal constitute the environmental situation where information requirements have to be defined and satisfied. Both of these descriptions are conseptual models of the real world. The information needed to reach the goal from the present situation can be seen as a conceptual construct which is semantically connected to both models. In a situation where information requirements are defined an important problem is how the information requirement definition is related with both of these models.

The semantical relation between these models defines the structure of the environmental situation. The relation between models depends on whether concepts in one model are deducible from concepts in another model or not. By enumerating different alternatives it is possible to define a set of structurally and semantically different classes of environmental situations.

The term 'information' is in the literature used in many different senses. A very detailed analysis of several different conceptions of information has been made by Nauta [16]. A more practically oriented survey has been made by Stamper [21]. In order to analyse the concept of information or to use that term in a specific meaning it is necessary to define the context which will be used.

The purpose of this paper is to analyse, using only one aspect of the notion of information, the problem of stating information requirements in a certain environmental situation and to define a classification of structurally and semantically different environmental situations. The problems of the analysis are:

1. Which kind of logical and semantical structures may be comprised in the environmental situation of information requirement definition.
2. Which are the logical and/or semantical limitations in each class of environmental situations when defining information requirements.

The importance of the classification of environmental situations is in the fact that in each class the limitations and the methodology for defining information requirements seem to differ from the limitations and from the methodology to be used in another class. This classification forms a basis for the analysis of the methodology for information requirement definition.

The analysis made in this paper indicates that in the problem of stating information requirements there are several areas where present data base management systems cannot help. The analysis also indicates that present data base management systems are quite primitive tools for handling complex information requirements as these systems are constructed to manipulate physical data items, not concepts or semantics of data items.

In the next two sections the basis concepts and conceptual constructs will be introduced. They will constitute the basis for the analysis presented in the rest of the paper.

In section 4 the environmental situation for stating information requirements will be formally defined, and the problem of stating information requirements will be formulated. In this section the logical and the semantical structure of the environmental situation will be defined and the classification of different structures will be developed. Some examples will be given.

In section 5 the relation between the environment and the definition of an information requirement will be analysed.

Section 6 contains a short summary.

2. BASIC PRINCIPLES AND CONCEPTS

2.1. Preliminaries

In the following the term <u>object</u> will be used as a general term to denote anything which is under observation. <u>Objects</u> may be concrete or abstract. Let O designate a set of objects o_i, $i = 1,2,\ldots,n$. Every object o_i has a set of properties p_{ij}, $j = 1,2,\ldots,n_i$, which characterizes that object. The <u>type</u> of an object o_i is defined by those of its properties p_{ij} common to all <u>elements</u> in O together with the set of operations which are defined in O and which are applicable to elements of O.

The term association will be used as an undefined basic term to express that there is a coupling between two or more distinct objects, which may be of the same or different type. This means that two or more objects are connected with each other to form a more complex object which will be called a construct. An association between two objects o_i and o_j may be direct or indirect. A direct association means that there are no other objects between the two connected objects o_i and o_j. An indirect association means that there is at least one other object o_k between the two connected objects o_i and o_j. The detailed description of an association can be given with a set of rules which describes the limitations which must hold between objects.

A construct may consist of an unlimited number of objects and it may be unlimitedly complex. Let K designate a construct and let C designate the set which consists of objects from which the construct is made of and the null object. The structure S_K of the construct K can be described as the subset of the cartesian product $\overset{i=n}{\underset{i=1}{X}} C_i$, i.e.

$$S_K \subseteq \overset{i=n}{\underset{i=1}{X}} C_i \quad .$$

The structure S_K of the construct describes the existence of associations beween objects.

2.2. Different approaches to abstraction

The real world and the phenomena within it can be described using data. Also abstract or illusory things can be described as data. However, data are related with the real world in two different ways. On one hand, there is a relation of semantical meaning between data and the real world, and on the other hand data are itself a part of the real world.

For the analysis of data and information requirements there are two different approaches. One approach, which may be called a semiotic approach, is based on the study of systems of signs [5, p.47, 15, p.95, 16, p.17, 17]. The other approach, which may be called a principle of abstraction levels, is based on the systematic process of abstraction in which properties of data are abstracted in the sequence which is defined by their relative abstractness [9, 10].

In the analysis of data using the semiotic approach three 'realms' or 'levels' can be identified: the linguistic, the conceptual and the physical level [5, p.57]. The linguistic level is concerned with the language, components of the language such as proper names, terms, phrases, sentences and other linguistic constructs as well as rules concerning these components. One important property of an instance of a linguistic construct is that it has a physical existence together with some other physical properties.

The conceptual level is concerned with concepts and conceptual constructs, such as propositions, theories, conceptual models etc. Although it may be impossible to find a complete definition of the notion of concept, I say that a concept is a pattern or a logical construct created by human thinking. In this paper it is postulated that concepts exist in the same sense as numbers. It is also possible to say that concepts are abstract objects which are materialized in physical brain processes of human thinking. In other words, for each concept there is a physical surrogate materializing that concept. The question of materializing concepts will not be analyzed here in more detail.

By using concepts people tend to outline, organize or analyse the abudance of things and phenomena observed in the real world.

The physical level consists of the set of all physical entities and of the set of all phenomena within the set of physical entities, such as producing a new entity, change of properties of an entity, and all kinds of physical process. It is important to maintain a clear distinction between the conceptual level and the physical level. For example, although it is possible to identify bundles of objects in the physical level, sets are concepts belonging to the conceptual level.

The discerning of the linguistic level and the conceptual level from the physical level is a purely theoretical distinction because both of these levels can be analyzed also from the physical point of view, and, in fact, they are only a part of the physical reality. Their special status is based on the functions of objects on these levels and on the relations between the objects on these levels and other parts of physical reality. Figure 1 depicts these levels, some objects on these levels, and relations between these levels [5, p.58].

The relations between different levels are the relation of designation and the relation of reference. The relation of designation holds between some objects on the linguistic level and their correlates, if any, on the conceptual level. It is an asymmetrical sign-idea relation. In general it is not a one-to-one relation. The relation of reference holds between some members of either the linguistic or the conceptual level and their correlates, if any, on the physical level. The relation of reference is an asymmetrical relation.

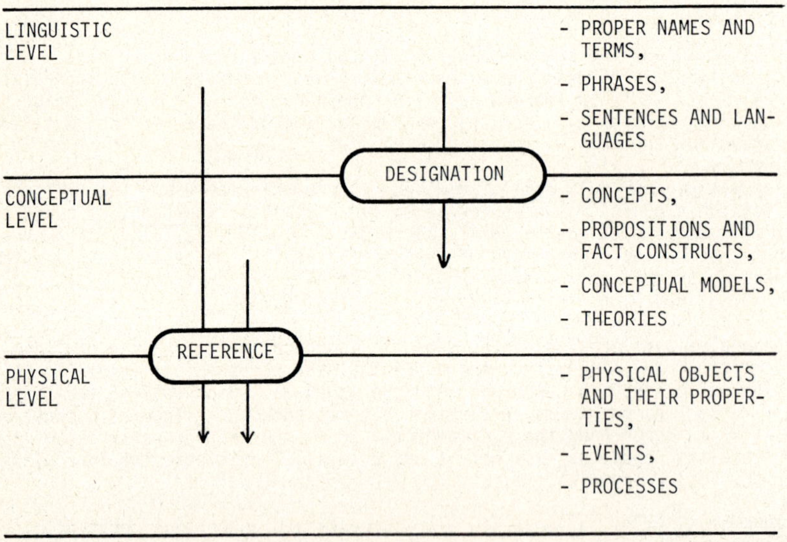

Figure 1. Different levels, their contents, and relations between them

If a proper name (on the linguistic level) or a concept (on the conceptual level) has a real correlate in the physical level, we shall say that the proper name or the concept refers to that entity or thing. The union of the two relations, that of designation and that of reference, may be called denotation [5, p.58]. A term is the name of a concept. It is a linguistic entity which can be used to designate the concept.

The principle of abstraction levels means that a collection of data can be described with the hierarchically arranged set of models in which each model has been constructed using such a set of modelling concepts that within each set the abstractness of the modelling concepts is (almost) equal, but the sets differ from each other in the abstractness of their modelling concepts. The hierarchy of models is arranged in such a way that the most concrete modelling concepts are on the lowest level of the hierarchy and the most abstract modelling concepts are on the highest level of the hierarchy.

In this context modelling concepts are conceptual abstractions of properties of data and/or relations between these properties. The concepts referring to properties and relations between them can be classified into four different classes which are called abstraction levels. Each class of concepts is a set of modelling concepts on one level in the hierarchy of models. On each abstraction level there are some basic modelling concepts, from which it is possible to derive a set of other modelling concepts which belong to this abstraction level [9, 10].

On the lowest level of abstraction modelling concepts refer to the physical properties of instances of data, such as the location of an instance, the length of an instance, etc. On the second level, modelling concepts refer to properties of data which are defined on the basis of representation rules of a given representation language together with values (concepts) to be represented. On the third and fourth level, modelling concepts refer to concepts and values used to describe the real world. The details of the third and fourth level will be given in subsequent sections.

The semiotic approach coincides with the principle of abstraction levels in many respects. However, the usage of these approaches is quite different. The semiotic approach is mainly used when studying data as a part of a language. It is also used when studying relations between data and their users, as well as relations between data and the real world described with those data. The principle of abstraction levels is mainly used when designing files, data bases and data base management systems [9, 10, 25]. In the following, the analysis of the conceptual basis of the problem area presented in this paper will be made using mainly the semiotic approach.

The main part of this paper concerns the conceptual level (the third and fourth abstraction level). The linguistic level and the physical level will not be analysed in detail.

2.3. Concept, conceptual construct and representation

Concepts are described using definitions. A definition is a linguistic expression, which associates a new concept - the definiendum - with the set of old, i.e. already known, concepts - the definiens - in some specific way. The definition describes the properties of a new concept with the help of properties of old concepts. A derived concept is a concept the properties of which have been derived from the properties of other concepts in a way described in the definition of that concept. However, within the system of concepts a set of basic concepts is always needed. A basic concept is a concept the 'contents', i.e. the intension, of which cannot be analysed or described using other concepts of the same conceptual system. Basic concepts are either completely undefined, or vaguely defined, intuitively understandable concepts, or they are described using an ostensive definition (for the ostensive definition, see [19, p.117]).

There are two basically different situations for defining concepts. Without going any deeper into philosophical details of the problem of concept definition, these situations are shortly described in the following. In both situations some methods for defining concepts are identified.

In one situation the definition of a basic factual concept states a correspondence rule between a set of concrete objects on the physical level and a concept to be defined on the conceptual level. This correspondence rule can be created either by the method of ostensive definition or by giving a set of semantical rules which are expressed as sentences in the metalanguage [23, p.11].

The formalization of the correspondence rules between the physical level and the conceptual level is a complex and problematic task involving many deep philosophical questions. Therefore it will not be analysed here in more detail. For the purposes of this paper I take the view that the definition of a basic factual concept is a partial mapping from the physical level into the conceptual level. In other words, for each basic factual concept there exists a mapping from the physical level into the conceptual level.

In another situation the definition of a derived concept can be described as an operation defined on the set of concepts. If C is a set of concepts, then a definition of a concept can in general be described in the following way

$$\text{Definition} : C^n \to C , \quad n \geq 1 .$$

The generality of a definition depends on the selection of the domain of the mapping. The problem of generality of concept definitions will not be analysed here in more detail.

It is possible to construct several different sets of basic types of concept definitions, which can be used to form more complex definitions. These basic definition types will be called concept operations. Concept operations are operations defined in the set of concepts. They can be used to construct an intension of the result concept of the operation from the intensions of concepts used as arguments of that operation. The two basic types of concept definition identified by J.M. Smith and D.C.P. Smith: aggregation and generalization, are examples of this situation [21].

A concept is either factually referential or factually non-referential, i.e. it either refers to some factual thing or it does not [6, p.39]. For example, numbers are factually nonreferential concepts. The concept 'car' refers to a factual thing.

Let C designate a set of concepts and let V designate a subset of C, i.e. $V \subset C$. The elements of V, which are called values, are all of the same type. The value v, $v \in V$, is a concept which is selected from a given set V by some operation t, e.g. measurement, classification or calculation. The type of a value v can be, for example, numerical or logical, but it is not limited to these two possibilities only.

The definition of a value, which describes the properties of this value in relation to the system of other values, is usually implicitly contained in some branch of the mathematical or logical theory or in some other conceptual system. The definition of a value may also contain a set of auxiliary rules, which are not part of that theory, but in a specific context express certain properties of the set V, e.g. the maximum and the minimum values of the set.

A conceptual construct is composed of a set of (basic or derived) concepts and/or of a set of other conceptual constructs which are connected with each other with the aid of associations. The difference between a derived concept and a conceptual construct is not always very clear and it will not be analysed here in more detail.

There are many kinds of conceptual constructs, e.g. propositions, conceptual models and theories. In order to use them in the communication between different people, it must be possible to represent them as linguistic expressions. A representation language or a notation is any generally known or agreed language which is suitable for representing values, concepts and conceptual constructs. A representation of a value is a linguistic expression which with the aid of physical signs materializes the value according to the rules of a given representation language.

Conceptual constructs are represented as sentences. A sentence is a linguistic expression which represents a conceptual construct and consists of one or more terms, zero or more representations of values and zero or more special linguistic components. The syntactic structure of a sentence is based on the structure of the conceptual construct to be represented and on representation rules of the representation language.

2.4. Fact constructs

On the conceptual level the real world is described using fact constructs. A fact construct is a conceptual construct (proposition) which is either a composition of different concepts or a pair of a concept and the value associated with it [11, p.32, 12]. The fact construct of the former type consists of two or more concepts associated by one or more additional concepts. This type of fact construct is called a CR-fact (concept-relation fact). Figure 2 shows an example of a CR-fact [12].

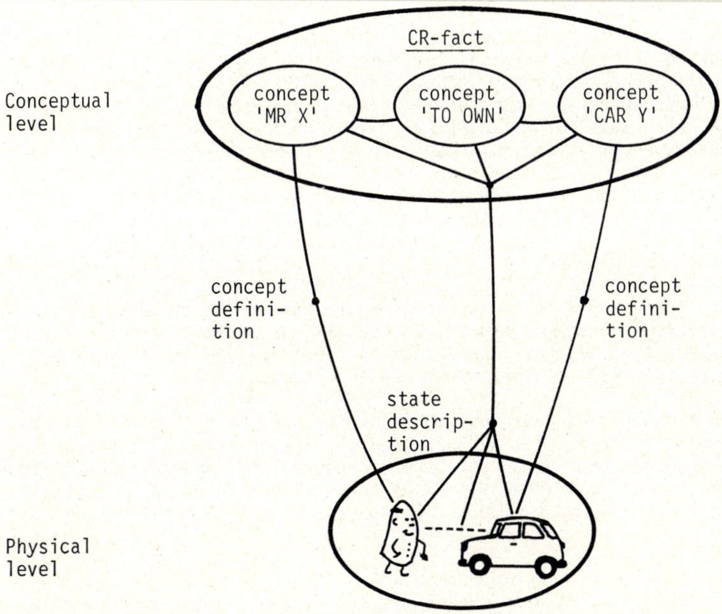

Figure 2. An example of the CR-fact.

In figure 2 there are two physical objects in the physical level (Mr X and car Y) and an association of certain type between these objects. The association consists of a set of different actions which Mr X has a right to perform with the car Y.

There are four different mappings from the physical level into the conceptual level. Three of these mappings are concept definitions which define the concept of 'Mr X', the concept of 'car Y' and the concept of 'to own'. The definition of 'Mr X' and the definition of 'car Y' describe the properties of these objects. The definition of 'to own' describes the set of different actions which the owner has a right to perform with the object which is owned. This definition has not been shown in figure 2.

The fourth mapping is a state description function which maps (a part of) the state of the real world into the set of conceptual constructs. In this example the conceptual construct selected by the state description function is a CR-fact which consists of concepts 'Mr X' and 'car Y' associated by the concept 'to own'.

The fact construct of the second type is a conceptual construct which is composed of two concepts and an association between them. One concept describes the part of the real world we are interested in. It is constructed by the concept definition which maps objects in the real world into the set of concepts. The other concept is a value which is selected from the set of values V by the state description function. It describes the state of the real world in that respect which is defined by the concept definition. In other words, the concept definition and the state description function must semantically correspond to each other in addition to that they share the same domain. In practice the state description function is some operation, e.g. measurement or classification. This type of fact construct is called a CV-fact (concept-value fact). Figure 3 shows an example of a CV-fact [12].

In figure 3 there is one physical object, Mr X, in the physical level. There are two different mappings from the physical level into the conceptual level: the concept definition and the state description. In the example the concept is 'the weight of Mr X'. The conceptual meaning of 'weight' is a complex conceptual construct which associates this concept with the system of other concepts and relations between these concepts. The value selected by the state description function is '75'. It is the result of an operation, which contains weighing Mr X with a scale and translating the analogue result into a digital form according to a set of specified translation rules. The method of weighing and the set of translation rules connect the value with the complex conceptual system which defines the units of weighing, e.g. grams, kilos, etc.

On the linguistic level each fact construct is represented as a sentence. For each concept in the fact construct there is a term in the sentence. The structure and syntactic form of the sentence corresponds to the structure of the fact construct according to the rules of the representation language.

The concept of data can be defined using concepts defined above. Data is a construct which is composed of a fact construct and a representation of that fact construct [12]. Both of these components are necessary. A representation without a corresponding fact construct is only a character string without any specific meaning. On the other hand, it is impossible to express a fact construct without a representation.

A data definition is a linguistic expression which describes or prescribes properties of given data, e.g. the terms used to designate the concepts in question, the definition of the concepts, the representation of the corresponding fact constructs, relative or absolute locations of these representations, etc.

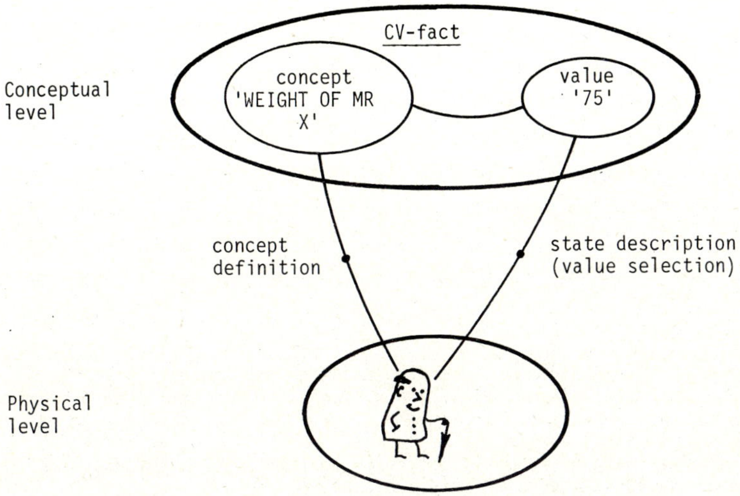

Figure 3. An example of the CV-fact

In the following only conceptual constructs will be examined. However, in principle it is always possible to produce one or more sentences which represent a given conceptual construct.

3. KNOWLEDGE AND INFORMATION

3.1. Conceptual model and knowledge

Let Ω designate a set of objects w_i, $i \in I$, and A designate a set of associations $a_j(w_1,w_2,\ldots,w_n)$, $j \in I$, between objects. An object w may be a physical object or an abstract object. The world to be described, i.e. the universe of discourse W is the union of Ω and A, i.e. $W = \Omega \cup A$. Time will not be considered here, irrespective of its importance in the actual situation.

Let C designate a set of concepts and conceptual constructs in Ω. All factually referential concepts or conceptual constructs c_i in C refer to some other elements in W. For simplicity in the following both concepts and conceptual constructs will be termed as concepts if there is no specific reason to separate them.

A subject S is a person who has a capability of receiving and interpreting messages sent by other persons. He has also a capability of storing and manipulating concepts.

A concept base C_S of the subject S is a subset of C and it consists of all basic and derived concepts known to S. It may contain both factually referential and factually nonreferential concepts.

If F_1 is a set of CR-facts known to S and F_2 is a set of CV-facts known to S, then a fact-base F_S of the subject S is the union of F_1 and F_2. In the following it will be assumed that all fact constructs in the fact base refer to some subsets of W.

Let C_S^F designate a subset of C_S consisting of all factually referential concepts which are contained in the fact constructs in F_S and let V^F designate a subset of C_S consisting of all values which are contained in the CV-facts in F_S. Concepts in V^F may be either factually referential, e.g. classes, or factually nonreferential, e.g. numbers. The intersection of C_S^F and V^F is not necessarily empty.

The union $C_S^F \cup V^F$ is a subset of C_S. Thus it is possible that the subject S knows concepts which are not contained in any fact construct in the present fact base F_S. The set of these concepts will be designated by U.

A knowledge base K_S of the subject S is the union of the concept base C_S and the fact base F_S. It consists of all concepts, conceptual constructs and fact constructs known to the subject S. The internal structure of the knowledge base can be described as in figure 4. In figure 4 fact constructs are represented by arcs which are labelled with the names of corresponding sets of fact constructs. The arcs correspond to associations between concepts.

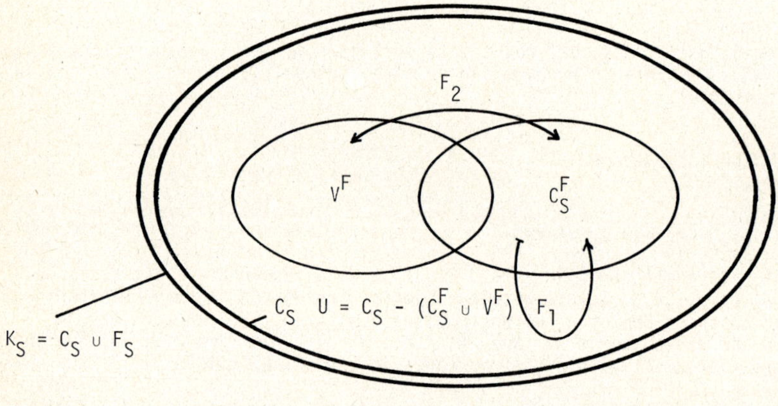

Figure 4. Description of the contents and the internal structure of the knowledge base of the subject S.

A fact construct in the set of fact constructs may be connected by an association with some other fact constructs in the same set, or it may be isolated. It may also be logically or semantically consistent or inconsistent with other fact constructs in the same set of fact constructs. The meaning of the terms connected, isolated, consistent and inconsistent will be interpreted in a normal, obvious way without analyzing and defining them here in more detail.

If all fact constructs in a set of fact constructs are directly or indirectly connected with all other fact constructs in that set, then the set of fact constructs is completely connected. If all fact constructs in a set of fact constructs are consistent with all other fact constructs in that set, then the set of fact constructs is completely consistent.

A conceptual model C_M of W, or of some part of W, is a completely connected and completely consistent set of fact constructs.

If at least one fact construct in the completely connected set of fact constructs is inconsistent with some other fact construct, then that set of fact constructs will be called an inconsistent conceptual model of W, or of some part of W.

3.2. Manipulation of conceptual constructs

Both concepts and fact constructs are abstract objects on the set of which it is possible to define operations and to apply some rules of inference for manipulating them. In the following the main principle is that within the set C it is possible to identify several different types of concepts. For the manipulation of concepts of different types, a different set of operations and logical inference rules is needed for each type.

In the rest of the paper the following simplification will be applied although it is not completely consistent with what has been said earlier. However, it preserves all the important problems and in the complete case it is a relatively straightforward task to take this simplification into account. It will be assumed that values are always numbers or logical truth values and concepts in CR-facts are never numbers or truth values.

Based on this simplification, the inference system IS will be defined. It consists of two parts: an inference system for concepts and CR-facts, and an inference system for CV-facts.

An inference system for concepts CIS is a set which consists of
a) a set CO of concept operations and
b) a set CIR of inference rules for concepts.

Inference rules for concepts are rules which can be used to make inferences concerning the meaning or other properties of concepts. These rules are important for example when constructing new conceptual constructs to satisfy certain logical or semantical requirements.

By applying concept operations to concepts in the concept base C_S it is possible to derive new concepts. An extended concept base EC_S is the union of the set C_S and the set of all concepts derivable from the set C_S with the set of concept operations CO.

Calculation operations are operations defined on the set of values V. They can be used to derive a new value from the values used as arguments of the operations.

Because of the nature of CV-facts there are restrictions in the derivation of new CV-facts. If C_1 and C_2 are CV-facts and a new CV-fact C_3 is to be derived from C_1 and C_2 by applying a concept operation and a calculation operation to them, then the semantics of the result c^* of the concept operation has to correspond to the semantics of the result v^* of the calculation operation. In other words, the operations applied to CV-facts to produce a new CV-fact have to preserve a semantical correspondence between the concept component and the value component of the resulting CV-fact. Figure 5 shows the situation graphically.

An extremely simple example in figure 5 shows three CV-facts, C_1, C_2 and C_3. In C_1 the concept component c_1 is the number of apples in the basket and the value component v_1 is a numerical value 5. The concept component c_2 of C_2 is the number of bananas in the same basket and the value component v_2 is a numerical value 3. By applying a calculation operation called addition, it is possible to get the sum 8 of value components 5 and 3. The concept component c^* of C_3 corresponding to the value 8 is a result of a concept operation which might be called concept intersection. The concept component c^* is the number of fruits in the basket. In figure 5 the semantical correspondence between the concept component and the value component of a CV-fact has been represented by dotted lines.

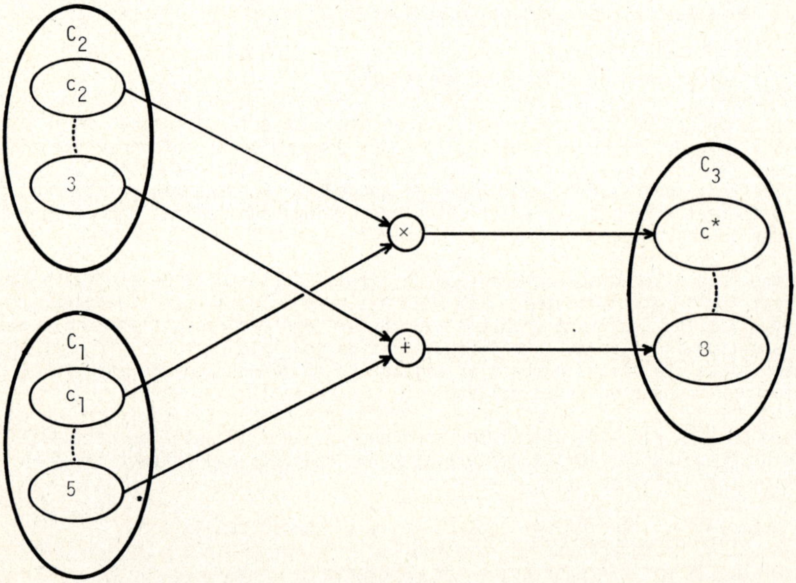

Figure 5. Semantical correspondence between the concept component and the value component in CV-facts.

The requirement of preserving the semantical correspondence between the concept component and the value component of the resulting CV-fact is very difficult to analyse and therefore the analysis will not be presented here. However, it is an important requirement because it prevents from deriving fact constructs which are logically derived correctly, but semantically nonsense.

A CV-fact f is derivable from a given set F of CV-facts if and only if:

a) the concept c contained in f can be derived with concept operations from concepts contained in the set F,
b) the value v contained in f can be derived with calculation operations from corresponding values contained in the set F,
c) each couple of a concept operation and a corresponding calculation operation used to derive f preserves the semantical correspondence between the components of the result.

Let F^{cv} designate a set of CV-facts. A fact operation 0^f is a couple of concept operation and calculation operation which defines on the set F^{cv} a mapping

$$0^f : {F^{cv}}^n \to F^{cv}, \quad F^{cv} \subseteq F_S, \qquad n \geq 1 .$$

in such a way that the resulting CV-fact is derivable in the sense described above.

An inference system for CV-facts FIS is a set which consists of
a) a set FO of fact operations and
b) a set FIR of inference rules for CV-facts.

An inference system IS is a union of CIS and FIS. It can be used to derive all concepts and conceptual constructs which are derivable from a given set of concepts and fact constructs.

An extended knowledge base $EK_S = \langle K_S, IS \rangle$ is the union of K_S and the set of all concepts and fact constructs which are derivable from the knowledge base K_S with the inference system IS.

The concepts described above can be applied in the data base management field in a rather straightforward way. However, there are some considerable differences between the present data base management technology and the ideas presented in this paper.

The set of definitions of concepts contained in the set C_S^F together with the set of definition of associations between these concepts correspond very closely with what is usually termed as conceptual schema of a data base (see for example several papers in [18]). Similarly, representation of values corresponds with what is usually called a data base. The set of definitions of concepts contained in the concept base C_S is a part of the content of a data dictionary. The representation of the knowledge base K_S corresponds to the union of the data dictionary and the data base.

Present data base management technology is lacking in the ability to manipulate conceptual constructs. In other words, concept operations are missing. Therefore, it may be very difficult to define, analyse and control the conceptual content of a data base or of reports produced by a data processing system.

3.3. Information

The concept of information is always related with a communication situation where the sender sends messages (linguistic expressions) to the receiver. This situation can be analysed from many different points of view (see [17], chapters 3 and 4). However, the question of the nature of information concerns always something which is carried by a message.

A set of messages (which may contain only one message) can be analysed using any of the following approaches:

1. Linguistic approach which makes it possible to analyse the surface structure and the deep structure of a message (see [7, 13]).
2. Semantic approach which makes it possible to analyse the conceptual content of a message (see [6]).
3. Statistical approach which makes it possible to analyse different statistical properties (both linguistic and semantic) observable within a single message as well as within a set of messages (see [17, 20]).

All these approaches can be used as a framework in developing the definition of the concept of information. In the following the statistical approach will be dismissed because it is mainly oriented towards the analysis of the syntactic structure of a message. This is not intended to mean denying the importance of the statistical approach in general. Similarly, the linguistic approach will be dismissed because only very few linguistic aspects are important in the context of this paper.

The concept of information will be defined in the following using the semantic approach. This approach has earlier been used as a basis for many excellent works. For some examples, see [1,2,8]. However, the approach used in this paper is not completely equal with that used in the semantic information theory by Bar-Hillel, Carnap, Hintikka and others, although there are some similarities. The concept of information to be developed in this paper will be based on the concepts defined in the preceding text.

In the following it will be assumed that the sender of a message has knowledge K^M and the receiver of a message has knowledge K_S such that $K^M \neq K_S$ and $K^M \cap K_S \neq \emptyset$. It is necessary that the intersection of K^M and K_S is not empty because otherwise the communication would not be possible at all. The intersection $K^M \cap K_S$ will be designated by K_S^M .

A message M is a set of sentences. The conceptual content M_S of a message M is a conceptual construct which has been constructed in such a way that concepts and/or fact constructs in it either belong to the set K_S^M or are derivable from K_S^M in a way which has been defined in the message itself.

The restriction included in the definition of the conceptual content of a message M guarantees that the receiver can always interpret the whole message. The question concerning the nature of the concept of information carried by a message is now the following. If the message consists of a conceptual construct and its representation, what is the information carried by that message?

The problem can be approached from two directions: from the senders point of view or from the receiver's point of view.

The sender constructs a message with a certain purpose in his mind. He selects components of the conceptual content M_S on the basis of this purpose. From the information point of view it is a crucial question how he selects the components to be inserted into the conceptual content of a message. If the components are exactly those which form the intended purpose of the message, there will be no problems. On the other hand, if the sender intends that the 'intended content' of a message is to be derived from the actual conceptual content by the receiver of the message, a lot of problems will arise. These problems will not be analysed here, but a conclusion from the analysis can be made. In general, the sender cannot be sure that the receiver will find out the intended content of the message because of the differences in the knowledge and inference systems of the sender and of the receiver.

On the receiver's side there is an aspect of newness which is crucial for the definition of the concept of information. If the conceptual content M_S of the message contains something which is not yet contained in the knowledge of the receiver, then the receiver will get information from the message. The consequence of this interpretation is that information is always defined in relation to the receiver, never in relation to the sender.

Two different types of information can be identified: immediate information and derived information.

If K_S designates the knowledge of a receiver and M_S the conceptual content of a message M, then the immediate information I_I received from the message can be expressed as the difference

$$I_I = M_S - K_S \quad .$$

If C designates a set of concepts and conceptual constructs and IS is an inference system, then the information space I, which can be described by an ordered couple <C,IS>, is the set of those concepts and conceptual constructs which either belong to the set C or are derivable from it with the aid of inference system IS.

The concept of derived information can now be easily defined.

If M_S designates a conceptual content of a message M, C^d designates an information space $<K_S,IS>$ and C^{dM} designates an information space $<K_S \cup M_S,IS>$, then the derived information I_D received from the message M can be expressed as the difference

$$I_D = C^{dM} - C^d \quad .$$

This conception of information could be called subjective information because it is based on the previous knowledge of the receiver. It is the kind of information which is important in the following chapters.

Formally the definition of derived information is closely related with the definitions of relative measures of information presented by Hintikka [8, p.8]. However, the interpretations of these definitions are quite different. Because the approach used by Hintikka is based on the use of the concept of logical probability, the formulas given by him define the measure of relative information. The concept I_D specifies a set of concepts and conceptual constructs.

4. THE DEFINITION OF INFORMATION REQUIREMENTS

4.1. Basic concepts

In order to analyse the problem of stating information requirements it is necessary to distinguish the situation which is the basis for information requirement definition from the result of the definition process which describes the desired information. The situation in which the information requirement is actually defined will be called an environment. The definition which describes the desired information will be called an information demand.

In order to define information requirements subject S, who needs information, has to relate with each other two conceptual models, M and M', which describe the real world. Conceptual model M' is a part of a goal G. The goal is a construct which describes the state of the real world to be reached in the future, when it has to be reached, how it has to be reached, at which cost it has to be reached, and so on. M' describes the state of the real world at a moment specified in the goal definition. Subject S needs information to reach that goal. Conceptual model M describes the state of the real world at a moment when information is needed. In a design situation it might be called a hypothetical knowledge of subject S, because it is assumed that subject S has that knowledge at a moment when he needs information.

The relation between the goal and the (hypothetical) knowledge can be described as a conceptual construct C_{MG}, which connects the goal and the knowledge. An inference system IS can be used to define that relation. Subject S has to select the most important part of this conceptual construct and to formulate its description as an information demand.

An information demand S_I is a set of sentences which describes the requested information I.

An environment E of information requirement is a construct consisting of the conceptual model M, the goal G and the inference system IS.

It follows from the definition of the concept of information that subject S has to describe as an information demand something that he does not know yet. However, he knows his own knowledge and the goal G. In addition to that he may have some attitudes, desires etc., which may have an effect on the definition of information requirements. He has to be able to conclude which information would solve his problem and to describe it as an information demand. Attitudes and desires will not be taken into account in the rest of the paper, although they are important in practice.

4.2. Environment of information requirement definition

The components of an environment in a simple case are: the conceptual model M, the conceptual model M', the goal G which contains the model M' together with some other specifications of when and how the future state has to be reached, and the inference system IS.

If the operations and rules contained in the inference system IS form a coherent totality which concerns concepts and fact constructs (in M and M'), it is justifiable to call that totality a theory. A theory will be designated by T.

The components and the logical structure of an environment in a simple case can be described as in figure 6.

Because the model M contains only fact constructs and the model M' contains only hypothetical fact constructs, the theory T will be needed to define some important aspects of both models. It will be assumed here that the same theory T applies to both models.

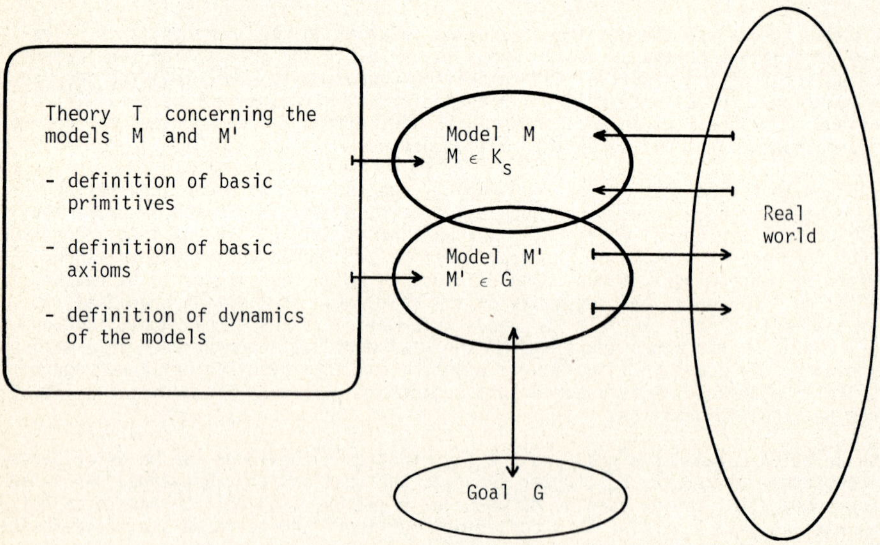

Figure 6. Logical structure of an environment in a simple case.

The theory T contains all ontological postulates concerning the models M and M', e.g. definitions of basic primitives, definition of basic axioms and rules describing the possible dynamics of the models. The theory T also contains different derivation rules and transformation rules as well as derived rules (theorems) which are derived from basic axioms and rules with the aid of derivation rules. Transformation rules can be used when replacing objects with other objects.

In a practical situation the model M may be divided into two separate parts. One part is the knowledge K_S of subject S. The other part is a set of data which describes some part of the real world and is external to subject S. In order to use external data, subject S must know its conceptual content but he may not be aware of values.

In addition to the case described above, it is possible to have an environment where only one conceptual model exists. This case normally appears only in a design situation where the other model is under development.

4.3. The semantic structure of an environment

Conceptual models M and M' may logically and semantically be related with each other in many different ways. The semantic structure S_E of an environment consists of all semantic relations between concepts and fact constructs in M and concepts and fact constructs in M'.

The following logical or semantical characteristics will be used as a basis in defining structural classes of different environments:

1. The existence of models M and M' in an environment.
2. Let C_M designate the set of concepts in the model M and $C_{M'}$ designate the set of concepts in the model M'. The characteristic feature of an environment is the existence of common concepts in the sets C_M and $C_{M'}$.
3. Let F_M designate the set of fact constructs in the model M and $F_{M'}$ designate the set of hypothetical fact constructs in the model M'. The characteristic feature of an environment is the unequality of the sets F_M and $F_{M'}$.
4. The semantic derivability of concepts and fact constructs in the model M' from the concepts and fact constructs belonging to the model M.

A classification based on these characteristics is shown in table 1. The classification consists of five classes of which some are further divided into subclasses.

In class 1 the environment consists of the conceptual model M and of the theory T applicable to the model M. A typical example of an environment in this class is an account data base in an accounting system. Events in the real world are classified according to a given conceptual schema, and fact constructs describing these events are grouped together according to this classification.

In class 2 the environment consists of both models M and M'. In this case the set C_M is equal with the set $C_{M'}$, but the set F_M differs from the set $F_{M'}$. In principle it is possible that there are several different sets $F_{M'}$, each containing a different set of fact constructs. A typical example of an environment in this class is a budget data base of an organisation. There may be several budgets for different time periods and the conceptual structure of each budget is the same, but values associated with concepts are different.

In class 3 sets C_M and $C_{M'}$ are different and therefore also the structures of the models M and M' are different. The intersection of the sets C_M and $C_{M'}$ is not empty, i.e. there are some concepts which appear in both models. In this

Class	M	M'	C_M vs. $C_{M'}$	Other specifications
1	$M \neq \phi$	$M' = \phi$	1° C_M	2° F_M
2	$M \neq \phi$	$M' \neq \phi$	1° $C_M = C_{M'}$	2° $F_M \neq F_{M'}$
3 a	$M \neq \phi$	$M' \neq \phi$	1° $C_M \neq C_{M'}$ 2° $C_M \cap C_{M'} \neq \phi$	3° $\forall c' \in C_{M'} - C_M : C_M \vdash c'$ 4° $\forall f' \in F_{M'} - F_M : F_M \vdash f'$
b	- " -	- " -	- " -	3° $\exists c' \; (c' \in C_{M'} - C_M \wedge C_M \vdash c')$ 4° $\exists f' \; (f' \in F_{M'} - F_M \wedge F_M \vdash f')$
c	- " -	- " -	- " -	3° $\forall c' \in C_{M'} - C_M : C_M \nvdash c'$ 4° $\forall f' \in F_{M'} - F_M : F_M \nvdash f'$
4 a	$M \neq \phi$	$M' \neq \phi$	1° $C_M \neq C_{M'}$ 2° $C_M \cap C_{M'} = \phi$	3° $\forall c' \in C_{M'} : C_M \vdash c'$ 4° $\forall f' \in F_{M'} : F_M \vdash f'$
b	- " -	- " -	- " -	3° $\exists c' \; (c' \in C_{M'} \wedge C_M \vdash c')$ 4° $\exists f' \; (f' \in F_{M'} \wedge F_M \vdash f')$
c	- " -	- " -	- " -	3° $\forall c' \in C_{M'} : C_M \nvdash c'$ 4° $\forall f' \in F_{M'} : F_M \nvdash f'$
5	$M \neq \phi$	$M' \neq \phi$	1° $C_M \neq C_{M'}$	2° $\exists c \; (c \in C \wedge C_M \cup C_{M'} \vdash c)$ 3° $\exists f \; (f \in F \wedge F_M \cup F_{M'} \vdash f)$

Table 1. Classification of environments

class there are three subclasses which are defined on the basis of the semantic relation between the set C_M and concepts belonging to the difference $C_{M'} - C_M$. These subclasses are the following.

a) All concepts c'_i in the set $C_{M'} - C_M$ are derivable from the concepts in C_M with the inference system CIS. Formally, $\forall c' \in C_{M'} - C_M$: $C_M \vdash c'$, where $\vdash$ means that c' is derivable from concepts in C_M. In a similar way all fact constructs f'_i in the set $F_{M'} - F_M$ are derivable from the fact constructs in F_M with the inference system FIS. Formally, $\forall f' \in F_{M'} - F_M$: $F_M \vdash f'$.

b) There is at least one concept c' in $C_{M'} - C_M$ which is derivable from C_M with the inference system CIS and at least one fact construct f' in $F_{M'} - F_M$ which is derivable from F_M with the inference system FIS.

c) There are no concepts in $C_{M'} - C_M$ which are derivable from C_M with inference system CIS and no fact constructs in $F_{M'} - F_M$ which are derivable from F_M with the inference system FIS.

An example of an environment in this class is an organization in which all statistical data in reports describing the activities of the organization are conceptually on a relatively low level and the goal definition of the organization is based on the concepts on a much higher level in such a way that only some concepts in the reporting system are common with the concepts in the goal definition.

In class 4 the sets C_M and $C_{M'}$ are different and separated. Also in this class it is possible to identify three different subclasses which are similar to subclasses in the class 3. An example of an environment in this class is an organization in which there is a conceptual gap between the set of concepts used in the reporting system and the set of concepts used in the goal definition. The main difference between classes 3 and 4 is in the methodology which can be used to analyse and manipulate information requirements. This problem will not be analysed here in more detail.

In class 5 the sets C_M and $C_{M'}$ are different but not necessarily distinct. Both models M and M' are logically in the same situation and the model M' is not regarded as a goal but as an additional, defined fact base. In other words, the object of interest is the information space $\langle M \cup M', IS \rangle$. A typical example in this class is a design situation in which the information system of a department (model M) has to be adapted to some external information system (model M') in such a way that the concepts and fact constructs inferred from each of these models will not conflict with each other.

4.4. The problem of stating information requirements

The problem of stating information requirements can be seen as a task of finding and defining a conceptual construct C_{MG} which is related with models M and M' and satisfies certain requirements. Depending on the structural class of an environment it may be related with one or both models.

The problem of stating information requirements is different in each structural class of the environment but in any case the solution has to satisfy some general requirements.

1. It must be possible to decide on the basis of an information demand S_I and the environment E that the satisfaction of the information demand S_I will help to reach the goal G. This requirement will be called a requirement of relevance.

2. It must be possible to decide on the basis of an information demand S_I and the environment E that is it possible to derive the required information from the environment. This requirement will be called a requirement of producability.

On the basis of these two requirements the problem of stating information requirements can be split into two parts: the production problem and the relevance problem. The situation can be depicted as in figure 7.

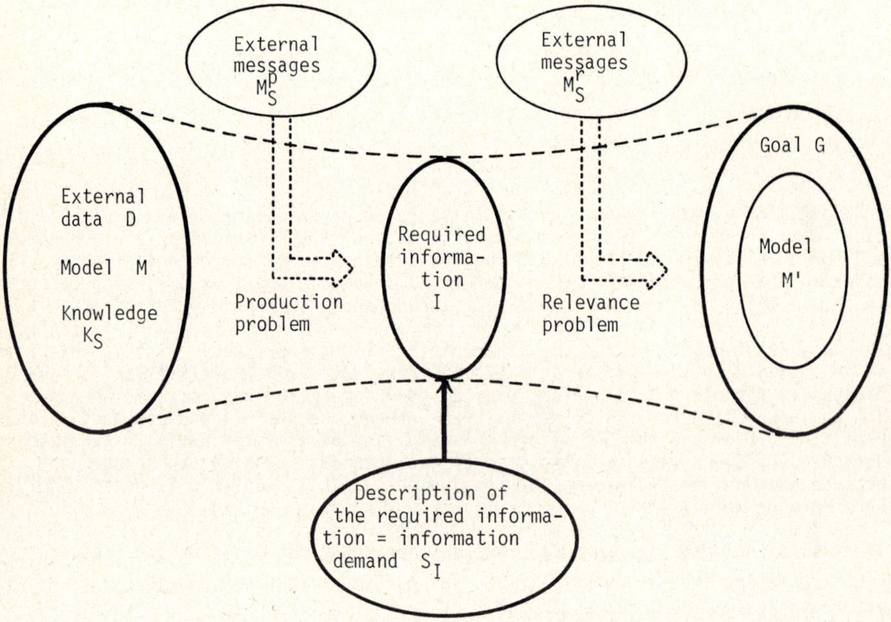

Figure 7. The relation between the environment and the solution to the problem of stating information requirements.

In figure 7 the model M consists of two parts: the knowledge K_S of the subject S and external data D which is not completely known by the subject S but is accessible to him. Figure 7 contains also two sets of external messages, the sets M_S^p and M_S^r, which may be needed to solve one or both of the subproblems. The set M_S^p may be needed to solve the production problem and the set M_S^r to solve the relevance problem.

The problem of stating information requirements is solved if both the production problem and the relevance problem are solved in such a way that the solution of one problem at the same time is also the solution of the other problem.

5. RELATIONS BETWEEN THE ENVIRONMENT AND THE INFORMATION DEMAND

An information demand S_I may be related with the environment E in many different ways depending on the contents of models M and M' as well as on the content of the information demand itself. In search for the solution of the problem of stating information requirements, the knowledge concerning the type of this relation may be crucial because the selection of methods to be used in solving the problem depends on the type of the relation between the environment and the information demand to be defined.

The <u>object of an information demand</u> may be a concept, a fact construct or a set of these in the model M, or it may be a derived concept, derived fact construct or a set of these based on the union of the model M and a set of external messages M_S^p . The set of external messages may be empty.

Because the information described by the information demand S_I must be relevant with respect to the goal, the process of solving the problem of stating information requirements proceeds in general 'backwards', i.e. the object of an information demand will be defined in a very late phase of work.

The classification of different relations between the information described by an information demand and the environment in the environment class 3 is described in figure 8. The identifiers of classes correspond to the identifiers of subclasses in table 1 in such a way that classes in this figure are numbered within each subclass of table 1.

In figure 8 the arrows between models and the required information I represent the solution of subproblems of the problem of stating information requirements. In some cases also external messages are needed to complete the solution.

A simple example of an information requirement in the class 3.b.2 can be described as in figure 9. The model M' specifies the situation in which monthly salaries have been paid for each employee on the basis of the number of hours worked last month and their hourly wage. The model M contains the work history of all employees. The information requirement of a cashier is that he must know how much money he has to pay for each employee.

The solution of the relevance problem is almost obvious because the concepts in the model M' and the concept component of the required information I are very close to each other. The amount of money has to be interpreted to mean the amount of the monthly salary of an employee.

The solution of the production problem has to be searched by using the usual methodology of information analysis. The purpose of the information analysis is to find out if the required CV-fact (information I) can be derived from the CV-facts in the model M.

A more complicated example of an information requirement in the class 4.c.3 is the case where the model M' specifies the level of the job satisfaction of employees to be reached at time t+n. The model M describes the history and the present state of the production system and of the economy of the company. The problem of managers is to develop the company in such a way that the goal will be reached.

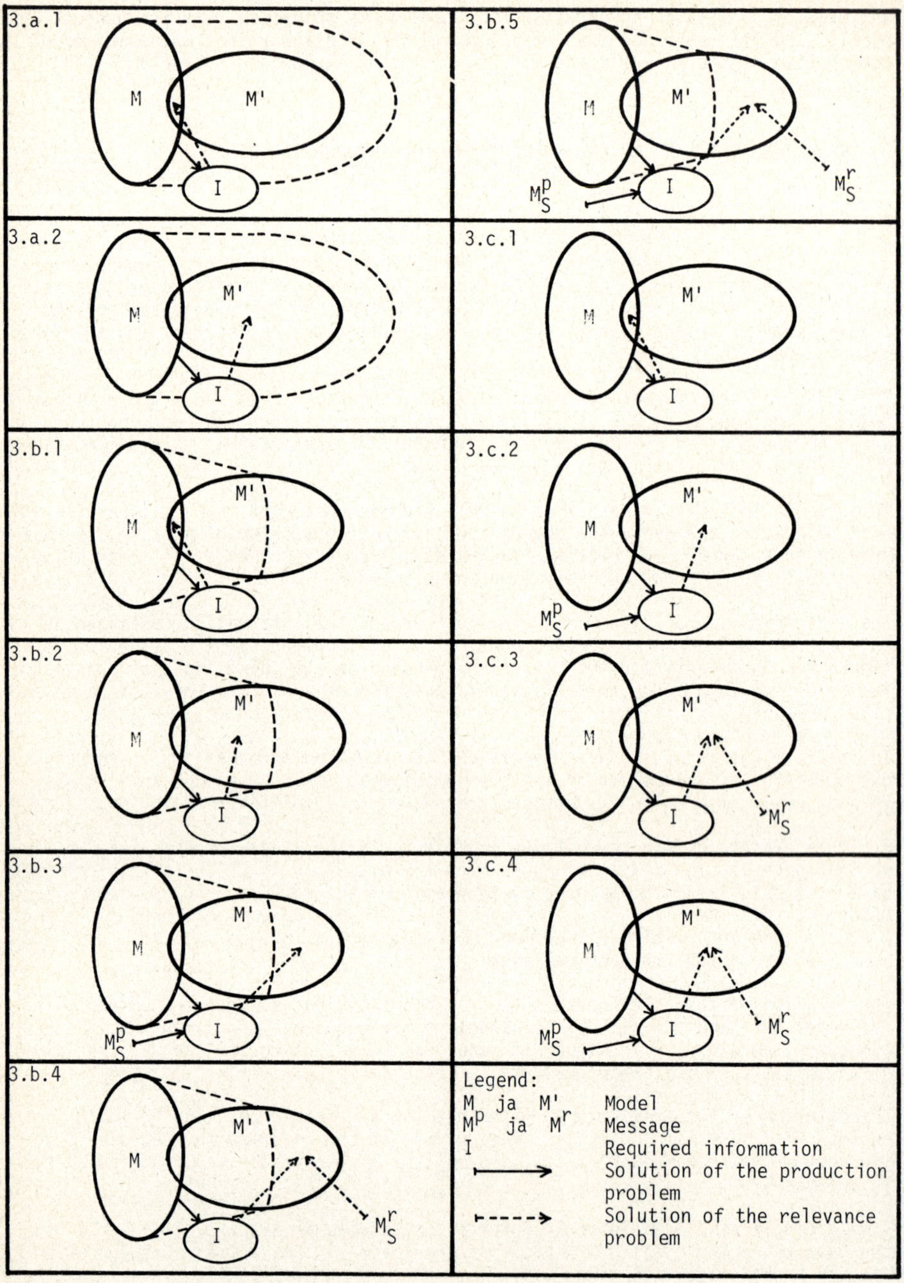

Figure 8. A classification of relations between the environment and the required information in the environment class 3. The area marked with the dotted line contains all the concepts and fact constructs derivable from the model M.

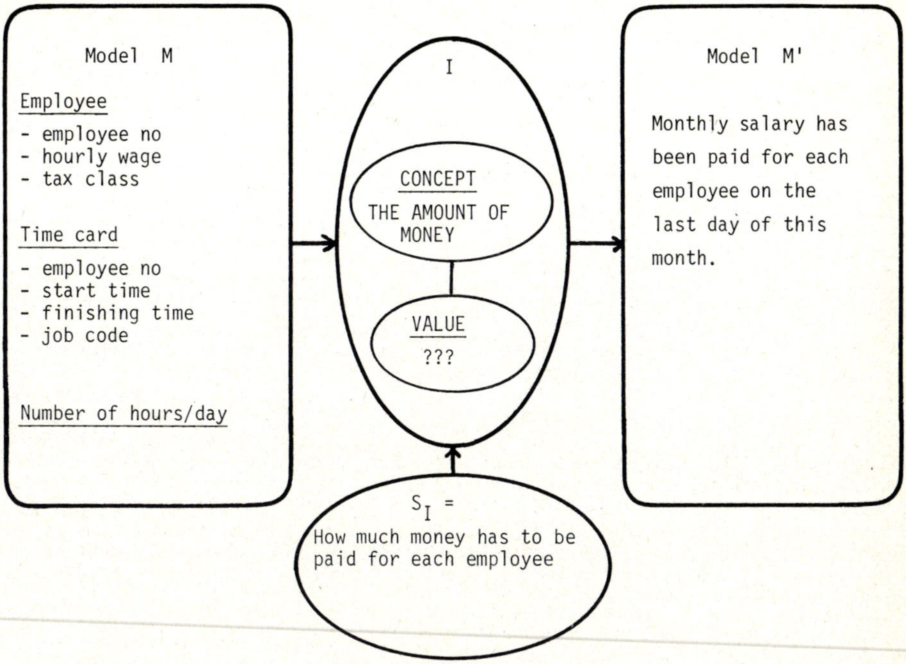

Figure 9. The information requirement of a cashier (an example).

In this case it is clear that the concepts in M' cannot be completely derived from the concepts in M. Managers have to define an information requirement specification in such a way that required fact constructs can be derived from the model M. In addition to this they will need at least some external messages for solving the relevance problem.

As the description of their information requirements managers may specify they will need a description of the trend of evolution of the production system and of the economy of the company. External messages will explain how the job satisfaction is related with the economic situation of a company as well as how the job satisfaction is related with the structure and functioning of the production system.

The two examples presented above are on a rather crude level. Therefore their classification is not absolute but depends on the concepts which are included in the models on the more detailed level. The first example may belong to the class 3.b.3 as well and the second example may belong to the class 3.c.3 if the models have some common concepts.

In this context the methodology needed to solve the problem of stating information requirements will not be analysed. However, some comments may be in order.

On the basis of a preliminary analysis there seem to be considerable differences between methods which must be used in different classes. These differences appear in starting point of the search process as well as in procedures which are used in the search for the solution.

In general, the methods to be used are more or less heuristic procedures which are based on the conceptual descriptions contained in the environment, i.e. the model

M and the goal G. A partial mechanization of these procedures seems to lead into the field of artificial intelligence.

Because of the size and complexity of any practical situation, efficient tools are needed to store and manipulate descriptions of the components of the environment. Present data base management and data dictionary systems are steps in this direction but at the moment they are far too primitive to be of any real help in the task of defining and analysing information requirements.

6. SUMMARY

In this paper the concept of information has been defined and the problem of stating information requirements has been analysed. The solution of the problem of stating information requirements is based on the relationship between the goal and the present knowledge of the subject. The solution consists of the solutions of two subproblems.

It is possible to identidy several different structural classes of environmental situations in which the information requirement will be defined. It is also possible to identify several different classes of relationships between the information demand and the environment. These two classifications are important in the development of methods and tools for stating and satisfying information requirements.

REFERENCES:

[1] Bar-Hillel, Y., Language and Information. Addison-Wesley, London, 1964.

[2] Bar-Hillel, Y., Carnap, R., An Outline of a Theory of Semantic Information. Research Laboratory of Electronics, Technical Report No. 247, MIT, 1952.

[3] Blumenthal, S.C., Management Information Systems: A framework for planning and development. Prentice-Hall, Inc., 1969.

[4] Bubenko, J.A. Jr, Berild, S., Lindencrona-Ohlin, E. and Nachmens, S., From Information Requirements to DBTG-Data Structures. ACM FDT 8, No. 2, 1976, pp. 73-85.

[5] Bunge, M., Scientific Research I. The Search for System. Springer-Verlag, Berlin 1967.

[6] Bunge, M., Treatise on Basic Philosophy, Volume I. Semantics I: Sense and Reference. D.Reidel Publishing Company, Dordrecht 1974.

[7] Chomsky, N., Deep Structure, Surface Structure, and Semantic Interpretation. In Steinberg, D.D., Jakobovitz, L.A. (eds.), Semantics - An Interdiciplinary Reader in Philosophy, Linguistics and Psychology, Cambridge, University Press 1971, pp. 183-216.

[8] Hintikka, J., On Semantic Information. In Hintikka, J., Suppes, P. (eds.), Information and Inference. D.Reidel Publishing Company, Dordrecht, 1970, pp. 3-27.

[9] Kangassalo, H., Stratified Description as a Framework of the File Description. (in Finnish). In DIFO-vuosikirja 2/1973. DIFO-tutkimus ry., Tampere 1973.

[10] Kangassalo, H., Conceptual Structure of the File Design Problem: a general view. Scandinavian Workshop on Data Base Schema Design and Evaluation. Røros, Norway, February 1975.

[11] Kangassalo, H., On Defining and Satisfying Information Requirements. (in Finnish), A thesis for the degree of licentiate in philosophy. University of Tampere. 1978.

[12] Kangassalo, H., Conceptual Foundation for Data Base Management Terminology. A contribution to the ISO/TC 97/SC 5/WG 3 DBMS -meeting in Helsinki, October 1978, Document number ISO/TC 97/SC 5/WG 3 781007.

[13] Katz, J.J., Fodor, J.A., The Structure of a Semantic Theory. Language, Vol. 39, No. 2, (1963), pp. 170-210.

[14] Lucas, H.C. Jr., Information Systems Concepts for Management. McGraw-Hill Book Company, 1978.

[15] Lyons, J., Semantics, Volume 1. Cambridge University Press, 1977.

[16] Morris, C., Signs, Language and Behavior. Prentice-Hall, Inc., New York 1946.

[17] Nauta, D. Jr., The Meaning of Information. Mouton, The Hague, 1972.

[18] Nijssen, G.M. (ed.), Architecture and Models in Data Base Management Systems. North-Holland, Amsterdam 1977.

[19] Robinson, R., Definition. Oxford University Press, Oxford, First edition 1954.

[20] Shannon, C., Weaver, W., The Mathematical Theory of Communication. Urbana, Ill., University of Illinois Press, 1949.

[21] Smith, J.M., Smith, D.C.P., Database abstractions: aggregation and generalization. ACM Trans. on Database Syst. 2, 2 (June 1977), 105-133.

[22] Stamper, R., Information in Business and Administrative Systems. B.T. Batsford, London 1973.

[23] Tuomela, R., Theoretical Concepts. Springer-Verlag, Wien 1973.

[24] Working Group of the ADP-institute: Building a Data Processing System. (in Finnish). Publication No. 25 of the Finnish Data Processing Association, Second edition, Vaasa 1975.

[25] Yeh, R., Data Base Design - an approach and some issues. Symposium on Database Design and Software Engineering. Chalmers University of Technology and the University of Göteborg, September 5-7, 1978.

Formal Models and Practical Tools
for Information Systems Design
H.-J. Schneider, Editor
North-Holland Publishing Company

AN EVENT-BASED DESIGN METHODOLOGY SUPPORTED BY DREAM

William E. Riddle

Department of Computer Science
University of Colorado at Boulder
Boulder, Colorado 80309

A methodology for the architectural design of software systems is composed of three interrelated facilities. First, there must be some means of capturing the requirements for the system in some primarily non-procedural specification. Second, there must be some means for describing potential modularizations of the system in some primarily pseudo-procedural design which captures the essential detail concerning the modules' interfaces and their interactions. Finally, there must be some means of determining whether a system design appropriately meets the system specification. In this paper, we present a design methodology based on the use of event and event sequence descriptions. We first give a brief definition of the Design Realization, Evaluation And Modelling (DREAM) system and its description language as they relate to an event-based design method. Then we define the design method and give a simple example.

INTRODUCTION:

Many methodologies have recently been advanced for the disciplined, orderly development of software systems. Each has as its basis a development method (or process for the gradual, evolutionary development of a software system) which serves to decompose the overall synthesis task into a sequence of smaller, more manageable steps. Many methodologies lend additional help to software developers in the form of guidelines, maxims or techniques that serve to support the method which they provide. A few offer help for the analysis which must be done to assure that the developed system delivers the functional capabilities which are required and does so within the performance and economic constraints which have been levied against the system.

A particularly effective way in which a development methodology may be delivered to software design practitioners is as a computerized support system. Systems of this type (e.g., [1], [2], [3], [4], [5], [6], [7], [8], [9], [10], [11], [12], [13], [14], [15], [16]) provide a language for the precise, but abstract, description of systems at intermediate points in their development when completely detailed descriptions cannot be given. This language then allows the definition of various development techniques and the provision of computerized aids supporting these techniques.

In our own development support system, called the Design Realization, Evaluation And Modelling (DREAM) system [12], we have focused upon providing help for the development of concurrent software systems (that is, those systems having parts which may be perceived as operating asynchronously and in parallel, even if the system actually executes in a uniprocessor environment). We have additionally focused upon providing analysis aid which is highly integrated with a top-down design method, so that system developers may gradually develop their confidence in the appropriateness of a system in tandem with developing the system itself.

In this paper we discuss the DREAM system and one of the development methods which it supports. In the next section, we narrow the scope of consideration to that phase of the software development life-cycle for which DREAM has been developed. We then discuss description languages in general and the DREAM description language in particular. Then, after outlining the DREAM system and discussing the types of computerized aid it provides, we outline a variant of the traditional top-down design method which the DREAM system provides and give a short example of its use.

ARCHITECTURAL DESIGN PHASE:

The software system development process may be divided into three major phases.[1] Chronologically first among these is the requirements definition phase during which the users' requirements are expressed in terms of the system's expected functional capabilities as well as in terms of performance and economic constraints upon the system. Chronologically last is a phase which may be called the algorithm design phase, during which the system's processing algorithms and internal data structures are developed to the level of detail needed to permit compilation.

Intermediate to these two phases is a phase which we call architectural design. During this phase the system's gross organization is specified in terms of a hierarchically structured collection of modules, each of which plays some well-defined role in the delivery of the system's functional capabilities. In addition to the delineation of the modules, their interfaces and interactions are defined in order to specify the coordination needed to assure the delivery of the expected functional capabilities and the observance of the constraints which have been levied upon the system.

The synthesis task during design[2] is therefore the development of a modularization for the system and the definition of strategies for interactions among the modules. The associated analysis task is to assess the strategies with respect to the system's requirements with the intent of certifying that if the modules operate and interact as specified then the requirements will be satisfied.

SOFTWARE DESIGN DESCRIPTION LANGUAGES:

The description task during architectural design is a modelling task that is only superficially similar to the traditional programming task encountered during the algorithm design phase. Modelling shares with programming the need to specify some details concerning the processing performed by the system. But this specification should be abstract with respect to specific mechanisms for implementing the processing. Stated differently, the specification should be expressed in requirements-oriented terms which reflect the effect of system operation rather than implementation-oriented terms reflecting the system's actual operation and, therefore, the cause of the observable effects. There is the need, therefore, for languages which are considerably different from programming languages and, in this section, we discuss the attributes of such design description languages.

Because of the need to highlight module boundaries and interactions, a design description language needs to be behavior-oriented rather than operation-oriented. A behavior-oriented language supports the abstraction of a module by allowing the description of the effect of the module's operation without the description of the manner in which this effect is caused. One approach to abstraction is to allow descriptions that are projections of the actual modules within the system. In a projection, the operational details of the module are suppressed, resulting in a description which focuses upon the module's overall behavioral characteristics. Another approach to abstraction is to allow a description which is orthogonal to the system's implementation description in the sense that the description may form associations among the elements of the system that are completely different from those formed by the system's internal, physical organization. Thus, the modules may be merely logical entities rather than physical entities. A final approach to behavioral abstraction is to allow descriptions that are non-procedural in that they describe the effect of the module's processing without specifying an algorithm for achieving the effect.

> Example: Assertions [15] are non-procedural projections of the modules they describe. They are orthogonal to the implementations of the modules in that they do not necessarily imply that one procedure must exist for each set of input/output relations defined by an assertion -- one generalized module could conceivably implement many sets of input/output relations.

The need to be able to investigate the interactions among the modules and the interplay among the various strategies implies that design description languages should be analysis-oriented. An obvious criterion is that descriptions be unambiguous, so that formal analysis techniques may be defined which derive information about the overall operation of a collection of interacting modules. Descriptions should also be outward-directed, specifying the characteristics of a module that are pertinent to its interactions with other modules, again so that characteristics of the overall operation of a collection of modules may be uncovered. Finally, descriptions should be redundant, specifying a behavior either from different points of view -- for instance, from the point of view of both the supplier or user of some processing facility -- or with respect to different sets of concerns -- for instance, with respect to desired properties of the overall operation as well as with respect to the operation of the individual modules.

> Example: Several recently defined programming languages -- such as Euclid [19], CLU [20], and Alphard [21] -- satisfy many of these criteria. They each have a well-defined semantics and hence lead to unambiguous descriptions. Redundancy is allowed either through the incorporation of assertions which allow formal verification, such as in Alphard, or the use of data abstractions and strict typing which lead to useful compile-time checks, as in CLU. Outward-directed descriptions are generally allowed through axioms, as in Alphard and Euclid, which allow the effect of a sequence of operations to be deduced.

Design description languages should also be modification-oriented so that descriptions may be easily augmented, as new decisions are made, or returned to a previous state should decisions be reversed. Descriptions should be modular so that self-contained descriptions of different aspects of the system may be separately specified. They should also be hierarchical so that the descriptions may be iteratively elaborated. It is also usually desirable to allow incremental descriptions so that fragments of the overall description may be prepared in an arbitrary order. This is sometimes contradictory with the desire to have hierarchical descriptions, but only when it is required (sometimes unnecessarily) that the order in which portions of the description are developed corresponds to the nesting structure of the hierarchy.

> Example: Algolic programming languages admit hierarchical, modular descriptions and the current trend toward incorporating data abstraction constructs, as for example in CLU, enhances programming languages with respect to these criteria. Incremental descriptions are not easily achieved in block-structured languages (and are somewhat inconsistent with the idea of structured programming), but can be achieved in languages which use the idea of guarded commands [22].

Finally, design description languages should be guidance-oriented in that they should allow descriptions which help guide the further design (and eventual implementation) of the system but do not overly constrain the design (or implementation) decisions remaining to be made. Descriptions should therefore be non-prescriptive such that they capture the decisions already made but do not prescribe the manner in which the resulting properties of the system should be achieved. Although non-prescriptive, descriptions should also be inward-directed, helping the designers to discover the options that are possible and feasible for ensuing decisions. It is sometimes beneficial to allow attribute descriptions in which various properties of the system are described positively by indicating the values that they may assume or negatively by indicating the values that are not to be allowed.

> Example: Assertions are non-prescriptive and frequently inward-directed since they describe a procedure's function as the conjunction of constraints and can therefore indicate different cases which should be handled. Assertions could also be used to give attribute descriptions which specify the range of permissible values for each attribute.

The examples have indicated that contemporary programming languages have moved in the direction of design description. Partially this is because programming is also algorithm design; partially, it is in recognition of the need to perform analysis in order to produce reliable programs. But programming languages are rarely acceptable design languages because they are inherently operation-oriented and specify behavior only implicitly through procedures for achieving the behavior.

THE DREAM DESIGN LANGUAGE:

As a basis for the DREAM system, which we discuss in the next section, we have developed a design description language called the DREAM Design Notion (DDN) which possesses many of the characteristics delineated in the last section. In this section, we discuss the major facilities available in DDN and indicate how these give rise to the various characteristics. The discussion here is brief and without examples. Some brief examples are given later -- others and more detailed discussions of the DDN facilities are given in the cited references.

DDN descriptions are of classes of components within a system [23]. Class-oriented descriptions were introduced in the SIMULA language [24] and have been incorporated in a wide variety of computer-oriented description schemes ([14], [20], [21], [25], [26], [27], [28]). DDN allows parameterized descriptions so that some of the details of a member (or instance) of the class may be specified when the member is created. This facility allows the specification of many different types of variation among members of a class. For example, it allows the description of system components which have a variable number of subcomponents (such as the class of multiple-task programs), a variable number of output linkages (such as the class of message transmitters in a computer network), or variable types of subcomponents (such as the class of stacks).

Class definition constructs facilitate the hierarchical definition of a software system since the designers are encouraged to think of the system as decomposible into subcomponents which are members of a set of classes and which are themselves decomposible into subcomponents which are members of other classes. They also facilitate projection and orthogonality since a class serves to collect together all of the information pertinent to a collection of components and hence leads to descriptions which highlight those characteristics common to the collection rather than particular to its members. Finally, class definition facilities allow modular descriptions which may be incrementally developed since fragments of a class definition may be prepared in any order. In sum, class definition facilities primarily enhance the modification orientation of the language.

As implied above, a system must be hierarchically decomposed into its subcomponents to be described in DDN -- components are composed of sub-components which are composed of sub-subcomponents, etc. The tree-like system organization which results is often natural in describing the details of a system's algorithmic processing as indicated by the usefulness of structured programming ([29], [30]) for program description. The tree-like organization is not appropriate, however, in situations in which sharing occurs either because of the nature of the system (as in shared database systems such as online reservation systems) or because of a desire to layer the system into levels of virtual machines (as in many current operating systems).

To allow non-tree-like organizations, DDN contains instantiation control constructs [23]. Using these constructs, the designers may specify that components which are described, for clarity of description, as distinct are actually a single component in the final system configuration. These constructs are similar in effect to equivalencing constructs such as found in the Fortran programming language, but do not allow components of differing types to be "overlaid". They are also similar in effect to the aliasing constructs typically provided by parameter passing mechanisms and capability-based addressing schemes, but are not intended to be effected by the transmission of addresses at run-time. Thus, the constructs provide for the description of sharing relationships that are determinded by the system's configuration and which do not vary during system operation.

The instantiation control constructs contribute primarily to the inward-directedness of DDN since they allow explicit description of the system's eventual physical configuration. They also contribute by allowing the implicit description of all of the contexts in which a given component is to function, thus leading the designer of the component to consider how the component should be implemented so as to efficiently and effectively function in the various contexts.

The instantiation control constructs also lead to orthogonal, modular descriptions since logically different parts of the system may be separately described even though they share common subparts. The constructs may then be used to separately describe the sharing relationships among the parts. This also tends to lead to incremental descriptions.

Components in a DDN description are considered to execute concurrently and asynchronously and there are two major types of components [11]. <u>Subsystems</u> are those components which (logically at least) operate concurrently, interact freely but in a way acceptable to both parties to any interaction, and collectively provide the system's functional capabilities ([31], [32]). <u>Monitors</u> also operate concurrently, but provide data storage capabilities and possess built-in mechanisms that may be used to synchronize the potentially conflicting demands placed by other components [50]. The DDN view of a system is therefore that it is composed of hierarchically organized collections of sequential processes which interact through shared data objects which individually contain the necessary synchronization code.

This parallel-world view of systems enhances the clarity of system descriptions in the following way. It is generally recognized that complex systems may be more easily comprehended if they can be broken into simpler, smaller parts which interact in well-defined ways [33]. When this is done, then an understanding of the system's operation may be obtained by first understanding the parts and then understanding the interactions among the parts. As evidenced by recent texts on operating systems ([34], [35]) and recently developed methods for structuring artificial intelligence systems [35], decomposition of a complex software system is easier when the parts operate concurrently and interact asynchronously.

In terms of the characteristics delineated in the previous section, the parallel-world view primarily facilitates modularization. It also allows abstractions to be more easily constructed, since it facilitates projection of the intermodule interactions and the overall effect of the interactions by allowing the suppression of detail concerning how the interaction is accomplished. Finally, it allows outward-directed descriptions which focus upon overall properties of the system which derive from the interactions among the components.

In collections of concurrently operating components which interact via shared data structures, it is common for the shared data structures to be used for message exchange. This form of interaction is distinguished in DDN and constructs are provided for explicitly describing the message generation and utilization characteristics of subsystems and the message flow among the subsystems. This message transfer view leads to descriptions which are orthogonal, projective and outward-directed, allowing as it does focus upon the logical characteristics of module interdependencies and interactions.

The final set of DDN description facilities are those for the non-procedural specification of overall system operation through the definition of behavior by the algebraic specification of sets of sequences of events [37]. Arbitrary events may be defined such as "program added to schedule queue" or "legal access made to database" and sequences of events which the designer wishes to allow may be specified by constructs ([38], [37]) which are extensions to those found in regular expressions and similar to those defined for path expressions ([39], [40]) and flow expressions [41].

The event sequence expression constructs of DDN have been included primarily to allow analysis. They provide a redundant, outward-directed description which may be checked for consistency against the operational descriptions of the component interactions [42]. As a descriptive scheme, however, they also provide for the non-procedural, non-prescriptive, projective and orthogonal description of the operation of collections of subsystems.

THE DREAM DESIGN SUPPORT SYSTEM:

Precisely-defined design description languages of the sort discussed in the previous section can serve as a basis for the delivery of several types of aid to software design practitioners. Tools, or computerized techniques providing this aid, are most effectively delivered as a set of coherent, integrated facilities within a design support system. These tools may be classified as follows:

> <u>bookkeeping</u> tools provide aid in recording the current state of the development, in modifying and augmenting this record, and in returning it to a previous state if decisions are reversed
>
> <u>supervisory</u> tools provide aid in assuring that practices and procedures that are deemed beneficial are actually followed
>
> <u>management</u> tools provide aid in assessing progress and making resource allocation decisions
>
> <u>feedback</u> tools provide aid in measuring the characteristics of the system under development for the purpose of detecting errors, gaining confidence in the appropriateness of the decisions that have been made, and guiding the further development of the system

The DREAM system is organized as depicted in Figure 1. (This organization has been patterned after that developed for the Tools for Program Development (TOPD) system [8].) Central to the system is a database in which information is stored in textual form, organized into <u>textual units</u> or fragments of description which individually specify different aspects of the system. Textual units are organized hierarchically -- for example, a textual unit describing a class of subsystems is composed of textual units which describe the subcomponents comprising each subsystem, the interfaces through which messages flow, the message transmission

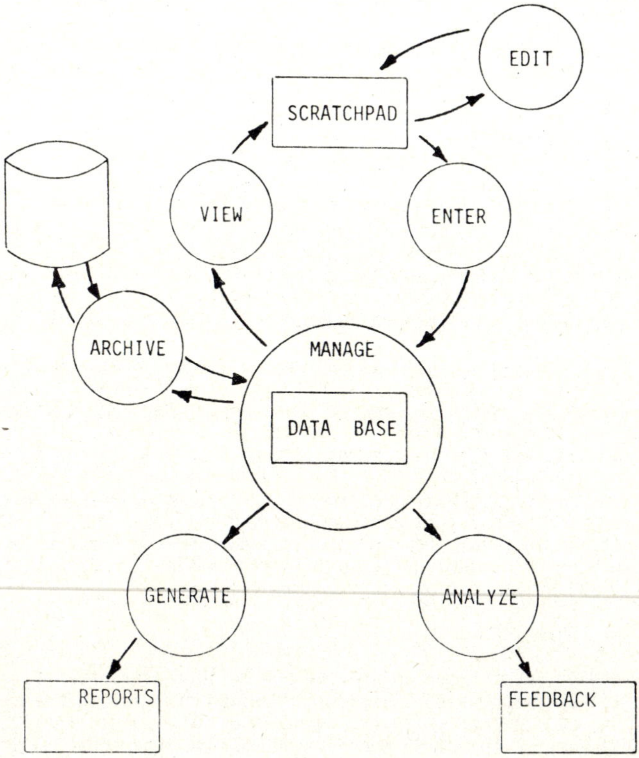

Figure 1.
Organization of the DREAM System

activities performed, and other aspects.

Several bookkeeping tools are provided as information insertion and retrieval mechanisms. Mechanisms for augmenting and modifying the information in the database on a textual unit basis facilitate the gradual evolution of the system's design while the current description is constantly available. Textual units which are to be added to the database (using ENTER) are prepared with the aid of a text editing facility (EDIT) and may be altered versions of units which have been copied from the database (using VIEW). Modifications to the database never result in the deletion of textual units which were previously entered -- thus designers have all of the previous versions of the design available and may back up to any previous point merely by retrieving the description which corresponds to that point and reentering it, thus making it the current description. Problems caused by having an ever-expanding database are eliminated by an archiving mechanism (ARCHIVE) which may be used to copy the database to external, offline storage, retaining only the latest version of each textual unit in the database itself.

DREAM does not currently provide any supervisory aids since one of the intents of the system is to allow the experimental determination of the efficacy of various aids and hence none were pre-defined in the system. DREAM has, however, been designed with the aim of allowing these aids to be easily added to the system as mechanism (within MANAGE) which control the flow of information into and out of the database. For example, documentation standards can be enforced by requiring that each textual unit be accompanied by a documentation unit when it is entered. Or, the principle of information hiding could be enforced by permitting designers access to only some of the information regarding components which they did not personally design. Or, a particular design method could be enforced by requiring that items in a design description be entered in a particular order.

Nor does DREAM currently provide any management aids, primarily because it is not clear what these aids should be. DREAM does provide a basis for management aids (such as GENERATE) as long as they can be formulated in terms of summary reports concerning the completeness or rates of change of the information in the database.

It is in the area of analysis aid that DREAM has been developed to provide the most aid. The analysis aids (such as ANALYZE) that are under development provide feedback analysis [43] in which information concerning the characteristics and properties of the system under design is derived and presented to the designers to be used in formulating rigorous arguments about the design's correctness or incorrectness. The only aid of this sort provided in the current DREAM system is a syntax checking mechanism, providing a check that is a necessary pre-requisite to any other analysis. The aids that are contemplated will span a broad spectrum (discussed in detail in [44]), from simple ones such as cross-reference generators to sophisticated ones which derive predictions of run-time characteristics by either analytic [42] or simulation [45] techniques.

AN EVENT-BASED DESIGN METHOD:

With the DREAM design support system and the DDN design description language, we have attempted to lend support to a variety of design styles rather than enforce our own style. A major reason is that we wish to be able to use the DREAM system to quantitatively measure the differences among various approaches to design. An equally important reason, however, is that we are not confident that we could define a method that was universally applicable across the full spectrum of systems which may be addressing using the DREAM system.

Our predilection toward top-down design methods is, however, quite evident in DREAM and DDN. We feel that these methods are the most effective to use since they allow designers the opportunity to introduce detail as warranted by consideration of a system's requirements rather than by consideration of aspects of the processing domain.

In using DDN to describe a variety of existing software systems ([46], [47], [48], [49], [50], [51]), we have found that it admits an interesting and novel variation of the traditional top-down design method. We call this variation the event-based design method and it is the purpose of this section to describe it in some detail and make some observations as to its value.

As with most design methods, the event-based design method consists of a design step which is applied iteratively. This basic step is graphically represented in Figure 2. The first task is to identify, on the basis of the partial design prepared by previous steps, events which are pertinent to the aspect of the system which is to be addressed at this design step. Then, the partial design is used to develop constraints upon the occurrences of these events which are necessary to assure that the system operates as required or intended. The next task is then to define system components which can produce the delineated events, and the final

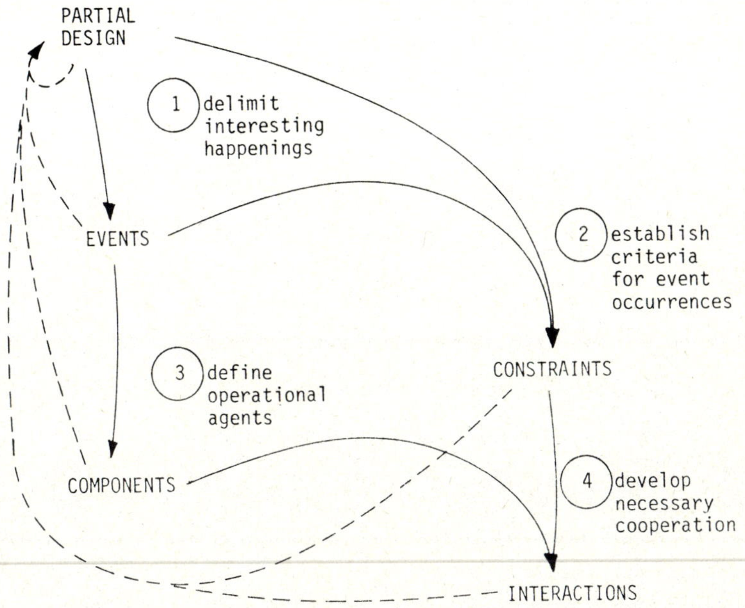

Figure 2.

Basic Steps in Event-based Design Method

task is to develop the interactions among the components which lead to the observance of the constraints.

Each design step therefore consists of the initial specification of the required behavior to be exhibited by the part of the system under consideration at this step. After this specification is prepared, the step is then completed by defining modules and module interactions which produce this required behavior.

As an example, consider the design of an on-board system for the in-flight monitoring of an aircraft's engines, and specifically that step at which we detail the interactions needed to call the attention of the pilot to the heating up of one of the engines. We hypothesize a partial design that includes the requirements of interest at this step, namely: there are four engines; a hot engine is to be signalled to the pilot by sounding an audio-alarm device; and signalling the existence of one hot engine should not block the recognition of another engine heating up and the signalling of this to the pilot. Notice that at this step we cannot focus exclusively on only the software parts of the system but must also consider non-software parts.

The events identified at this design step are defined, using the DDN language, in Figure 3. They correspond to four interesting "happenings" of concern at this step

```
EVENT DEFINITION;
   heat up: DESCRIPTION; temperature of an engine becomes greater
            than or equal to 150 degrees F END;,
   ring: DESCRIPTION; audio-alarm device sounds END;,
   notice: DESCRIPTION; monitor recognizes that engine has heated
            up END;,
   handle_hot_engine: SEQUENCE(heat up, notice, ring)
   END EVENT DEFINITION;
```

Figure 3.

and reflect aspects of the system that an external agent could observe during system operation. In addition to three "primitive", undecomposed events, we have defined the overall event of handling a hot engine as a sequence of instances of the three primitive events.

The constraints of interest at this point are recorded in Figure 4, again using

```
DESIRED BEHAVIOR;
   SEQUENCE(heat_up, notice, ring),
   POSSIBLY 4 CONCURRENT
     (SEQUENCE(heat_up, notice, ring))
   END DESIRED BEHAVIOR;
```

Figure 4.

the DDN description technique. First, we have established that every time an engine heats up, this is noticed by the monitoring system and the alarm is sounded. The second constraint reflects the requirement that the handling of hot engines be able to be carried out concurrently in the case that another engine heats up when one hot engine is being handled. In this description, the constraints are expressed in terms of desirable properties of the sequences of the sequences of events which occur during system operation. In approaching the description task this way, the desired effect is non-procedurally and non-prescriptively being specified.

Figure 5 gives a DDN definition of the components suggested by the events that have been defined. Notice the components are ones which operate concurrently and that both hardware and software components are specified.

The interactions among the components are defined, in message transmission terms, in Figure 6. Parts are defined and "plugged" together to establish the communication pathways, and the control process models specify the message transfer among the components. It should be emphasized that message transmission is being used to model the interactions among the components and that the interactions may actually take place using some other mechanism. Note that programming-language-like

```
SUBCOMPONENTS;
   engines ARRAY[1::4] OF [engine],
   monitors ARRAY[1::4] OF [engine_monitor],
   alarm OF [audio_device]
   END SUBCOMPONENTS;
```

Figure 5.

```
[engine_monitor]: SUBSYSTEM CLASS;
   request_status: OUT PORT;  END OUT PORT;
   receive_status: IN PORT;
      BUFFER SUBCOMPONENTS; signal OF [status_signal]
         END BUFFER SUBCOMPONENTS;
      END IN PORT;
   sound_alarm: OUT PORT;  END OUT PORT;
   observe: CONTROL PROCESS;
      MODEL;
         ITERATE SEND request_status;
                 RECEIVE receive_status;
                 IF signal = is_hot
                    THEN notice: NULL;
                                 SEND sound_alarm;
                    END IF;
                 END ITERATE;
         END MODEL;
      END CONTROL PROCESS;
   END SUBSYSTEM CLASS;

[status_signal]: MONITOR CLASS;
   STATE SUBSETS;  is_ok, is_hot  END STATE SUBSETS;
   END MONITOR CLASS:

[engine]: SUBSYSTEM CLASS;
   status_request: IN PORT;  END IN PORT;
   status_report: OUT PORT;
      BUFFER SUBCOMPONENTS; signal OF [status_signal]
         END BUFFER SUBCOMPONENTS;
      END OUT PORT;
   report: CONTROL PROCESS;
      MODEL;
         ITERATE RECEIVE status_request;
                 MAYBE heatup: SET signal TO is_hot;
                    ELSE       SET signal TO is_ok;
                    END MAYBE;
                 END ITERATE;
         END MODEL;
      END CONTROL PROCESS;
   END SUBSYSTEM CLASS;
```

```
[alarm]: SUBSYSTEM CLASS;
   ring_request: IN PORT;  END IN PORT;
   ringer: CONTROL PROCESS;
      MODEL;
         ITERATE RECEIVE ring_request;
                 ring: NULL;
                 END ITERATE;
         END MODEL;
      END CONTROL PROCESS;
   END SUBSYSTEM CLASS;

CONNECTIONS;
   FOR ALL i IN [1::4];
      PLUG (engines[i]|status_request, monitors[i]|request_status);
      PLUG (engines[i]|status_report,  monitors[i]|receive_status);
      PLUG (engines[i]|sound_alarm,    alarm|ring_request);
      END FOR;
   END CONNECTIONS;
```

Figure 6.

constructs are used to define the interactions. Also note that models of the hardware are specified to record the capabilities that are required -- the engines, for example, must have sensors and be able to "send out" status signals upon demand. Finally, note that the events identified at the beginning of this design step have been related to specific points during the operation of the system by labelling statements with the event identifiers.

We feel that the event-based design method outlined in the previous discussion formalizes the general practices of many software designers and that this formalization leads to several benefits. The greatest benefit comes from the provision of an important additional facility -- the definition of events and constraints. This facility allows the gradual reduction of requirements to precise statements oriented to the system's evolving modularization.

Another benefit, which we only briefly argue here, is the ability to verify the design as it evolves. The constraints developed at each step provide a redundant specification against which the newly designed operation of (part of) the system may be checked. In our example, we could use the pseudo-procedural descriptions given in Figure 6 as input to a simulator and thereby derive sequences of event occurrences. These sequences may then be compared to the desired sequences as stated in Figure 4. Of course, simulation is not in general sufficient since one needs to know all possible sequences of events that may arise. It is possible to derive a description of all possible sequences but the comparison is not, in general, feasible [42]. We are continuing our research in this area, seeking algorithms for subcases which span a wide variety of naturally occurring situations.

CONCLUSION

We have described a variation of the traditional top-down design method that utilizes the concepts of event and event sequence definition. At each step, criteria for system modules being elaborated at that step are extracted from the existing design and precisely stated using the event and event sequence constructs. The step is then completed by detailing the interactions among newly-designed and existing modules necessary to satisfy the criteria. The opportunity then exists to analyze the new, partial design to assure that the criteria are met before proceeding to the next design step.

The event-based design method arose in the process of our assessment of the effectiveness of the DREAM development support system and its description language, DDN. We have not extensively used it in design experiments, but have conducted two simple experiments in order to refine its definition. We have found it natural and easy-to-use, and feel that it both formalizes the practices of design practitioners and provides a basis for the integration of analysis with synthesis during software system design.

REFERENCES:

[1] Ambler, A.1., Good, D.I., Browne, J.C., Burger, W.F., Cohen, R.M., Hock, C.G., and Wells, R.E. Gypsy: A language for specification and implementation of verifiable programs. Software Engineering Notes, 2, 2 (March 1977), 1-10.

[2] Baker, J.W., Chester, D., and Yeh, R.T. Software development by step-wise evaluation and refinement. SDBEG-2, Software and Data Base Engineering Group, Dept. of Computer Sci., Univ. of Texas, Austin, January 1978.

[3] Campos, I., and Estrin, G. SARA aided design of software for concurrent systems. Proc. 1978 National Computer Conf., Anaheim, Calif., June 1978, pp. 325-336.

[4] Davis, C.G., and Vick, C.R. The software development system. IEEE Trans. on Software Engineering, SE-3, 1 (January 1977), 69-84.

[5] Estrin, G., and Campos, I. Concurrent software system design, supported by SARA at the age of one. Proc. 3rd International Conf. on Software Engineering, Atlanta, Georgia, May 1978, pp. 230-242.

[6] Estrin, G. Application of machine descriptions to design of concurrent systems. In Moneta, J. (ed.), Information Technology, JCIT3/North-Holland Pub. Co., 1978.

[7] Good, D.I. Constructing verified and reliable communications systems. Software Engineering Notes, 2, 5 (October 1977), 8-13.

[8] Henderson, P., Snowdon, R.A., Gorrie, J.D., and King, I.I. The TOPD System. Tech. Report 77, Computing Laboratory, Univ. of Newcastle upon Tyne, England, September 1975.

[9] Moriconi, M.S. A system for incrementally designing and verifying programs. ICSCA-CMP-9, Certifiable Minicomputer Project, Inst. for Computing Sci. and Computer Applications, Univ. of Texas, Austin, December 1977.

[10] Pearson, D.J. CADES - Computer aided design and evaluation system. Computer Weekly, (July/August 1973).

[11] Riddle, W.E., Wileden, J.C., Sayler, J.H., Segal, A.R. and Stavely, A.M. Behavior modelling during software design. IEEE Trans. on Software Engineering, SE-4, 4 (July 1978), 283-292.

[12] Riddle, W.E., Sayler, J.H., Segal, A.R., Stavely, A.M., and Wileden, J.C. DREAM - A software design aid system. In Moneta, J., (ed.), Information Technology, JCIT-3/North-Holland Pub. Co., August 1978.

[13] Robinson, L., Levitt, K., Neumann, P., and Saxena, A. A formal methodology for the design of operating systems software. In Yeh, R.T. (ed.) Current Trends in Programming Methodology, Vol.I, Prentice-Hall Inc., Englewood Cliffs, N.J., 1977.

[14] Snowdon, R. Interactive use of a computer in the preparation of structured programs. Thesis, Univ. of Newcastle upon Tyne, England, 1976.

[15] Teichroew, D., and Hershey, E.A. PSL/PSA: A computer-aided technique for structured documentation and analysis of information processing systems. IEEE Trans. on Software Engineering, SE-3, 1 (January 1977), 41-48.

[16] Van Horn, E.C. Software evolution using the SEER data base. Digital Equipment Corp., Maynard, Massachusetts, June 1978.

[17] Peters, L.J., and Tripp, L.L. A model of software engineering. Proc. 3rd International Conf. on Software Engineering, Atlanta, May 1978, pp. 63-70.

[18] Manna, Z. Mathematical Theory of Computation. McGraw-Hill, New York, 1974.

[19] Popek, G.J., et al. Notes on the design of Euclid. Software Engineering Notes, 2, 2 (March 1977), 11-18.

[20] Liskov, B., Snyder, A., Atkinson, R., and Schaffert, C. Abstraction mechanisms in CLU. Comm. ACM, 20, 8 (August 1977), 564-576.

[21] Wulf, W.A., London, R.L., Shaw, M. Abstraction and verification in Alphard. In Schuman, S.A. (ed.), New Directions in Algorithmic Languages, IRIA (1975).

[22] Dijkstra, E. A Discipline of Programming. Prentice-Hall, Englewood Cliffs, N.J., 1976.

[23] Riddle, W.E. Hierarchical description of software system organization. RSSM/40, CU-CS-120-77, Dept. of Computer Sci., Univ. of Colorado at Boulder, November 1977.

[24] Dahl, O., and Nygaard, K. SIMULA - An Algol-based simulation language. Comm. A.C.M., 9, 9 (September 1966), 671-678.

[25] Henderson, P. Finite state modelling in program development. Proc. 1975 International Conf. on Reliable Software, Los Angeles, April 1975.

[26] Liskov, B.H., and Zilles, S.N. Specification techniques for data abstractions. IEEE Trans. on Software Engineering, SE-1, 1 (March 1975), 7-19.

[27] Parnas, D.L. A technique for software module specification with examples. Comm. ACM, 15, 5 (May 1972), 330-336.

[28] Wirth, N. The programming language PASCAL. Acta Informatica, 1, (1971), 35-63.

[29] Dahl, O., Dijkstra, E., and Hoare, C.A.R. Structured Programming, Academic Press, N.Y., 1973.

[30] Wirth, N. Program development by step-wise refinement. Comm. ACM, 14, 4 (April 1971), 221-227.

[31] Riddle, W.E. Abstract process types. RSSM/42, CU-CS-121-77, Dept. of Computer Sci., Univ. of Colorado at Boulder, December 1977 (revised July 1978).

[32] Riddle, W.E., Sayler, J.H., Segal, A.R., Stavely, A.M., and Wileden, J.C. A description scheme to aid the design of collections of concurrent processes. Proc. 1978 National Computer Conf., Anaheim, Calif., June 1978, pp. 549-554.

[33] Simon, H.A. The architecture of complexity. Proc. Am. Phil. Soc., 106, (December 1962), pp. 467-482. Also in Simon, Sciences of the Artificial, MIT Press, Cambridge, 1969.

[34] Brinch Hansen, P. The Design of Concurrent Processes. Prentice-Hall, Englewood Cliffs, N.J., 1977.

[35] Habermann, A.N. Introduction to Operating System Design. SRA, Chicago, 1976.

[36] Fennel, R., Lesser, V.R. Parallelism in artificial intelligence problem solving: A case study of HEARSAY II. IEEE Trans. on Computers, C-26, 2 (February 1977).

[37] Wileden, J.C. Behavior specification in a software design system. RSSM/43, COINS Tech. Rep. 78-14, Dept. of Computer and Info. Sci., Univ. of Massachusetts, Amherst, July 1978.

[38] Riddle, W.E. An approach to software system behavior description. To Appear: J. of Computer Languages.

[39] Campbell, R.A., and Habermann, A.N. The specification of process synchronization by path expressions. In Lecture Notes in Computer Science, 16, Springer Verlag, Heidelberg, 1974.

[40] Habermann, A.N., Path expressions. Computer Sci. Dept., Carnegie-Mellon Univ., Pittsburg, June 1975.

[41] Shaw, A.C. Software descriptions with flow expressions. IEEE Trans. on Software Engineering, SE-4, 3 (May 1978), 242-254.

[42] Riddle, W.E. An approach to software system modelling and analysis. To appear: J. of Computer Languages.

[43] Riddle, W.E. A formalism for the comparison of software analysis techniques. RSSM/29, Dept. of Computer and Comm. Sci., Univ. of Michigan, Ann Arbor, July 1977.

[44] Stavely, A.M. Design feedback and its use in software design aid systems. Proc. Software Quality Assurance Workshop, San Diego, November 1978.

[45] Sanguinetti, J.W. Performance prediction in an operating system design methodology. RSSM/32 (Ph.D. Thesis), Dept. of Computer and Comm. Sci., Univ. of Michigan, Ann Arbor, May 1977.

[46] Cuny, J. A DREAM model of the RC 4000 multiprogramming system. RSSM/48, Dept. of Computer and Comm. Sci., Univ. of Michigan, Ann Arbor, July 1977.

[47] Cuny, J. The GM terminal system. RSSM/63, Dept. of Computer and Comm. Sci., Univ. of Michigan, Ann Arbor, August 1977.

[48] Riddle, W.E. DREAM design notation example: The T.H.E. operating system. RSSM/50, Dept. of Computer Sci., Univ. of Colorado at Boulder, April 1978.

[49] Segal, A.R. DREAM design notation example: A multiprocessor supervisor. RSSM/53, Dept. of Computer and Comm.Sci., Univ. of Michigan, Ann Arbor, August 1977.

[50] Riddle, W.E., Sayler, J.H., Segal, A.R., Stavely, A.M. and Wileden, J.C. Abstract monitor types. Proc. of Specification of Reliable Software Conf., Boston, April 1979.

[1] The distinction of phases which we use here is a simplified version of the many, diverse distinctions that have been made by others, for example by [17].

[2] For the remainder of this paper we use the term design to refer to architectural design.

Formal Models and Practical Tools
for Information Systems Design
H.-J. Schneider, Editor
North-Holland Publishing Company

EVENT DIRECTED PROGRAM EXECUTION FROM DECLARATIVE SPECIFICATIONS

Paul LINDGREEN *)

Abstract: This paper reports an approach where the task of administrative computer application systems is defined and described in a declarative manner, so that executable programs can be generated directly without the need of any manual algorithm construction. The basic idea behind the approach is the recognition of events as a means of specifying the dynamic properties of datamatic systems. Events are declared and defined and are referred to as triggers of the various operations and processes that constitute the system. A commercially available design and implementation tool employing this idea has been in practical use for several years. It has evolved through a number of iterations and generalizations, which have not only lead to a more powerful tool but also to a clarification af some of the principles behind the approach.

Contents:

*) The reported work was supported by and carried out at A/S REGNECENTRALEN, Copenhagen. Authors present address:
DSB, Organization Office, Kalvebod Brygge 3o, 4,
156o Copenhagen V.

1. Introduction.

The topic of this paper is to investigate some descriptional problems arising in the phase of the design of datamatic systems, where the information analysis is finished: The task of the system is defined in all details and the remaining activity is to program a computer to perform the task. The paper will not evaluate programming in its traditional sense, but rather indicate how a change to non-algorithmic specifications enables a properly formed task description to serve as the program itself.

A complete formal description of the task of a datamatic system is primarily a description of its output, that is, its elements and, how they are structured. The elements can be described as functions of elements from a database and/or from input. This implies the necessity to refer to a database description and to an input description. The input description may be an integrated part of the task description or it may be elements of one or more descriptions from other (possibly manual) systems.

Regardless of the method employed in the task description, it probably differs much from the result of the programming process. This may be the main reason why the programming often turn out to be a costly part of datamatic projects. The author is convinced that this is so, because the programming languages traditionally used are algorithmic by nature. The implementation could be much simplified if the burden of proper algorithm construction was removed, or at least reduced.

One way to obtain this is to recognize events as a mean to express the dynamic properties of programs. The first part of the paper evaluates this possibility on a hypothetical level, by means of examples.

The other part, however, describes elements of a real tool which uses the ideas in a practically applicable way.

2. Event Directed Processing.

The execution of a process on a computer is governed by information present in what traditionally is called a program. In the computer itself the program is represented as an ordered set of 'machine instructions' and stored as bit patterns which are interpreted by the CPU. The instructions define the operations to be executed and the operands to be operated on. Furthermore for each instruction executed there is always defined a successor to be executed nest, unless the process is 'disturbed' by an interrupt.

The external representation of a program is a text expressed in some programming language. In most cases the program constitute an algorithm, possibly with one or more sections where the involved operands are declared. An algorithm consists of a number of statements, which in principle are equivalent to the machine instructions Although a single statement normally will comprise operations corresponding to the execution of several instructions, the successor principle is the same. After the execution of any statement the programming language will uniquely define the next statement to be executed. In most languages the rule is, that, unless an explicite statement says otherwise, the successor is always the next statement in the lexicographical order.

These well-known algorithmic principles appear to be fundamental in some sense: Man has used algorithms for many purposes long before computers were invented, and when new persons learn programming it seldom seems to be the algorithmic principle which causes troubles.

The naturalness of algorithms together with the algorithmic nature of the computer itself are probably the main reasons why most known programming languages are procedural and apply the lexicographical order to define the dynamic properties of the process which the program describes. One main drawback of this principle is that the condition for executing a statement is extremely implicite - loosely spoken: a statement is executed only when you happen to be at its location in the program.

There is, however, another way it can be done - a way which is more convenient when you try to decompose your system requirements.

The alternative principle can be illustrated by considering the following simple program:

```
begin
  read (a);
  b:=a+3;
  print (b);
end
```

According to a well established algorithmic tradition this means the following 'operations' to be executed:

1) the reading of an external value into the variable a
2) the assignment of the sum of a and 3 to the variable b
3) the printing of the value of b.

Now consider the following transscription of the program:

```
begin
  on assignto b: print (b);
  on assignto a: b:=a+3;
  on start     : read (a);
end
```

We note that the new program basically consists of the same three statements, but each statement has been preceded by a specification of an event to trigger its execution. Furthermore the statements have intentionally been rearranged to show that their order is immateriel. This principle constitute one of the main advantages of the approach, because it enables the designer (or programmer) to specify the statements in the order in which it is most convenient. Since system analysis and a possible documentation often progress from output via process to input, it may ve useful to have the freedom to do so, also when the datamatic specifications are prepared.

However, although it probably illustrates the alternative principle quite well the above example is rather inconvincing - at least in two aspects:

- realistic programs are never that simple and trivial
- the necessary specifications seem to indicate a drastic increase in the amount of program text.

Undoubtedly, if only straightforward methods for event specification, as those shown, are applied the idea will die as soon as the users recognize what is required from them. Fortunately - as will soon be obvious - the amount of text can be reduced to even less than the corresponding algorithm. Let us therefore look at a slightly more realistic example:

Consider a system which shall process a set of records representing customer orders and produce a survey showing for each customer the total value of ordered items (as far as the information is present in the records). Each record refer to the sale of a given amount of a given item and contains, among others, the fields 'customer_no', 'sales_value'. There may be any number of records for each customer. Let us suppose that an underlaying file system or DBMS is able to access the records sequentially according to increasing values of 'customer_no'. A possible algorithm to produce the survey could be:

```
old_customer_no := total_value := 0;
while more records do
  readnext (customer_no, sales_value);
  if customer_no = old_customer_no then
      total_value := total_value + sales_value
  else
      begin
        comment a new customer was recognized;
        print (char(newline), old_customer_no, total_value);
        total_value:= sales_value;
        old_customer_no:= customer_no;
      end;
end do;
```

(The clever programmer may relax: The author is aware of an obvious flaw in the algorithm. We shall return to it.)

Now, how could this be transformed to declarative statements with events as triggers? One possible formulation could be:

```
on idle              : readnext (customer_no, sales_value);
on end customer_no   :
  print(
      char(newline),
      customer_no,
      accum sales_value over customer_no);
```

Note: At this point we are not discussing linguistic elements in any language and far less syntactical matters. The examples are chosen entirely to illustrate ideas and concepts. End of note.

The first statement is equivalent to the while loop specification with the readnext operation. The trigger 'idle' could be regarded as a kind of standard event, which occurs whenever the processing caused by all previous events have ceased.

The second statement performs the printing just like the algorithm - except that the above-mentioned flaw has been removed due to the trigger 'end customer_no'. The flaw in the algorithm is that the survey will start with a dummy total line for the imaginary customer number zero. The event specification is composed of an operator 'end' with the ordering field 'customer_no' as operand. This event will occur once for each customer number when the last record with that number is read. This corresponds to the 'else' situation in the algorithm, apart from the fact that 'end customer_no' will not occur before the first customer is processed. In this way no dummy total is printed.

In the algorithmic print statement a variable 'total value' is referred, which by properly scattered statements around in the program is secured to have the correct value when it is used. In its declarative counterpart all the necessary information is specified where it is used by means of an accumulation operator 'accum' and a range or resetting operator 'over'. We shall return to these operators later on. At this point a more important question must be dealt with.

Most readers undoubtedly will say that the arguments above in favor of the declarative approach are unfair. Any reasonable programming language provides a procedure mechanism which is everything that is needed. All the algorithmic statements could be embodied in a procedure declaration, which possibly could be separately translated and even stored in a library. Done so, the program can be reduced to a single statement 'produce_customer_survey' if the procedure is declared with that name.

To do it that way is rather absurd. Nothing is really gained if a procedure is so ad hoc that it can only be used in one situation. However, the point remains that one example can never prove that the introduced operators and event definitions are not equally ad hoc and in practice only usable in that example. Furthermore, let us assume that they really have reasonable general, modular, and/or basic properties to justify them as candidates for elements in a declarative language. Is it then possible to define a whole set of such elements, which on the one hand is very limited, orthogonal in nature, and based on a few and simple concepts, and on the other hand sufficient complete to cover a whole class of applications? Finally, is it possible to implement the ideas resulting in practical applicable tools?

As mentioned before, this section should only show event directed specifications as an alternative possibility. A formal language satisfying the above listed demands has been developed at Regnecentralen in Copenhagen and will be discussed in the second half of the paper. Before that, some comments about the background may place the approach in the right perspective.

3. A Historical Interlude.

In a paper at the 'Norddata' Conference in 1969 in Stockholm the author presented some principles and features of a general system language, EDDAP, to be used by system planners for exact description of the tasks of datamatic systems (see ref. 1). The paper was bases on some attempts to describe application systems in a way where the ambiguity of the natural language was avoided through a formalism. In the paper it was postulated that a compiler could be produced that automatically would generate executable programs from such a formal description and a plan to reach the goal was outlined. The first step was to finish and describe the language and let people try to use it as a purely descriptive tool to ease the communication with the programmers. Based on experience from this step, the construction of a system language compiler should be initialized.

The plan failed!

The language was finished and it was even applied in the description of a few systems. The programmers seemed to be happy with the result because they had a well defined reference document to specify what they should do. But the lack of any real motivation for the system people to use it, soon caused the new tool to be abandonned. The time schedules for the system planners did not take into account that it takes time and effort to be precise. An informal way of communicating with the programmers seemed easier and faster. Consequently the burden of beeing precise was left to the programmers and in this way the system people could keep up with the scedules. The result was that no compiler project was started up.

This looks like a management failure. It is a well-known 'fact' that from a technical point of view the management never knows what the real problem is and even less what the right solution is. In this case the right solution, as the author (of course) argued, was to implement the compiler and thereby avoid the manual programming phase. On hindsight, which is possible now several years later, the author is convinced that the only way to secure proper use of formal methods is that programs can be generated automatically. On the other hand, hindsight also tells another story: Based on what has been implemeted since then of compilers for various subsets of such a system language (and after several iterations and refinements of methods) we know that it can be done now. But at that time a compiler project of the proposed kind would have lead to a disaster.

The way to this admission and to the present know-how has been via three successful projects all concerned with declarative languages, but in each case in a much less ambitious scale. The projects, which have been reported in ref. 2, tried to combine the development of practically applicable tools with a certain amount of research in techniques and methods. The tools developed were:

- a DBMS, called SODA with declarative specifications of access patterns (see ref. 3)
- a lexical scanner, called COMET, for compiler construction with declarative specifications of the source language syntax
- a processing system, called GENIUS, for administrative applications with restricted types of input, but with declarative specifications of output, DB-access, and computations.

The last mentioned tool is the primary basis for the following more elaborate description of event directed processing.

4. GENIUS.

4.1 Survey.

GENIUS is an acronyme for the Danish words meaning 'general level-oriented output system' which pretty well describes the intentions with the first version of the system which was announced as a flexible tool to be used for producing report programs in administrative systems. It was created in the first half of 1975, when the author was assigned responsibility for the development. This became the opportunity to recover some of the ideas burried in the old EDDAP language. They were now put into a more viable frame.

To be more specific: A subset of EDDAP was extracted which covered the necessary printing possibilities (layout, format, calculations, etc.) and this was defined to operate in an event directed virtual machine. Its basic function was defined as to read a sequence of transactions represented as records of various types stored in a file, and compare specified, so-called criteria fields according to which the records are ordered.

The criteria fields constitute a hierarchy, so that the most significant fields are common for all the record types while the least significant are permitted to depend on the record type. Whenever a new record is read its criteria fields are compared with the corresponding criteria fields in the previous record. This will result in a sequence of 'match' or 'no match' situations, and these situations constitute the basis for the occurrence of the events that may be specified to trigger the required operations of the system.

In general an event, as the concept is used here, can be defined in the following way:

An event is a recognized, well-defined situation or change of state in a system.

The above-mentoned so-called criteria events will occur according to the following scheme: The comparison process proceeds in the direction from higher to lower levels and will continue until a 'no match' situation is recognized or until the list of comparable criteria field is exhausted. When a 'no match' situation is recognized on some level this per definition implies 'no match' on all lower levels. For each criteria field two potential events are defined - one called the 'end event' and one called the 'new event'. They will both occur in a 'no match' situation indicating the last record with the current value of the criteria field and the first record with a new value respectively. *) Accordingly when a 'no match' is recognized the 'end event' will occur before the 'new event'.

In this way every reading of a transaction may cause the occurrence of several or none criteria events. However, independent of the comparisons, one event is defined always to occur - one referring to the type of transaction just read. This event is called the type event.

*) We have already explained an event of the 'end' type in the customer survey example in section 2.

The system must secure that the various print operations, calculations etc. are executed in a well-defined order. Therefore a fundamental principle is always applied: Two events will never occur simultaneously. Upon every reading GENIUS will force the events to occur in the following sequence:

1) All 'end events' (if any) referring to criteria fields in the record at hand in order from lowest level to that one where no match was recognized by the comparison.

2) All 'new events' (if any) referring to criteria fields in the new record in order from the level where no match was recognized to the lowest level.

3) The type event referring to the new record.

The operations declared to be triggered by these events will then be executed accordingly. See Figure 1.

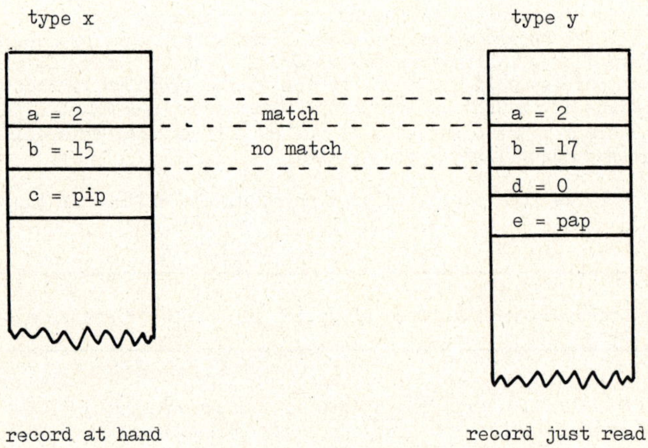

Figure 1.

A comparison between two consecutive transactions of different type where a 'no match' is recognized for the criteria field 'b'. This will cause the following series of events to occur:

end c, end b, new b, new d, new e, type y

Each of these events may or may not trigger the execution of operations.

Many aspects of the above-mentioned principles from the first GENIUS version are also found in other known report generator systems. This is not surprising since they reflect basic elements in well-known solutions to a set of common datamatic problems. However, in the later versions of GENIUS this rather narrow view of events has been broadened through a series of generalizations. This has changed GENIUS to what reasonably could be regarded as a first iteration of a general system language implementation. In order to see this we must turn and see how the principles are reflected in the GENIUS language.

4.2 The Initial GENIUS Language.

The user - that is, the system designer or programmer - who wishes to employ GENIUS to produce a program for some application must prepare what is called a GENIUS description. This consists of two parts - declarations of the relevant input transactions and declarations of operations to be executed during an activation.

The input transactions may either be declared directly in the description by a specification af all the involved fields constituting the various record types, or - what is normally used - the transactions are defined by reference to record types in a common database description (schema). Whatever method is employed the declarations define a set of variables corresponding to the transaction fields and are referred by the field names. These variables serve as images of the corresponding fields in the following way: When a new transaction is read and all operations triggered by the possible end events have been executed, the values from all the transaction fields of the new record are transferred to the corresponding variables. A value remains in a variable until another transaction is read which contains a field with the same name. In this way operations triggered by 'end events' can refer to the 'old' values while operations triggered by all other kinds of events will refer to 'new' values.

The transaction type declarations define the set of criteria fields which are used in the comparison process. Also these fields are associated with variables, but besides this their names are used to identify the appropriate criteria events. One of the common criteria fields is designated a special meaning. It contains a number which identifies the transaction type and is used for references to type events. For example the event 'type 3' will occur after the possible criteria events if a transaction with the value 3 in the type field has been read. Different transaction types may be defined as the same or different record types in the DB description.

The section with operative declarations contains a set of so-called definition statements which may be specified in any order, the user may wish. Each statement defines an identifier and associates a type and meaning to it. The identifier may denote a part of the output text (the report to be printed), an expression to be evaluated, or a variable to be assigned a calculated value. A definition statement is terminated by a semicolon and is composed of the following units:

- the identifier to be defined
- a possible trigger
- a definition symbol
- a definition body

The meaning of these units will become obvious if we consider the example in Figure 2:

```
payment                          = price * amount;

product_line on end item_no     .= print(
      1 lo t *    : 'item'
       18 n 5     : item_no
       26 n 3.2   : payment
       4o n 5.2   : accum sales_value over customer_no
     case sales_code of (
         1: price_details
         2: product_description
     else : sales_survey)                 );

sales_value on type 3            = if code = 5 then payment else 0;
```

Figure 2: An Example of Definition Statements from a GENIUS Description.

The second statement defines a part denoted 'product_line' of some report. This part is generated whenever the event 'end item_no' occurs. It consists of five sub parts, four of which are individual fields and a fifth one which depends on the value of 'sales_code' and which is defined in statements not shown here.

Here we shall not evaluate the many formatting and printing possibilities of GENIUS (if interested, see ref. 4) but just explain, that the first field is the constant text 'item', which appears on a new line from position lo. The next field in position 18 is the numeric value of the criteria field 'item_no' (which will have a new value in the next transaction - a fact we know, because it was the event 'end item_no' that triggered the current operation). The third field in position 26 is the value of the expression 'payment' defined in the first statement. This expression is now evaluated and formatted with two decimals in the field.

The fourth field is the value of an anonymous accumulator defined to contain the sum of all occurrences of 'sales_value' for a given value of 'customer-no'. The accumuland must either be a variable associated with a numeric transaction field or, as here, a so-called <u>event variable</u> defined in a statement to be assigned when a specified trigger occurs. In the first case the accumulator is incremented whenever a transaction occurs that contains the corresponding field. In the second case the accumulation is performed on the same trigger just after the assignment. In our case the result is a conditional accumulation of payment.

It is important to note that it is illegal to accumulate the value of 'payment' directly, since it is not associated with an event that can trigger its accumulation.

The resetting of an accumulator is triggered by an event which must be specified after the over operator. In our case the name of a criteria field is specified, implying the corresponding 'new event'. To be meaningful here it must be assumed that several type 3 transactions may appear for each value of 'customer' since the accumulated 'sales_value' is assigned - and thereby accumulated - triggered by the event 'type 3'.

The last part of 'product_line' is conditional and determined by the value of 'sales_code'. The case operator selects one of the specified identifiers which must be defined elsewhere in the description by means of the print operator but without a trigger. This statement is then evaluated (with possible references to further print levels) before the current statement is resumed. In our case it is finished and then GENIUS will take care of the next operation to be activated by a trigger.

Although this example ignores several aspects, it should give the reader a fair idea of the language as it appeared for the users in the first version. However, it could be mentioned that also a number of other useful operators were available. Most of them served to simplify the task of preparing a GENIUS description, for example by providing a general applicable shorthand notation for the calculation of often used administrative and accounting concepts. Also a general count operator was provided. It keeps track of the number of occurrences of a specified event in a manner equivalent to the accum operator.

4.3 The First Improvements.

The first versions of GENIUS became an immediate success - especially among non programmers, who were not used to the algorithmic way of expressing a process. Many simple as well as complicated reports could now be specified in a rather easy and straightforward way as long as the structure of the report could be reflected in the sequence of transactions and in the levels of the criteria fields. And this was the case for a surprisingly great part of the possible reports. Programmers, on the other hand, found that a lot of freedom was removed from them, and they pointed out several cases where it was awkward to solve a problem with GENIUS but rather easy if an ordinary programming language was used.

Slowly experience was gained among consultants and other system people, who constituted the main group of users, that, indeed, some tasks - often extremely relevant - could not be described properly in GENIUS. The author was presented with several problems and also with some proposals for new elements in the language which seemed to solve the problems. A few of these ideas was implemented as simple extensions because they reflected the lack of a relevant independent feature, but two main classes of problems were not so easily removed:

The first one appeared with reports of the ordered sequential kind, possibly with many details on several levels, which at the end should present a summary, but ordered according to other criteria than the first part. A well-known programming technique, which could be called scatter storing, provides a simple solution to most of these problems. It involves the possibility to assign, accumulate or count in random elements of arrays and afterwards to refer to the elements in an ordered sequential manner. However, the first version of GENIUS provided no means to utilize this technique.

The second class of problems appeared disguised in various ways, but often it could be tracked down to an apparent lack of proper events. The potential events defined by a given set of transactions and criteria fields were not always sufficient to express the necessary dynamic characteristics.

If the idea of event directed processing was as viable as the author steadily believed, it should be possible to incorporate in the GENIUS language a few elements which provided the necessary facilities. A continuous analysis of user problems during nearly two years extensive use of GENIUS indicated that the two mentioned problem areas were fundamental.

Due to the origin of GENIUS it seemed natural to look in the original system language for the solution. It then turned out that in EDDAP the second class of problems was clearly recognized and the basic idea for solution provided. However, apart from some vague working notes the first class of problems were completely ignored. This is a further reason why the original one-iteration-EDDAP project would never have succeeded.

To keep a long story short: During the summer and fall of 1977 a set of more or less inspiring ideas were considered, dismissed or evaluated through numerous fruitless as well as fruitful attempts to define the new elements. The demands are well-known from any formal language design, but they are not easy to satisfy all together:

- conceptual economy and orthogonality
- operational simplicity and generality
- backward compatibility
- naturalness

The design process led to a very satisfactory result, because not only the new elements were invented, but so much know-how was gained about the fundamental principles that the new version was simpler to explain than the old one.

The new elements comprised:

- user defined events
- new standard events
- array counters and accumulators
- scan ststements

A user defined or derived event is defined in a statement with a reference to another event - basic or derived itself - combined with a logical expression.

```
special_ customer *= new customer for which balance > 10000;
```

In this example an event named 'special_customer' is defined to occur whenever the event 'new customer' occurs, provided the value of 'balance' is greater than 10000. Since two events never occur simultaneously a further rule is needed to define the order of occurrence for the primary and the derived events. This has been defined so that if the primary event is an 'end event' or is derived from such one (through any number of levels) then the derived event will occur before the primary event, otherwise after. User defined events can be referred in all situations where so far only basic events could be used.

Three standard events were introduced to further simplify the descriptions. One of them, denoted 'trans', is of special interest here, because it illustrates the intensions to generalize the concepts. It is defined to occur after the possible criteria events whenever a transaction is read, independent of its type. This event provides the possibility to define derived events reflecting arbitrary classes of transactions, for example so:

```
debit_transaction *= trans for which payment > 0;
```

In this way it is easy to see that the originally introduced type event is nothing but a special case of this much more general facility. For example the event 'type 3' is equivalent to the user defined event:

```
type_3 *= trans for which trtype = 3;
```

Where 'trtype' is the name of the field declared to contain the transaction type. On this background it is surprising to note, that also the concept of the 'trans' event is just a special case of a more general principle, as we shall see in the next section.

The solution to the scatter storing technique comprises the introduction of array counters and accumulators and a new type of statement defining a sequential scan of a specified range. So far we have talked about single accumulators (and counters) defined to be increased and reset on certain events, but now the user may specify for example:

```
accum (month max 12) payment over year;
```

It defines an anonymous accumulation array with 12 elements, which are increased whenever a new instance of 'payment' appears. When this happens the current value of the identifier 'month' is used as index to select the proper element in which the accumulation shall take place. Normally, both the index and the accumuland will be present in pairs in transactions, but they may as well be defined by proper expressions (the accumuland via an event variable).

This generalization from simple to array accumulation (and counting) will take care of the scatterwise collection of values, but normally such values are required to be used in a well defined order - often according to increasing values of the index. In ordinary programming language this is taken care of by a for/do statement of some kind. In GENIUS it was solved accordingly, but 'in the spirit' of event directed processing. The solution is <u>the scan statement</u>, as shown in the following examples:

```
period on end year *= scan month max 12;
short_element      *= scan element while
                            length(element) < height (element);
```

A scan statement defines what could be called an array or 'a burst' of events. These events will occur immediately after each other, and for each occurence a variable specified after the scan operator is increased by one. Before the first event the variable will be reset to zero. The burst or scan will stop when a specified value is reached or when a logical condition becomes false. Each scan can be triggered either by a specified event or by reference from a print statement just like one print statement can be activated from another.

The events defined by scan statements may be used like other types of events and therefore also to trigger the printing of the contents of arrays. Since a variable is increased for every occurence of the event it is assumed to be used as index directly or in an index expression. This provides everything which is necessary to take care of array printing, but the scan statement is in no way bound or restricted to this application. A scan event may trigger another scan and thereby provide a general multilevel framework, for example, for the production of all kinds of tables or analytical surveys etc.

4.4 The Incorporation of Data Base Operations.

GENIUS was born as a report generating system and its only input was a stream of transaction records assumed to be ordered properly. The production of report programs uses a fair part of the ressources in ADP and this justifies the development of a special tool for that purpose. On the other hand, other kinds of datamatic processing are needed as well. Therefore, on the background of its success it seemed natural to consider extensions to GENIUS to cover primarily DB operations - especially that input is taken directly from the DB if this is relevant.

As mentioned in section 3 a DBMS called SODA has been developed. It provided all the necessary operations in a very convenient way, but one problem was that SODA was developed to be activated from ordinary programs. Could it be used in a declarative environment as well, and how could it fit into the existing GENIUS language?

As explained in ref. 3 SODA applies two fundamental access principles:

- record access via references to so-called record sets
- field access via locally declared variables.

A record set is declared in a local data description (sub schema/external schema) as a set of one or more record types. Record sets may be single or they may be subscripted, in which case the set is partitioned and each subset associated with a so-called mother record in another set. This reflects one-to-many relations in the information structure (conceptual schema).

For each set a mapping between variables and record fields is specified. It defines the relevant fields when a record of the set is accessed and the variables through which the field values are accessed. This is in fact the principle again with field image variables, but where it in GENIUS is restricted to a one-way/one-to-one mapping, is it in SODA implemented in full generality.

Two quite different ideas inspired the author to the solution which finally defined a beautiful symbiosis between GENIUS and SODA.

The first idea was a proposal by Zahle (ref. 5) to combine the simplicity of the relational DB approach with the one-record-a-time principle known from DB navigating systems, as for example the CODASYL DBTG. One important advantage of the proposal is that the complexity of a FIND operation with its complex currency concepts is avoided. It is described to work in an algorithmic host language environment and is based on references to relations with proper logical expression as restrictions, but this caused no problems: We have already seen how algorithmic statements can be transformed to declarative ones, and the SODA record set was an obvious substitute for a relation. The proposal involved two operators 'fetch' and 'scan' which accesses a single record and a whole set of records respectively. They both permitted the specification of any operations on each accessed record.

The second idea originated from some incomplete theoretical studies which were done in relation to the EDDAP project. They were concerned with the notion of complementary events. Assume some GENIUS description with two transaction types, so that the universe of possible type events after the reading of a transaction consists of 'type 1' and 'type 2'. The complementary event to 'type 1' is then 'type 2' and vice versa. So far, this was not reflected in the GENIUS language, but when a single record is accessed in a DB, two possible results must be considered: The record is in the DB, or it is not in the DB. This presents two complementary events.

The synthesis of the above-mentioned ideas resulted in the following extensions to the GENIUS language:

1) The GENIUS description is provided with a reference to a local data description in which the relevant record sets and necessary field image variables (with mapping to record fields) are declared. These variables can be used freely all over the GENIUS description.

2) The scan operator of GENIUS is generalized to cover not only arrays, but also the scanning of record sets. By reference to a declared record set, each record of the set is accessed sequentially and each access will cause the scan event to occur. The increase of a scan variable is omitted, but the while condition is permitted for record sets also.

3) The event definition statement used for derived events is extended to define the access of a single record in a record set by a 'get' operation. The access may be triggered by an event, or it may be activated by reference. The necessary identifying values of key fields is supplied as usual for SODA in selected variables specified in the declaration of the record set. Upon the access, the defined event will occur if the record is present in the DB, otherwise the complementary event will occur. This is referred by the operator 'not' before the event identifier.

4) The DB operations 'create', 'put' and 'delete', which in principle do not communicate back, are permitted as elements in a print operation. For obvious aestetic reasons it is syntactically permitted to use the operator 'do' instead of 'print', but this has no functional influence.

Provided with these DB operations, GENIUS must be regarded as a general datamatic tool and not just an advanced report generator. However, once more the introduction of a new operational possibility has resulted in a more general view of the basic functions in the system. The reader may remember how the introduction of the standard event 'trans' and the declatation of derived events simply turned the original type event into just a special case of a more general feature.

Now, the same happens with the 'scan' operator. The basic function of GENIUS to read a sequence of transactions is, in fact, nothing but a scan of a record set defined to comprise the transaction record types. A set of criteria events can be defined for each record set scan based on possible ordering or identifying fields in the involved records. The 'trans' event will then be replaced by the user defined scan event. The only basic event necessary will be the standard event 'start' which occurs once when the system is activated.

The recognition of a generalization like this provides great support to the 'scan' operator as a fundamental element in the language.

5. Concluding Remarks.

The naturalness with which DB operations were integrated in GENIUS indicates that event directed program specification is a viable principle and a possible alternative to the traditional algorithmic way. GENIUS can be further developed to cover the reading of unprocessed text, for example from input terminals. The recognition of any information element on any level from such a text is also equivalent to the occurence of an event, and this can easily be used to trigger required operations. A proposal for the necessary linguistic elements to describe such input structures has been reported in ref. 6 and a partial implementation thereof is described in ref. 2.

The experience with the GENIUS system through more than three years shows that people, who are not traditional programmers, will learn to use the system very fast. The notion of events and the principles of how they can be used as triggers, is nearly instantly understood, but, naturally, it will take some time before the syntax and the details of the various operators in the language is completely mastered. Programmers, on the other hand, will often need some time to emancipate from their traditional way of expression. However, once they have accepted the fact, that it is unnecessary to construct a proper algorithm in order to have something done, they are usually very happy with the tool.

Experience furthermore shows that, as the demands to the application systems change, it is much easier to maintain a GENIUS description than a traditional program. It is also an advantage that it is often the consultant/system designer himself who maintain the descriptions, so that communication to and dependence upon a programmer is avoided. One could then ask: What will become of the programmers? Will they join the rows of unemployed? The answer is probably, that they will appear in new roles with new tools.

References:

[1] Paul Lindgreen: Exact Definition of Datamatic Problems. Norddata Conference. Stockholm June 1969.

[2] Paul Lindgreen: Declarative Languages. Data, Copenhagen April 1977.

[3] P.Lindgreen, E.Rosenberg: SODA - A Flexible Scheme for Database/Program Interface. International Computer Symposium Liege April 1977.

[4] GENIUS Manual. RCSL 21-V041 Regnecentralen, Copenhagen April 1978.

[5] T.U.Zahle: SCAN - A Simple Record-at-a-time DML for the Relational Data Model. International Conference on Database Management Systems. Milano, June 1978, p 115-126.

[6] Paul Lindgreen: INFORMAL - A Comprehensive Method for Input Data Description. Norddata Conference, Helsinki, June 1976.

Formal Models and Practical Tools for Information Systems Design
H.-J. Schneider, Editor
North-Holland Publishing Company

END-USER TOOLS FOR INFORMATION SYSTEMS REQUIREMENT DEFINITION

G.M. NIJSSEN[1] F.J. VAN ASSCHE[2] J.J. SNIJDERS[2]

1 Control Data and University of Brussels
2 Control Data Belgium

ABSTRACT

In this paper we will very briefly describe the major principles and overall framework of an approach to information systems. The major characteristics of this approach are its completeness and its simplicity, and a clear distinction of the three areas of effectiveness, namely information analysis, programming and computer resources. Experience with this approach during the recent two years permits the provisional conclusions that with this new approach it is possible to materialize significant increases in information system building and maintenance productivity. Furthermore, this approach permits the users to be very actively involved in the problem specification or requirement definition.

Once we have this overall model for information systems design, we will describe some recently developed computerized tools to be used for designing and maintaining the object systems grammar. In our opinion the object systems grammar is the most abstract information systems requirement specification. In order to have the end-users involved in the specification process, it is very essential to have some tools which permit the dynamic update of the requirements definition as well as providing all the useful reports. This set of tools, called ISDIS (Information Systems Design and Implementation System), permits the end-user to be directly involved in the requirement definition; ISDIS contains a formal language for stating the requirements and is at the same time used as documentation system as well as tool for information analysis. ISDIS contains two concepts which permit the precise description of various levels of abstraction of the problem definition as well as the cooperation of several groups of information analysts working on a very complex problem.

With respect to information system requirement specification, it is our experience that this new approach forces the user and information analyst to get the requirements right before application programming starts.

1. INTRODUCTION

In this paper we will describe the practical results of a computerized aid in information systems requirement specification. For reasons of brevity we will limit ourselves to describe the tools which only apply to the most abstract problem description, sometimes referred to as object systems grammar.

In section two we will describe the basic axioms and concepts for an overall model for information system design and the complete architecture for informationbase management systems as a result of it.

In section three we will illustrate what this approach means for ISDIS (Information Systems Design and Implementation System) and what the objectives and scope of it are.

In section four we will describe why it is needed to distinguish two kinds of conceptual schema, one being the information systems grammar, and one being the object systems grammar, and how they are related.

In section five some analysis and end-user tools needed for the information systems requirements definition are described.

In section six some aspects of dynamic update capabilities are described as well as their relationship to the people involved.

In section seven we concentrate on the large number of different retrieval reports needed in a practical environment.

The last section contains the major conclusions.

2. THE OVERALL MODEL FOR INFORMATION SYSTEMS DESIGN

The first axiom of our approach has been given the name ENALIM (Evolving NAtural Language Information Model) and is as follows:

> Each communication between a human being and an information system, as well as each communication between any two information systems can be considered to consist of a set of natural language sentence instances (reference 4).

And furthermore we postulate that each communication between two programs can be considered to consist of a set of natural language sentence instances.

The consequence of this assumption is that we now have a unifying approach to such seemingly different things as information systems, databases, programming, distributed systems and data dictionaries.

The unifying aspect is that <u>all</u> traffic between two processes (people, programs, information systems) can be described in the same way.

Without any loss of generality we can define that a natural language sentence instance consists of a set of elementary sentence instances, bound together by the sentence connective "and".

In our opinion, it is not so important which formal tool - the predicate or the set - is selected to describe this elementary sentence instance. The critical aspect is that one deals with a linguistic construct, the elementary sentence instance.

These sentence instances communicate some knowledge about one or more objects. Very essential is the fact that only sentence instances make up the traffic, and not object name instances. This means that only sentence instances can be the object of an update or retrieve command. Therefore one can prescribe the allowable traffic by defining the

- elementary sentence types
  . object name types
  . constraints on sentence populations and on transitions from one population to another.

But how is this prescription enforced in today's information system? A large part of the prescription is handled by the application program (some of it is often referred to as data validation) and the remaining part is prescribed in the schema. The principle of the INSYGRAM (INformation SYstems GRAMmar) approach is that 100% of the prescription is in one (conceptually) central contract and 0% in the application program (reference 4).

The result of ENALIM and INSYGRAM is that we now can speak of a framework of conceptual information systems which consist of three components, namely

a. a prescriptive grammar which is the only and complete description, prescribing which (natural language) sentence instances may enter and reside in the informationbase which contains at each moment in time a set of sentence instances. This prescriptive grammar we give the name conceptual schema.

b. an informationbase instance which consists of a set of sentence instances allowed by the prescriptive grammar and existing at a certain moment in time.

c. an interaction or application program which may modify the informationbase instance (or state) but only if the resulting new informationbase instance (or state) is permitted by the conceptual schema, or which may retrieve from the informationbase instance.

If we want to add to this framework the possibilities to handle and optimize computer resources, independently of the conceptual schema, then we have to introduce another schema, called an internal schema. This is a set of rules describing how the sentence instances of the informationbase are physically stored. The independence is obtained by introducing a conceptual-internal transformation.

If we furthermore want to add the possibilities to handle and optimize programming, independently of conceptual and internal aspects, we introduce another schema, called an external schema.

This is a set of rules describing how sentence instances of the informationbase can be viewed by a program. The independence of the external view of the other views is obtained by introducing a conceptual-external transformation.

This architecture as presented in figure 2.a is given the name COEXISTENCE architecture because it permits the coexistence of various external schemata and various internal schemata while the correctness of the informationbases is completely under the control of the conceptual schema.

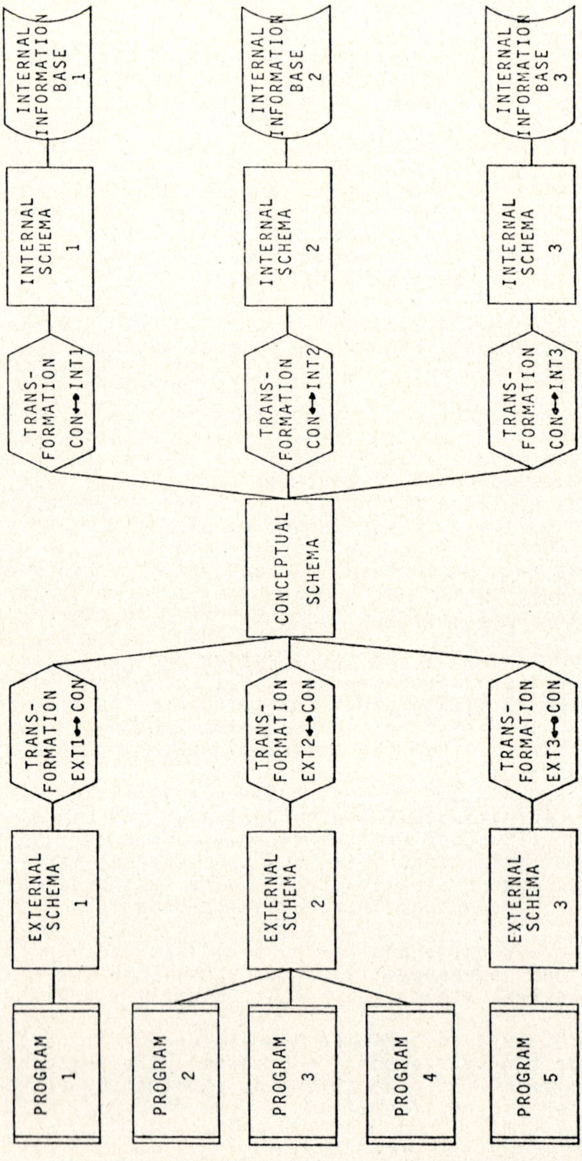

Figure 2.a

3. ISDIS

The objectives of ISDIS are first to control and support the whole information system development cycle, i.e. information analysis, design, programming, testing, conversion and maintenance, and help everyone who is involved in it, and second to control and support the operation of this information system.

The scope of ISDIS ranges over the complete information system as described above and the information system environment, i.e. hardware, system software and users.

For the development of ISDIS, which itself is an information system, we followed the ENALIM and INSYGRAM approach. If we simplify the architecture of figure 2.a we can illustrate (see figure 3.a) how both systems relate to each other. The conceptual schema of the user is contained in the informationbase of ISDIS. ISDIS itself has a conceptual schema and a number of application programs which execute the tasks fulfilling the objectives described above. By doing so the following advantages of the informationbase approach are gained on the level of the user-informationbase as well as on the ISDIS level:

- the correctness of the information in the informationbase is guaranteed by the (INSYGRAM) conceptual schema approach.
- many users can share the common informationbase.
- it gives users the flexibility to extend their application areas while the existing application areas keep going without change.
- it gives users the flexibility to integrate two separate application areas which are already using the informationbase approach while keeping the return on investment of the original two information systems.
- it gives the opportunity to substantially increase the information analysis productivity.
- it gives the opportunity to increase the programming productivity by a factor of 2.
- it gives the opportunity to reduce the reprogramming expenses by more than 50 percent.
- any formatted information system can be done much better in this way.

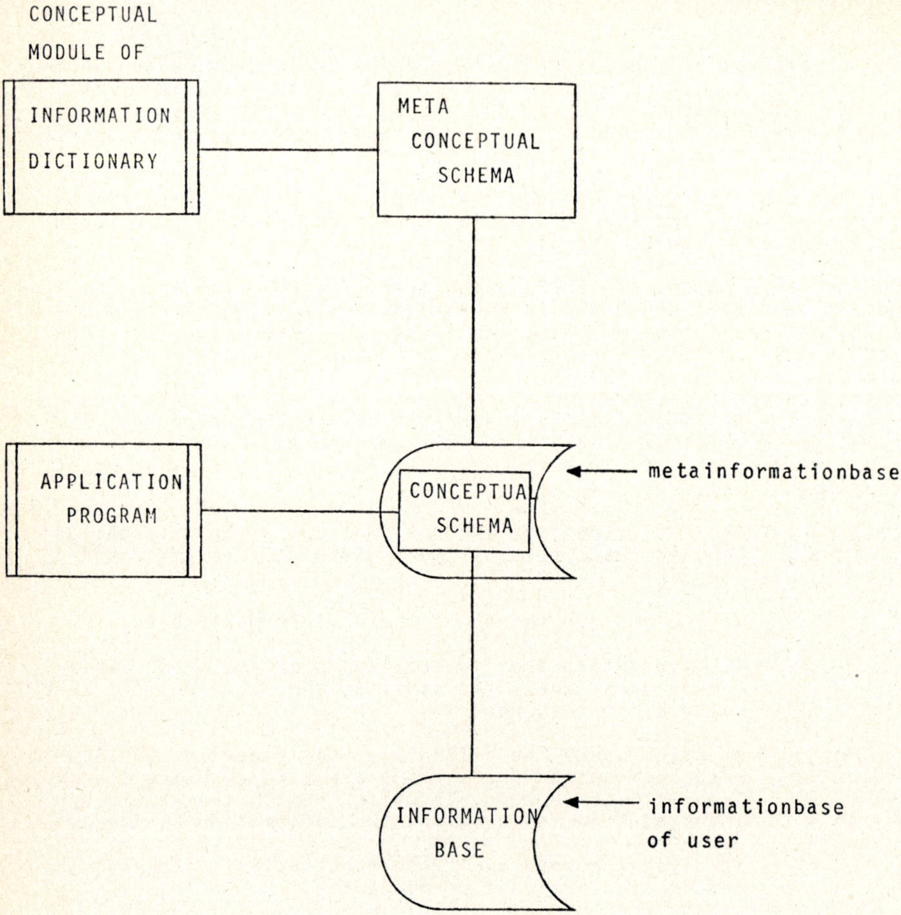

Figure 3.a

4. BASIC CONCEPTS FOR THE OBJECT SYSTEMS GRAMMAR

Before describing the recently developed computerized tools to be used for designing and maintaining the object systems grammar we have to clarify what an object systems grammar is and why it is needed.

A conceptual schema as defined in the ENALIM and INSYGRAM approach is a set of rules specifying the set of allowable informationbase states and the set of allowable transitions. It is obvious that in such a conceptual schema one has abstracted from programming or computer considerations. But is this conceptual schema the highest level of abstraction? In our opinion there is one more level of abstraction, namely the one in which one abstracts from the naming conventions with respect to object instances. The result is that then one no longer deals with sentences but with abstract sentences, or ideas. In sentences one deals with object names, in ideas with objects. This abstraction will result in a more stable problem description. One could say that the grammar which prescribes the communication in sentences is an information systems grammar. We have given another definition for the information systems grammar above, namely it is a set of rules specifying the set of all allowable informationbase states and the set of allowable transitions. We now may say that if we abstract from the names in the informationbase, we get the "object system base" or idea base. Analogously we may define that there is a set of rules specifying the set of all allowable object system states and the set of all allowable transitions. This set of rules prescribes the "communication in ideas" and is an OBject SYstems GRAMmar (OBSYGRAM).

Figure 4.a contains a table with the few aspects of the information and idea grammar.

schema name	grammar name	manipulatable construct	world with
idea base schema	OBJECT SYSTEM GRAMMAR	IDEA	things (objects)
information base (sentence base) schema	INFORMATION SYSTEM GRAMMAR	SENTENCE	names of things (object names)

Figure 4.a

We have seen before that a sentence base schema consists of

- sentence types
  - . object name types
  - . constraints

and now we may add that an idea base schema consists of

- idea types
  - . object types
  - . constraints

In figure 4.b are illustrated the idea base and sentence base schema and the transformation in between. During the information analysis phase, this transformation is an abstraction from object names to objects, but during the design phase this transformation "forces" the users to be aware of the fact that he must take decisions how names are assigned to objects; this latter aspect is neglected in too many information systems design approaches.

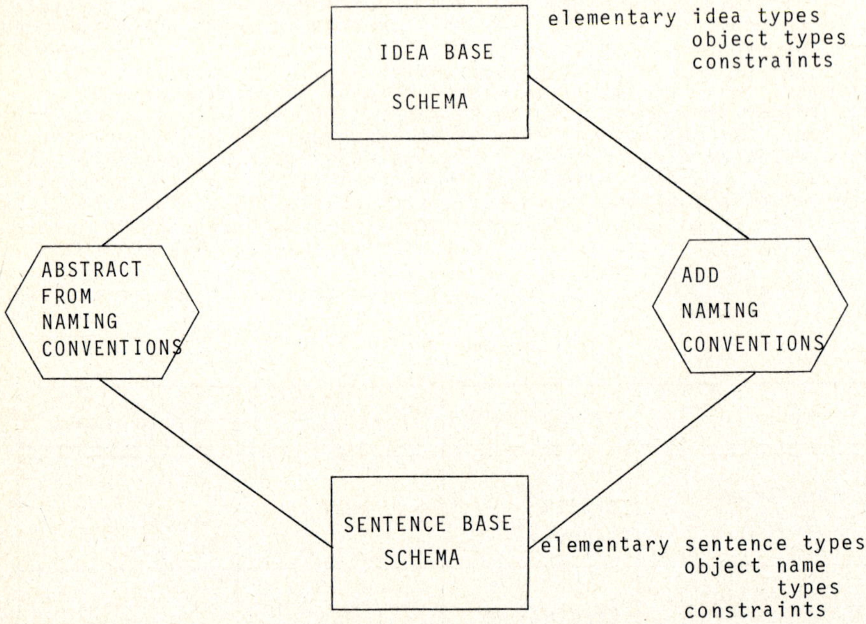

Figure 4.b

5. ANALYSIS AND END-USER TOOLS

In this section we will describe concepts and tools which in our opinion are necessary if one really wants to master complex and large information system requirements definitions, having many persons involved in the specification process.

5.1 Names and user defined names

Each basic concept in ISDIS has a name, which is called the preferred name and most of them can be given a synonym name, called the user defined name. Working with many groups of persons requires that each group may use its own names. User defined names are of special importance if one wants to integrate two or more existing information systems while permitting the users to use their own, well-familiar names.

5.2 Descriptions and designators

The descriptions and keywords are important features for analysis, detection of redundancy of definitions, documentation and control of an information system. Every basic concept can have a textual description of the general contents and purpose of it. The designators are more short identifiers, optionally constructed from a controlled list of keywords.

5.3 SCOPE

Probably the most practically useful concept is the concept we have given the name "scope". A scope is defined as an arbitrarily specified subset of the idea types and (referred) object types. This concept permits us to concentrate the attention on any part of the idea base schema. Applying the conceptual schema approach in practice, we found that the concept of SCOPE is a must. If not available, one gets such reactions as: "this approach deals with too many details", "this approach cannot be used to have various groups work together", "this approach is not attractive to management", etc. Figure 5.3.a gives an idea type diagram of an idea base schema, in which two scopes, called SCOPE-PROJECT and SCOPE-EMPLOYEE are defined.

5.4 ZOOM

The definition of the concept SCOPE shows that this is a very powerful "concentration" or "abstraction" tool. Sometimes, however, one wants a somewhat different tool for purposes of "concentration" and "abstraction", and this concept we have given the name ZOOM. A ZOOM is defined as an ordered set of scopes, such that the lowest level of the ZOOM contains the largest number of idea types, and for each higher level contains successively less idea types. For a given idea base schema there may be any number of ZOOMs and there is no restriction such as overlap etc. The concept of ZOOM can be illustrated by figure 5.4.a. There we have two ZOOMs, called ZOOM-A and ZOOM-B. The first level of ZOOM-A contains only idea type c, the second level c and j, the third level c, d and j, the fourth level a, c, d, e, i and j and the fifth and lowest level in ZOOM-A contains the idea types a, b, c, d, e, f, g, h, i and j. ZOOM-B has only 3 levels, idea type j belongs to level 2, 3, 4 and 5 of ZOOM-A, and to level 3 of ZOOM-B.

5.5 Status control

With most of the concepts a proposed status or an approved status is associated. Apart from this ISDIS needs the capability of a test status, and production status in order to test changes without affecting the normal operations. However, something in proposed status can not be in production status at the same time. E.g. if we wish to test out a modification in a program, a test version must be provided.

5.6 History and version control

Since there is a timelag between the moment of updating the information system requirement specifications and the dissemination among all users, one must keep track of several versions. The control of these versions is of course of no little importance. Furthermore, keeping track of the whole analysis and maintenance history of the basic concepts is instructive and very worthwhile as documentation.

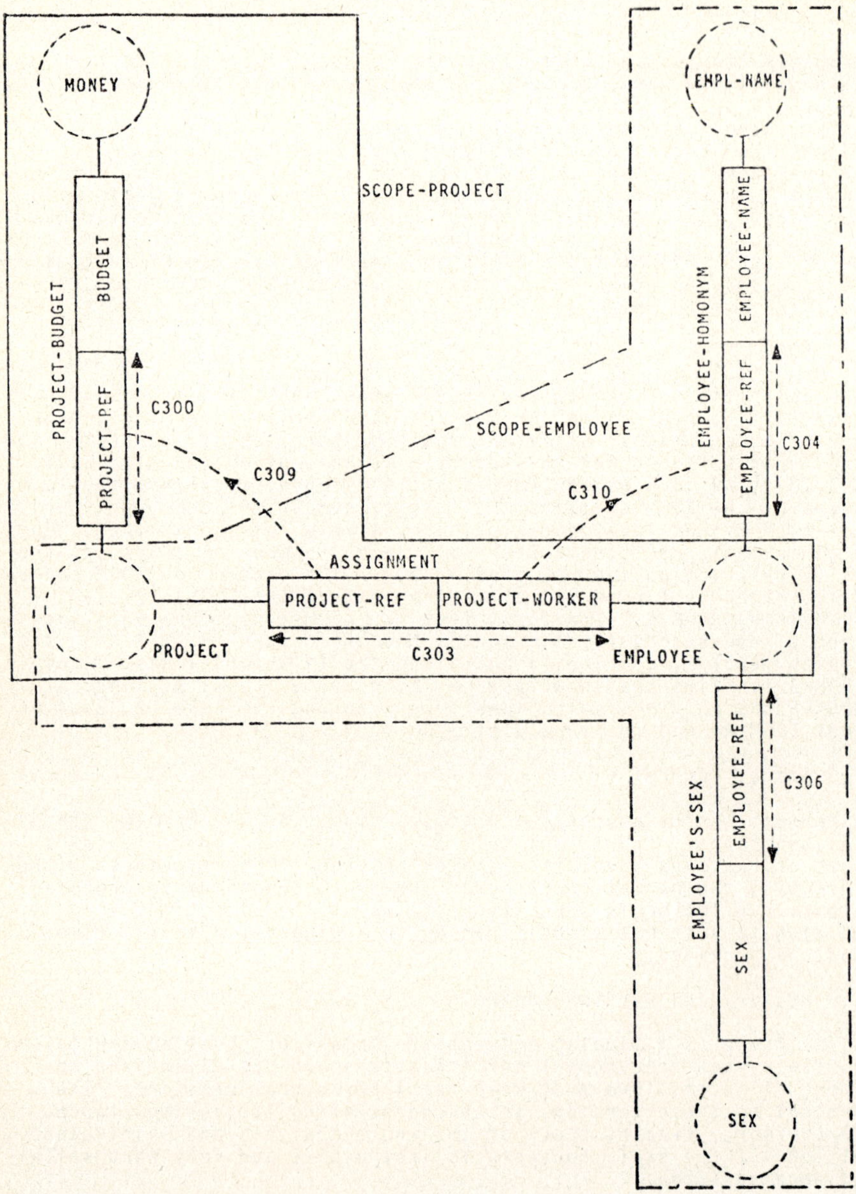
MONEY
BUDGET
PROJECT-BUDGET
PROJECT-REF
C300
SCOPE-PROJECT
C309
SCOPE-EMPLOYEE
EMPL-NAME
EMPLOYEE-NAME
EMPLOYEE-HOMONYM
EMPLOYEE-REF
C304
C310
ASSIGNMENT
PROJECT-REF
PROJECT-WORKER
PROJECT
C303
EMPLOYEE
EMPLOYEE-REF
C306
EMPLOYEE'S-SEX
SEX
SEX

Figure 5.3.a

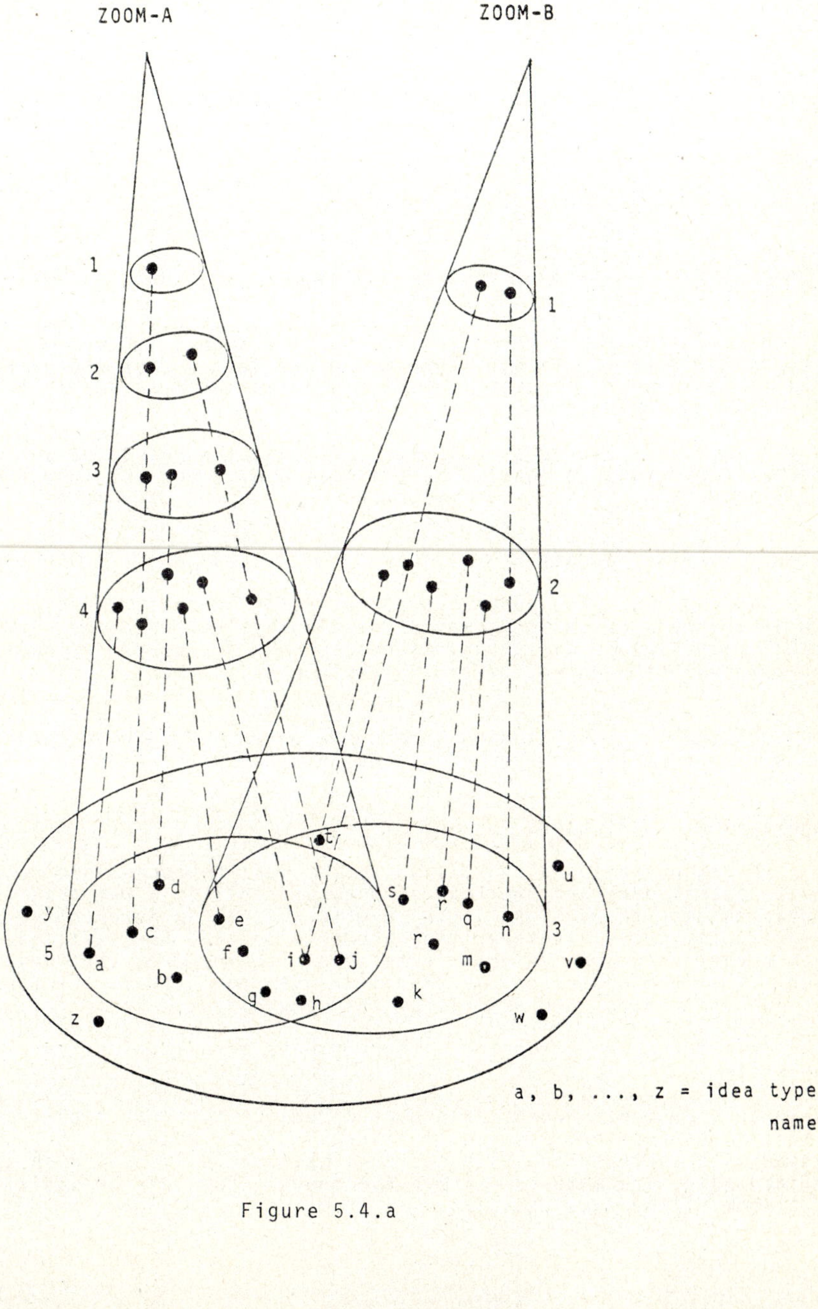
ZOOM-A
ZOOM-B
1
2
3
4
5
1
2
3
a
b
c
d
e
f
g
h
i
j
k
m
n
q
r
r
s
t
u
v
w
y
z
a, b, ..., z = idea type name

Figure 5.4.a

6. DYNAMIC UPDATE CAPABILITIES

Updating

The update functions of the information dictionary include the addition, deletion and modification of such things as objects, ideas, constraints, users, databases, zooms, scopes, etc. ISDIS requires that the update is done in such a way that the information contained within the dictionary (meta informationbase) remains consistent.

Let us examine this consistency requirement. For example, consider additions: the addition of a constraint presupposes the existence of the idea types which are referred to; the addition of an idea type presupposes the existence of the object types which are referred to. Now consider deletions: the deletion of an object type can cause several idea types and constraints to be deleted (in the jargon called a strong delete). For modifications: the modification of the name for an idea type must be effected everywhere this idea is referred to (note: a modification implies the same as a deletion and an addition).

As a result, the user does not always realize the effect of an update. Therefore he must be kept informed of the total impact of every operation.

Batch or on-line update

Both batch and on-line update capabilities are necessary because the environment of the information dictionary system can be either batch or on-line or mixed. Furthermore, both are used for loading and maintenance whenever we are in a mixed environment.

Experience indicates that initially blackboard, paper sheets, etc. are used and that the loading often is a batch job. The more stable the meta informationbase becomes, the more the on-line environment will be used for update functions.

Regular and casual users

An information analysis and design system must be accessible both to the casual user and the regular one, and this in a way that is convenient for them. Experience reveals that in an interactive program, the users, whenever they are able to take the initiative themselves, show some resistance to spoon feeding from the computer side. The more a user becomes familiar with the system, the more he likes to control the stimuli of the communication himself.

Therefore there is a need for different ways of communication with the system.

Table 6.a, 6.b, 6.c and 6.d show how an object-type, an idea-type, a constraint-type and a scope of figure 5.3.a is added to the system in a conversation with a casual user while also Spanish user defined names are entered. Table 6.e shows a part of the addition of a zoom of the same example.

```
DO YOU WANT TO ADD
 1. OBJECT TYPES
 2. IDEA TYPES
 3. CONSTRAINTS
 4. SCOPES
 5. ZOOMS
OR
 6. DO YOU WANT TO CONTINUE ?
TYPE EXACTLY ONE NUMBER.
? 1

OBJECT TYPE 000001 OF SCHEMA "TEST"
WHAT NAME (AND USERNAME) DO YOU WANT TO USE FOR THIS OBJECT TYPE ?
? MONEY,DINERO
WHAT DESCRIPTION DO YOU WANT TO USE FOR THIS OBJECT TYPE ?
? INTERESTING
? ƀ
DO YOU WANT TO ENTER ANOTHER OBJECT TYPE ?
? YES
```

Table 6.a

The addition of an object type

```
DO YOU WANT TO ADD
 1. OBJECT TYPES
 2. IDEA TYPES
 3. CONSTRAINTS
 4. SCOPES
 5. ZOOMS
OR
 6. DO YOU WANT TO CONTINUE ?
TYPE EXACTLY ONE NUMBER.
? 2

IDEA TYPE 000001 OF SCHEMA "TEST"
WHAT NAME (AND USERNAME) DO YOU WANT TO USE FOR THIS IDEA TYPE ?
? PROJECT-BUDGET,PRESUPUEST-DEL-PROYECTO
WHAT DESCRIPTION DO YOU WANT TO USE FOR THIS IDEA TYPE ?
? ƀ
YOU NOW HAVE TO GIVE NAMES FOR THE TWO ROLES OF THIS IDEA TYPE
AND INDICATE THE RESPECTIVE OBJECT TYPES THEY REFER TO.
== FIRST ROLE ==
ROLE 000001 OF SCHEMA "TEST"
WHAT NAME (AND USERNAME) DO YOU WANT TO USE FOR THIS ROLE ?
? BUDGET,PRESUPUESTO
WHAT DESCRIPTION DO YOU WANT TO USE FOR THIS ROLE ?
? ƀ
ENTER THE NAME OF THE OBJECT TYPE TO WHICH THIS ROLE REFERS.
? MONEY
== SECOND ROLE ==
ROLE 000002 OF SCHEMA "TEST"
WHAT NAME (AND USERNAME) DO YOU WANT TO USE FOR THIS ROLE ?
? PROJECT-REF,REFERENTE-A-PROYECTO
WHAT DESCRIPTION DO YOU WANT TO USE FOR THIS ROLE ?
? ƀ
ENTER THE NAME OF THE OBJECT TYPE TO WHICH THIS ROLE REFERS.
? PROJECT
```

```
THIS IDEA TYPE HAS TWO VALID ROLES NOW ; IT IS ACCEPTABLE
IF IT GETS AT LEAST ONE UNIQUENESS CONSTRAINT.

CONSTRAINT 000001 OF SCHEMA "TEST"
WHAT NAME (AND USERNAME) DO YOU WANT TO USE FOR THIS
UNIQUENESS CONSTRAINT ?
? AT-MOST-ONE-BUDGET-PER-PROJECT.PRESUPUESTO-UNICO-POR-PROYECTO
WHAT DESCRIPTION DO YOU WANT TO USE FOR THIS UNIQUENESS CONSTRAINT ?
? ƀ
ENTER THE NAME(S) OF THE ROLE(S) WHICH MUST OCCUR IN THIS
 UNIQUENESS CONSTRAINT.
? PROJECT-REF
? ƀ
DO YOU WANT TO ENTER ANOTHER UNIQUENESS CONSTRAINT FOR THIS IDEA TYPE?
? NO
EVERYTHING IS FINE WITH THIS IDEA TYPE.
LET@S GO ON NOW.
DO YOU WANT TO ENTER ANOTHER IDEA TYPE ?
? YES
```

Table 6.b

The addition of an idea type and his uniqueness constraint

```
DO YOU WANT TO ADD
 1. OBJECT TYPES
 2. IDEA TYPES
 3. CONSTRAINTS
 4. SCOPES
 5. ZOOMS
OR
 6. DO YOU WANT TO CONTINUE ?
TYPE EXACTLY ONE NUMBER.
? 3

CONSTRAINT 000005 OF SCHEMA "TEST"
WHAT NAME (AND USERNAME) DO YOU WANT TO USE FOR THIS CONSTRAINT ?
? NO-ASSIGNMENT-WITHOUT-EMP-NAME.NO-ASIGNACION-SIN-NOMBRE-EMP
WHAT DESCRIPTION DO YOU WANT TO USE FOR THIS CONSTRAINT ?
? ƀ
THIS CONSTRAINT WILL BE OF TYPE
 1. UNIQUENESS
 2. SUBSET
 3. EQUALITY
 OR
 4. EXCLUSION
TYPE EXACTLY ONE NUMBER,PLEASE.
? 2
YOU NOW HAVE TO SPECIFY THE DOMAIN OF THIS SUBSETTING CONSTRAINT.
ENTER THE IDEA TYPE NAME.
? ASSIGNMENT
ENTER THE NAME(S) OF THE ROLE(S) WHICH MUST OCCUR IN
 THIS CONSTRAINT-SET.
? PROJECT-WORKER
```

```
? ƀ
YOU NOW HAVE TO SPECIFY THE RANGE OF THIS SUBSETTING CONSTRAINT.
ENTER THE IDEA TYPE NAME.
? EMPLOYEE-HOMONYM
ENTER THE NAME(S) OF THE ROLE(S) WHICH MUST OCCUR IN
 THIS CONSTRAINT-SET.
? EMPLOYEE-REF
DOMAIN AND RANGE HAVE GOT THE SAME NUMBER OF ROLES
SO , EVERYTHING IS OK. LET@S GO ON NOW.
DO YOU WANT TO ENTER ANOTHER CONSTRAINT ?
? YES
```

Table 6.c

The addition of a subsetting constraint

```
DO YOU WANT TO ADD
 1. OBJECT TYPES
 2. IDEA TYPES
 3. CONSTRAINTS
 4. SCOPES
 5. ZOOMS
OR
 6. DO YOU WANT TO CONTINUE ?
TYPE EXACTLY ONE NUMBER.
? 4

SCOPE 000001 OF SCHEMA "TEST"
WHAT NAME DO YOU WANT TO USE FOR THIS SCOPE ?
? SCOPE-PROJECT
WHAT DESCRIPTION DO YOU WANT TO USE FOR THIS SCOPE ?
? NO COMMENT
? ƀ
YOU NOW HAVE TO SPECIFY THE CONTENTS OF THE SCOPE BY ENTERING
THE NAMES OF THE EXISTING OBJECT AND IDEA TYPES YOU WANT TO HAVE
IN THIS SCOPE : YOU CAN ALSO ENTER THE NAMES OF THE SCOPES
THAT HAVE TO BE COPIED INTO THIS SCOPE.
ENTER SCOPE NAME(S) , PLEASE .
? ƀ
ENTER OBJECT TYPE NAME(S), PLEASE
? PROJECT
? MONEY
? EMPLOYEE
? ƀ
ENTER IDEA TYPE NAME(S), PLEASE
? ASSIGNMENT
? PROJECT-BUDGET
? ƀ
DO YOU WANT TO DEFINE ANOTHER SCOPE ?
? YES
```

Table 6.d

The addition of a scope

```
ZOOM 000001 OF SCHEMA "TEST"
WHAT NAME DO YOU WANT TO USE FOR THIS ZOOM ?
? ZOOM-INCREMENTAL
WHAT DESCRIPTION DO YOU WANT TO USE FOR THIS ZOOM ?
? ƀ
HOW DO YOU WANT TO INSERT THE LEVELS OF THIS ZOOM
 1. INCREMENTAL (STARTS WITH FEWEST OBJECT TYPES AND IDEA TYPES)
 2. DECREMENTAL (STARTS WITH GREATEST NUMBER OF OBJECT AND IDEA TYPES
TYPE EXACTLY ONE NUMBER , PLEASE.
? 1
*
* ATTENTION!!
* EACH LEVEL OF A ZOOM IS CONSIDERED AS A SCOPE.
*

LET@S START WITH THE TOP LEVEL.
SCOPE 000003 OF SCHEMA "TEST"
WHAT NAME DO YOU WANT TO USE FOR THIS SCOPE ?
? MINI
WHAT DESCRIPTION DO YOU WANT TO USE FOR THIS SCOPE ?
? ƀ
YOU NOW HAVE TO SPECIFY THE CONTENTS OF THE TOP LEVEL BY
ENTERING THE NAMES OF THE EXISTING OBJECT AND IDEA TYPES YOU WANT
TO HAVE IN THIS TOP LEVEL ; YOU CAN ALSO ENTER THE NAMES
OF THE SCOPES THAT HAVE TO BE COPIED INTO THIS TOP LEVEL.
ENTER SCOPE NAME(S) , PLEASE .
? ƀ
ENTER OBJECT TYPE NAME(S), PLEASE
? MONEY
? PROJECT
? ƀ
ENTER IDEA TYPE NAME(S), PLEASE
? PROJECT-BUDGET
? ƀ

DO YOU WANT TO ENTER ANOTHER LEVEL FOR THIS ZOOM ?
? YES
SCOPE 000004 OF SCHEMA "TEST"
WHAT NAME DO YOU WANT TO USE FOR THIS SCOPE ?
? PROJECTS
WHAT DESCRIPTION DO YOU WANT TO USE FOR THIS SCOPE ?
? ƀ
THE PREVIOUS LEVEL IS NOW COPIED INTO THIS LEVEL.
YOU CAN NOW INCREASE THIS LEVEL BY SCOPES,OBJECT TYPES AND IDEA TYPES
ENTER SCOPE NAME(S) , PLEASE .
? SCOPE-PROJECT
? ƀ
ENTER OBJECT TYPE NAME(S), PLEASE
? ƀ
ENTER IDEA TYPE NAME(S), PLEASE
? ƀ
```

Table 6.e

The addition of a zoom

7. RETRIEVAL REPORTS

Apart from the update capabilities discussed in previous sections, ISDIS must be equipped with a large diversity of parameterized retrieval reports. Such a diversity is essential if we wish to allow the user to retrieve very specifically that information he wants and no more.

7.1 Catalog reports

These are formatted (edited) lists of concepts with optionally their descriptive attributes. The most important catalog report for the idea base schema is the edited list of it (or part of), which contains an object type division, an idea type division and a con straint division. Table 7.1.a shows the report of a part of the example object base schema i.e. of the scope named SCOPE-PROJECT.

```
*************************************************************************

        ISDIS   RELEASE 1,LEVEL 3  USING  CDC-CYBER-EDMS

                   REPORT GIVING A SCOPED LIST

*************************************************************************


                          SUMMARY OF THE REQUEST
                          ......................

               DATE:  79/05/09          TIME:  13:05
               ONTOLOGICAL SCHEMA IS TEST
               KIND OF RETRIEVAL: LISTING
               THIS REPORT GIVES A FULL LISTING
               OF SCOPE :SCOPE-PROJECT


                                ACTUAL REPORT
                                .............



OBJECT TYPE DIVISION
    OBJECT TYPE NAME IS MONEY
    OBJECT TYPE NAME IS PROJECT
    OBJECT TYPE NAME IS EMPLOYEE
```

```
ELEMENTARY IDEA DIVISION
     IDEA NAME IS PROJECT-BUDGET
          INVOLVED OBJECT TYPE NAME IS MONEY
              ROLE IS BUDGET
          INVOLVED OBJECT TYPE NAME IS PROJECT
              ROLE IS PROJECT-REF
     IDEA NAME IS ASSIGNMENT
          INVOLVED OBJECT TYPE NAME IS PROJECT
              ROLE IS PROJECT-REF
          INVOLVED OBJECT TYPE NAME IS EMPLOYEE
              ROLE IS PROJECT-WORKER


CONSTRAINT DIVISION
     CONSTRAINT NAME IS AT-MOST-ONE-BUDGET-PER-PROJECT
          ROLE PROJECT-REF
                              IN IDEA PROJECT-BUDGET
                                       IS UNIQUE
     CONSTRAINT NAME IS ONLY-ONCE-THE-SAME
          ROLE PROJECT-REF
          ROLE PROJECT-WORKER
                                                     CONCATENATED
                              IN IDEA ASSIGNMENT
                                       IS UNIQUE
     CONSTRAINT NAME IS ASSIGNMENT-ONLY-IF-BUDGET-OK
          ROLE PROJECT-REF
                              IN IDEA ASSIGNMENT
                                       IS SUBSET OF
          ROLE PROJECT-REF
                              IN IDEA PROJECT-BUDGET


************************************************************

                                END OF REPORT

************************************************************
```

Table 7.1.a

7.2 Cross reference reports

These are formatted (edited) lists of concepts together with the concepts they reference. Table 7.2.a shows the report of the ideas referencing the object types EMPLOYEE and PROJECT within the scope SCOPE-EMPLOYEE.

```
**********************************************************************
*                                                                    *
*        ISDIS   RELEASE 1,LEVEL 3  USING  CDC-CYBER-EDMS            *
*                                                                    *
*    REPORT SHOWING WHICH IDEAS REFERENCE A GIVEN OBJECT TYPE        *
*                                                                    *
**********************************************************************

                        SUMMARY OF THE REQUEST
                        ======================

              DATE:  78/11/16          TIME:  10:04
              ONTOLOGICAL SCHEMA IS TEST
              UTILITY REQUEST IS CROSS-REFERENCE
              THIS REPORT CONSISTS OF INFORMATION
              ABOUT FOLLOWING OBJECTS :
                        =*= EMPLOYEE
                        =*= PROJECT
              OF SCOPE :   SCOPE-EMPLOYEE
              AND IS GIVEN IN ALPHABETICAL ORDER

                              MESSAGES
                              ========

      *** FOLLOWING REQUESTED OBJECTS ARE NOT IN THE GIVEN SCOPE :
              MONEY

                            ACTUAL REPORT
                            =============


          *      OBJECT TYPE IS:    EMPLOYEE

                       REFERRED IN:

             -      IDEA TYPE: ASSIGNMENT

             -      IDEA TYPE: EMPLOYEE-HOMONYM

             -      IDEA TYPE: EMPLOYEE-SEX

          *      OBJECT TYPE IS:    PROJECT

                       REFERRED IN:

             -      IDEA TYPE: ASSIGNMENT

**********************************************************************
*                                                                    *
*                           END OF REPORT                            *
*                                                                    *
**********************************************************************
```

Table 7.2.a

7.3 KWIC-KWOC reports

The keyword in context (KWIC) report is an index-like list of the descriptions and the concept it is describing, according to the relevant words in the description. The keyword out of context (KWOC) report is an index like list of the designators and the concepts which are designated.

7.4 Diagrams

From all reports, diagrams induce probably best the general semantics of a schema. Figure 7.4.a shows a diagram of the example object base schema produced by a plotter.

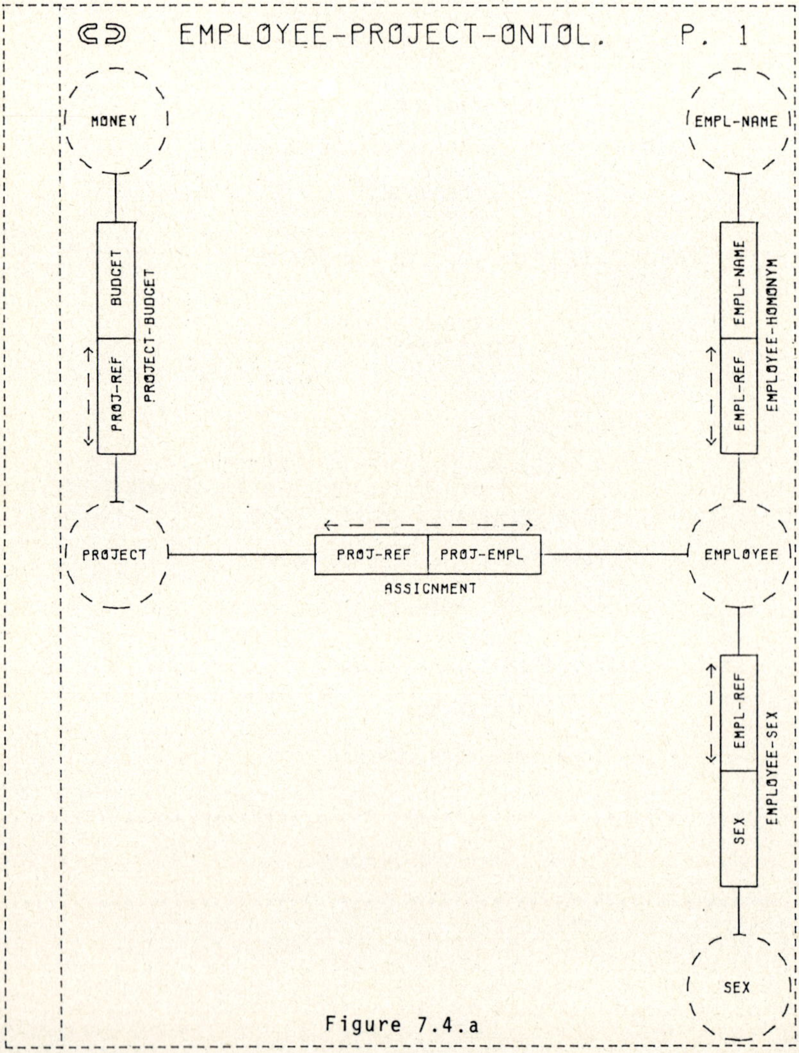

Figure 7.4.a

7.5 Control reports

These reports serve an administrative and statistical purpose showing cardinalities, frequencies, etc. Table 7.5.a shows the report with cardinalities of the example object base schema.

```
*****************************************************************

   ISDIS   RELEASE 1,LEVEL 3  USING  CDC-CYBER-EDMS

               STATISTICAL REPORT

*****************************************************************


               SUMMARY OF THE REQUEST
               ----------------------

       DATE:  79/05/09            TIME:  13:07
       ONTOLOGICAL SCHEMA IS TEST
       KIND OF RETRIEVAL: STATISTICS
       THIS REPORT GIVES STATISTICAL INFORMATION
       ON THE ENTIRE ONTOLOGICAL SCHEMA

                    ACTUAL REPORT
                    -------------


       THE ONTOLOGICAL SCHEMA HAS

             5 OBJECTS

             4 IDEAS

             8 ROLES

             6 CONSTRAINTS
                  4 OF TYPE UNIQUENESS
                  2 OF TYPE SUBSETTING
                  0 OF TYPE EQUALITY
                  0 OF TYPE EXCLUSION

             6 SCOPES

             1 ZOOM


*****************************************************************

                    END OF REPORT

*****************************************************************
```

Figure 7.5.a

7.6 History and impact reports

Apart from the reports which give you a view of the actual status of the information system, history reports can show how the status was one year ago, who made modifications, when, etc. Also a vision on the consequences of a planned change is revealed in impact reports. Table 7.6.a shows of the example object base schema the impact of the delete of an object type.

```
DO YOU WANT TO DELETE
 1. OBJECT TYPE(S)
 2. IDEA TYPE(S)
 3. CONSTRAINT(S)
 4. SCOPE(S)
 5. ZOOM(S)
 6. THE  ENTIRE  ONTOLOGICAL SCHEMA
OR
 7. CONTINUE
TYPE EXACTLY ONE NUMBER , PLEASE
? 1

ENTER OBJECT TYPE NAME(S), PLEASE
? SEX
? \
I HAVE NOT DELETED ANYTHING YET.
IF DELETION WOULD TAKE PLACE, THE FOLLOWING WOULD BE DELETED


   OBJECT TYPE DIVISION
       OBJECT TYPE NAME IS SEX
           USER NAME IS SEXO


   ELEMENTARY IDEA DIVISION
       IDEA NAME IS EMPLOYEE-SEX
               USER NAME IS SEXO-DEL-EMPLEADO
           INVOLVED OBJECT TYPE NAME IS EMPLOYEE
                   USER NAME IS EMPLEADO
               ROLE IS EMPLOYEE-REF
                       USER NAME IS REFERENTE-A-EMPLEADO
           INVOLVED OBJECT TYPE NAME IS SEX
                   USER NAME IS SEXO
               ROLE IS SEX
                       USER NAME IS SEXO
```

```
CONSTRAINT DIVISION
    CONSTRAINT NAME IS AT-MOST-ONE-SEX-PER-EMPLOYEE
        USER NAME IS A-LO-SUMO-UN-SEXO-POR-EMPLEADO
         ROLE EMPLOYEE-REF
           USER NAME IS REFERENTE-A-EMPLEADO
                         IN IDEA EMPLOYEE-SEX
                         USER NAME IS SEXO-DEL-EMPLEADO
                                  IS UNIQUE


DO YOU MAINTAIN YOUR DELETION REQUEST? TYPE YES OR NO.
IF YES, THE DELETION WILL BE AS DESCRIBED ABOVE,
OTHERWISE, NOTHING WILL BE DELETED!!
? NO
```

Table 7.6.a

7.7 Ad hoc reports

The reports described above can be obtained as full listings or for a part of the schema specified ad hoc in an interactive way. Table 7.2.a is an example of an ad hoc report.

8. SUMMARY AND CONCLUSIONS

In this paper we have first made an effort to describe an overall framework for information systems. Such a framework can greatly help the discussions on which concepts are the best at the conceptual, external and internal schema level. The use of such a framework and associated tools has proven to be a more effective tool to get better information systems requirements definitions. The work reported in this paper is part of a longer term research and development project which has as aim the optional use of the computer during all stages of information systems life cycle, i.e. analysis, design, programming, testing, conversion and maintenance. So far the part of the system which is operational consists of some 25000 lines of source statements using an advanced database management system and COBOL, FORTRAN and PASCAL, all extended with a simple yet powerful DML. The results obtained from limited tests in a few practical projects are encouraging, but much work is still to be done.

REFERENCES

(1) Falkenberg, E., Concepts for Modelling Information, In: Modelling in Data Base Management Systems, Proceedings of the IFIP Working Conference held in Freudenstadt, Germany, January 5-8, 1976, North-Holland Publishing Company, (Amsterdam 1976).

(2) Fillmore, C., The Case for Case, In: Universals in Linguistic Theory, Bach and Harms (eds), 1-90.

(3) Nijssen, G.M., On the Gross Architecture for the Next Generation Database Management Systems, In: Information Processing 77, Proceedings of the 1977 IFIP Congress, Toronto, Canada, North-Holland Publishing Company, Amsterdam.

(4) Nijssen, G.M., Modelling in Data Base Management Systems, Invited paper to be presented at Euro IFIP 1979, September, London; Proceedings by North-Holland Publishing Company, Amsterdam.

(5) Wittgenstein, L., Tractatus Logico-Philosophicus, Routledge Kegan Paul, London.

Formal Models and Practical Tools
for Information Systems Design
H.-J. Schneider, Editor
North-Holland Publishing Company

CONSTRAINT SPECIFICATION IN EVOLUTIONARY DATA BASE DESIGN

G.BRACCHI^, A.FURTADO^^, G.PELAGATTI^

^^Departamento de Informatica
Pontificia Universitade Catolica do Rio de Janeiro
Brazil

^Istituto di Elettrotecnica ed Elettronica
Politecnico di Milano, Italy

In this paper the problem of collecting and specifying conceptual and quantitative requirements for data base design is discussed.
The elements that should be included in requirement analysis are illustrated, and their relevance to the subsequent phases of logical and physical data base design is shown.
Particular emphasis is devoted to the problems of defining static and dynamic constraints, and of specifying requirements on the evolution of the data base during its life-cycle.

1. INTRODUCTION

We have recently seen the emergence of a number of different methodologies for the design of data base applications /1-2/. These approaches tend to concentrate on only a few partial aspects of the design problem; hence, they reflect different views and models of the design process.

However, every methodology must include a phase of requirement analysis, that provides initial input to all the subsequent phases of the design process.

Requirement collection and specification for data base design may be seen as a special case of the well known problem of gathering and stating requirements for information systems /3/. It is aimed at an analysis of the requisites of the users and of the enterprise regarding the content and use of the data base, in order to make explicit the necessary components of the data base as well as the data and processing needs of all potential users.

The purpose of this paper is to discuss the various requirements that should be collected and specified in data base design, and to show their relevance to the subsequent phases of constructing, integrating, and optimizing abstract models or schemas (logical design), and of mapping these models into storage level representations of data for a given particular data base management system technology (physical design).

The framework that will be proposed is independent of the specific design methodologies and of particular data base technologies.

Section 2 will discuss the elements that have to be collected and specified in requirement analysis; many of these elements have already been discussed by other authors /4-6/. Hence, in this paper only the new aspects will be emphasized.

Section 3 will deal specifically with the problem of specifying static and dynamic constraints and of enforcing them in practical data base implementations.

Section 4 will be concerned with the specification of requirements on the evolution of the data base during its life cycle.

Section 5 will finally discuss the quantitative parameters that must be collected for use in the subsequent design phases.

2. ELEMENTS OF DATA BASE REQUIREMENT ANALYSIS

The elements that have to be determined in performing requirement analysis may be subdivided into two classes: the conceptual requirements, that refer to logical properties of information structures, information processes and their evolution, and the quantitative requirements, that refer to statistical measures.

This section will deal with conceptual requirements, while quantitative requirements will be treated in Section 5. The elements that have to be collected in the analysis of conceptual requirements can be grouped in three Schemas, that are represented in Table 1:

Evolution Schema

- Events
- Rules for modification of Data and Functional Schemas

Data Schema	Functional Schema
- Entities	- Operations
- Relationships	- Transactions
- Attributes	- Parameters
- Static Constraints	- Dynamic Constraints

Table 1 - Elements of the Conceptual Requirements

- The data schema, where entities, relationships and attributes are described, and where static constraints are formulated;
- the functional schema, where operations, trasactions and parameters are described, and where dynamic constraints are formulated;
- the evolution schema, which is related to the possible transformations of the other two schemas.

As far as the data schema is concerned, the notions of entities, relationships and attributes are well known /7-8/. Static constraints are those constraints which characterize a valid state of the data base, and therefore can be checked at the current state, without referring to other states.

The functional schema reveals a strong parallelism (duality) with the data schema. This duality is useful as a reminder that considerations made on one schema may be as well applied to the other schema.

The operations that we shall consider are elementary update and interrogate primitives. The elementary update operations are listed below; instances of entities are represented by e, e', while r is a relationship, and a, a' are expressions giving values of attributes.

create e
delete e
link e to e' via r
unlink e from e' via r
modify a of e to a'
modify a of r (e, e') to a'.

The elementary interrogate operations that we will consider here are the following:

find e with a
find e from e' via r
retrieve a of e
retrieve a of r (e, e')

Note that the modification of an attribute includes changing its value from/to undefined to/from defined. Normally the update operations require the execution of a previous interrogate operation. The above sets of operations have been introduced in order to facilitate the statement of quantitative requirements that are needed in the subsequent data base design phases (see Section 5).

The update and interrogate operations correspond respectively to Parnas' O - and V - functions /20, 21/, which have been used for a formal characterization of states and transitions.

Transactions represent execution relationships among operations which together would accomplish some meaningful effect. Both operations and transactions have parameters, noting that a transaction may require parameters other than those needed by its constituent operations.

One uses operations and transactions in order to produce a transition from one data base state to another (note that pure interrogate operations change only currency indicators, users' variables, flags and other auxiliary elements).

Dynamic constraints are those that characterize the valid state transitions.

Often the current data and functional schemas have to be adapted to external events occurring in the real world. The evolution schema would contain as much information as possible on the predictable external events and would also include means for replacing the data and functional schemas and for converting the data base system accordingly.

A simple example will be introduced now and will be used throughout this paper in order to illustrate the notions that will be discussed. The example considers a school which offers a summer course.

We do not claim that the example is fully realistic, and also many details will be omitted for the sake of brevity. It is assumed that a previous analysis of activities involved was performed; it may have proceeded by integrating different users' views /1/, or as the work of an enterprise administrator /7/.

Assume that from this initial study the following data schema has emerged:

entities

c - courses
s - students
t - teachers

relationships

s takes c
t teaches c

attributes

of c : c # - course number
ti - title
d - description
of s : s # - student number
of t : t # - teacher number
of takes : g - grade

static constraints

sc 1 - there can be at most 4 courses
sc 2 - courses must have course number and course title defined; the description may or may not be defined
sc 3 - students must have student number defined
sc 4 - teachers must have teacher number defined
sc 5 - there can be no more than 30 students taking a course
sc 6 - a grade must be an integer between 0 and 10,
sc 7 - a teacher must teach exactly one course

....

The above specified set of static constraints contains only those constraints which are independent of database evolution and is therefore only partial. An example of a static constraint which is instead depedent on evolution is the following: "there must be at least 2 courses". This constraint is static because it characterises a valid state of the database, but this constraint is meaningful only after some particular event has occurred, for instance the event "begin enrolment". This fact will be stated in the evolution schema (see Section 4).

The following functional schema is also established:

operations (with their parameters)

create c
delete c
....
link s to c via takes
....
retrieve g of takes (s, c)
modify g of takes (s, c) to g'
....
find s with s #
....

transactions (with their parameters)

prepare summer program / involves creating courses and teachers and linking them /
enroll s # in c #
....
obtain grade of s # in ti
....
raise grade of s # by 'K'
....

dynamic constraints

dc 1 - teachers cannot be deleted
dc 2 - a teacher cannot be unlinked from the assigned course
dc 3 - grades can be modified only if they are undefined and the new grade is defined, or if the new grade is higher than the current (defined) grade
dc 4 - if a student has a defined grade less than 5 in a course, he must be unlinked from the course
dc 5 - if a student has all grades defined and their average is less than 6, he must be unlinked from all courses and deleted
....

A graphical representation of the data and functional schemas for our summer-school-example (not including static and dynamic constraints) is shown in figures 1 and 2. A comparison of the two figures emphasizes the idea of duality between the two schemas.

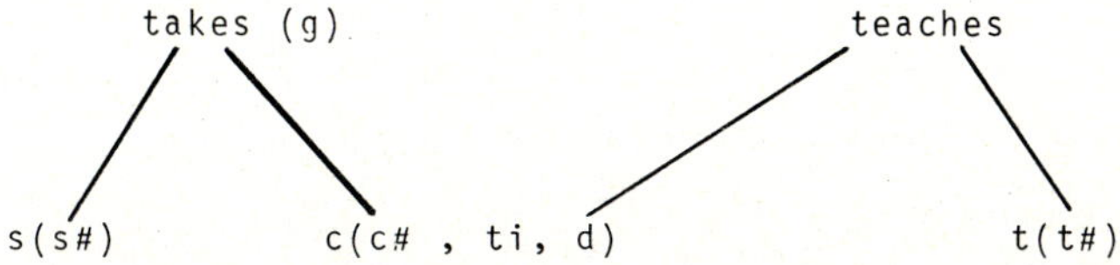

Fig. 1 Relationships with common entities; the attributes of entities and relationships are shown within brackets

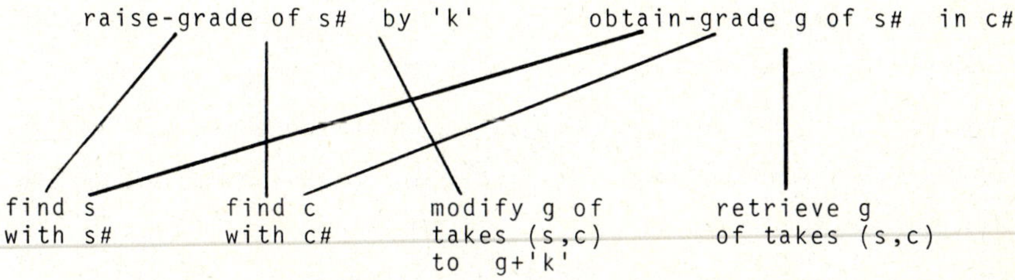

Fig. 2 Transactions with common operations

3. CONSTRAINT SPECIFICATION AND CHECKING

3.1 Static constraints

A classification of the most important static constraints is shown in figure 3; in the same figure a reference is also given to the corresponding constraints of the summer school example. Static constraints have to do with the existence of entities and relationships among entities, with permissible values of attributes, and with diverse cardinality considerations.

The existence of an entity may depend on the fact that certain attributes have defined values, or on some other condition imposed on such values. It may also depend on the fact that the entity participates in certain relationships. The number of entities of a given type may be bounded.

The existence of relationships among entities may depend entirely or partly on conditions imposed on the entities, or on the existence of other relationships involving them, or on the definiteness (or some other condition) on the values of the entities and relationship attributes.

The relationship in some cases can exist only if the conditions hold, (see the notions of mandatory/optional, automatic/manual membership, and delete modes in the Codasyl proposal /9/).

Cardinality considerations on relationships impose bounds on the number of related pairs (or n-tuples if non-binary relationships are considered), and on the number of entities that can be related to a given entity via the relationship.

Permissible values of attributes can be restricted by requiring that they be drawn from some well-known set (e.g. positive integers, by enumeration, by range, by format, etc.).

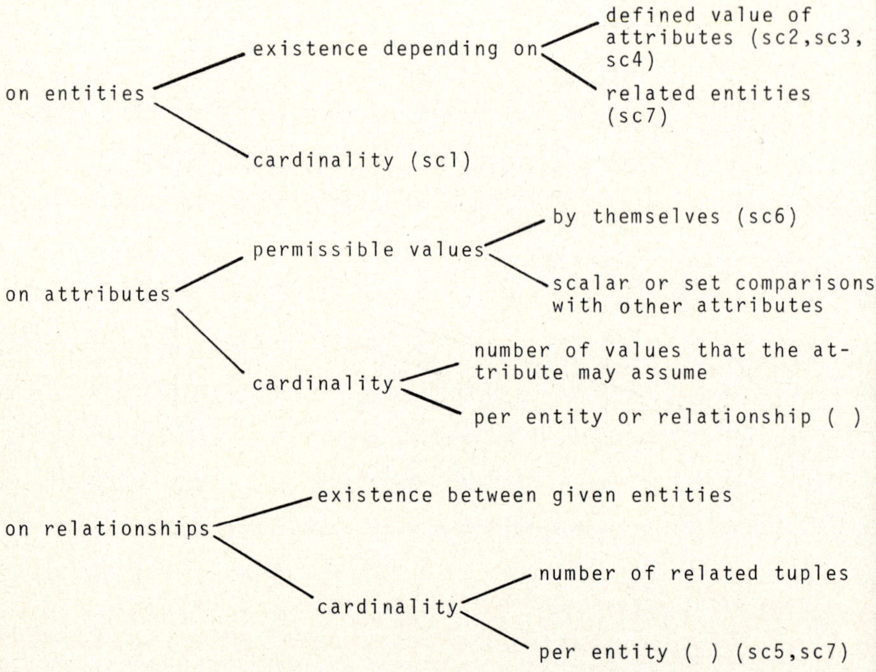

( ) includes functional dependencies as a special case

Fig. 3 Static constraints

They can also be restricted by requiring that they satisfy some scalar or set comparison expression, involving constants, attributes of the same or other entity or relationship, and functions such as MIN, MAX, AVG, TOTAL. etc.

Cardinality considerations on attributes refer to the number of values, and especially to the number of values they may assume per entity or relationship. Functional dependencies /10/ are obviously cases of cardinality restrictions on relationships or on attributes.

The same constraint may belong to two different classes. For instance sc7: 'a teacher must teach exactly one course', is both a constraint on the existence of the entity 'Teacher' and a constraint on the cardinality of the relationship 'Teaches' per entity 'Teacher'.

3.2 Dynamic constraints

Dynamic constraints have to do with the possibility or necessity of executing operations or transactions, with permissible values of parameters, and with diverse frequency considerations.

The dynamic constraints on the possibility of executing operations are shown in Fig. 4, where a reference is also given to the corresponding constraints of the summer school example. The duality between the data and the functional schemas suggests some interesting considerations, and particularly the fact that for operations p and g we may have that:

p can be executed only if g was executed

p must be executed if g was executed

that are constraints very close to the "prerequisite" and "implies" arcs of semantic networks /11/, referring to the possible or necessary existence of relationships among entities.

The most striking difference between static and dynamic constraints is that the latter may involve a comparison between elements of more than one state, usually the current state and the new intended state.

Also note that the only if and the if formulations in fact correspond to the logical implication

$$p \rightarrow g$$

which fails whenever p holds and g does not, and the way to distinguish between them is to add t_1 and t_2, expressing instants of time, requiring that $t_1 < t_2$ (t_1 precedes t_2). We can now write

a. $(p, t_2) \rightarrow (g, t_1)$

b. $(p, t_1) \rightarrow (g, t_2)$

which read:

a. the execution of p implies that g was executed before (only if formulation);

b. the execution of p implies the subsequent execution of t_2 (if formulation).

General form:

1) operation p can be executed only if condition b is true
2) operation p must be executed if condition b is true.

Condition b can be:

1) always True or False (dc1, dc2)
2) a predicate involving data of the current and of the new state (current and new refer to the state before and after execution of p) (dc3, dc4, dc5)
3) a predicate involving the fact that another operation q was executed

Fig. 4 Dynamic Constraints on the possibility of executing Operations

This stresses the time-dependence of dynamic constraints.

3.3. Enforcing constraints

Static constraints can be checked, at a given current state, by executing some auditing program. They can also be enforced dynamically. For example, a maximum cardinality constraint on entities can be translated in terms of frequency of creates (minus the frequency of deletes) permitted. More generally, we may perform tests before an operation or transaction is executed, and trigger other operations, so that (assuming that the current state is valid) the new state will also be valid.

Dynamic constraints can only be enforced through an auditing program if history of past states is also kept in the data base. They can normally be checked as the operation or transaction is executed, noting that the 'only if' conditions will correspond to tests and the 'if' conditions to triggers. One exception is a constraint of the type "an employee that has been fired cannot be hired again", for which historical data must be kept.

If all transactions that may be useful on a certain data base can be known at design time, it is desirable to take advantage of the following strategy for enforcing both static and dynamic constraints, and in fact ensuring that violations will not occur: implementing modules based on one (or more) transactions; such modules would incorporate tests and would include all operations (and transactions) that are related by 'if' constraints; moreover, allowing users to interact with the data base (for update purposes) only through such modules. This strategy should characterize the so-called goal-oriented systems /3/.

If this cannot be done, then a similar (but costlier) enforcement of constraints is still possible through some mechanism that adds pre-programmed tests and actions to certain users' requests, such as the assertions/triggers of System R /12/ and the query modification device of INGRES /13/.

The precedence rules established by dynamic constraints can be used also for determining which operations or transactions are to be executed serially or in parallel.

Constraints are extremely important to all phases of data base design because (like a grammar) they define what configurations can arise and what transformations can be performed. When designing the records, normalization through functional dependencies considerations is fundamental, requiring that each record (tuple in a relation /10/) expresses a single fact; similarly, when designing a module, we may use the execution 'only if' and 'if' precedences to construct modules with functional (or at least procedural) strength /14/. The 'data-coupling' notion of /14/ has also a parallel in the realm of data: records should not have information-carrying links, beeing joinable only on comparable attributes, as the composition of modules should ideally be done through parameter passing only.

Constraints point to the impossibility of considering certain operations and their effects in isolation. Besides considering the intended effects on certain indicated data, we are led to consider other prerequisite or implied operations and other data elements; in particular, access to the <u>constraining set</u> of data /15/ (i.e., data that are not affected by the intended change, but are part of the expression of a constraint) must be ensured, and the cost of this access must be considered. It is clear that the operations required for accessing the constraining set must be considered in database design in the same way as all other operations; therefore their frequency and other quantitative parameters have to be collected, as it will be shown in Section 5.

The relevance of the determination of constraints with reference to many aspects of database has been shown. It must be observed that it is very difficult to ensure that the set of constraints provides a complete and consistent specification of valid states and transitions. In particular, once a set of constraints has been specified, one has to verify that:

1. the set is self consistent - constraints cannot contradict each other; e.g.: if we require that a teacher cannot be disassociated from a course, we should not have a constraint permitting in some cases the deletion of a course to which a teacher has been assigned;
2. the closure of the set is well understood - from certain constraints others may be inferred; it is desirable to define a "minimal" set of constraints where no constraint that may be deduced from others is included, but it is also necessary to know the deducible constraints in order to make sure that no unexpected (perhaps unwanted) situations will arise; e.g.: if there can be no more than 4 courses, and there can be no more than one teacher per course, and any teacher must be assigned to a course as soon as he is created, it follows that the school can hire at most 4 teachers;
3. the set is complete with respect to the needs of the enterprise activities - constraints mirror rules that regulate real-world activities, hence they should cope with the needs of these activities one may find that a self-consistent set lacks a constraint which should instead have been included, unless an assumption is made that it is not important to check this constraint, or that in practice it would never be violated; e.g., it is not realistic to have a course with no students enrolled, but we may know as a fact that there will always be enough students enrolling in each course.

Very subtle errors can occur, especially with dynamic constraints of the "trigger" type. For instance, the statement of the two constraints dc4 and dc5 in the summer-school-database could lead to an erroneous implementation, because the condition of dc5 can be tested only if the action triggered by dc4 has not been executed yet. Therefore constraint dc4 should be changed in the following way: if a student has all grades defined and constraint dc5 has already been checked and a grade is less than 5 in a course, then he must be unlinked from the course.

4. THE EVOLUTION SCHEMA

If we consider a single unchangeable pair of data/ functional schemas, what we have in a data base system are states which can be transformec into other states through transitions, the legitimate states and the allowable transitions being defined respectively by static and dynamic constraints.

However, the schemas may be required to evolve under the pressure of external events; for example, new types of entities may be introduced or some new constraints may be added, or a transaction can be dropped, etc.

One may be more or less able to <u>predict</u> and therefore to plan for the changes. In certain cases there is a cyclic regime, in which every cycle has a number of calendar dates at which different pairs of schemas should become current. Another special important case of predicted change is the gradual implementation of an information system.

Unpredicted evolution may include changes in the enterprise policies precipitated by unanticipated changes of market conditions, or of the legislation etc. In this paper we do not consider unpredicted evolution, in which, for example, new entity types not recognized in the design phase would have to be added. This involves in fact a new design and leads to the area of maintenance.

Our interest is restricted to data base systems for which the requirements have all been laid down at the design phase and considered in the system implementation, but with the problem that not all components are necessarily active at all phases and that changes in the constraints may impose a different behaviour at each phase. Therefore in this paper the expression "evolution of a database system" means the ability of the system to exhibit different predicted configurations and behaviours as a response to different real world situations associated with previously defined external events. It is the job of the enterprise administrator to signal the occurrence of an external event. The relevant events for the life of the summer school database example are listed in figure 5. Although the characterization of events has a certain degree of arbitrariness, depending on the free decision of the enterprise administrator to signal or not their occurrence, one may identify some meaningful properties of events which include:

- the calendar date of occurrence, or some time delay with respect to another event; or, if the event is not determined by time, the characterizing circumstances, as for example the fact that other institutions have entered the market, or even information extracted from the data base;
- total or partial precedence between events, and the pattern of the possible sequences; the summer school database example follows a cyclic pattern, assuming that during each year the same sequence is repeated (fig. 6). Other typical patterns would be 'complete', 'tree with backtracking', etc.

end of database initialization (DI)
begin enrolment (BE)
end enrolment (EE)
classes start (CS)
deadline for dropping courses (DDC)
classes end (CE)
exams (EX)
deadline for grades being assigned by teachers (DGA)
certificates awarded (CA)

Fig. 5 Events for the summer-school-database

As an event is signalled, the current data/functional schema pair α is replaced by another pair β. It is possible to characterize β in one of the following ways:

- by enumerating the differences between β and α (or between β and some 'initial' pair α_0);
- by a complete description of β without referring to other pairs.

The possible differences between schemas are either the activation or deactivation of components (entities, relationships, attributes, operations, transactions, parameters) or the modification of the sets

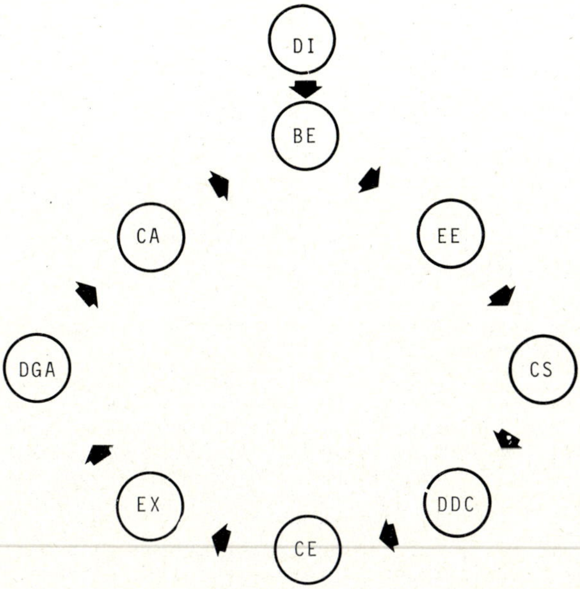

Fig. 6 Cyclic pattern of events for the summer-school-database

of static and dynamic constraints. In any case, one must be careful in order to make explicit all other differences which are consequences (side-effects) of the intended ones; thus, the deactivation of an entity will deactivate its attributes, the relationships involving it, the operations and transactions that manipulate it, other operations including an access to it as part of the constraining set, etc. ..; constraints referring to the deactivated entity will be suspended, and there may be a lengthy propagation of such side-effects, as other dependent entities are consequently deactivated, etc.

In Table 2 some data/functional schema changes associated with some events in the summer-school-database-example are listed.

So far we have considered the fact that after an event the data/functional schemas of the database are changed; in fact evolution rules are characterized by changes at the schema level, while operations and transactions defined in the functional schema operate at the instance level. Nevertheless, when a change at the schema level occurs, it has some immediate effect at the instance level, e.g., if a constraint is modified, then the state of the database must be adapted to the modified constraint. Therefore it is also necessary to specify some 'provisions for conversion' which describe the necessary adaptations. Conversion is a difficult problem which has implications at all levels and may impact users in severe ways /16/.

Whenever possible, one should try to specify the provisions for conversion taking into consideration the situation at each possible previous phase.

Referring to the evolution rules for the summer-school-database that are shown in Table 2, for instance one should add the following provision for conversion: 'at event <Deadline for Grades being assigned by Teachers> check that all grades have a defined value, otherwise.. ...'. This fomulation alters the previously stated static constraint 'a grade must be an integer between 0 and 10 or be undefined'.

This example leads to an important remark: while it is reasonable to suppose that all components of the data/functional schemas are defined only once and simply activated or deactivated, the same is not reasonable for constraints, because they show a complex structure which is modified during evolution (although conceptually it would be possible to define for example two constraints of the type $C_1 = A \vee B$ and $C_2 = A$, and to state that at some event C_1 must be deactivated and C_2 activated, it is however more convenient and clear to say that the constraint $A \vee B$ has been modified to A).

For the above reasons one should define in the data/functional schemas only those constraints which apply to the initial state or those which are independent on any evolution.

The evolution schema, together with the data/functional schemas, constitutes a part of the data directory /17/, which may be regarded as a meta-database. Through the data directory the external events are communicated and handled according to the evolution rules.

5. COLLECTING QUANTITATIVE REQUIREMENTS

In conducting the conceptual design quantitative information must be collected to be used in the subsequent phases to produce a concrete implementation.

It is outside the scope of this paper discussing how the database design should be conducted; therefore we will refer to the existing literature on file and database design /1-5,18/ and we will simply say that we must collect all the parameters which are commonly considered as inputs to design. However, since different authors collect their parameters referring to different system models, we have transposed these parameters to our model.

Table 3 shows the quantitative parameters which should be collected together with the components of the data schema. Clearly such information is similar to the cardinality bounds imposed by static constraints. However, cardinality bounds are absolute (logical) limits, whereas here statistical measures such as expected values (averages) and variances are needed.

Considering now the parameters which refer to the components of the functional schema, there is general agreement that the transactions have to be predefined and their frequencies determined. For the other component one can recognize two different approaches: one approach /5/ defines the transactions as queries and derives the file design from the parameters of the data components and from the queries' frequency and complexity; the other approach /4/ defines the transactions through a specification of the elementary operations which constitute them, and collects the quantitative parameters associated with each elementary operation. The former approach appears to be more suitable for the design of a database system based on dynamic optimization of non predefined queries, since the parameters on data components can be collected for all components, while the latter approach allows a more detailed collection of parameters referring to specific transactions and ensures a better static optimization.

Event	Desired Actions	Side-effect Actions
1) Certificates Awarded	deactivate-entity: Student	deactivate-relation: Takes deactivate-attribute: S# (Stud.number) deactivate-attribute: G (grade) : (deactivate all operations and transactions referring to the above elements of the data schema)
2) Begin Enrolment	activate-entity: Student activate-relation: Takes activate-attribute: S# activate-attribute: G : (activate operations and transactions)	
3) Deadline for Grades being assigned by Teachers	modify-constraint sc6 to: 'a grade must be an integer between 0 and 10'	
4) Deadline for dropping courses	deactivate-operation: unlink s from c via takes	
: :	:	

Table 2 - Some Evolution Rules for the summer-school-database

for each entity type

- number of instances of an entity type
- number of instances of an entity type associated with one instance of another entity type via a certainrelationship
- number of instances of an entity type selected through one value of an attribute

for each relationship

- number of pairs (or n-tuples) associated via the relationship

for each attribute

- size of the possible values
- number of different values

Table 3 Quantitative parameters of the data schema

for each operation

- frequency of execution
- frequency of execution inside each transaction

for each transaction

- frequency of execution

for each parameter (and subsequently accessed data elements)

- which elements are used for access only and which are processed

Table 4 Quantitative parameters of the functional schema

A combination of the two approaches would suggest to design the database in order to optimize the most important transactions, while keeping in mind that unforeseen queries will happen. In table 4 the quantitative parameters which are associated with the components of the functional schema are listed. Through the study of the quantitative characteristics of the functional schema (and of the data elements involved in transactions and operations), we are led to associate more closely the data and the functional analysis. As pointed out in /19/, access takes two main modes:

a) access by content addressability, whereby entities are located through the values of their attributes, using some hashing or indexing techniques;

b) access by relatability, which navigates through the relationship links.

The above two modes are expressed in our model by the two possible forms of the find operation that were defined in Section 2. Some authors /4/ point out that one should also find out if certain attributes or links are searched in some fixed order, which would lead to implementations where ordering is used to enhance efficiency. Ordering has not been considered in our model, because it appears to be more an implementation issue than a logical requirement.

Conceivably, one can start with the data analysis, defining the data organization and then trying to optimize the access algorithms; one can instead start with the functional analysis, and try to find for the given algorithms the best data organization. The fact that this choice is feasible (and that attempts to define at once the best algorithms and data organization do not seem realistic) is strongly suggestive of duality as found in operations research problems.

So far we have considered the quantitative parameters associated with the components of the data/functional schemas, without considering the effects of constraints and evolution rules. Constraints affect the quantitative parameters primarily because constraint checking is usually a very expensive operation. We suggest to consider constraint checking as an activity with its own elementary operations and associated parameters, and to distinguish two different cases;

a) constraints which are checked when executing an operation or a transaction can be enforced by considering the elementary operations which are required to access the "constraining set" of data

b) constraints which are checked by auditing programs can be treated as transactions.

In both cases, as far as the specification of quantitative parameters is concerned, we have reduced the problem of data base design with constraint checking to the same problem without constraints.

Let us finally remark that the information contained in the evolution schema is also important for the implementation of the database. First of all, provisions for conversion are analogous to transactions and can be treated in the same way. Secondly, knowing what components are active at each phase, it becomes possible to determine what files should be on line, and which are the peaks of activity with respect to transactions. Finally, it has to be recognized that being the data base system variable, it also has varying requirements. Knowledge of predicted evolution transforms measures (quantitative parameters)from points to discrete or continuous functions of time, where external events are relevant.

6 CONCLUDING REMARKS

Existing work on data base design methodologiesconcentrates on different and generally partial aspects of the design problem.

However, requirement analysis is a necessary prerequisite for every methodology.

This paper has presented an integrated approach to requirement analysis. It showed that conceptual requirements may be collected in three different schemas (meta-databases): the data schema, where entities, relationships and attributes are described, and where static constraints are formulated; the functional schema, where operations, transactions and parameters are described, and where dynamic constraints are specified; and the evolution schema, which is related to the possible transformations of the other two schemas. The duality existing between the data and the functional schema has been shown.

The need for the collected requirements in both logical and physical data base design has been illustrated, and the role of quantitative requirements in design optimization has been finally demonstrated.

The framework that has been presented is independent of specific data models, design methods, and data base technologies. It can be used as the conceptual foundation of an integrated methodology for collecting and expressing the different requirements that are needed to take the specific design decisions.

REFERENCES

/1/ Yao, S.B., Navathe, S.B. and Weldon, J.: An Integrated Approach to Logical Database Design, in:Proc. N.Y.U., Database Symposium, New York, (May 1978).

/2/ Fry, J.P. and Teorey, T.J.: Design and Performance Tools for Improving Database Usability and Responsiveness, in: Schneidermann B. (ed.) Databases: Improving Usability and Responsiveness, (Academic Press, 1978).

/3/ Sibley, E.H.: Components of Problem Statement Languages, ISDOS Working Paper # 61, University of Michigan, (1972).

/4/ Mitoma, M.F. and Irani, K.B.: Automatic Data Base Schema Design and Optimization, in: Proc. Conf. on Very Large Databases, Framingham, Mass. (Sept. 1975).

/5/ Yao, S.B. and Merten, A.G.: Selection of File Organization Using an Analytic Model, in: Proc. Conf. on Very Large Databases, Framingham, Mass. (Sept. 1975).

/6/ Kahn, B.K.: A Method for Describing Information Required by the Database Design Process, in: Proc. 1976 ACM SIGMOD Int. Conf. on Management of Data, ACM, New York, (June 1976).

/7/ ANSI/X3/SPARC/STUDY Group Data Base Systems, Interim Report, ACM/SIGMOD Newsletter, fdt, 7, 1, (Dec. 1975).

/8/ Chen, P.P.S.: The Entity-Relationship Model - Toward à Unified View of Data, ACM Transactions on Database Systems, 1, 1 (March 1976).

/9/ CODASYL, Data Base Task Group Report, (ACM, New York, 1971).

/10/ Date, C.J.: An Introduction to Database Systems, (Addison-Wesley, Reading Mass., 1977).

/11/ Roussopoulos, N. and Mylopoulos, J.: Using Semantic Networks for

Data Base Management, in: Proc. Conf. on Very Large Databases, Framingham, Mass. (Sept. 1975).

/12/ Astrahan, M.M. et al.: System R: Relational Approach to Data Base Management, ACM Trans. on Database Systems, 1, 2, (June 1976).

/13/ Stonebraker, M.R. et al.: The Design and Implementation of INGRES, ACM Trans. on Database Systems, 1, 3 (Sept. 1976).

/14/ Yourdon, E.: Techniques of Program Structure and Design, (Prentice-Hall, Englewood Cliffs, New Jersey, 1975).

/15/ Hammer, M.M. and McLeod, D.J.: A Framework for Semantic Integrity, in: Proc. II Int. Conf. on Software Eng., (Oct. 1976).

/16/ Fry, J.P. et al.: Stored-Data Description and Translation: A Model and Language, Information Systems, 2, 3, (1977).

/17/ Report of the British Computer Society Data Dictionary Systems Working Party, Data Base, 9, 2 (Dec. 1977).

/18/ March, S.T. and Severance, D.G.: A Mathematical Modeling Approach to the Automatic Selection of Database Design, MISRC-WP-78-02, University of Minnesota, (1978).

/19/ Tsichritzis, D.C. and Lochovsky, F.H.: Data Base Management Systems, (Academic Press, New York, 1977).

/20/ Robinson, L. and Levitt, K.N.: Proofs Techniques for Hierarchically Structured Programs, CACM, 20, 4, (April 1977).

/21/ Yeh, R.T. and Baker, J.W.: Toward a Design Methodology for DBMS: A Software Engineering Approach, in: Proc. Conf. on Very Large Databases, Tokio, (Oct. 1977).

Formal Models and Practical Tools for Information Systems Design
H.-J. Schneider, Editor
North-Holland Publishing Company

A NEW SYSTEM ANALYSIS METHOD BASED ON THE STS (SOCIO-TECHNICAL SYSTEM) APPROACH(*)

Adriano DE MAIO and Emilio BARTEZZAGHI
Istituto di Ricerca Intervento sui Sistemi Organizzativi, Milan
and Politecnico di Milano, Milano, Italy
Gianni ZANARINI
Tema S.p.A. and Università di Bologna, Bologna, Italy

The diagnosis and evaluation of the failures and the problems of computer-based information systems suggest the need for a review and a reframing of current design techniques. This paper presents a new method based on socio-technical approach, which covers the early stages of information system analysis and design. The suggested method has been divided into phases or steps: identification of the object of the analysis; procedure analysis; verification of critical problems in view of procedure analysis; variance analysis; effectiveness/efficiency evaluation; map of variances; identification of objectives and constraints of the information system; indications about the suitability of organisational interventions. As an example, a case study is briefly presented step-by-step.

1. INTRODUCTION

A critical evaluation of the results obtained by computer-based information systems points out that a large amount of "failures" or, at any rate, many unexpected problems arise during the life cycle of a system.

The most important causes of this situation appear to be:

a) The "rationality" of EDP technology usually prevails in the system design and development process. In other words, the "real" functioning of the "process" to which a computer-based information system is applied is subordinated to the operating rules of the "computer" system. Sometimes this attitude leads to an increase in rationality (i.e. more efficiency) of the automated process, but in most cases it leads to the growth of major contradictions within the real organisational system.

(*) This contribution is part of a research on the organisational aspects connected with the analysis and design methodology of computer-based information systems conducted by the Istituto di Ricerca Intervento sui Sistemi Organizzativi (Institute of Action Research on Organisational Systems), Milan. A. De Maio, E. Bartezzaghi, O. Brivio, C. Ciborra and G. Zanarini carried out the research work. The research was partially supported by Tema S.p.A., Bologna, and Politecnico di Milano, Milan, Italy.

b) The frame of reference adopted by system designers is a "systemic" one with regard to EDP aspects, but it is "non-systemic" with regard to the real world (the process to be partially or totally automated). That implies also that a minimal amount of attention is devoted to "indirect" effects (cost and benefits) and to process dynamics.

c) Specifically, the interactions within the organisation (changes induced by the automation process and reactions which tend to modify automation specifications) are barely examined and analysed. In general they are completely neglected during the design process and interactions are not foreseen.

d) User's participation in the design process is usually inadequate. The user is involved mainly in securing the systems designer. The systems designer's ideal is to obtain written and signed specifications from the users at the end of the specification definition phase.

If the preceding diagnosis and evaluation are correct, the need for a review and a reframing current design techniques and methodology becomes evident. [1] [2] [3]

Instead of defining new types of approach, it seems convenient to use other methods previously experienced, and specifically the STS approach, as a base.

The reasons for such a choice appear to be:

a) STS thinking provides methods commonly used in organisational analysis which aim at focusing the interaction between technology and organisation (structure and organisational behaviour).

b) The Socio-technical System approach is, by nature, a systemic method and, at the same time, it focuses on the behaviour of the real system in all its aspects, both social and technological, and in a dynamic context.

c) The method requires a great involvement of all interested persons and organisational units. This is due to the fact that:

. the method cannot give any specific content by itself; it provides only the lens for observing things, not their representation;

. a greater insight into the "process" under consideration is required;

. the "process" is examined from different points of view, depending on the actors involved and on various technical, managerial and organisational parameters and variables.

Given these basic characteristics of the STS approach, the main causes of failures as previously defined, are removed and it is more reasonable to foresee the success of the automation process.

In what follows an analysis method based on the STS approach is put forward. At present it is being tested in a number of organisations. Four case studies and three applications have been carried out in the following areas:

-production and inventory control in a small-sized electronics firm, belonging to a multinational company;

- inventory and distribution in a middle-sized chemical company;

- production control in a middle-sized firm in the footwear sector, producing shoes at customer's order;

-production control in a furniture factory (large batch production);
- production and distribution control in a new division of a large food company, owned by a multinational holding;
-telecommunication plant set up and maintenance;
-accounting department in a large consumer goods company.
In five of these firms the computer was already in use. In all the areas examined the way of operating of the organisation can be regarded as quite "organic", thus not specifically suited for traditional analysis methods which tend to rely on the study of already formalised procedures.

Four cases have actually been developed strictly following the method herein proposed (see [4], [5], [6], [7]). In the following pages, the first of these cases is summarised step-by-step.

2. THE ANALYSIS METHOD

In the analysis and design phases of a computer-based information system, the proposed method represents a tool the users and analysts can use to analyse the present organisational and information systems and build a "map" of all the major problems which possible computer applications must cope with. Furthermore, it provides a means to simulate the organisational and economic consequences of the implementation of the EDP procedures and/or organisational redesign.

In short, the method

- analyses organisational and information problems,
- provides a representation of the interdependences between problems and effects,
- provides a tool for the qualitative simulation of the consequences of EDP applications,
- gives criteria of relevance in order to choose information flows to be examined in a more structured way.

The procedure for the suggested method has been divided into phases or steps.

The main criterion used to identify the phases consisted in the possibility to define a specific output (product) that might be transmitted and verified. Each phase is also unitary from the standpoint of the role played by the participants in the analysis and design work, that is neither the participants nor their relevant roles change within a single phase. Phases are in both a logical and temporal sequence. The whole process however is not linear, but the possibility and, in some cases, the necessity is envisaged to go back to previous phases. The type and number of iterations depend on the specific case for which the procedure is used. Also, the need for a formal redefining of the iterated phase must be evaluated from time to time. Finally, the aggregation of several phases may prove convenient. That happens when the complexity of the problem is not as great.

Each step is analysed sequentially according to:

a) the objectives to be reached by executing the step and the produced output (report);

b) comments on how the step must be run: well defined elements will be provided for some steps while only general suggestions will be supplied for others. In fact, the steps have different design levels;

c) the emphasis on main problems, partly solved and partly open, present when the steps are performed. Some of these problems are technical-theoretical in nature and some are strictly operative. Both are emphasised to draw the user's attention to the most difficult situations for which the results could not be as satisfactory as expected.

d) identification of the participants in a single step and their role. Participant identification is based on their own characteristics and executive responsibilities within the organisation under examination.

3. THE STEPS OF THE METHOD

3.1. Step One: Identifying the Object of the Analysis

3.1.1. Objectives

- Singling out the client's objectives and hypotheses. The scope and range of the analysis as the client proposes it (explicitly or not) must be specified: where and why it is thought as expedient to analyse the information system as a whole or, more specifically, either to introduce an automated I.S. or to modify an existing one, and which results the client expects to obtain with regard to specific problem areas.

- Defining the organisational unit including all the problem areas identified in the above stated way, called "reference organisational unit".

- Outlining the "process" within the selected organisational unit and correlating the main problems identified in the above stated way with the opportunities and problems relating specifically to the I.S. and possibly to its automation. The result is a problem interaction system ("map of critical problems") which, among other things, prevents a solution to a given problem from making another problem more acute at a later stage.

- Identifying the significant variables and pinpointing those which could be termed "exogenous", thus acting as constraints for the problem solving process. The variables to be considered are:
a) those influencing the identified problem
b) those controlled to a large extent by decisions external to the organisational area considered.

That some variables will be regarded as "exogenous" instead of "internal" depends on organisational considerations only, that is on the reference organisational area selected. Conversely, the identification of the significant variables allows verification and perfection of such a selection.

Output

i) A document (report) including:
   a) a detailed statement of the subject of the study
   b) description of the process
   c) identification of significant variables (internal/exogenous)

ii) "map of critical problems"

3.1.2. Execution

The step is mostly executed through:

a) interviews with the person in charge of the reference organisational area and with the persons in charge of other internal units, particularly those involved in the identified problems;

b) an examination of the available documents.

It does not seem appropriate to specify more detailed techniques for this step. This is so not because it is a particularly simple activity but because the execution depends completely on the professional experience of the analyst, on his skill in interpreting formal documents and on his ability as a schemer of the interview. At any rate this is a preliminary step and so the risk of dwelling on the problems as the client senses them is very small since during the following step a check of this step is possible. The method includes a step (Step 3) in which such a check is specified formally.

3.1.3. Problems

- The main conceptual and methodological problem regards the identification of the "reference organisational area". It is of the utmost importance to make that definition in the proper way because the organisational reference(s) play(s) a leading role in applying the method correctly, thus in the successfulness of the method. The extreme situation is when the problems identified are "transversal" with regard to the organisation as a whole. In other words, there are no specific units responsible for the correct solution of the problem. In the circumstances the organisational unit having the maximum aggregation is the top management. It should be noted also that, except when very simple problems are tackled - in which case the use of sophisticated methods of analysis is likely to be irrelevant - a certain degree of "transversality" is always present. Thus, if the definition of reference organisational area is applied too strictly, the top management risks being always identified as the reference. That would make the method impracticable de facto. Thus by reference organisational area we mean the organisational unit that:

a) in most cases is in a position to face the problem and that however controls the majority of variables affecting the problem; and

b) is able to define the expected results, thus to validate the objective the information system, be it automated or not, should reach.

- Another open question regards the identification of the "process". If the problems refer to production processes (broadly understood as all processes of physical transformation of an input into an output) describing the flow from the methodological-conceptual point of view is not difficult at all. If on the contrary the problem regards support activities (e.g. accounting operations) one should not consider as the "process" the information handling and processing modes (whose analysis will be the subject of following sections, namely of Step 2), but the production processes upon which the considered activity rests.
Production processes shall be examined however in terms of the activity considered (referring to the previous example, in terms of official duties and certification, typical of the accounting function).

3.1.4. Participation

It has been said already (3.1.2.) whom the analyst should contact during this step. The role played by:

a) the top person in charge of the reference organisational area;
b) the persons in charge of the other organisational units involved, and
c) the analyst.

The analyst's role consists of prodding the discussion and of bringing all problems to the surface. On the contrary, it is not up to the analyst to define or provide indications as to what the real problems are. In fact it is better to define, pinpoint and share said problems also during the following steps, with reference to the actual operative procedures and to the production process.

The persons in charge of the other units should supply data and, if possible, participate in, discuss and share the final definition of problems and opportunities. The decision on the final acceptance of the map of critical problems and of the objectives is up to the top manager of the organisational unit involved.

3.1.5. The case study

As an example, we will describe step-by-step in a very short way one of the pilot case studies. It is the last and the simplest of them. The others are more complex especially as regards problems in the definition of the reference organisational area which we did not experience in the present case due to the size of the firm.

The firm produces office furniture and has 83 employees. The product lines, consisting of unit modules, are three:

- a medium quality level (with respect to the market) wood furniture line, which represents about 90% of the internal production

- a high quality level wood furniture line (about 10%)

- a metal furniture (with wooden working tops) line, which is only partially assembled and distributed by the firm.

There are two kinds of items:

- laminated (3 colours)

- veneered (black or other colour bay oak, rosewood, walnut)

The production process flow is indicated in fig. 1.

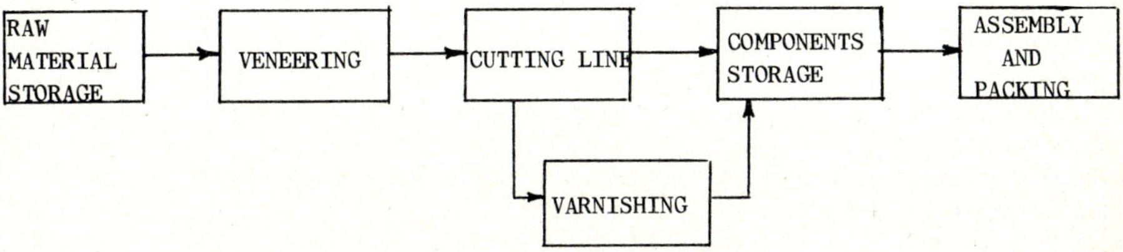

Fig. 1 PRODUCTION PROCESS FLOW

There are two kinds of orders: "routine" orders from end customers or dealers and "large" orders or turnkey supplies. Special parts, i.e. not standardised items, are often required essentially in the "large" orders. The "routine" orders are accepted on the basis of an average delivery time; the components are assigned to each order and the orders are accumulated for the next assembly plan. The "large" orders have a strictly defined delivery time; a complete production plan is defined both for the cutting line and the assembly line. For the "routine" production a cutting line programme (with lot size different for laminated or veneered components corresponding respectively to about three month and six month consumption) and an assembly plan (monthly and weekly) are defined.
The organisational structure, not formalised, may be described as in fig. 2.

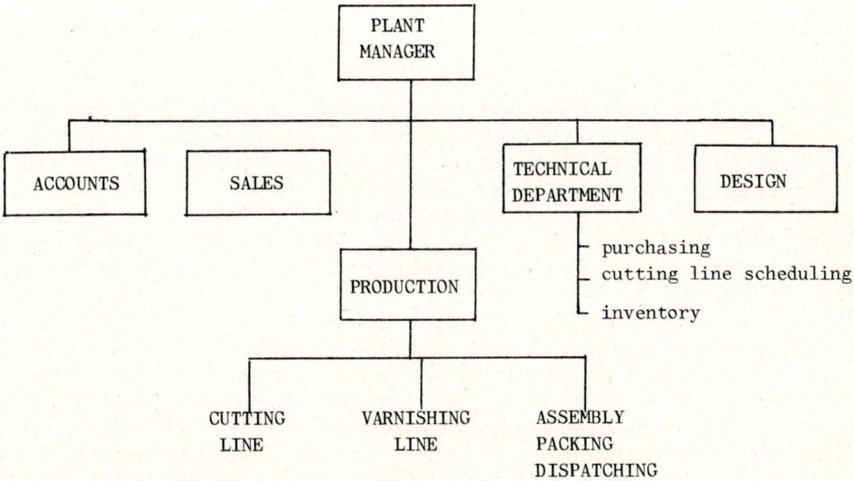

Fig. 2 ORGANISATIONAL STRUCTURE

The identified problems are
- the average delivery time for the "routine" orders is long
- delivery delays are frequent for the "routine" orders
- there is a lack of knowledge and control of work in progress, plant load, idle time etc.
- there are continuous changes in programmes; interventions by exception are often necessary
- there is often lack of parts and/or items when the final assembly and dispatching occur
- a particular coordination effort is often needed for "large" orders and/or special parts production

These problems are significant only for the main line of products (the medium quality line) and for the cutting line and assembly (not for varnishing).

The general objectives stated by the management for the information systems were a better knowledge about the production process state, more efficiency and the reduction of the organisational stress. The interventions already planned at the moment of the case study were the automation of accepting customer orders and the inventory control.

3.2. Step Two: Procedure Analysis

3.2.1. Objectives

- Checking how the problems identified in the previous step are faced and solved. This check aims at considering the real procedure of the organisation and at the same time highlighting any existing formal rules and their application instructions. More specifically, it is necessary to detect how these are transmitted, understood and applied at the different levels and in the various organisational units involved.

- Then verifying whether the real operating procedure differs from formalised procedures, if any.

- Collecting as many elements as possible in order to verify the definition and cruciality of the problems. Actually it should be detected whether the variables qualified as "significant" do in fact have a role in the real process. Failing this, an overall verification should be carried out. In that way additional elements would be available for an evaluation of what the criticality of the problem consists of, as the same can be defined in many different ways, i.e. based on the presence of undesirable effects, on the presence of marked deviations from a hypothetical "normal" situation etc.

- Linking the way problems are tackled or, in other words, the decision-making process to the organisational structure (who decides and how within the organisational context). In establishing said link it will appear clear to what extent it is suitable to maintain, in the description of procedures, a sufficiently realistic organisational "thickness". As a matter of fact, when the procedures are all considered at the same level one loses sight of one of the basic functions of the organisational structure in which each position coordinates the positions immediately below, thus being responsible for the link between the internal operative procedures of organisational units of such a level. Two levels of procedures are then identified in this hypothesis.

- Finally, detecting the main "variances" - related to the problems - that have been and should be analysed.
These data serve as the input to Step 4 (variance analysis).

Output

- Description of first-level procedures (who makes what and in relation with whom).

- Description of the main information flows related with each procedure.

- Drawing of the "procedure graph", that is the graph highlighting the links between different procedures (2nd level procedures).
- List of variances.

3.2.2. Execution

- The problems and processes to which the problems refer are taken as a starting point. The activities carried on to tackle and solve the problems are then identified. The procedure is thus defined as a set of activities carried on in order to take decisions regarding a given problem.

- Then the Elementary Organisational Units (EOU) are identified. From the operational point of view an EOU is an organisational unit controlling almost totally at least one decision variable qualified as relevant during the identification step (Step 1).

- Then the first-level procedures are identified, that is procedures executed mostly within a single EOU.

- The links between first-level procedures are then defined, thus identifying second-level or coordination procedures.

- The procedure graph is finally drawn to highlight:

a) which are the main variances within single 1st level procedures (1st level variances);

b) which are the "interconnection points" between procedures or, in other terms, which are the factors causing the switching from one procedure to another;

c) which are the main variances of 2nd level procedures (2nd level variances).

3.2.3. Problems

- How the procedure is defined.
By procedure we mean a set of activities usually carried on to solve a given problem. Some activities may be emphasised or overlooked (a typical example of the latter possibility is when possible alternatives are predetermined) to suit the characteristics of the problem. Moreover, for a decision process to be qualified

as procedure a certain degree of "repetitiveness" of the process itself is required so that some behaviour "standards", though not formal, may be defined.

- Which are the EOU, or at what level the organisational analysis stops. The decision on the minimum aggregation level based on the procedure analysis does not lie with the analyst but only with the client. Consequently an a priori evaluation is not feasible as it needs to be confirmed by data emerging from the analysis.

- Which are the variances.
First-level variances can be defined as variances present in the aspects of the process that are controlled by a first-level procedure. This fact suggests, among other things, that the minimum organisational level at which the analysis stops is determined by the need for a thorough examination of the process aiming at identifying all the relevant variances.

Second-level variances, that is present in second-level procedures, may be produced both outside and inside first-level procedures that have been examined. As to the former, it is not necessary to examine them thoroughly but just to detect them since they are, by definition, outside the reference organisational unit. As to the latter, they must coincide with the interconnection points between first- and second-level procedures. On the contrary, all interconnection points are not necessarily variances (actually in some cases they consist of standard actions - typical "clock" mechanisms - that should not be regarded as variances).

To sum up, it can be said that:

- all variances to be analysed are variances of the process to which the considered procedures refer;

- first-level variances are the variances present in the process appearing within first-level procedures;

- second-level variances are the variances requiring a control through a second-level procedure.

- It should be stressed that the definition of EOU and the distinction between first and second level are not definitive. These concepts and the method of analysis must be applied in a modular way.

For example, if P_a and P_b are two first-level procedures (at a given phase of the analysis) and $P_{a,b}$ a second-level procedure interconnecting them while being controlled by a higher level organisational unit, nothing prevents $P_{a,b}$ from being regarded as a first-level procedure in another phase and the corresponding organisational unit from being regarded as "elementary". In principle more than two organisational levels could be also considered. As stated, the method however can be applied in a modular way. Consequently, there is no limit whatsoever to the number of organisational levels one might consider.

3.2.4. Participation

Both the persons in charge of the EOU concerned and those in charge of any other higher level organisational units involved by the procedures participate in the analysis.

It is better to analyse each single procedure separately until a draft of the graph is drawn. Once all procedures are examined and the procedure graph is drawn it is necessary to verify them once more together with all persons involved, possibly during plenary meetings.

The final graph should be accepted by all participants. Following a first check, adjustments and a further probing of some procedures are likely to prove necessary.

3.2.5. The case study

The first level procedures, regarding a single stage of production process (assembly, cutting linc, order accepting, purchasing) or a specific period of time or a specific output ("routine" or "large" orders) are:

A) Order dispatching
B) Fortnightly control of cutting line programme
C) Cutting line programme
D) Assembly plan
E) "Large" orders procedure

As an example, the flow chart of procedure A is presented in fig. 3 with the indication (dotted circles) of the occurring variances.

The second level procedures, which regard how to pass from a first level procedure to another and/or to apply a first level procedure are (see the procedure graph in fig. 4):

1. Coordination between assembly and cutting line (joint programming; priority verification etc.)
2. Adjustment of cutting line programme (coordination between market and production and also between different production plans, e.g. laminated and veneered components)
3. Linking of production plans (internal) with "administrative" operations (such as purchase solicitation)
4. Linking of "routine" activities with "large" order production
5. Coordination of production plan for one or more "large" orders and routine production
6. Linking of order acceptance with order scheduling and dispatching
7. Procedure "B" startup "clock" (fortnightly)
8. Procedure "D" startup "clock" (month, week)
9. "Normal" procedure "C" startup
10. Coordination of special parts production
11. External production coordination
12. Coordination between market (solicitations by clients) and assembly

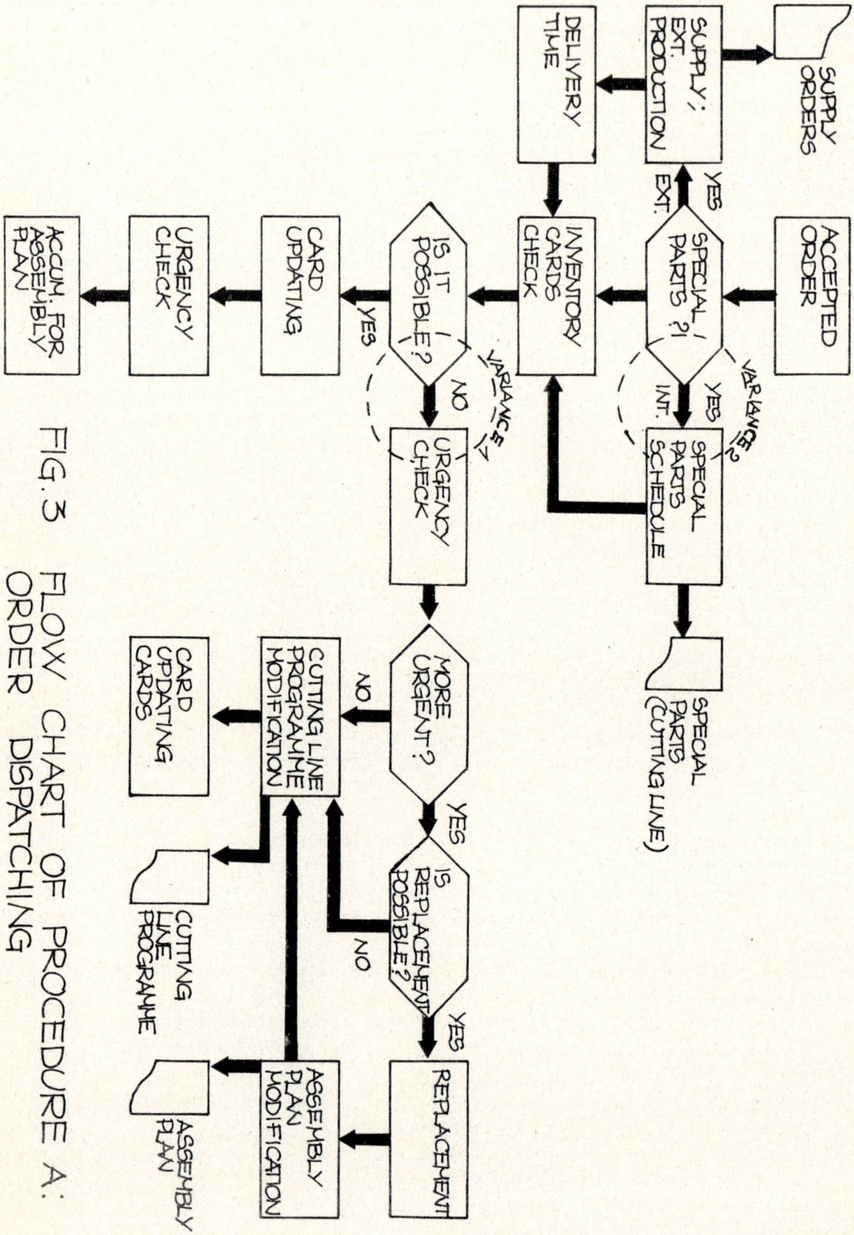

FIG. 3 FLOW CHART OF PROCEDURE A: ORDER DISPATCHING

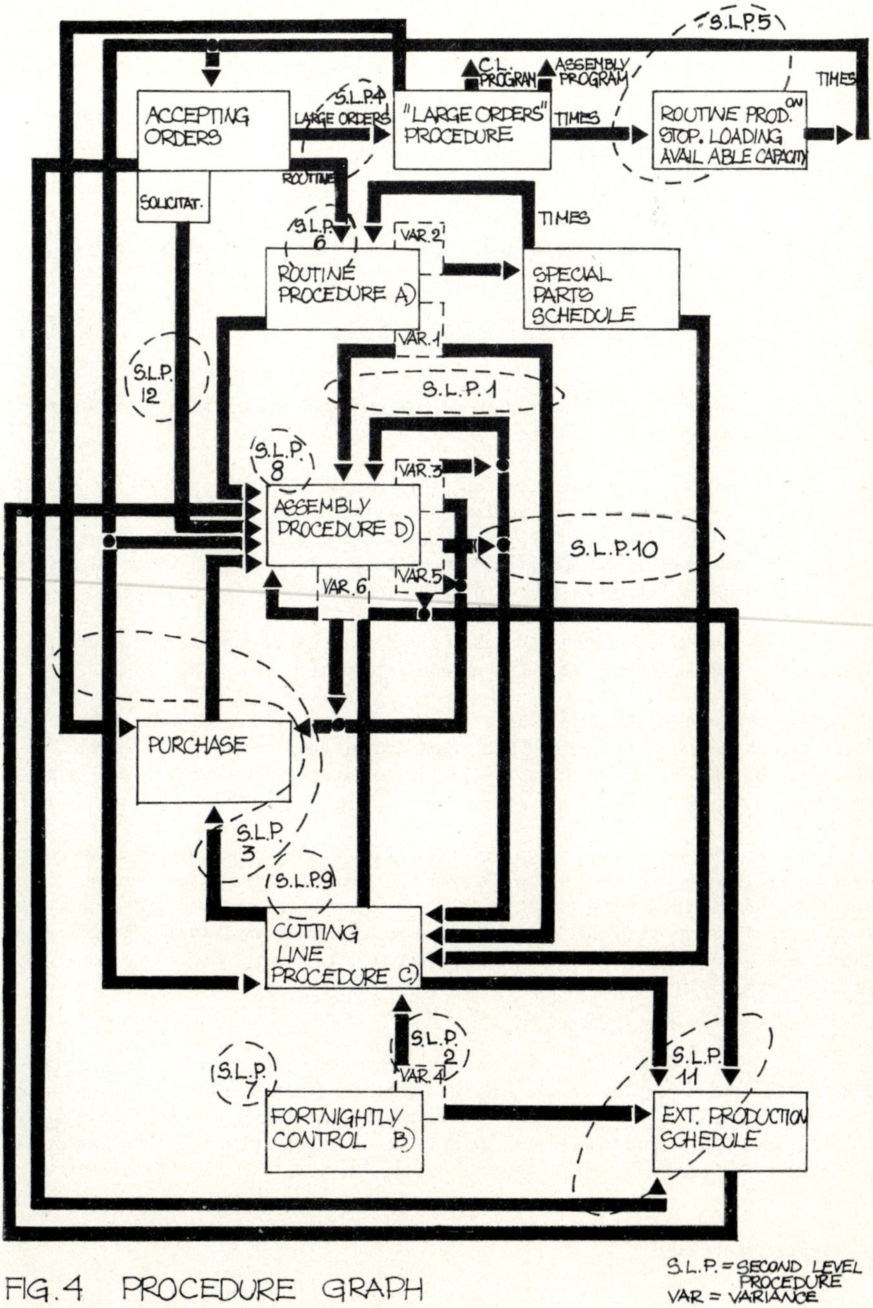

FIG. 4 PROCEDURE GRAPH

The identified variances are:

1. Lack of materials (components) desumed from inventory cards
2. Special parts required
3. Lack of materials for assembly (even though recorded on inventory cards)
4. Market variance: fluctuation in order volume
5. Production defects of special parts
6. Order priority variations

All these are second level variances. The first level variances are not significant.

3.3. Step Three: Verification of Critical Problems in view of Procedure Analysis

3.3.1. Objectives

- Clarifying why the real operating mode differs from established procedures, if any.

- Verifying whether the identification of problems holds out against the detailed analyses of procedures. In particular, verifying:

  - whether the identification of the significant variables and their qualification (exogenous or internal) is valid or they do need further control;

  - the reasons why the selected problems can be regarded as critical (that is specifying what the criticality degree consists of);

  - whether any problems should be eliminated or any new ones included (e.g. because a problem was found to be irrelevant and/or easy to solve or, on the contrary, because the process analysis highlighted any new problem originally unveiled);

  - for what areas, in conclusion, an exhaustive analysis needs to be carried on because it is reasonable to state that within them the information element is all-important for the understanding and decision making process. More specifically, it should be ascertained whether "exogenous" variables actually do not affect the problem too heavily and so whether the present situation could be improved significantly just by modifying them.

Output

The output is a report reviewing what has been done during the first three steps. It may be regarded as an end item. At times the analysis work may even end at this stage to skip directly to the definition of information system constraints and objectives (Step 7). The report presents the results after the analysis, namely:

- critical problems
  - which
  - why

- relevant procedures
  - descriptions
  - who manages them
  - their relationship

- which aspects require action on the information system

- what variances are to be analysed thoroughly.

3.3.2. Execution

This step requires the use of the procedure graph and its analysis together with all persons involved in the data collection steps.

Of course the procedure graph is to be read along with the map of critical problems and in view of the problems and opportunities characterising an information system (be it automated or not).

3.3.3. Problems

- The verification of constraints due to exogenous variables points out the importance given to the organisational aspects. By focusing attention on who holds the control of decision variables one is able, among other things, to verify where action is required to reach any significant result and thus to understand whether given actions (a typical example is the automation of procedures or anyway the introduction of a computer) are basic or just marginal.

- The analysis also highlights the variance degree between established procedures (it does not matter very much whether they are written or not) and the real operating mode. To gain a better insight into the extent - theoretical and practical - of said variances, one should refer to the following rough description of how organisational structures operate.
Any organisational unit may be roughly viewed as operating according to a model lying between two extreme situations:

a) a strictly bureaucratic structure in which (conceptually at least) a "decision table" is provided with a list of all the events likely to occur on one side and the corresponding actions to be taken on the other side;

b) structure "based on results", in which the conceptual table contains on one side the variables and parameters to be watched (instead of the possible events) and opposite the opportunities to be seized (instead of actions to be taken). Of course a close mechanistic relationship between the two sides does not exist. Each organisational unit "negotiates" in advance the objectives to be reached (once the constraints have been defined and the levers controlled) and eventually "justifies" the results attained.

If these two structures are taken as extreme examples it could be said that quite often the actual operating mode of the organisations is much nearer to b) than one would expect. That is neither an advantage nor a disadvantage per se, but the analysis may help to make the situation better or worse.

For example, if the real organisation de facto brings about more satisfactory results than those resulting from the implementation of a formal organisation, any EDP action based on the latter certainly would worsen the situation. Vice versa, the action could be designed to improve the way the real organisation operates. Thus, if in that case the analysis was only limited to the formal aspect, it is almost certain that the conclusions would lead to negative results.

Identifying and setting out clearly the real organisation however is not just a technical and aseptic work. It often means establishing a conflict between different organisational units and questioning the distribution of real power and formal authority within the organisation (regarding the definition of real organisation see [8]).

3.3.4. Participation

The execution of this step is very complex.

It is here that any possible conflicts between different units begin to emerge patently, quite often involving the analyst himself.

At any rate, even when he is faced with these dangers, the analyst always must perform as comprehensive a comparison as possible of the analysis findings with all persons who supplied data in order to be able to continue his work. In fact a general agreement and belief must exist on what has been found so far in order to prevent the following analysis from being distorted.

Among other things some problems may happen to prove fictitious, being due either to a lack of communication or to a different interpretation of the same event. In these cases the efficacy of this step can be verified immediately.

3.3.5. The case study

Schematically we have:

- the market policy is "towed" by demand;
- about the production planning: the cutting line programme is too rigid and, on the contrary, the assembly plan actually consists of the execution of the order backlog and is continuously modified according to priorities;
- about the inventories: the actual state of inventory is not known; it is impossible to solicit in advance (for special parts production, external production, raw material supply); the updating of inventory cards is made on the basis of programmes and orders and not of the actual "load" and "unload" of the storage; in this way, inventories do not separate different sub-systems but, on the contrary, increase the difficulties and transfer variances;
- the coordination between "routine" and "large" orders procedures regards: materials, machine load, assembly time;
- there is a lack of coordination because often different people intervene in the same problem.

3.4. Step Four: Variance Analysis

3.4.1. Objectives

- Pointing out the control circuits for each variance and emphasising the main characteristic parameters, such as: loop closure, response delays, required control means, intervening roles, "primary" effects caused by an inadequate or incomplete control, and "secondary" effects due to the control activity itself.

- Emphasising specifically the structure of the information network within the control circuit: what information are used, by whom, how and with what response delays.

Output

A card for each variance, containing the following data:

- variance description;
- possible causes;
- observed "symptoms" of the variance: which, by whom and how (it is important to focalise what information are necessary and how these should be handled so that the signal and its relation of cause and effect with the variance are perceived);
- control: who holds the control, how, decision making in defining control activities (based on which information, defining which alternatives, based on which objectives, under what constraints);
- primary effects, that is the main effects occurring when a limited or no control is performed;
- secondary effects, that is what generates, how concomitantly, the execution of control activities (variance absorption).

3.4.2. Execution

The most appropriate method is the one usually used for the analysis of control circuits of variances (occurring in production processes) in view of organisation designs. In such a case, a preliminary analysis carried out with the help of the people concerned is followed by a direct study (observation) of the process, by its control and then by a reproposal (possibly amended) of the analysis already done.

The only basic difference (in this context) is the possibility of a lower amount of field observation due to the lesser consequence of the technological aspects of the process.

3.4.3. Problems

- The main theoretical problem regards the already underlined difference between first- and second-level variances. The control circuits of the respective variances in fact take on a different meaning. The result is what could be named a multilevel control system ("hierarchical control system"). At this stage it takes on a particular significance the execution of an analysis of the consistency between operational procedures and organisation structures, particularly in the sense of a check for the correspondence between a formal organisation hierarchy

and a control system hierarchy.
Also the step of problem identification and of their allocation to specific organisational areas should be verified following this approach.

- Another problem has to do with the "information" variable within the control circuit.
From our point of view and with regard to the objective of the analysis two elements should be brought into a particular prominence, viz.:
  - what information are processed
  - how these information are handled (that is, based on which implicit or explicit model).
The latter element is often dealt with in a diminishing way within strictly formal descriptions of information flows.

3.4.4. Participation

As stated under 3.4.2. the experience gained by using variance analysis methods allows to formulate the following two remarks:

- the involvement within the analysis process should be as wide and thorough as possible;

- conflicts may arise among the involved people - both between them and with the analyst - because the method aims at giving prominence to particularly significant elements - not always recognised - of a "well known" reality.
Consequently this activity may trigger off conflicts between different organisational units and lead to a new mooting about power distribution within the organisation.

3.4.5. The case study

The scheme of variance control table adopted in this case is the following:

VARIANCE	CAUSES	DETECTION	CONTROL	ABSORPTION	EFFECTS	CRITICAL FACTORS
Description		how? who?	how? who? required info.	how is it possible?	primary, secondary	

As an example, we report the control table for variance 1 (fig. 5).

3.5. Step Five: Effectiveness/Efficiency Evaluation
3.5.1. Objectives

- Defining the main objectives to be reached and the main constraints to be respected. For these objectives and/or constraints, exact and quantifiable indicators may be available (e.g. production costs, delays, order loss etc.) as it mainly happens with "management events". At times it may prove necessary to keep to more qualitative judgment and evaluation factors (such as organisational stress, demotivation, conflicts etc.) mainly when "organisational events" are con-

VARIANCE	CAUSES	DETECTION	CONTROL	ABSORPTION	EFFECTS	CRITICAL FACTORS
1-Lack of materials desumed from inventory cards	Sudden and high change in consumption of a given item since the last control (max. 15 days before) That may result from uncontrollable market events (e.g. a concentrated demand)	-Check of cards for an accepted order Who: Technical Dept. (card updating)	It consists of different steps: 1-Urgency check. If "low" the order is filed in the next production plan. If "high" step 2 applies. 2-Replaceability check. If it can be replaced by an order still to be passed to assembly (a low priority one of course) the order is replaced. Otherwise step 3 applies. 3-The control cannot be performed anymore within procedure A. Check for the possibility to divert material/time destined to other orders in assembly. If assembly requests are changed the information are maintained for changes in the cutting programme. Otherwise step 4 applies. 4-Quantity and priority change in the cutting line programme. Who: Tech. Dept.,Assembly Shop Foreman. Required information: .orders being filled . priorities .cutting line programme progress	It is guaranteed by: a)possibility to delay delivery to the "weaker" client (if the delay is too long the client might be lost). b)the possibility to change the cutting line programme and assembly plan (flexibility against higher costs and in-factory "troubles")	.Control type 1-2 The effects concern the delivery (delay) of the order in question or of the replaced order. .Control type 3 Delay in replaced order. Cutting line and assembly reprogramming. .Control type 4 Cutting line reprogramming. Delayed delivery of the order in question	.Order urgency(*) .Market trends (*)The "high" or "low" urgency also is a function of the time up to the start of the new cutting line programme (or fortnightly control)

FIG. 5 CONTROL TABLE FOR VARIANCE 1

sidered.

- Assessing the consistency of the identified objectives and constraints with the list of problems identified at the beginning of the analysis. If necessary, a new assessment of the problems and/or a better identification of the objectives and constraints should be carried out.

- Establishing a relationship between primary and secondary effects of variance control circuits and the identified objectives and constraints. In that way the less significant effects could be discarded, leaving only the other ones under prominence.

- Identifying the "fitness" of the control of the various variances as against the effects. Specifically, as a first approximation, efforts could be concentrated on the "efficiency" level relative to first-level variance control circuits and to the "effectiveness" degree relative to higher level variances.

- Identifying the weak or strong points or at any rate the elements characterising the information flow relative to the efficiency and effectiveness of control loops.

Output

- List of objectives and constraints with the specification, when possible, of the indicator selected for each one and the reason for it.

- List of the effects to be kept under observation.

- Evaluation of variance control circuits relative to the effects.

- Identification of information flows compared with the efficiency and effectiveness level of the various control circuits.

3.5.2. Execution

The table of variances shows the primary and secondary effects of the control.

Thus the passage from these effects to the efficiency and effectiveness indicators becomes simple. Then the evaluation of how the control is actually performed and consequently of what main effects do occur is carried out. Thus the strong and weak points of the various control systems are identified. Again by means of the table of variances it is possible to identify what main data are present, which is the structure of the information flow and which relationships do exist with the actually operating control circuits.

All this enables to assume, fairly rapidly, to what extent the information flow influences the efficiency/effectiveness of the control.

Except for particularly complex cases, this step is executed jointly with the next one.

3.5.3. Problems

- The indicator identification and selection problem is neither rapid nor easy to solve. It happens quite often that the same events, when interpreted and analysed quantitatively, are largely shared, while they cause serious and intense conflicts when a more specific and quantitative evaluation is performed.

- The previously mentioned difference between efficiency and effectiveness - the former being attributed to the way first-level circuits are controlled and the latter to higher level circuits - is an abstraction that in some cases could be farfetched. Such a distinction stems however from the following considerations. The higher level circuits define how first-level circuits interconnect to one another and which of them operate in the various situations. Thus, at least as a first approximation, they should be regarded as those vouching for the extent to which general objectives are reached. On the contrary, first-level control circuits basically are in charge of making the most of the available resources for a well-identified process, in which case the term "efficiency" is mostly used.
It is only too true, however (though such an argument goes beyond this specific context) that the effectiveness also consists in setting up as best as once can a set of instruments and methods allowing a high efficiency level to be reached. On the other hand, a good level of efficiency is the pre-requisite for the attainment of a proper level of effectiveness. In such a sense, a clear-cut distinction between effectiveness and efficiency cannot be made.

- The indicators identified in order to define objectives and constraints, and consequently the effects, should be verified in terms of their overall consistency too. Thus any priorities among the objectives to be reached and also any possible relations between the indicators should be detected.

- Finally, as far as the information flow is concerned, in the sense mentioned above, it is necessary to point out the presence of a learning process (memory) that in many cases cannot be identified easily since it often is based on unestablished implicit models. In that connection what has been said extensively about the control circuit analysis schemes applies. [9]
The latter fact is charged with theoretical, as well as operational implications. Actually, with regard to that problem also the objectives set by single decision makers that do not coincide with or do not perfectly match company objectives should be pointed out and considered. We will just observe here that currently there are no satisfactory established organisation design and analysis schemes allowing consideration of conflicting objectives explicitly. The discrepancy between formal organisation and real organisation however can disclose their presence. It is thus during this step that the reason of said discrepancy can be analysed in view of the processing performed so far (problem dealt with already under Step 3).

3.5.4. Participation

In identifying the most appropriate participation it should be considered that the main question concerns on the one hand the indicator definition process (which are they and what priorities they have) and on the other hand the prominence to be given to the "memory" present in control circuits. In that connection, taking into account what has been said before (3.5.3.) one can easily understand how this point may give rise to tensions and conflicts.

3.5.5. The case study

The main effects are (listed at random):

1. Delivery delays
2. Modifications (quantity/sequence) of cutting line programme
3. Modification of assembly plan
4. Solicitations to suppliers
5. Problems and difficulties in coordination and management of external production and special parts production
6. Reworking of defective parts
7. Dispatching incomplete orders

These effects are analysed and evaluated in terms of specific costs or factors of organisational stress.

3.6. Step Six: Map of Variances and Effects

- Defining the relationships between variances and their respective control circuits.

That entails for example, the necessity to verify whether activities performed to control a given variance interact with other variances; whether any primary or secondary effect of a control circuit may in its turn represent a variance in other procedures; and whether some effects, primary or secondary, could render the control of other variances more critical.

- Analysing for each effect (organisational or managerial) which variances and relevant control processes influence it to a greater extent.

- Simulating the dynamics of the generated process by acting on a variance or a control circuit (e.g. by reducing or eliminating the causes of a variance by curbing its effects).

- Then collecting all the elements allowing to decide where and how it would be convenient to intervene on the information system.

Output

- Map of variances and effects pinpointing:
  - effects (managerial and organisational)
  - variances
  - relationships (generally complex) between variances and effects
  - critical factors for the control of a given variance.

3.6.2. Execution

All data required for the drawing up of such a map are obtained through the previous steps. For its specific use the map should be read at the same time as the variance table because the relationships with objectives/constraints and with effects (managerial and organisations) occur in the same way as the control is actually carried out. It should be noted that steps 5-6-7 may require several iterations depending on the complexity of the problem under examination.

3.6.3. Problems

The most interesting result emerging from the analysis and on which it is worthwhile to dwell concerns a systematic evaluation of the variances-control circuits-effects-objectives/constraints complex. At least two highly interesting possible situations can be pointed out in that connection.

a) First the existence of possible positive feedbacks, that is the occurrence of "cascade" effects whose evaluation is difficult when a detailed and overall analysis is absent.
Among other things that tends to render the identification of a law correlating given interventions and/or variances to the resulting effects (as measured by the above mentioned indicators) much more difficult. As a matter of fact the positive feedback leads to the need for the identification of a dynamic law whereas as a rule most relations of cause and effect are formulated statically.

b) The possible shift of criticity as a result of a given corrective action, that is the possibility that an action destined to improve given performances will bring about globally counterproductive results. In other words that means that such an analysis gives prominence to scarcely intuitive or even counter-intuitive phenomena or laws.

3.6.4. Participation

All remarks made with regard to Step 5 apply here, this step being a logical continuation of the previous one.

3.6.5. The case study

The map of variances and effects is reported in fig. 6.

The following considerations on the map are possible:

- the most significant "positive feedbacks" seem to be those between variance 1 and effect 2 and effects 1 and/or 2 and variance 5
- a "cascade" effect occurs between variances 1 and 3, effects 2 and 3 and variance 6
- the critical variances seem to be variance 3 and 6

Variance 3 is caused by lack of information. Variance 6 is caused by continuous programme modifications more than by external solicitations. It depends mainly on absorption and control of variances 3 and 1.

3.7. Step Seven: Identification of Objectives and Constraints of the Information System

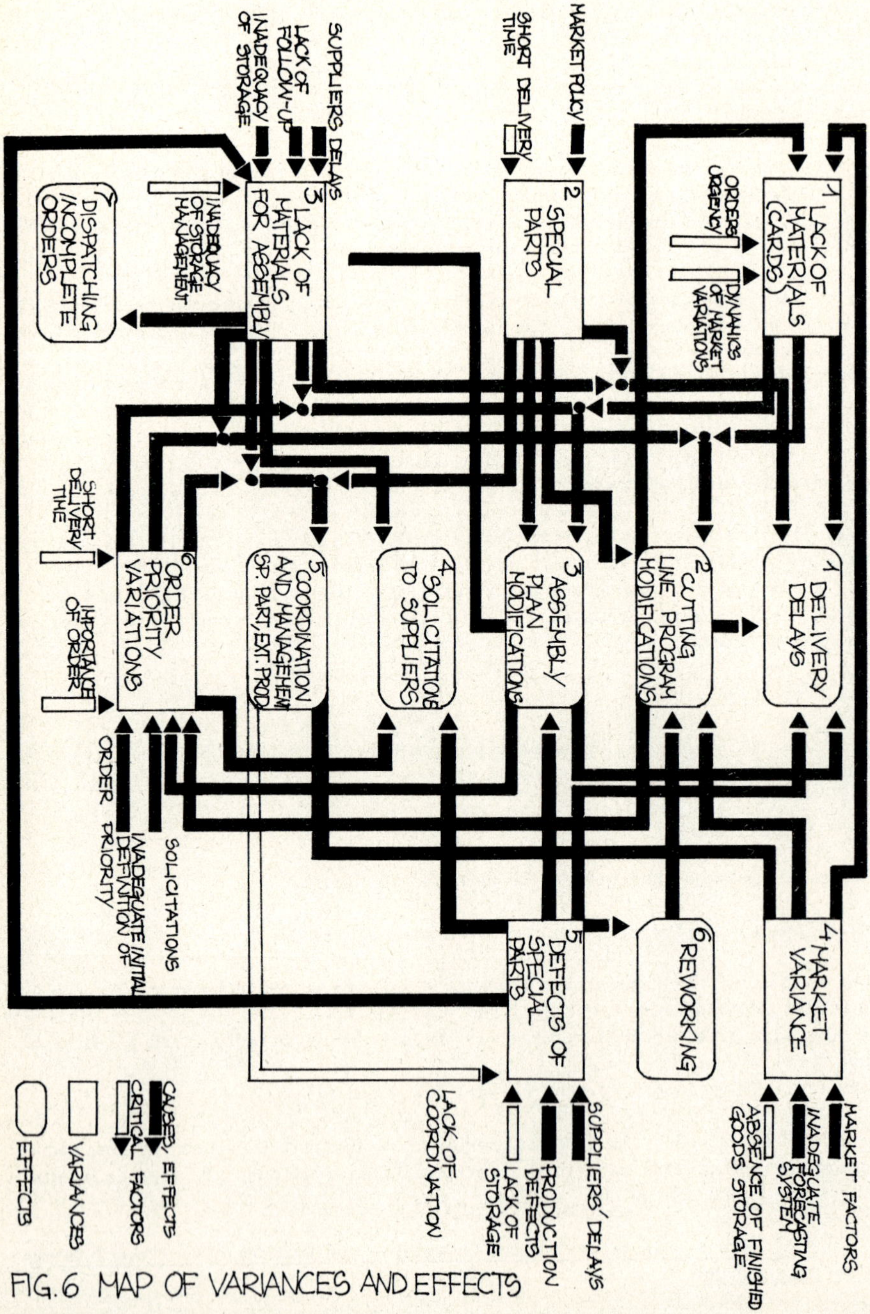

FIG.6 MAP OF VARIANCES AND EFFECTS

3.7.1. Objectives

- Defining the objectives and constraints of the information system in order to start the real technical/informative project immediately after.

- In particular, identifying if and how with regard to the unautomated information handling modes the introduction of a computer could involve rigidity and so results in a negative outcome or, conversely, which positive facts it could bring about.

Output

- List of the information that, when properly organised, help to decrease the critical state. From a strictly operational standpoint, definition of information flow and data file structures, of updating and processing modes, of communication times of the data enabling such an objective to be reached, and to what extent the objective itself can be reached. In that connection both the consequence of exogenous variables - already mentioned - and the complexity of real systems, as stated under the previous step should be kept in mind.

3.7.2. Execution

The required information will be found in the map described in Step 6 and in the analysis of the Information System (relevant to critical events) under Step 5.

3.7.3. Problems

No special problems exist here. We would like to remind, however, what has been said about the "memory", which is something showing a high specific critical status. As already said, the memory is not easy to identify though it plays quite an important role in real control circuits. For that reason the argument could be reversed, that means underlining how important it is not to ignore, or rather, to use well both during the analysis and during the following possible design of information systems such a characteristic of control circuits that makes them quite different from simple "automatic" adjustment loops also from the point of view of performance.

3.7.4. Participation and utilisation criteria

What has been said for the previous step applies here too.

3.7.5. The case study

The identified objectives and constraints for information system design are:
. the elimination of variance 3 (lack of materials for assembly) is possible: this requires not only an inventory control system based on the recording of the actual storage loading and unloading, but also the cutting line production follow up for anticipating the knowledge of when the requested material will enter the inventory (and the same criteria apply to purchasing and external production)
. the cutting line production follow up is useful also for a better knowledge of work in progress, plant load and to define a delivery time for "routine" orders in

a better way
. the reduction of variance 1 is connected to the improvement of the forecasting and production planning systems (the follow-up procedure will help)
. the reduction of variance 6 is possible as a consequence of the elimination of variance 3 and of an improved p lanning system.

3.8. Step Eight: Indications about the Suitability of Organisational Interventions

3.8.1. Objectives

- Based on the elements collected during the analysis, evaluation of whether it would be suitable to supplement the design of the Information System (or even to preface it) with a more thorough organisation analysis (irrespective of any indication as to who will conduct the analysis), in view of a possible redesign.

Output

- A conclusive section of the final report in which opportunities and problems connected to an organisational intervention would be assessed in qualitative terms.

3.8.2. Execution

By examining the variance map one may assess whether a change in the structures of control circuits (that is in the competence of organisational units) could result in significant results. Of course that would be a qualitative appraisal largely based on the analyst's intuition and experience in similar contexts.

3.8.3. Problems

The first problem consists in the difficulty to formulate indications as to changes in an organisation that the client will not interpret as an undue interference in an unauthorised sector. Sometimes, however, the analyst is confronted with the opposite problem, i.e. how to preserve his specific professional role when he is asked disguisedly for the technical legitimation of an organisation transformation already provided for.

On the other hand the methodology suggested here has a share (in both cases) in finding a neither provocative nor collusive working method that simply may point, based on the work carried out, to the suitability of an investigation of organisational aspects.

The second problem concerns the analyst's organisational training, which should be good enough to prevent him from falling into a naive technicalisation. In fact it is clear that the analogy with the control of processes, used throughout the method, is a powerful work tool. On the other hand, as already stated, the model should not be mistaken for the reality, thus ignoring all truly organisational aspects substantiating the real operative mode.

3.8.4. Participation

During this step the participation is limited by necessity to top people of the client's organisation. The problem of an enlarged participation will be tackled later on if the proposal is accepted.

Acknowledgements

The authors should like to record their thanks to the other two members of the research group for their specific contribution. They are also very grateful to the colleagues of the Istituto di Ricerca Intervento sui Sistemi Organizzativi for their helpful advice and suggestions, and to all the firms that gave them the opportunity to carry out the case studies they used to define the method.

References

[1] R.P. Bostrom and J.S. Heinen, MIS Problems and failures: a sociotechnical perspective, MIS Quarterly, Sept. 1977, 17-32 and Dec. 1977, 11-28.

[2] E. Mumford, F. Land and J. Hawgood, A participative approach to forward planning and system change, Impact of science on society, Vol. 28, 3, July-Sept. 1978.

[3] A. DeMaio, E. Bartezzaghi, O. Brivio, C. Ciborra and G. Zanarini, A socio-technical approach for design and changing technology: the EDP case, forthcoming (in Italian).

[4] E. Bartezzaghi and A. De Maio, An application of STS approach methodology to a furniture firm (in Italian), RSO report, 79-11.

[5] A. De Maio and G. Zanarini, Information system design for a new division of a large firm (in Italian), RSO report, 79-13.

[6] A. De Maio, Information system design for telecomunication plant installation groups (in Italian), RSO report, 79-14.

[7] G. Zanarini, Information requirements for an accounting department (in Italian), RSO report, 79-15.

[8] F. Butera, La divisione del lavoro in fabbrica (Marsilio, Venice, 1978) (in Italian).

[9] E. Bartezzaghi, C. Ciborra, A. De Maio, P. Maggiolini and P. Romano, Information systems and organisation: an empirical research, in: B. Gilchrist (ed.), Information Processing 77 (North-Holland, Amsterdam, 1977).

Formal Models and Practical Tools
for Information Systems Design
H.-J. Schneider, Editor
North-Holland Publishing Company

AN APPROACH FOR INVOLVING THE USERS IN THE SPECIFICATION OF INFORMATION SYSTEMS

Mats Lundeberg
Department of Administrative Information Processing,
University of Stockholm, Sweden

Abstract: This paper has two messages:

1 The users can control the specification of information systems by themselves - given suitable circumstances

2 The effectiveness of the specification process can be improved if it is performed on three levels (change analysis, activity studies, information analysis) instead of only on one level (information analysis)

The paper describes an approach for involving the users in the specification of information systems on the three levels change analysis, activity studies, and information analysis. The practical experience of using these three levels of specification is that it is much more work effective than starting with information analysis at once.

1 INTRODUCTION

1.1 THE SIGNIFICANCE OF THE PAPER

Two important messages of this paper are:

1 *The users can control the specification of information systems by themselves - given suitable circumstances*

2 *The effectiveness of the specification process can be improved if it is performed on three levels (change analysis, activity studies, information analysis) instead of only on one level (information analysis)*

Information systems shall only be developed if they can support human beings in facilitating or improving some of their activities. The development of information systems can thus be seen as part of the development of the activities in organizations. The persons responsible for the activities - the users - should also control the development of these activities. They should therefore also control the development of information systems to support the activities. In order to be able to do this, aids in form of working methods and description techniques are needed. Our experience is that the users can control the specification of information systems by themselves - given such aids and other suitable circumstances.

This paper describes an approach for involving the users in the specification of information systems on three levels:

1 *Change analysis* (in order to ensure that information systems are developed only when there really is a need for them)

2 *Activity studies* (in order to ensure that only such information systems are developed that give positive contributions to the activities of the organization in some way)

3 *Information analysis* (in order to ensure that information systems are developed in such a manner that the users understand what they contain and perform)

The practical experiences of using these three levels of specification are that it is much more work effective than starting with information analysis at once.

1.2 PURPOSE AND OUTLINE

The purpose of the paper is to describe the ISAC approach to information systems specification in an introductory manner. ISAC (Information Systems work and Analysis of Changes) is a research group at the department of Administrative Information Processing at the Royal Institute of Technology and the University of Stockholm, Sweden. Since 1971 research has been performed in the ISAC group around a new approach to information systems development with special emphasis on analysis and design of information systems. This work has been conducted in close contact with practical applications in different business companies and other organizations. The ISAC approach to information systems development has been described in [4], [5], [6], and [7]. This paper builds on these works and focuses on the specification part of information systems development.

The ISAC approach to information systems specification is described by:

- discussing some common problems in information systems specification in practice
- giving a short outline of the ISAC approach to information systems specification
- presenting parts of a case study of information systems specification
- summarizing the relations between the three levels change analysis, activity studies, and information analysis
- summarizing some experiences and possibilities in connection with the ISAC approach to information systems specification

2 SOME COMMON PROBLEMS IN INFORMATION SYSTEMS SPECIFICATION IN PRACTICE

Specifying information systems is an activity where many persons experience problems. In fact, empirical evidence suggests that the specification process is the bottle-neck in developing information systems in some cases. Examples of typical problems that are experienced in business companies and other organizations in Scandinavia in connection with specifying information systems are:

1 The communication between the different human beings that are involved does not work

2 Individual and varying specification methods are used

3 Poor and fast specifications sometimes result in other information systems being developed than those that are needed the most by the users

4 The specification process takes much more time than planned

5 Documentation from the specification process is missing or is incomplete or is not possible to understand

Some of these problems are typical not only for specification of information systems but for information systems development work in general. The discussion will however be concentrated to the information systems specification viewpoint. The problems are not independent of each other. The two first problems, for example, highly influence also the later problems.

The communication problems in the specification process exist mainly between users and systems analysts. Some of these communication problems may depend on the fact that these categories of people "speak different languages". Usually a number of other factors also contribute to the communication problems -- e.g., uncertainty concerning the problems that are to be solved and uncertainty about what the future will look like.

A concrete example of people not talking the same language is that common work methods often are missing in information systems development. The lack of generally accepted work methods increases the uncertainty about the development. The circumstance that individual and varying methods are used enhances the communication problems.

If the communication between the users and systems analysts does not work it may lead to poor specifications or that the specification process is hurried over too fast. Poor specifications may in turn result in the development of other information systems than those that the users really wanted. Instead, more or less conscious professional goals of the systems analysts can lead to the development of systems that are too ambitious in comparison with the users' needs. Another consequence of failing communication is that work takes longer a time than it should. A common example is that one has to start all over again because of missing guidelines the first time. Work is therefore delayed.

One result of information systems specification is by definition a documented specification. Despite this, parts of the documentation are often missing in practice. Information systems specification is found to be more abstract and hence more difficult than e.g. programming.

The examples of problems mentioned above indicate some of the difficulties in specifying information systems. *In summary, information systems specification is a difficult but essential work task in the development of information systems.* Two important needs in the specification process are:

1 *On the human side*, human beings need knowledge of how to clarify and specify problems and of how to communicate during this specification process

2 *On the subject matter side*, aids in form of working methods and description techniques for the specification process are needed

The ISAC approach to information systems specification is an approach which provides working methods and description techniques for the specification process. These working methods and description techniques help human beings to clarify and specify problems and facilitate the communication during the specification process. If you use the ISAC approach in your organization, you do not automatically solve all problems mentioned earlier. However, you may thereby take a significant step towards reducing some of them.

3 A SHORT OUTLINE OF THE ISAC APPROACH TO INFORMATION SYSTEMS SPECIFICATION

The ISAC approach to information systems specification consists of a work methodology from the needs, problems, and ideas experienced by the users to information analysis models. The information analysis models are the specifications for the subsequent data system design work. Methodology here refers to a number of manageable and coherent work steps including rules for what types of models and other documentation that are produced during these work steps. The documentation should be a natural part of the work and not something that is done afterwards.

Figure 3.1[1)] illustrates the relations between activities in an organization and the development of these activities. In the activities different problems and needs for changes constantly arise. Some of these you try to solve by developing the activities in the organization in various ways. When different development

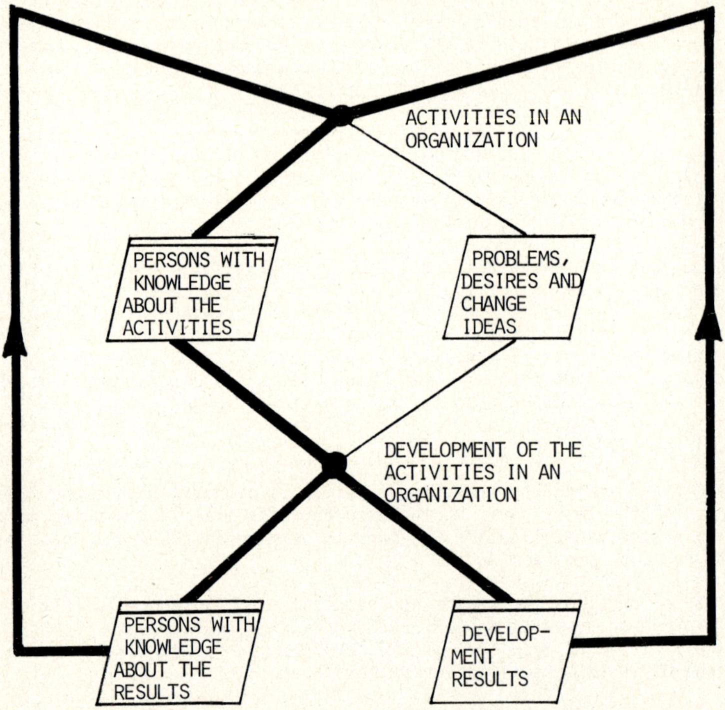

Figure 3.1 The relations between activities in an organization and the development of these activities

results have been implemented, new problems and needs for changes arise and so on. Figure 3.1 can be seen as a description of the learning cycle of an organization - a constant circulation between performing activities in the organization and developing these activities. The figure is very partial. The relations between the organization and its environment are, for example, lacking completely. One aspect is however stressed. The persons working with performing the activities in the organization learn much about these. This knowledge is an important resource when developing the activities in the organization. In the same way, the persons who participate in the development learn much in connection with this work. This knowledge is also an important resource when implementing the development results.

Figure 3.2[2)] illustrates information systems specification as part of the development of activities in an organization. The figure shows that we distinguish between change analysis and proper development as parts of the development of activities in the organization. The aim of change analysis is to clarify what kind of changes of the activities in an organization one should aim at. If the change analysis leads to the conclusion that the needs and problems of the users are of a different kind than the information systems kind, other development is performed instead.

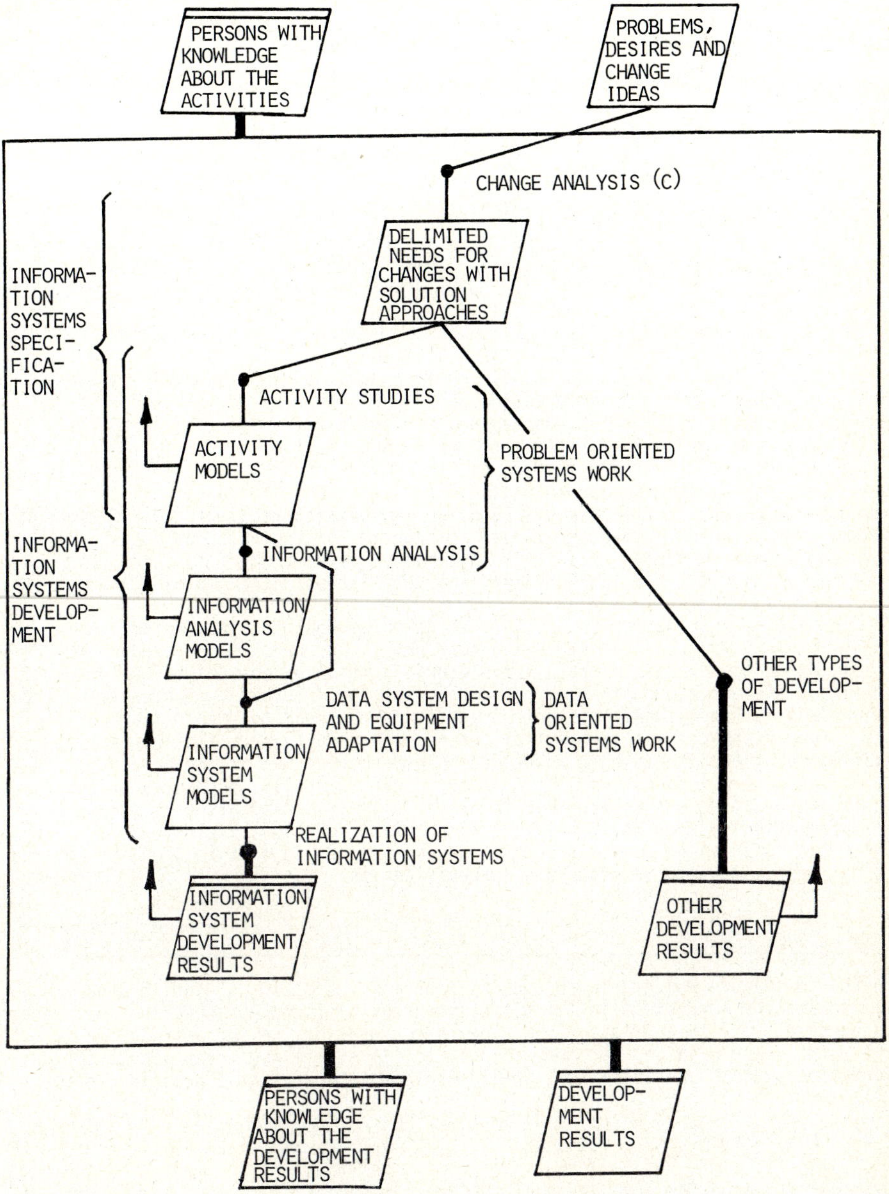

Figure 3.2 Information systems specification (change analysis, activity studies and information analysis) as part of the development of activities in an organization

Information systems specification is according to the ISAC approach performed on three levels: Change analysis, activity studies, and information analysis. A short presentation of these different areas will be given below.

The purpose of change analysis is to study the types of changes (improvements) that are needed in order to do something about the problems experienced in the activities of an organization. It is important to try and find the reasons behind the problems and not only the symptoms. The results from change analysis are a combination of development measures in order to cope with the defined needs for changes. Information systems development should be considered a suitable development measure only if the change analysis indicates that there are problems and needs in the information systems area. In this way, change analysis results in information systems specifications on a first, crude level. This level defines why information systems and not other measures are considered as solutions to existing problems and needs.

The purpose of activity studies is to delimit future information systems in the activities of the organization. The information systems should be delimited in such a way that they contribute to the solving of the problems of the different interest groups involved. In order to delimit information systems, one usually has to describe the activities in more detail than in the change analysis. Delimitation of future information systems should be made from the specific problems and needs that the users have and not using existing technical aids as a basis. The delimitation means that the input and output information sets of the information systems are defined, including relevant properties of the information sets. In this way, activity studies result in information systems specifications on a second, intermediate level. This level defines and delimits potential information systems.

The purpose of information analysis is to describe what the thus delimited future information systems shall contain and perform. The description is used in two different connections. On one hand it represents a means of communication for the affected interest groups in their discussion of the information contents. On the other hand it constitutes an exact basis for the succeeding data system design. The information analysis starts from the desired results from the information system. One then studies what is needed in order to arrive at these results. The structure of the information sets is also studied. Finally, necessary processes in the information system are described. In this way, information analysis results in information systems specifications on a third, detailed level. This level defines the information needs in detail and corresponds to what is usually referred to as a detailed information systems specification.

4 PARTS OF A CASE STUDY OF AN INFORMATION SYSTEMS SPECIFICATION PERFORMED ON THREE LEVELS

In [5] an example which goes through all the main chapters is used in order to illustrate the work steps in the different areas of the ISAC approach. The example is based on reality and taken from a dairy corporation (called Dairco). Parts of the Dairco case will be used here as well to illustrate the three levels of information systems specification. For a more comprehensive case description see [5].

4.1 CHANGE ANALYSIS

Dairco has a need for a revision of their order processing, invoicing and distribution activities. Dairco was formed by a number of merges during the past few years. This has lead to a situation where these activities are performed differently in different regions. What type of development should be chosen in order to develop these activities?

In Dairco a decision is made to set up a project group in order to find an answer to this question. The project group is put together with representatives and one systems analyst. Among the users in the project group there are "direct" users and "inbetween" users. The direct users come from different specialist functions at the central office. The inbetween users also come from the central office but represent the "end" users at the dairies indirectly.

None of these persons have performed change analysis earlier. It is therefore decided to have a learning program around change analysis, now that the project group has been established. Only the project group participates in the learning program, which takes place during three days and in a residential form. During these three days the basics of change analysis are treated. This includes method steps and description techniques. The project group then applies these methods and techniques to the problems in their own project. The learning program also turns out to be the real start of the project, now that work in the project group really begins.

The work then continues at Dairco until the following results are obtained:

1 An evaluation of the current situation

2 A chosen change alternative to be implemented in the future

3 A combination of development measures to implement the change alternative

The results of the evaluation of the current situation are the following needs for changes:

N1 Better order procedures
N2 Better distribution basis
N3 More effective order office work
N4 Common order system
N5 Better order entry equipment
N6 Better production planning basis

Three main change alternatives are discussed:

A0 *No change* (zero alternative), i.e. orders are brought to the office by the truck drivers

A1 Implement a *telephone order system*, where either the order personnel call the customers or the other way around

A2 Implement a *purchase proposal system*, where purchase proposals are sent to the customers

The project group proposes that Dairco continues to work with the purchase proposal idea. An overview of the relations between dairy, customer, and consumer in the purchase proposal system is given in figure 4.2 in the form of a so called A-graph (activity graph). Rules for how to interpret the different symbols in A-graphs are presented in figure 4.1. It should be noted that figure 4.2 has been drawn by the users themselves with the aid of the systems analyst in the project group.

The project group can now define necessary development measures in order to implement a purchase proposal system:

DM1 Information systems development
DM2 Continued organizational development

Information systems will be needed for the preparation and distribution of purchase proposals. Continued organizational development will be needed so that the personnel know how to work with the order processing activities in the future.

SYMBOLS IN A-GRAPHS	CORRESPONDENCE IN DESCRIBED ACTIVITY

REAL SET

SET OF PERSONS AND/OR MATERIAL.

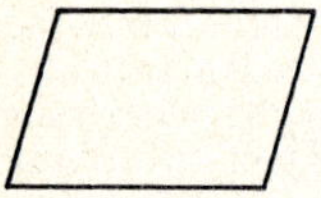

MESSAGE SET

SET OF MESSAGES, E.G. DOCUMENTS OR INFORMATION BY TELEPHONE.

COMPOSITE SET

SET COMPRISING PERSONS/MATERIAL AS WELL AS MESSAGES.

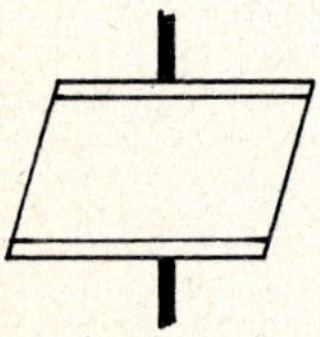

REAL FLOW

FLOW OF PERSONS/MATERIAL ONLY.

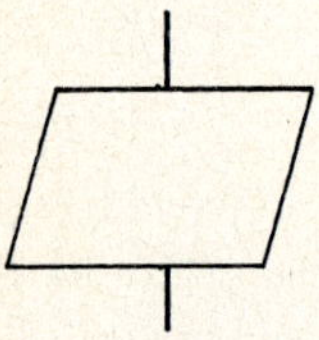

MESSAGE FLOW

FLOW OF MESSAGES.

COMPOSITE FLOW

FLOW OF PERSONS/MATERIAL AS WELL AS MESSAGES.

ACTIVITY

PEOPLE AND OTHER RESOURCES TAKE PART IN THE ACTIVITY.

ALL FLOWS ARE ASSUMED TO GO FROM TOP TO BOTTOM ON THE GRAPHS. ARROWS ARE NEEDED ON UPWARD AND (POSSIBLY) HORIZONTAL FLOWS ONLY.

Figure 4.1 Explanation of symbols used in A-graphs

dairco

Analyst
DOP
Subject
Purchase proposal system:
Relations between dairy,
customer and consumer

A - GRAPH
Date
1978-07-15

No PPO
Version 4

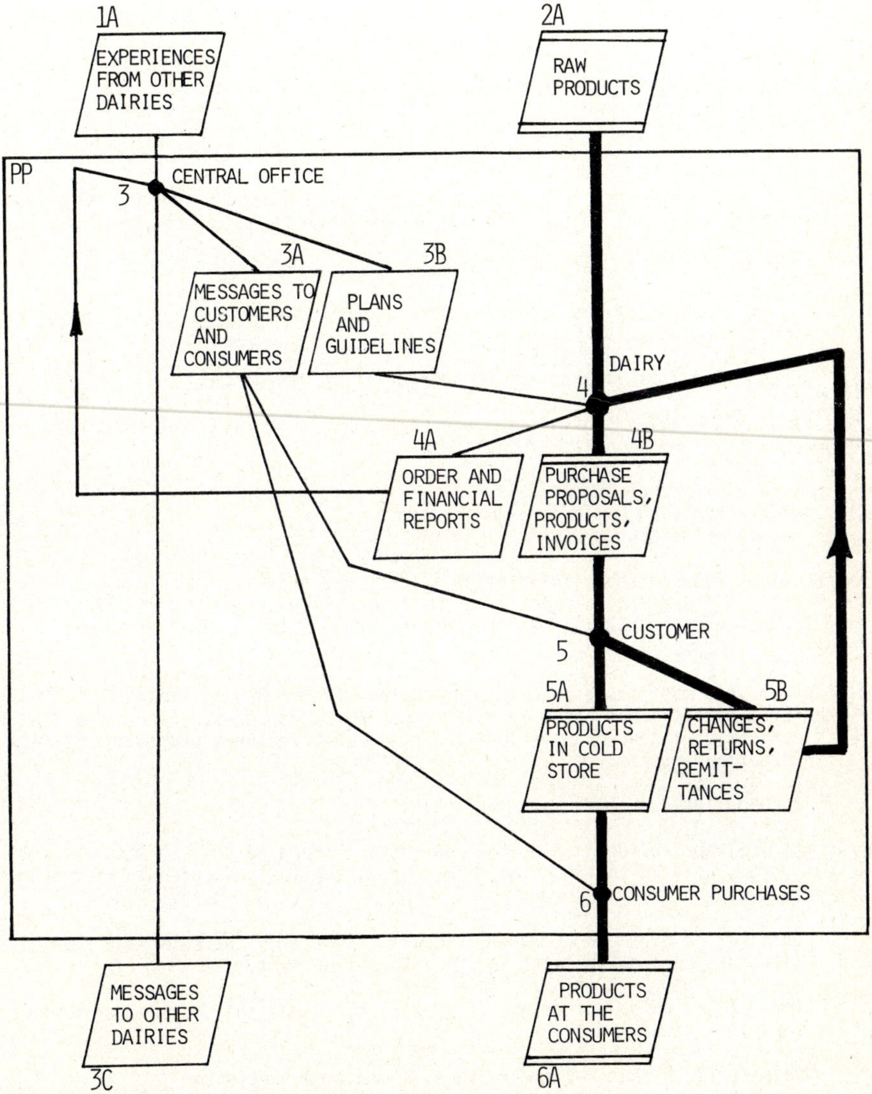

Figure 4.2 Relations between dairy, customer and consumer in the purchase proposal system (A-graph PPO)

The list of needs for changes given above, the A-graph in figure 4.2 and the defined development measures given above are concrete examples of information systems specifications on a first, crude level. The essential characteristic of this level is to define where and why information systems and not other measures are considered as solutions to existing problems and needs.

4.2 ACTIVITY STUDIES

In Dairco, the proposal of the project group is accepted. The project group thus continues with information systems development as one part of their work. The project group is satisfied with the way the learning program around change analysis was carried through. They would like to continue with a learning program in the same way during the information systems development. As to the information systems specification parts, a one week residential work period each is scheduled for activity studies and information analysis respectively. As before, method steps and description techniques are treated. The project group then applies these methods and techniques to the problems in their own project. The work with activity studies is then continued at Dairco until the following results are obtained:

1 A list of information subsystems of the purchase proposal system

2 A-graphs defining the relations between these subsystems including their inputs and outputs

3 A cost/benefit calculus for each information subsystem

The list of information subsystems of the purchase proposal system includes the following subsystems of order processing:

-1 Prognosis processing
-2 Order receiving and order summarizing
-3 Return processing

The relations between these information systems are shown in the A-graph in figure 4.3. Again, this A-graph has been drawn by the users with the aid of the systems analyst. The cost/benefit calculi are not included in this short description of the case.

The list of information subsystems shown above, the A-graph in figure 4.3 and the cost/benefit calculi (not shown here) are concrete examples of information systems specifications on a second, intermediate level, which defines and delimits potential information systems.

4.3 INFORMATION ANALYSIS

After the one week residential work period in the learning program with information analysis, this work is continued at Dairco until the following results for each information system:

1 Information precedence graphs (I-graphs) that show the relations among the different information sets in the information system

2 Information component graphs (C-graphs) that show the contents of these information sets

3 Process lists that define relevant information processes

4 Process tables that describe each process separately

An example of an I-graph is found in figure 4.5. The rules for interpretation of I-graphs are found in figure 4.4. Examples of C-graphs are found in figure 4.7.

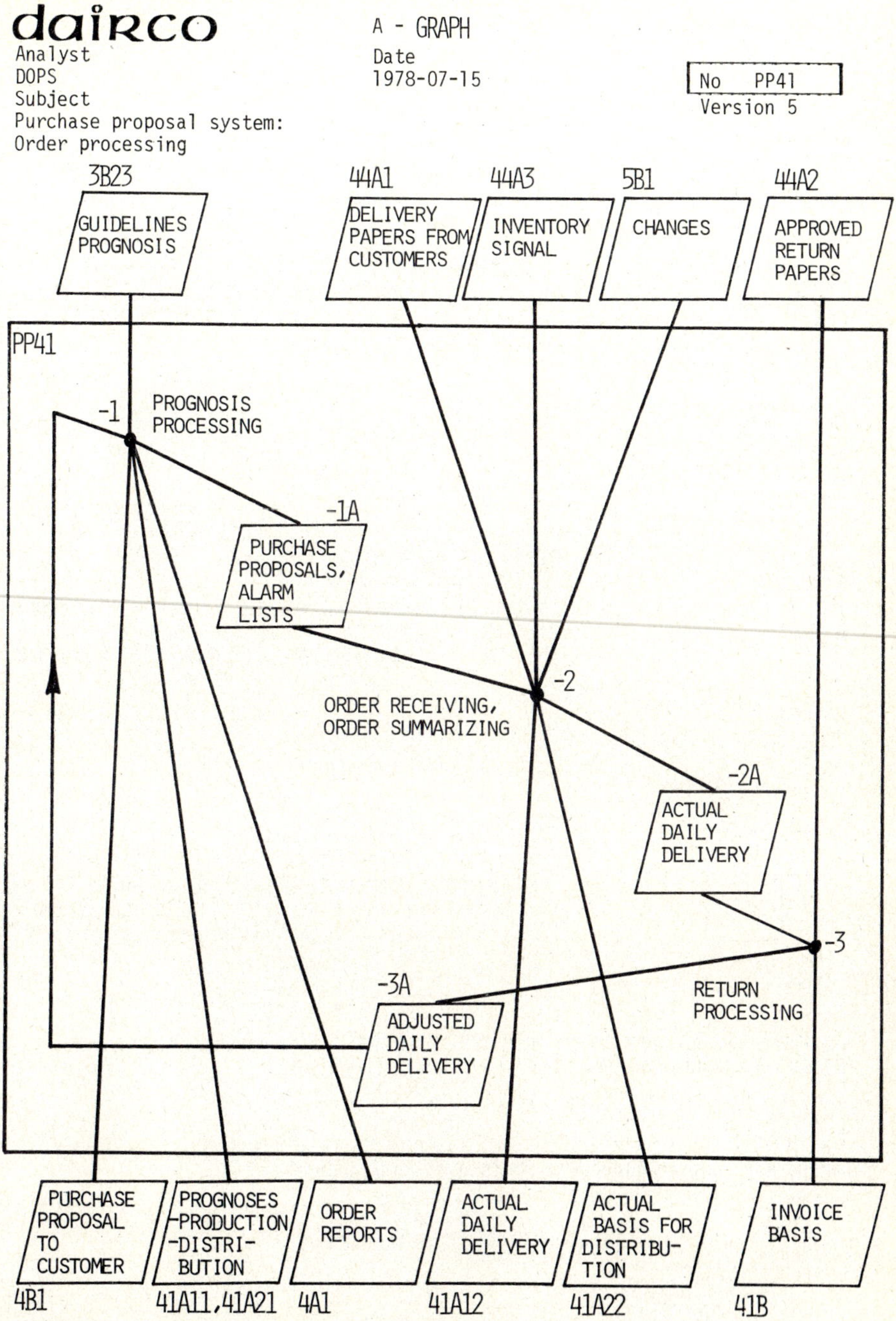

Figure 4.3 Order processing in a purchase proposal system (A-graph PP41)

SYMBOLS IN I-GRAPHS — CORRESPONDENCE IN DESCRIBED INFORMATION SYSTEM

INFORMATION SET

AN INFORMATION SET CONSISTS OF A NUMBER OF MESSAGES. AN INFORMATION SET IS DESCRIBED BY THE INFORMATION CONTENT IN THESE MESSAGES.

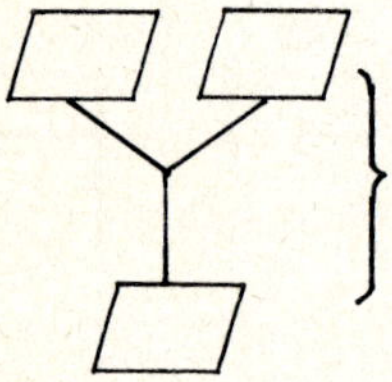

PRECEDENCE RELATION

RELATIONS BETWEEN INFORMATION SETS. THE PRECEDENCE RELATION IS ILLUSTRATED BY A NODE AND A NUMBER OF BRANCHES.

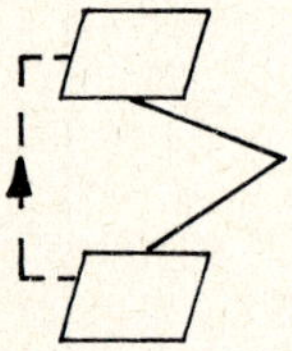

PERMANENT INFORMATION SET

AN INFORMATION SET WHICH EXISTS IN DIFFERENT GENERATIONS, I.E. WITH A SIMILAR STRUCTURE BUT WITH INFORMATION CONTENTS FROM DIFFERENT POINTS OF TIME.

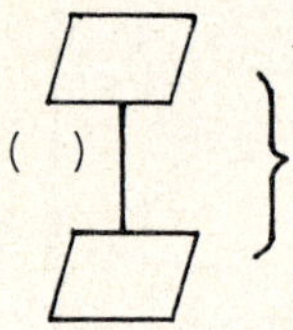

FICTITIOUS PRECEDENCE RELATION

TWO IDENTICAL INFORMATION SETS ARE SHOWN BY A FICTITIOUS PRECEDENCE RELATION, INDICATED BY THE PARENTHESES WITHOUT A REFERENCE CODE.

ALL FLOWS ARE ASSUMED TO GO FROM TOP TO BOTTOM ON THE GRAPHS. ARROWS ARE NEEDED ON UPWARD AND (POSSIBLE) HORIZONTAL FLOWS ONLY.

Figure 4.4 Explanation of symbols used in I-graphs

dairco I - GRAPH

Analyst DOPS | Date 1978-07-15 | No PQ4 Version 4

Subject Prognosis processing

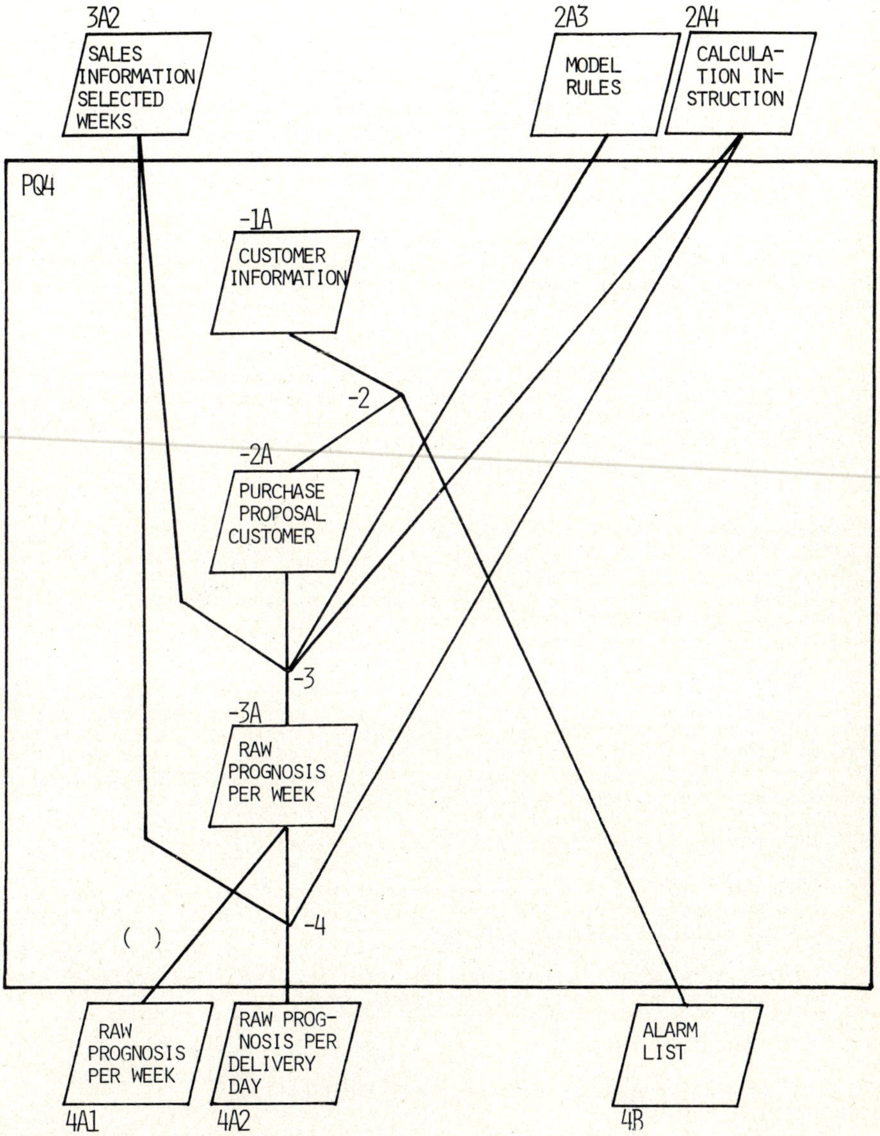

Figure 4.5 I-graph PQ4

The rules for interpretation of C-graphs are found in figure 4.6. From figure 4.5 the following processes can be defined:

-2 Selection of purchase proposal customers and production of alarm list
-3 Calculation of raw prognosis per week
-4 Spreading of raw prognosis to delivery days

A process table describing the first of these processes in the form of a decision table is found in figure 4.8.

Together with the list of processes above the I-graph, C-graphs and process table in figures 4.5, 4.7, and 4.8 represent a concrete illustration of a detailed information systems specification.

4.4 SOME EXPERIENCES FROM THE DAIRCO CASE

In general terms, the Dairco case can be said to be a successful project. The users controlled the project and arrived at specifications which clearly expressed their intentions. The number of iterations in drawing the graphs was less than in other cases where only information analysis had been performed without change analysis and activity studies.

However, to illustrate the difficulties in specifying information systems, an unsuccessful episode from this project will also be introduced here. At a certain stage, the project group felt a little uncertain about how realizable one information system was and how the end users would react. After some discussion it was decided to implement a prototype system at one site. The idea was to gain experience for the real information system later on.

The project group had to make a large number of decisions about practical details in connection with the coming test period. One felt a great need to start the prototype test soon. Lack of time and stress came into the picture. This lead to a situation where parts of earlier produced documentation were overlooked in writing the computer programs for the prototype. Certain parts of the reports were omitted, a number of incorrect calculation rules were used in the programming etc.

What happened to the prototype? One started the test activities on time. But the prototype did not work as intended. After some time the prototype was taken out of use in order to adapt it to the users' specifications. The "new" prototype then worked as intended. A user reaction: "If we had looked at the ISAC drawings a little more into detail, our first test would have worked out from the beginning." The experiences from this episode underline:

- The importance of performing sufficient information systems specifications

- Time pressed and carelessly performed specification work leads to poor information systems that either have to be redone to a large extent or that are not used by the persons affected

5 SUMMARY OF THE RESULTS FROM CHANGE ANALYSIS, ACTIVITY STUDIES, AND INFORMATION ANALYSIS AND THE RELATIONS BETWEEN THESE

The results from change analysis can be summarized in three parts:

1 Evaluated activity model of the current situation with

- A-graphs

- Text pages with more detailed descriptions of the different parts of A-graphs

SYMBOLS IN C-GRAPHS

CORRESPONDENCE IN DESCRIBED INFORMATION SYSTEM

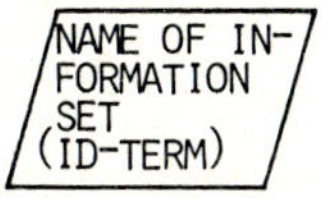

INFORMATION SET

INFORMATION SET OR INFORMATION SUBSET. IT IS GIVEN AN INFORMATION SET NAME FOLLOWED BY AN IDENTIFICATION TERM IN PARENTHESES. A TERM CAN CONSIST OF SEVERAL SUBTERMS. AN INFORMATION SUBSET IS IDENTIFIED BY THE IDENTIFICATION TERMS WITHIN PARENTHESES AND BY THE IDENTIFICATION TERMS "HIGHER" UP IN THE TREE STRUCTURE OF THE C-GRAPH.

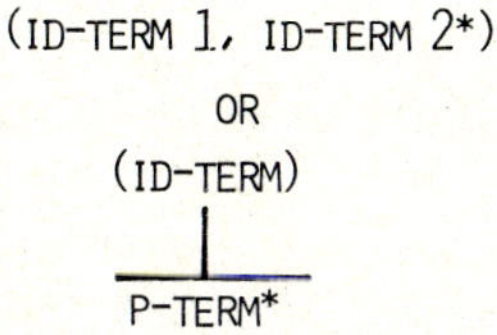

ITERATION

REPETITION OF SEVERAL MESSAGES WITH THE SAME IDENTIFICATION OR PROPERTY TERM BUT WITH DIFFERENT VALUES OF THIS TERM. THE ASTERISK (*) INDICATES THE TERM THAT HAS REPEATED OCCURENCES.

ELEMENTARY INFORMATION SET

AN INFORMATION SET WITH ONLY ONE PROPERTY TERM. THE IDENTIFICATION TERMS ARE GIVEN BY INFORMATION SETS "HIGHER" UP IN THE STRUCTURE.

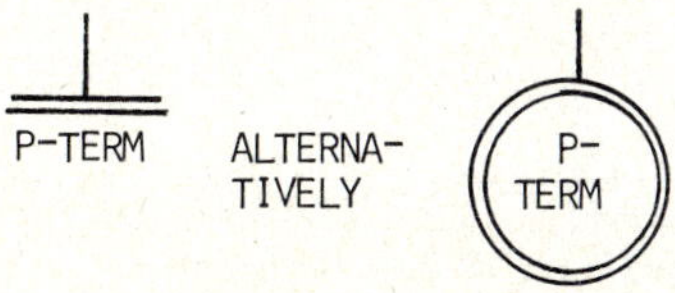

ALMOST-ELEMENTARY INFORMATION SET

AN INFORMATION SET THAT CONSISTS OF A NUMBER OF ELEMENTARY INFORMATION SETS WITH COMMON IDENTIFICATION TERMS. IDENTIFICATION TERMS ARE GIVEN BY INFORMATION SETS "HIGHER" UP IN THE STRUCTURE.

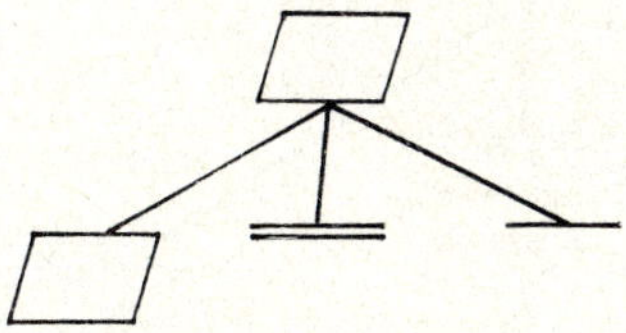

COMPONENT RELATION

DIVISION OF INFORMATION SET IN INFORMATION SUBSETS. TYPES OF COMPONENT RELATIONS (THE MESSAGE TYPES OF INFORMATION SETS AND THE TERMS OF MESSAGE TYPES) ARE INDICATED IMPLICITLY IN THE C-GRAPH.

Figure 4.6 Explanation of symbols used in C-graphs

dairco

Analyst
DOPS
Subject
Prognosis processing

C - GRAPH
Date
1978-07-15

No 2A4,41A,42A,4B
Version 3

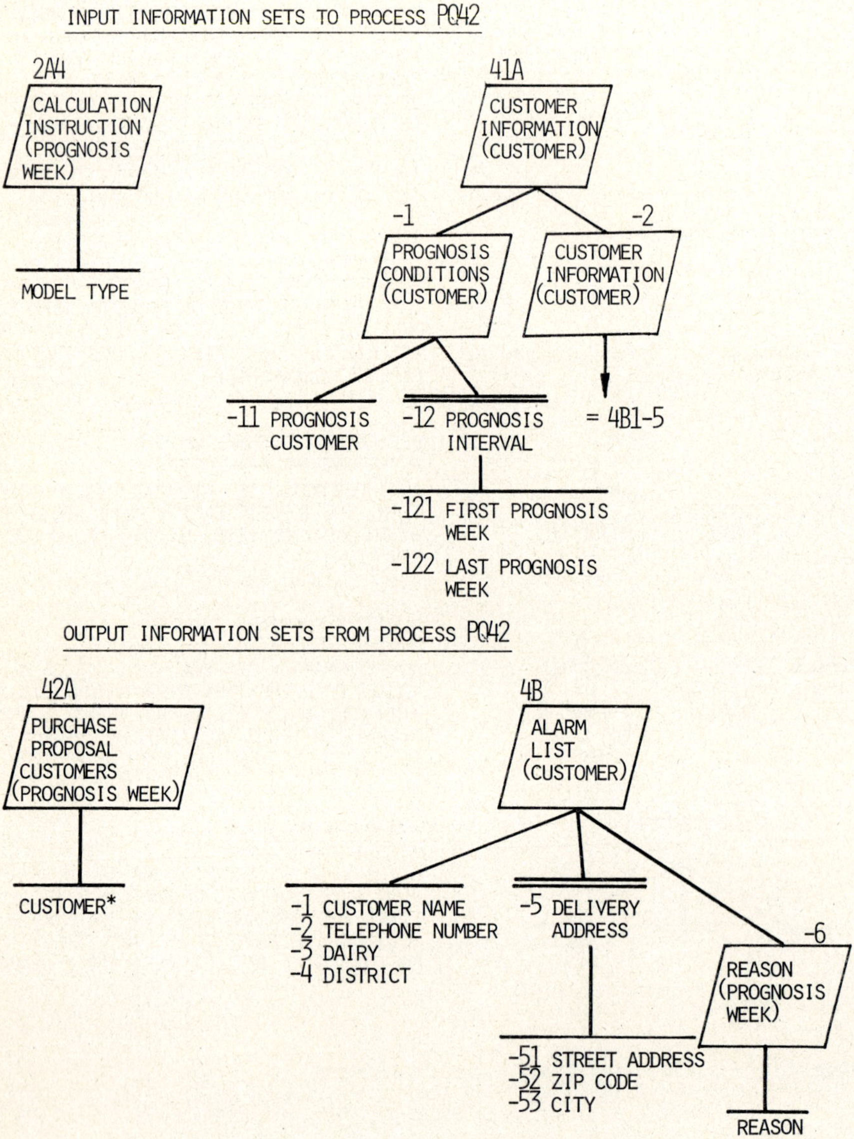

Figure 4.7 C-graphs of input and output information sets to process PQ42

dairco

Analyst DOPS	PROCESS TABLE Date 1978-07-15	No PQ42 Version 2
Subject Prognosis processing		

PREREQUISITES
FIND A MESSAGE IN 2A4. FIND MESSAGES IN 41A FOR THE <u>SAME</u> CUSTOMER.

CALCULATIONS	1	2	3
PROGNOSIS CUSTOMER IN 41A11?	N	Y	Y
FIRST PROGNOSIS WEEK (41A121) ≤ ≤ PROGNOSIS WEEK (2A4) ≤ ≤ LAST PROGNOSIS WEEK (41A122)		N	Y
4B1-5 := 41A2	X	X	
PROGNOSIS WEEK (4B6) := PROGNOSIS WEEK (2A4)	X	X	
REASON (4B6) := "NOT PROGNOSIS CUSTOMER"	X		
REASON (4B6) := "OUTSIDE PROGNOSIS INTERVAL"		X	
PROGNOSIS WEEK (42A) := PROGNOSIS WEEK (2A4)			X
CUSTOMER (42A) := CUSTOMER (41A)			X

Figure 4.8 Process table for process PQ42

- Property tables with descriptions of relevant properties in connection with the different parts of A-graphs
- Tables with needs for changes
- List of interest groups

2 Evaluated activity model of chosen change alternative with
- A-graphs
- Text pages to A-graphs
- Property tables
- Tables with needs for changes
- List of interest groups

3 Plans for chosen change approach with
- Chosen development measures
- Outline of relations between development measures
- Time schedules
- Resource plans

The results from activity studies can be summarized in two parts:

1 Activity models of information subsystems with
- A-graphs
- Text pages to A-graphs
- Property tables
- List of information systems
- Cost/benefit calculus for each information subsystem

2 Plans of information subsystems with
- Chosen information subsystems for continued development
- Outlines of relations between the development of different subsystems
- Time plans
- Resource plans

The results from information analysis are detailed information analysis models for each information subsystem analyzed. Such models consist of
- I-graphs
- C-graphs
- Text pages to I-graphs
- Term catalogues
- Process lists
- Process tables
- Property tables

The transition from change analysis to activity studies is indicated in figure 5.1. Figure 5.2 shows the transition from activity studies to information analysis.

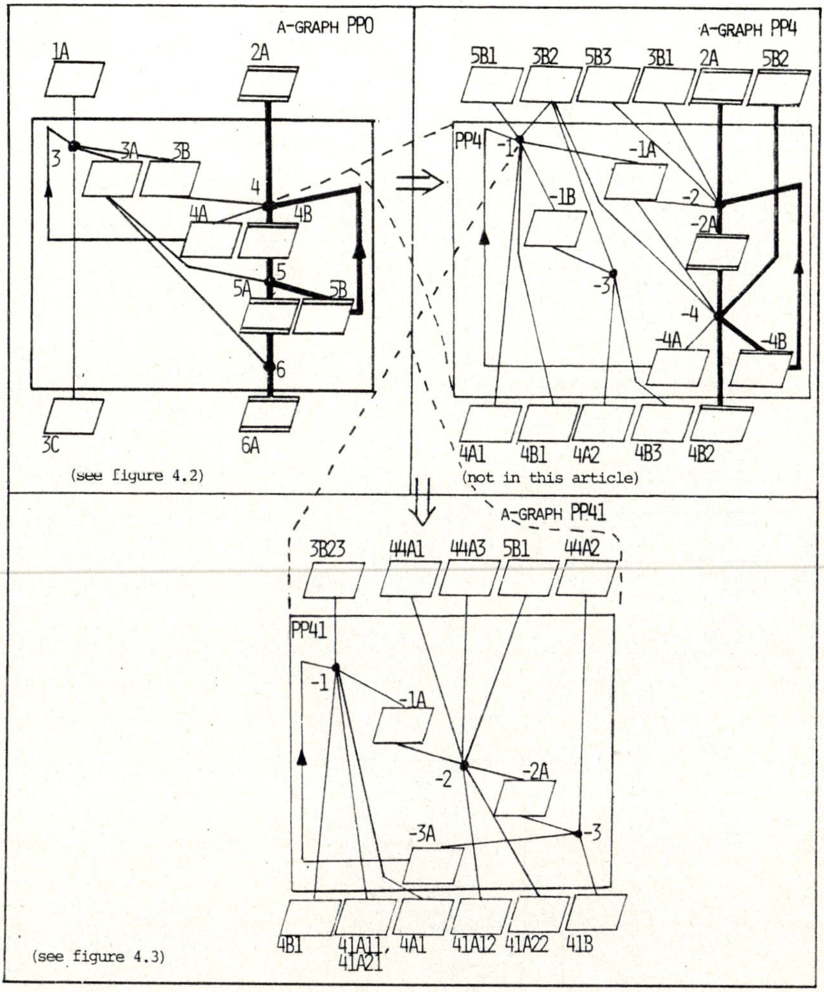

Figure 5.1 Transition from change analysis to activity studies: Preparation of detailed activity models

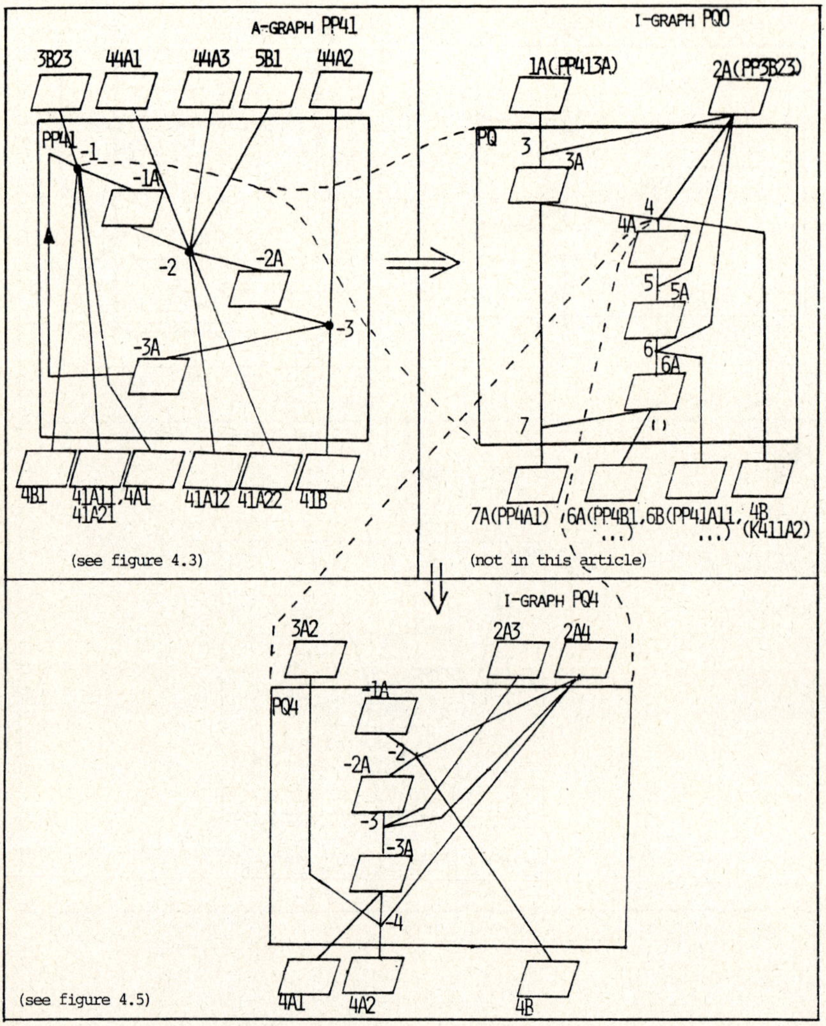

Figure 5.2 Transition from activity studies to information analysis: Preparation of detailed information analysis models

6 SOME POSSIBILITIES THAT THE ISAC APPROACH TO INFORMATION SYSTEMS SPECIFICATION OFFERS

Our *experience*[3)] shows that the following possibilities of the ISAC approach are essential in practical work with specifying information systems today:

The users can control the specification of information systems by themselves

The ISAC approach contains such structuring possibilities that the users themselves can describe and analyze their own activities, thereby understanding them better. After they have described and analyzed the activities, the next step is to describe possible future information systems that can facilitate or improve the activities. In doing this, you also give the information contents of the future information systems, thus specifying what the information systems shall do. The users have the best knowledge of the facts also in this case. No technical background or knowledge is needed in order to describe what the information systems shall do. The ISAC approach gives the users possibilities to perform this specification of information contents.

Information systems specification can be performed in a number of small, manageable and connected steps

To specify information systems is a difficult task. The subject area is comprehensive. Many complex problems have to be solved in connection with information systems specification. We think that the only way to solve complex problems is to divide them into subproblems until they become manageable. A requirement for this to work is that the solution to the subproblems gives the solution for the problem as a whole -- i.e., that the division in subproblems is coherent. The ISAC approach to information systems specification uses a partitioning in three levels. In each of these three levels there then is a number of steps that are performed, with each step using the results from the preceding steps. Together the chain of steps forms an integrated methodology for information systems specification.

It is possible to achieve good cooperation between different professional categories in the specification process

Good cooperation and good communication among human beings is an important prerequisite for successful information systems specification. The existence of a continuous chain of steps gives a clear picture of what everybody can contribute. This fosters a working collaboration between different interest and professional categories in the specification process, such as

- users
- problem oriented systems analysts

There are especially large possibilities of obtaining a good cooperation between different interest and professional groups in the specification process if in parallel with the ISAC approach one also works actively with the communication and learning process during information systems specification.

The advantages discussed here can have many important consequences for the way in which an organization specifies information systems in practice. We would therefore like to point out some of these:

Specification of information systems can become a natural part of the normal activities of the users

It often happens that many users are unfamiliar with their information systems. Some users do not understand completely what the information systems do. Others may think that the systems analysts bring up conditions and circumstances that have nothing to do with specification of information systems. With the ISAC approach, in which users can describe and analyze their own activities and specify the information systems by themselves, specification of information systems can become a natural part of the normal activities of the users and not something strange.

The problem oriented systems analyst can come to work as a catalyst

What is the role of the systems analyst in the ISAC approach? Will he or she no longer be needed when the users describe and analyze their own activities and specify the information systems by themselves? The systems analyst has in the ISAC approach the possibility to work as a catalyst -- i.e., a person who gives methods support when needed --, instead of an expert who knows best and who specifies the end results. Working as a catalyst is a very demanding task that calls for great skill, but it is also very stimulating and rewarding.

REFERENCES:

[1] Aamodt, M., Sørsveen, Å., Mennesker, kommunikasjon og konsekvenser (NORCOL, Oslo, 1977) (in Norwegian).

[2] Gunnerblad, G., Holmqvist, H., Possne, K., Organisk utbildning. Bakgrund, program, metoder (PA-rådet, Stockholm, 1974) (in Swedish).

[3] Langefors, B., Theoretical Analysis of Information Systems (Studentlitteratur, Lund, 1966, third edition 1973).

[4] Lundeberg, M., Goldkuhl, G., Nilsson, A., Information Systems Development - A First Introduction to a Systematic Approach, draft available from research group ISAC, Department of Administrative Information Processing, University of Stockholm, 106 91 Stockholm, Sweden (1978).

[5] Lundeberg, M., Goldkuhl, G., Nilsson, A., Information Systems Development - A Systematic Approach, draft available from research group ISAC, Department of Administrative Information Processing, University of Stockholm, 106 91 Stockholm, Sweden (1978).

[6] Lundeberg, M., Goldkuhl, G., Nilsson, A., A Systematic Approach to Information Systems Development - Part I: Introduction, Information Systems, Vol 4 (1979) no 1.

[7] Lundeberg, M., Goldkuhl, G., Nilsson, A., A Systematic Approach to Information Systems Development - Part II: Problem and Data Oriented Methodology, Information Systems, Vol 4 (1979), no 2.

[8] Nissen, H.-E., Andersen, E.S., Systemering - Verksamhetsbeskrivning (Studentlitteratur, Lund, 1978) (in Swedish, English translation with the title "Information Systems Development - Description of Activities" is planned).

[9] Rogers, C.R., Freedom to learn (Charles E. Merrill Publishing Co., Columbus, Ohio, 1969).

---

1) In this and later figures of development activities we describe different activities and the results from these. We also illustrate that persons participate in the activities. The activities are described with small filled circles, the results with rhomboids and persons with rhomboids with double lines on top. In such cases when the results include real objects (e.g. machines) these are also illustrated with double lines on top.

2) That some of the sets outside the frame in figure 2.4.2 only go to/from the frame and not to any special activity should be interpreted as if they go to/

from all activities inside the frame. The iteration arrows (⌐) shall in the same way be interpreted as if they go to all activities inside the frame. By having persons in this figure we once again emphasize that enterprise development including change analysis and information systems development should be considered as a communication and learning process.

3) This section deals with experiences from practical applications of the ISAC approach. They are formulated as possibilities since the achievement of these results in practical applications depends on how you use the methods. Methods must not be applied mechanically.

Formal Models and Practical Tools
for Information Systems Design
H.-J. Schneider, Editor
North-Holland Publishing Company

VERBAL MEASURES AND INSEPARABLE MULTIDIMENSIONAL UTILITY IN SYSTEM EVALUATION

Janet EFSTATHIOU*, John HAWGOOD*, Vladislav RAJKOVIČ‡

*University of Durham, Science Laboratories, Durham DH1 3LE, England

‡"Jozef Stefan" Institute, University of Ljubljana, Ljubljana, Yugoslavia

In the evaluation of complex systems, many different performance criteria must be considered. The usual ways of doing this, by assessing partial utilities and aggregating them, have some theoretical and practical problems, which are discussed in this paper. To overcome these problems, a new approach to system evaluation is proposed, which introduces some concepts from fuzzy set theory and which may be accommodated within a participative design framework. Some practical applications are described.

Most existing methods for assessing comparative benefits of alternative policies or systems suffer from a theoretical weakness - that utility is calculated as a sum of partial utilities of different attributes - and from a practical disadvantage - that numbers are an unconvincing way of describing certain important subjective performance measures (comfort, convenience, prestige, job satisfaction, ...). The concepts of fuzzy reasoning and linguistic variables introduced by L.A. Zadeh |1| have been applied by many authors to alleviate the latter problem; in this paper it is suggested that they can also help to solve the former.

Utility can be regarded as a multidimensional function of all the different performance variables which should be taken into account by the decision maker. In most real cases, the variable axes are not orthogonal but, more fundamentally, the change in utility corresponding to a given change in any variable depends on the values of all the others at the working point, even if they can be held constant during the change being measured.

Human beings in ordinary life are quite accustomed to this and cope with it implicitly as a matter of course; difficulties arise only when the decision making process is to be made explicit and replicable. Attempts to use numerical aids to decision making tend either to relegate the "intangibles" to a secondary role outside the formal process, or to include them and accept aggregation methods which are known to apply only to small parameter increments.

The approach to participative system design developed by Mumford, Land and Hawgood |2| is based on the principle that people <u>should</u> design their own work systems and the empirical observation that they <u>can</u>. Because people already operating a system know its human aspects (often the real problem) better than any outside analyst, and because they will have to work any system devised as a solution, the participative approach has many potential advantages. But to participate effectively in system design people need tools - for system description, diagnosis, design, evaluation and implementation. The evaluation tool described by Mumford, Land and Hawgood |2| suffers from the two weaknesses mentioned above. In this paper it is suggested that this evaluation tool can be made both theoretically sounder and practically more acceptable in participative system design, by introducing verbal measures for the individual goals and a visual aid to help participants estimate total utility direct without any recourse to partial utilities of the separate goals. The heuristic utility estimation may then be coded as a "fuzzy algorithm".

1. Weaknesses of partial utilities

The formal theory of numerical utility has existed since 1944 with the publication of von Neumann & Morgenstern's axioms of rational behaviour. The rules for combining utilities to produce an overall utility value have been defined by Fishburn |3|. However, man is notoriously irrational and there has always been debate on this topic. Experimental psychology has shown that in judgemental tasks, behaviour may be fairly well predicted by addition of "utilities", but workers have shown that other rules such as conjunctive, disjunctive and lexicographic can also be used to model human behaviour. The judges insisted that they made use of complex interactions between the decision attributes, but the psychologists had little success when they added higher-order terms to their prediction equations.

To take account of these alleged higher-order interactions, decision consultants |4| also suggested the practical use of more exotic combination rules, but these too have no firm theoretical basis.

The foundation of any system of addition of partial utilities is that there must be strict independence of the utilities of different attributes. But we all know that this is rarely true, and the "higher-order interactions" which people told the psychologists they use are an example. It is important here to distinguish carefully between independence of the utility of attributes and the constraints of real life. For example, when choosing a car we may value its comfort and its prestige separately, but in practice it will usually be true that an increase in comfort implies an increase in prestige. In this case the utilities may be independent but because of the real world connection between comfort, prestige and cost, some combinations of comfort and prestige will not exist, e.g. high comfort and low prestige.

One source of the difficulties of traditional methods occurs when dealing with the "edges" of the decision space. When a particular attribute assumes high or low values, relative to the status quo, its importance may alter drastically. An attribute which might appear to be of minor importance now may become crucially important in deciding the success or failure of a project if its level of performance is changed much from the existing values. Similarly, little effort may be required to make considerable progress towards fulfilling a goal and reducing its importance, although it is seen as crucial now. So we could say that such models fail when attempting to model the entire decision space and are only suitable for small changes around the existing condition. In other words, by assuming that the weight or relative importance of each goal is constant no matter what, we will run into difficulties.

For example, we were asking a group of workers to evaluate the importance of a goal which was stated as "improving job satisfaction". To our surprise, they each ranked this goal well down the list, placing more altruistic goals above it in importance. When questioned about this, they replied that their job satisfaction was already high and did not need improvement. One wonders how much decrease in job satisfaction would have been tolerated before trouble would break out.

This example illustrates two points. Firstly, that weights are not constant over the whole decision space; changes do occur, particularly at high or low values of the attribute, i.e. the importance of an attribute depends on how much of it you have. Secondly, people tend to weight a goal according to their present environment. This is only to be expected, but one must beware when extrapolating to the extreme values.

We need to know how important different attributes are at their normal values, but we must also find out about interaction between goals at different levels.

We are really assuming two things when the weights are kept constant, although stating one implies the other. The first assumption has already been discussed, i.e. that the relative importance of the attributes does not change. The second assumption is that the trade-off rates between goals are constant too. This means that we are willing to exchange x units of one attribute for y units of another, regardless of the amounts of either attribute which we already possess. Again, we can verify by introspection or referring to the previous example of the prestige and comfort of a car that this will not always be so. Together, the contradiction of these two assumptions means that not only does the importance of any particular goal depend upon its level of achievement, it will depend upon the levels of all the other goals as well! The classic pattern of weighting and scoring of goals was difficult to cope with, so how are we to cope with a problem when the relative importance of the goals are interconnected in all manner of subtle non-linear ways?

2. Fuzzy description of subjective attributes

Natural language, by definition, is the closest parallel to the way our minds really work. Therefore a description in everyday simple language of what we think, for example, about utility of a given alternative comes most easily to us. If we want to express this in numbers there are at least two problems. Firstly, we have to translate our natural language to an artificial language of numbers. In participative decision making, this means that some people have to learn a new language of numbers. This is a waste of time and it is also difficult to express our meaning in a language we do not know well. Secondly, many concepts in our minds are too complex to be expressed by simple numerical values. Therefore if our natural language is used, there is no need to learn a new language (of numbers) and information is probably more realistically expressed.

But in practice how can everyday words be used instead of numbers? The simplest idea is to replace numbers with words directly, for example, if the utility scale is from 0 to 1, one can say "very high utility" is equal to 1, high utility is equal to 0.9, etc. (In practice these would in fact be numerical regions, rather than points, denoted by names.) In this simplified approach we can at least express transitions between one and another value. The theory of fuzzy sets, in particular that of linguistic variables, gives a better solution |1|.

Let us remain with the linguistic variable "utility". The set of its values is, for example:

(very high,high,medium high,...,acceptable,...)

This set of values can be finite or infinite and is usually called the "term set". We can if we wish establish meaningful correspondence between this term set and a set of numerical values from the interval [0,1] which is the base variable set of utility in our case. In terms of natural language, the meaning of words "very high", "high", etc. has to be defined. In terms of fuzzy sets, every linguistic value (element of the term set) is interpreted as a label of a fuzzy set, which represents a fuzzy restriction on the values [0,1] of the base variable set. A fuzzy restriction of meaning is characterised by a compatibility function denoting, for any value from the base variable set, a grade of membership of the linguistic value in hand. The grade of membership is a value in [0,1]. For example, the compatibility function of "high" utility grades of membership of elements of the base variable set could be the function presented below:

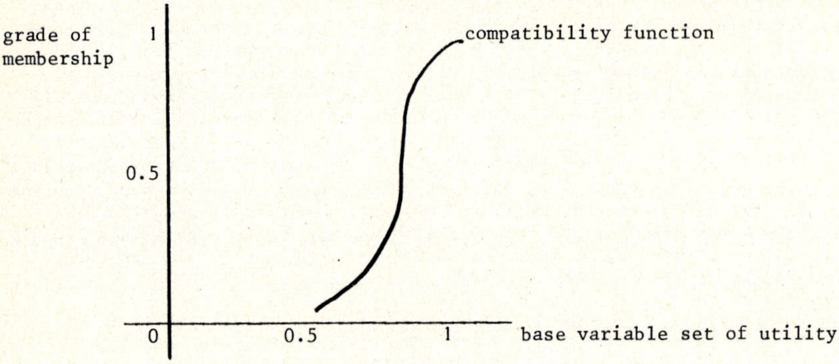

Figure 1

So a vocabulary presenting a common opinion of the meaning of linguistic values can be defined. After that we have a natural description tool and further calculations are possible on the base of fuzzy sets.

Knowledge about utility which is subjectively defined on performance space has been already taken as an example, when linguistic variables were introduced. Alternatives are evaluated and their values can also be expressed linguistically; "good but not very good" or in comparison "alternative A is not very much better than B", or "the best alternative C is much better than A". |5|

So people can communicate in the decision making process with predefined words. Words are denoted by fuzzy sets, which means that any calculations needed can be made using properties of fuzzy sets. Such calculations may not be numerical - precise fuzzy algorithms can be defined in words.

There are several problems connected with the practical use of fuzzy concepts. One is the need for common vocabulary, which is a problem also in everyday communication. In our proposal there is enough room for subjective opinion, but everyone has to speak reasonably similar language. Therefore at the beginning of the process the group we are working with has to define a common vocabulary, so that everyone means approximately the same thing by "high" utility or "small" size. This does not prevent subjective judgment of utility which everyone can still make.

We use verbal measures when necessary but not for their own sake. If people think that the classical numerical description is better, some variables can be described in numbers, as is usually the case with the variable "price". In our process a fruitful combination of numerical and linguistic variables is possible.

It is useful to have in mind that behind linguistic values there can be distributions of other values - for example, numbers - and that "serious" calculation is possible both with words and with numbers. In fact there is more information in words than in single numbers. Linguistic variables are less precise but they give a chance to replace classical precision (which does not work well in humanistic systems) with significance, clarity and simplicity.

Fuzzy concepts do not solve problems by themselves. Fuzzy set theory can be a useful tool in human decision making, especially in a participative context, but the key problem is in the implementation of the whole process in a way meaningful in real life.

3. Participative system design

The BASYC approach to benefit assessment for system change was one of the techniques developed for use by participative design teams by Mumford, Land and Hawgood |2|. As described in the paper just cited, the BASYC approach is subject to the criticisms made above - that benefits are estimated by adding partial utilities. Briefly, the BASYC approach was for a design team to identify detailed measurable system goals relevant to the interests of different groups, assign percentage weights according to the relative importance of the goals, define alternative system changes and score these on a 21-point numerical scale according to their likely impact on each goal. The sums for each interest group of the products of the weights and scores for all goals represented comparative utilities for the alternative strategies.

We are now suggesting that the process can be improved by replacing the numerical values which were previously used by verbal weights and measures and defining a "fuzzy algorithm" to derive a verbal utility direct from measures (without performing any scoring operation for the individual goals). Numerical and verbal measures can be mixed, each being used where most appropriate, as stated above.

The process we now recommend for participative system design incorporates the use of verbal measures, and also two key features of the systems approach devised by Checkland |6| and his collaborators at Lancaster. These two features are, first, a very clear distinction between the real world of the problem and the "concept world" where only the essentials of the system are modelled, and, second, a set of formal rules for "root definitions" of relevant systems and subsystems. The process as a whole follows the flow chart (Figure 2): the top half is mainly diagnosis and analysis, while the bottom half is design and assessment. Our main concern in this paper is with system evaluation, but a short description of the total process will next be given to help set it in context.

When a "problem area" is identified, whether this concerns long-range strategy, information system design or departmental procedures, we suggest that two teams should study it - a design team (mainly consisting of the people who will carry out the strategy, use the system or operate the procedures) and a steering group of representatives of other interests (managers of other departments, Trade Union officials, local Councillors, officers of user groups, ...) to define political and economic constraints and assure interdepartmental cooperation. It is useful - almost essential - to include in the design team someone with experience of the approach. If nobody in the relevant department has such experience, a professional system analyst may need to be called in - but as a trainer rather than as a practitioner.

Description of the overall situation is done both from the social (human) and from the organisational (technical) points of view - any computer hardware or software that may be involved being considered only as subsystems of the total "human activity system". Particular attention is paid to future contingency analysis of relevant economic, commercial or technological trends, of changing organisational aims and of the effects of uncertain predictions of machine performance or user behaviour.

Crossing the boundary into the "concept world" means making a conscious effort to see the broad picture from different points of view. Careful formulation of "root definitions" expressing the essential function of the overall system leads on to definition of goals relevant to different people and ways of estimating progress towards them. In some fields there are standard models to help - such as Enid Mumford's method for measuring job satisfaction |2|, but for most goals the design team will have to define appropriate "vocabularies" of words and/or numbers.

PARTICIPATIVE SYSTEM DESIGN

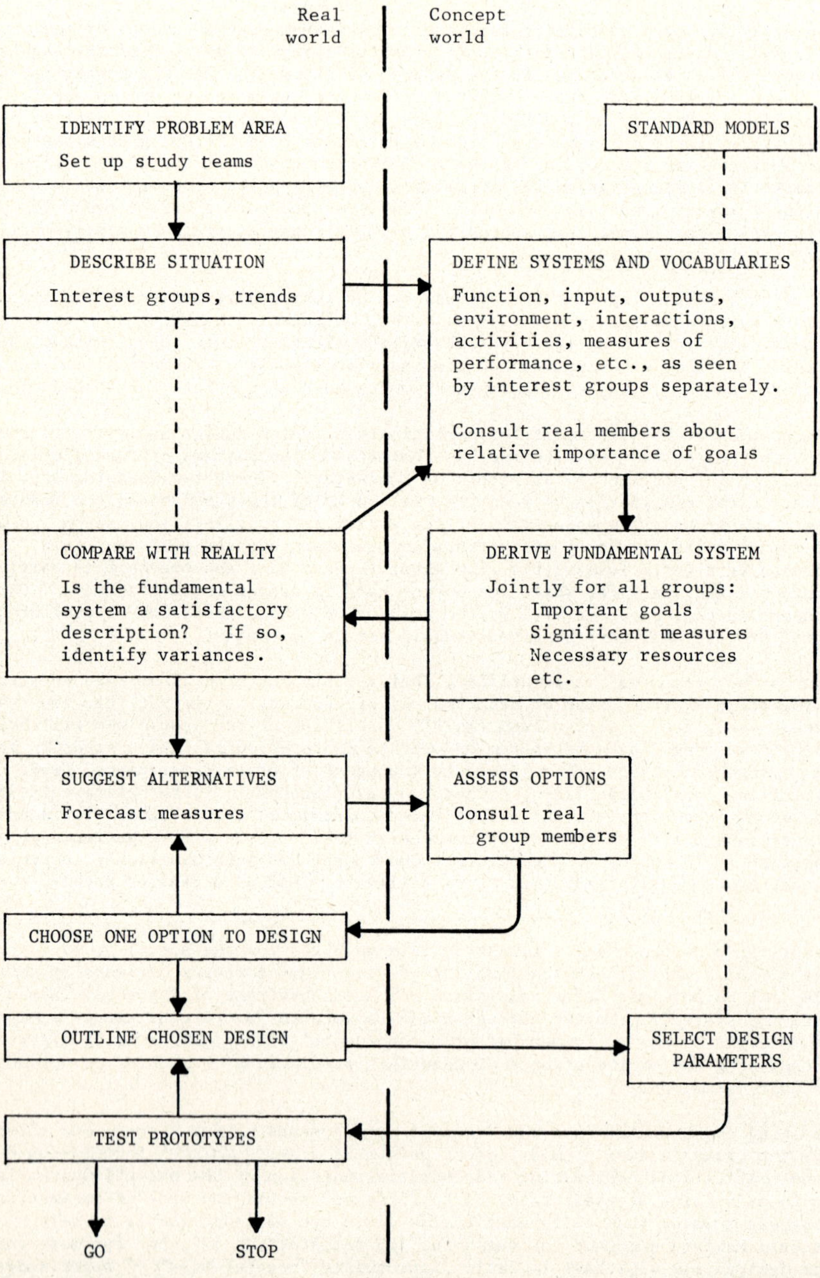

Figure 2

Real members of interest groups must be consulted about the relative importance of different goals to them: we have found verbal measurement using the scale "extremely important, very important, important, desirable, unimportant" much more acceptable than the percentage weights used before - but there is a need to warn people against a certain tendency to inflation whereby too many goals may get labelled "extremely important". The cautionary remark in Section 1 about weights not being constant also applies here - the present situation influences people's opinion unduly unless they are warned about the difference between weights for "improving" and "maintaining". While consulting representatives about priorities, the design team should also be checking that the "fundamental system" emerging satisfies them as a representation of the essentials of what the real-world situation should be. If not, further analysis and redefinition is required.

When a satisfactory concept of the fundamentals of the system has been achieved this represents a design aim. As a first step to a real-world solution, detailed diagnosis is needed of where current reality, as modified by identified trends, will fall short of this design aim. A very wide spread of possible alternative policies or systems is next sought, with a rough estimation of their likely effects on the objective and subjective measures. These alternatives need not - should not - all be obviously feasible ones at this stage, as it is necessary to explore the "edges of decision space", as mentioned in Section 1.

The box "assess options" in Figure 2 is a rough initial mapping of the multidimensional utility function, done once again in consultation with real members of the interest groups. They should be asked to rank the alternative policies as now described in terms of their effects on priority goals, and to give verbal estimates of the utility differences, such as "A is a little better than B, which is much better than C". A visual aid to this process is described in Section 5. Practical possibilities soon emerge - also sometimes conflicts between groups' interests, which rule out what had initially seemed an obvious solution.

The rest of Figure 2 is just a skeleton of the normal process of design and prototype testing of the system chosen as promising for implementation. The box "select design parameters" may involve the discussion of predicted goal measures with representatives of interest groups in the light of their reactions to pilot trials. For short-range adjustments of the policy, near the point in the multidimensional performance space chosen from the initial rough mapping, the additive and linear approximations of conventional utility analysis are usually acceptable.

4. Theoretical points

Previous techniques involving analysis of the multi-attribute utility of the alternatives have followed a two-stage process. The first stage consists of obtaining a separate utility for each attribute, and, in the second stage, these are combined to give an overall, aggregate utility. We propose |7| that these two stages should be collapsed together and treated as one process, which is the direct determination of the overall utility function, which we call Φ.

The determination of the utility function Φ requires an algorithm or decision rule for the coordination of different attributes, and for interpolation between different points.

There are many known rules to describe the process of decision-making, such as lexicographic, conjunctive, disjunctive, linear combination, etc. Formal decision-making techniques generally take one of these rules and apply it over the whole decision space, so over the whole range of the performance variables.

We would argue that it is wrong to take an arbitrary rule and apply it over the whole space, for two reasons. Firstly, we do not know that the preselected rule is correct or relevant to the decision-maker at hand, and secondly, even if a rule can be shown to be correct over one region of the decision space, we must be careful to check with the decision-maker that it remains applicable over the whole space. In other words, instead of adopting a rule as a general description of utility we should choose a rule for each particular case, and only by consultation with and observation of the decision-maker himself. We believe it is important to remember that each decision problem, with the people who comprise its decision-makers and interest groups, is unique and that it is an easy mistake to over-generalise.

Clearly, without an interpolation rule, it may become difficult fully to describe Φ, but once the decision-maker has made some preliminary statements, we can use fuzzy logic to test for their consistency. For example, using the user-chosen combination rules we can interpolate between points and check whether the utility at a particular point is independent of the pairs of points between which the interpolation is performed (see Figure 3).

Calculation of utility of point X under interpolation between utilities of pairs of points (A,C) and (B,D)

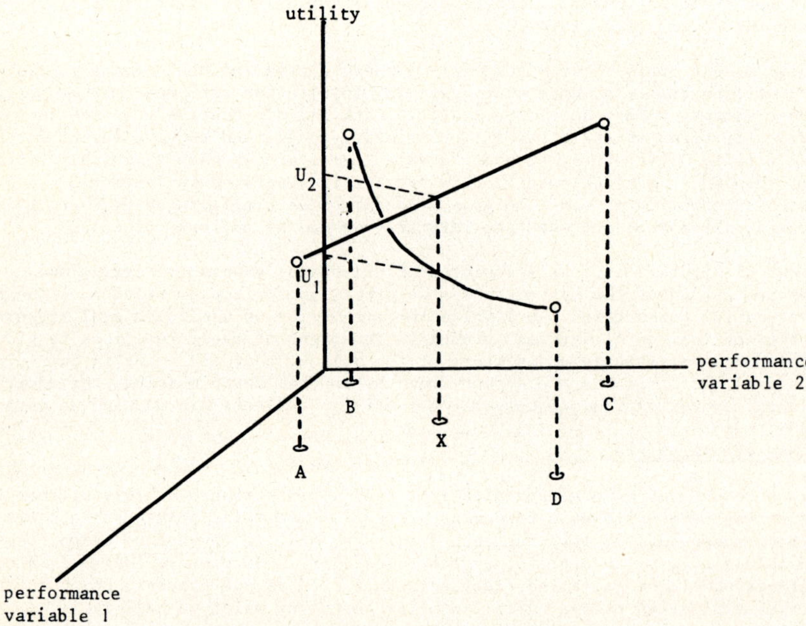

Figure 3

Any utility difference found may be negligible and due only to the vagueness inherent in such statements, or it may be due to a genuine oversight, which can be pointed out to the decision-maker and revised if necessary.

As a further check, we can trace through Φ and see how the overall utility changes as a function of our variable when all the others are held constant, to see what insight this provides on the decision-maker's statements.

Because we are working with fuzzy logic and as human decision-making is an imprecise process, a certain amount of inexactness will always be apparent.

This is only natural and can be tolerated. At first, wild disparity between utility assessments for the same point will have to be tracked down and presented to the decision-maker. This may indicate an incorrect statement of utility elsewhere, or that a performance variable which caused this utility difference has been omitted from the decision space. Either way, revision of the original statements will probably be necessary. However, after a certain amount of refinement, the decision-maker cannot be any more precise, and whatever inconsistencies are left will have to remain, as a description of how the decisions seem really to be made.

Another source of inconsistency is derived from intransitivity. Most other axioms of utility theory require some sort of transitivity of preference, one characteristic of the decision-maker as "rational man". Because such assumptions are not built into the determination of Φ, we can use transitivity to test how rational the decision-maker actually is. For example, we can show where loops are set up, defying transitivity, e.g.

$$d_1 > d_2 \text{ and } d_2 > d_3$$

$$\text{but } d_3 > d_1$$

where $>$ means "is preferred to" and d_i represents alternative i

or slightly differently,

$$d_1 \approx d_2 \text{ and } d_2 \approx d_3,\ d_3 \approx d_4 \ \ldots\ d_{n-1} \approx d_n$$

$$\text{but } d_1 > d_n \text{ when } n \geq 3$$

where $\approx$ is "indifferent to"

In the first case, such intransitivity suggests a mistake somewhere, and closer investigation may correct it. The decision-maker may realise his assessment of an alternative along its performance variable has been wrong, he may have omitted a relevant performance variable from his list or may realise the existence of a further decision rule. When detected, intransitivity can provide useful insights on the decision-maker's behaviour, which, one would hope, would resolve the inconsistency. The second case is less likely to require revision, and indicates the ever-present imprecision of human reasoning.

The determination of Φ requires the decision-maker to think carefully about how he makes his decisions. He must set down all the performance variables which influence him, and by how much at various levels, in combination with all the others. But instead of being forced to give precise numerical estimates of their importance and struggle with trade-off graphs, he can state how he feels as accurately as he can, in natural language. It is not necessary to assume that the decision-maker is a "rational man", but this hypothesis can be tested and the decision-maker shown where his behaviour appears to be intransitive or inconsistent, whereupon he may revise earlier statements, recall further performance variables, or leave the statements as they are.

Describing the alternatives and obtaining their utilities is a step of the decision-making process which is closely related to the determination of the utility function, and may become indistinguishable. As we try to determine Φ it may be necessary to postulate policies to achieve some points of the decision space, which would otherwise appear as infeasible to the decision-maker. In his statements about the utility of that point, the decision-maker will also be commenting indirectly on the policy. To make sure that this statement is reasonable, we would need to compare with those for neighbouring points, or postulate an alternative policy for the same point and test if the utility remains the same. If it differs, the reason why can again be revealing. In the same way as we used transitivity as a check on decision behaviour, we could use a rule such as "The utility of a point is independent of the policy used to take you there".

5. Practical applications

The authors are involved in several practical applications, including the following:

(a) One of us (VR) has been applying this approach to select computer hardware suitable for secondary schools. The work was partially supported by an interactive computer program, helping the construction of group utility knowledge. The decision process was conducted according to the following steps:

1) Identification of interest groups:

teachers, students, computer experts.

2) Identification of alternatives:

a) using computer in nearest existing computing centre (present situation),

b) a classroom with programmable calculators at school,

c) a microcomputer at school,

d) one terminal at each school connected to (university) computing centre,

e) a classroom with terminals connected to a minicomputer at each school,

f) classroom like (e) but for several schools together.

3) Definition of decision space:

up to 7 performance variables were identified:

a) usefulness for individual student problem solving - programming (PS),

b) usefulness for computer assisted learning (CAL),

c) usefulness for computer managed learning (CML),

d) usefulness for standard administration (ADMINIST),

e) ease of maintenance of equipment (MAINT),

f) convenience of location of equipment (LOCAT), and

g) price.

In discussion with groups, verbal measures for performance variables were set up. All the groups used the same vocabulary, but the number of relevant performance variables were different. For example, the students thought that only 4 variables were relevant to them:

DECISION SPACE LIST

PS=(v good,good,acc,poor)

CAL=(v good,good,acc,poor)

CML=(good,acc,poor,none)

LOCAT=(v conv,conv,l conv)

UTILITY=(ex,v good,good,r good,acc,cond acc,not acc)

4) Estimation of importance of performance variables:

every group made its own estimates of the importance of the variables.

5) Making logical statements about utility:

every group made logical statements about utility regarding different values of performance variables. For example, students said that:

i) utility is excellent (ex) only if all performance variables have maximum value.

ii) utility is acceptable (acc) if PS and CAL are at least "acc".

iii) utility is "not acc" if PS and CAL are "poor".

6) Utility knowledge tabulation

On the base of such logical statements the utility table presenting knowledge about utilities was constructed. At the beginning knowledge was simply entered in the table which was displayed interactively on a VDU. The students' initial table was:

PS	*CAL*	*CML*	*MAINT*	*LOCAT*	*PRICE*	*UTILITY*
v good	*v good*	*good*	*none*	*v conv*	*low*	*ex*
v good	*v good*	*acc*	*min*	*v conv*	*med*	*v good*
good	*good*	*poor*	*min*	*conv*	*med*	*good*
acc	*acc*	*poor*	*acc*	*conv*	*high*	*acc*
acc	*acc*	*poor*	*demand*	*l conv*	*high*	*cond acc*

To refine the table, different features of the program can be used. For example, different combinations of values of performance variables are generated and the decision-maker states the corresponding utilities; the decision-maker asks for utility of a given combination (program calculates the utility from existing knowledge); points (combinations) having equal utilities can be generated and displayed for the decision-maker. In this way a different table of utility knowledge was constructed for every group.

7) Evaluation of alternatives:

every alternative was measured for all performance variables and entered (to the computer) as n-tuple of linguistic values. The results were different utilities for each group. These utilities were discussed later in a joint meeting for making a joint collective decision.

The main good point was that the decision-making results and utility tables were displayed simply, giving a background for decisions which could be easily understood. The result was not only a selection of the best alternative, (e), but also a fruitful discussion on the relative utilities leading to further experiments with microcomputers, (c), and terminals, (d). It was also obvious why the existing situation is difficult. So, reasonable short and long term policies were suggested.

Following the described technique, we can state that the decision-making process (DMP) provides other results besides the selection of the best alternative. Such a DMP is a learning process, in which critical points can be identified and discussed. The technique documents the DMP in a simple way, which is especially useful in the implementation phase where some changes of characteristics of alternatives can happen.

(b) A group of secretaries in the management services division of a large chemical firm are engaged (with Enid Mumford's advice) in designing a word-processing system for their own use. One of us (JE) helped them to apply our approach to set objectives and measure their relative importance verbally. It was found that most of their goals were highly subjective (e.g. "maintaining trust", "increased knowledge", "more responsibility"). They were asked to rank order their list of goals in two ways, according to the importance of improving on the present level and according to the importance of preventing deterioration from the present level. Using verbal scales of importance, they were readily able to distinguish between weights for "improve" and "maintain".

(c) Two groups of public librarians in England and four in the USA are using this approach for planning what library and information services will best serve their communities in the next few years. A "visual aid" has been designed by one of us (JH) and used to represent verbal measures and their combination as multi-attribute utilities. The diagram (Figure 4) is essentially a rectangular plot of predicted performance of an alternative policy for a particular goal against importance of that goal to a particular group. The horizontal axis can be labelled "unimportant", "desirable", "important", "very important", "extremely important", working from left to right, while the vertical scale is different for each goal according to the appropriate attribute - in each case the words or numbers used at the bottom represent poor performance and those at the top represent very good performance. The plots of two different groups, when two alternative policies O and ● are being assessed for goals a,b,c,d, might be like this:

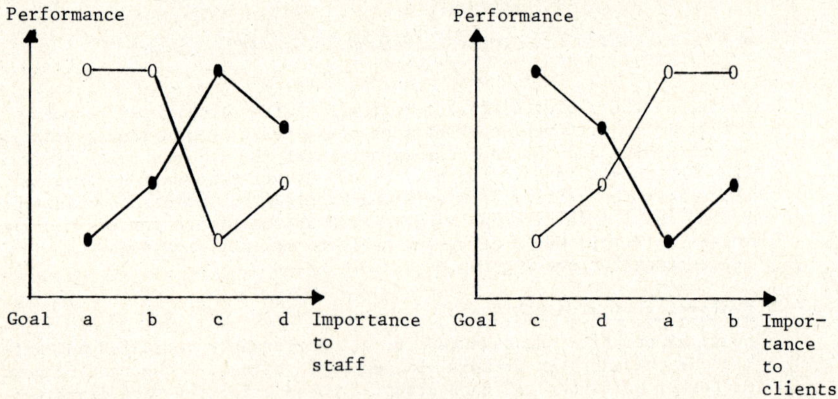

Figure 4

Relative acceptabilities of alternative policies by each group can usually be "seen at a glance" and depicted using a scale labelled "very much more acceptable ..... very much less acceptable". In Figure 4, Policy ● would clearly be better for staff and Policy O for clients.

A detailed proforma based on Figure 4 is being used successfully to help the public librarians; the main result so far has been that they realised their policies were not well enough defined. They have found little difficulty in weighting the goals or estimating relative multi-attribute utilities from the diagram - the problem has been more in agreeing on performance measures for the individual goals.

The development of decision aids, such as that described in this paper, reflects a change in the role and attitude of decision consultants. The consultant used to be called in from outside, given some facts and left to carry out his computer simulations and analyses until he could present management with a firm recommendation. In practice, this arrangement has a number of difficulties. The consultant is not familiar with the informal working of the organisation, and the human problems involved. He comes along with his own prejudices and value system, which will inevitably influence his recommendation.

With participative decision aids, the consultant does not have any role in making or even recommending the decision, but guides the decision-makers and their advisers on how to organise their thoughts so as to take the decision better themselves. By developing techniques which are simple and natural to use, the consultants can help the decision-makers to understand their own reasoning process a little better. The consultant assumes a passive role and is no longer active in making recommendations about decisions on the organisation's behalf.

As a general conclusion, we feel the method is very promising for practical use. Codifying people's heuristics into useful fuzzy algorithms is the next step that must be taken if theory and practice are to become truly complementary.

References

1 ZADEH, L.A. "The concept of a linguistic variable and its application to approximate reasoning - I, II, III", Information Sciences, 8, 1975.

2 MUMFORD, E., LAND, F. and HAWGOOD, J. "A participative approach to the design of computer systems", Impact of Science on Society, Vol.28, No.3, UNESCO, 1978.

3 FISHBURN, P.C. Utility Theory for Decision Making, John Wiley & Sons, New York, 1970.

4 DUJMOVIČ, J.J. "Preference scoring method for decision making: survey classification and annotated bibliography", Informatica 1977, Vol.2, pp.26-34.

5 BAAS, S.M. and KWAKERNAAK, H. "Rating and ranking of multiple-aspect alternatives using fuzzy sets", Automatica, 13, 1977.

6 CHECKLAND, P. "Towards a systems-based methodology for real world problem solving", J.Syst.Eng., Vol.3, No.2, Winter 1972.

7 EFSTATHIOU, J. and RAJKOVIČ, V. "Multi-attribute decision making using a fuzzy heuristic approach", to appear in IEEE Trans. on Systems, Man and Cybernetics, Vol. SCM-9, June 1979.

Formal Models and Practical Tools for Information Systems Design
H.-J. Schneider, Editor
North-Holland Publishing Company

THE ROLE OF THE TRIGGER IN SYSTEMATICS

Kit GRINDLEY

London School of Economics, London, England

In 1966, SYSTEMATICS (Grindley, 1966) was proposed as a language for describing information systems. This paper is in two parts. Part I reviews the basic principles in SYSTEMATICS theory which have emerged since that time. Part II illustrates some of the SYSTEMATICS' techniques which are now being employed and which make use of that theory.

The main purpose of the paper is to show that the identification of a particular type of input, called a Trigger, allows us to construct a special case of Precedence Analysis (Langefors, 1966) and that the basic process of systems requirements analysis and specification can be reduced to this special case, that of 'chaining outputs back to their triggers'.

PART I - A THEORY FOR AN INFORMATION ALGEBRA

A system consists of components and relationships. In order to build a model of a system we need to be able to identify and describe its components and to identify and describe their relationships. In this statement of SYSTEMATICS theory we look first at the components of information systems and then at their relationships.

1. Components

There is only one type of basic component in an information system. It is called an item.

Items	The smallest collection of signals which together play a separate part in the system

Consider the item Customer Address, e.g. 117 Rue St Christophe, Paris, France. The first thing to note that it is made up of individual digits and letters of the alphabet. These in turn may consist of 'bits' when stored in a computer. If we pursue this argument, it is doubtful if we could ever resolve what is the basic element of information. Fortunately it does not matter. For our purpose, if this collection of signals is always treated in one lump, we can consider the collection as a whole as being a basic component in the information system.

We further notice that the definition of any particular item is quite arbitrary. Customer Address consists of :

Number, Street, Town, Country.

If Customer Address is always used as a whole in the system, then the analyst defines it as an item. Later he may wish Town to play a part on its own. For example, Despatch Charges may vary according to Town. In this case the analyst defines Town as an item in its own right.

2. Relationships

There are five basic types of relationship between the items in an information system. They are :

Role

Association

Condition

Derivation

Trigger

Role

We have noticed that various collections of signals always play their part together in an information system. These collections are called Items. We now notice that certain Items always play the same part. We group these Items into sets called Data sets.

A Data set is a collection of all items which play the same part in the system.

We name each of these data sets, e.g.

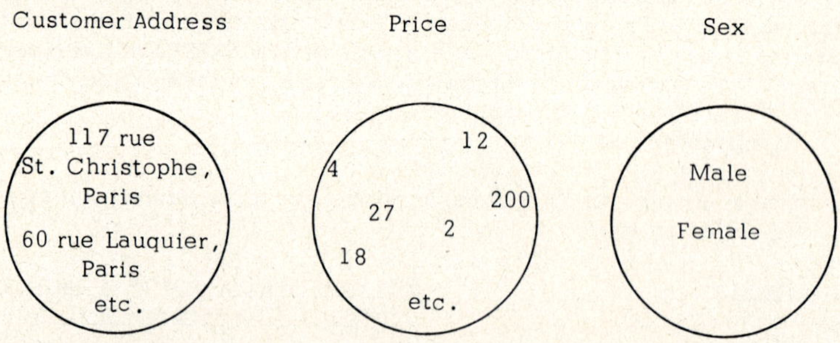

Fig. 1

Fig. 1 shows three data sets, Customer Address, Price and Sex. In the set Customer Address are all the items which play the role of Customer Address, in the set Price all the prices, etc.

Association

Take an item from the set Price, for example 18. On its own this is Data and is useless. It is when we know its association with items from other Data sets that it becomes useful; for example when we know that Price 18 is associated with Product Number 1004. Items from different Data sets which are associated are called Information (Price 18 is Data, Product No. 1004 is Data but 'the Price of Product 1004 is 18' is Information). We group associated items into a different type of set called an Information set.

An Information set is a collection of associated items.

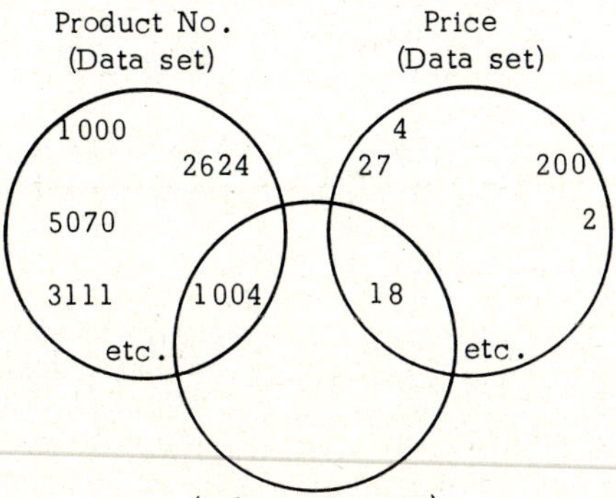

Fig. 2

Fig. 2 shows an Information set containing the associated items Product Number 1004 and Price 18, and illustrates the intersection of Information sets and Data sets. We now notice that there are two types of Information sets.

Given Information sets.

An Information set may be given to the system.

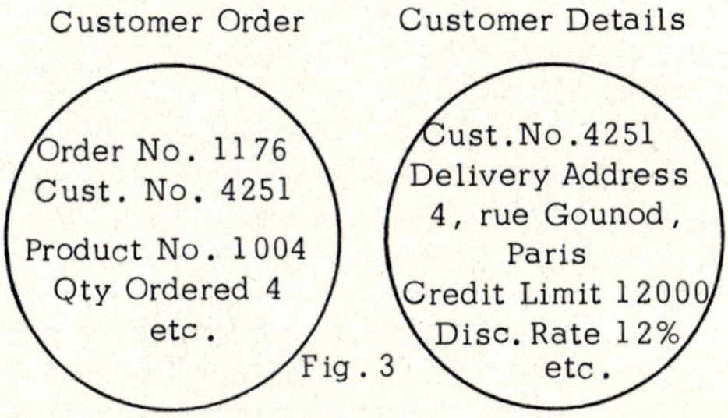

Fig. 3

In Fig. 3 we show two Information sets. The first is an example of a Customer Order, which is given to the system each time a customer places an order. The second is an example of Customer Details which is given to the system each time the company accepts a new Customer. The key point is that in each case the system is told that the items in each set are associated.

Derived Information sets.

An Information set can be derived by the system. This is done by <u>joining</u> two or more given Information sets on their common item.

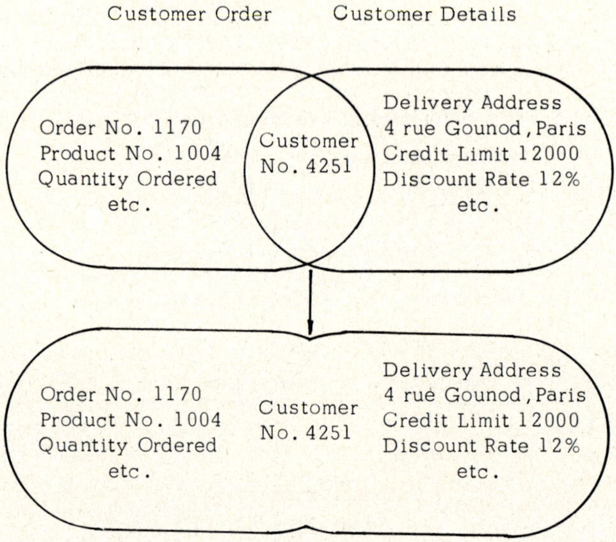

Fig. 4

Figure 4 shows the Information set Customer Order joined to the Information set Customer Details on the item they have in common, i.e. Customer Number 4251. The system thus derives a new Information set. It was given the information that Customer No. 4251 ordered four of Product No. 1004, and that Customer Number 4251's Delivery Address is 4 rue Gounod, Paris. It derives the information that four of Product No. 1004 are to be delivered to 4 rue Gounod, Paris.

<u>Conditions</u>

Conditions are rules given to the system for deriving Information sets. They are no more than a special case of given Information sets but are treated separately because they are so common.

	Rule 1	Rule 2	Rule 3
Sex	Male	Male	Female
Age	≥ 21	< 21	-
Sports Fund	15	10	5

Fig. 5

Figure 5 provides the rules governing Sports Fund Contribution in a decision table. We can consider each column to be a given Information set. We may then join these sets to other given Information sets.

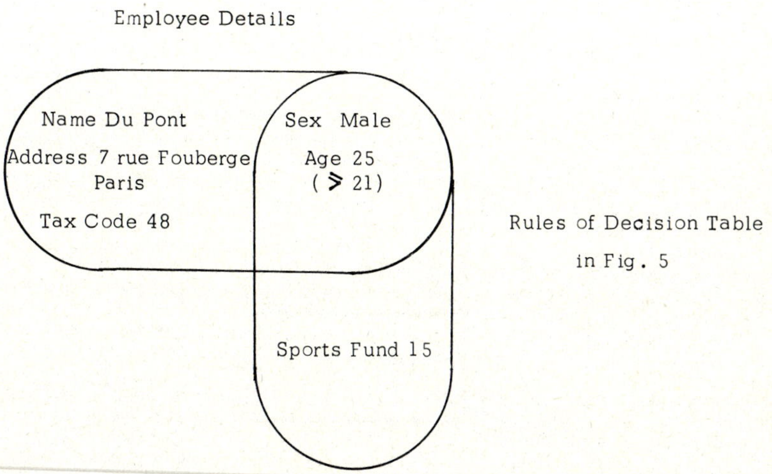

Fig. 6

Figure 6 shows that the system derives the Information that Du Pont contributes 15 to the Sports Fund.

Derivations

We have distinguished two sorts of Information sets, given and derived. We notice that a similar distinction can be made for Data sets. Many Data sets are given to the system, e.g. Customer Name, Customer Address, etc. But some are derived by the system, e.g. a payroll system would probably derive the set Gross Pay.

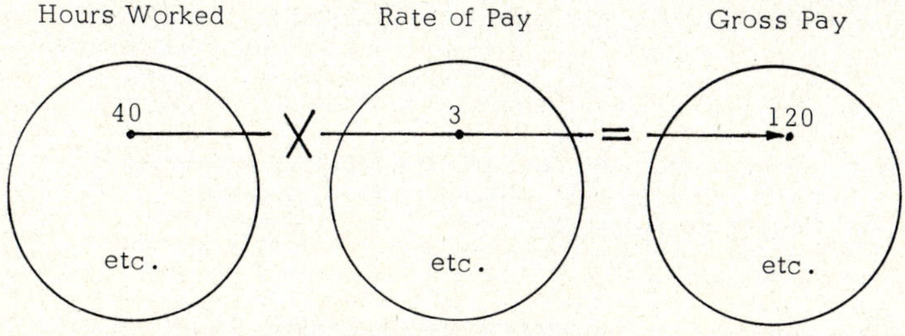

Fig. 7

Figure 7 shows that the derived set Gross Pay is in fact the result of a particular mapping of the given sets Hours Worked and Rate of Pay. We can state the general rule.

Any derived Data set is the result of a specific mapping involving one or more given Data sets.

Triggers

The four relationships we have described so far are all static relationships.

Figure 8 shows a dynamic model of an Information system.

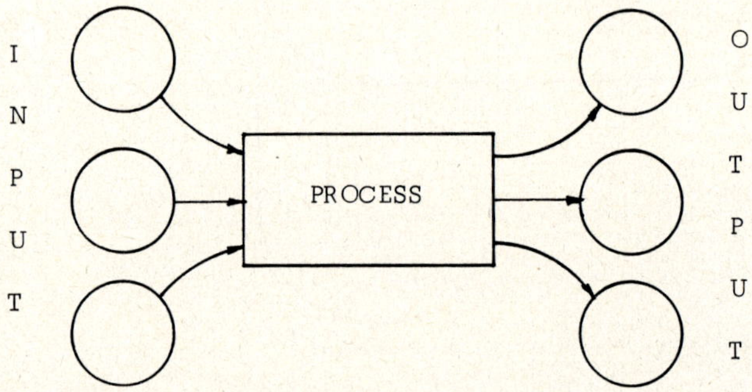

Fig. 8

This model illustrates that Information sets (inputs) are received by the system, processed, and Information sets (outputs) are produced, e.g. Orders come in are processed and Invoices are produced. We notice that the outputs are not produced spontaneously. Invoices are only produced as a result of an Order. Not all input Information sets inspire the production of an output, e.g. on receipt of Customer Details the system may do no more than store the related items contained in the set.

Those input Information sets that do inspire the production of an output are called Triggers. We may state two further rules :

> Every output information set is related to a Trigger.
>
> Every item in the output is the result of a mapping of the Trigger or of a derived Information set joined to the Trigger.

Figure 9 shows that the mapping may be of three types.

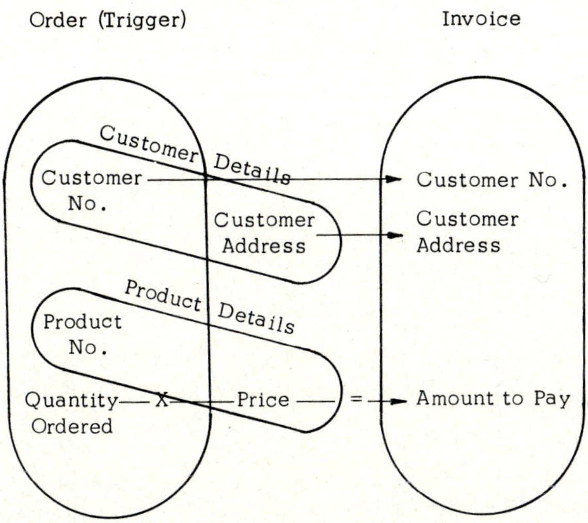

Fig. 9

These three types are as follows :

- the output item may be a member of the Trigger set, e.g. Customer Number is a member of Order;

- the output item may be a member of a derived Information set joined to the Trigger, e.g. Customer Address is a member of the derived Information set formed by joining Customer Details to Order by Customer Number;

- the output item may be the result of an operation on one or more items belonging to the Trigger or to a derived Information set joined to the Trigger, e.g. Amount to Pay is the result of a multiplication operation on two members, Quantity Ordered and Price, of the derived Information set formed by joining Product Details to Order by Product Number.

It is of interest to relate the basic concepts of SYSTEMATICS to the basic concepts of three of the generally accepted authorities in this field.

SYSTEMATICS	Information Algebra (Bosak, 1962)	Information Systems Theory (Langefors, 1966)	Relational Analysis (Codd, 1970)
Item	Property value		
Data set name	Property		
Data set	Property value set		Simple domain
Information set name	Entity		
Information set	Point in property space, also a set of such points		Row containing simple and/or non-simple domains
Derived relationships	Bundles		Joins
Derived items		Precedence Analysis	
Mapping the trigger		Precedence Analysis	

The only new concept appears to be that of the trigger itself.

In the remainder of this paper we show how the definition of triggers enables us to construct a simple, step by step approach to the task of systems analysis, design and specification.

PART II - SYSTEMATICS IN PRACTICE

In this part we build a model of an order processing system showing how SYSTEMATICS theory may be used in practice.

STEP 1 : Define the Outputs

Let us suppose the requirement of the system is to produce an invoice. Fig. 10 shows a form describing a possible invoice.

OUTPUT NAME	CONTENTS
Invoice	Order No. Customer No. Customer Name Customer Address
TRIGGER	Product No.
Order	Product Name Quantity Ordered Amount to Pay

Fig. 10

The items the designer wishes to be members of the Invoice Information set are listed down the right hand side of the form. The name of the Input Information set (Order) which is to trigger this output is also shown.

STEP 2 : Construct an Input Dictionary

The remaining steps consist of a discipline of analysing the relationship between the members of the output set Invoice and the members of its trigger set Order.

We may start by assuming that all the Invoice items are contained in the Order. Fig. 11 shows the situation where everything needed in the Invoice is given to the system on the Order.

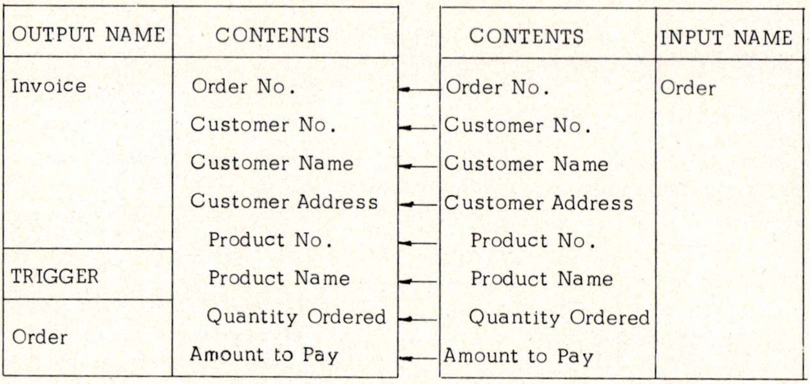

Fig. 11

Certain items on the Order remain constant whilst others change, however. For example Customer Name and Address are the same on all orders from that Customer. We can make an economy of input, therefore, if we feed these constants once only to the system, - and 'join' them to the Order items when they arrive.

Fig. 12 shows Customer Details containing Customer Number, Customer Name and Customer Address.

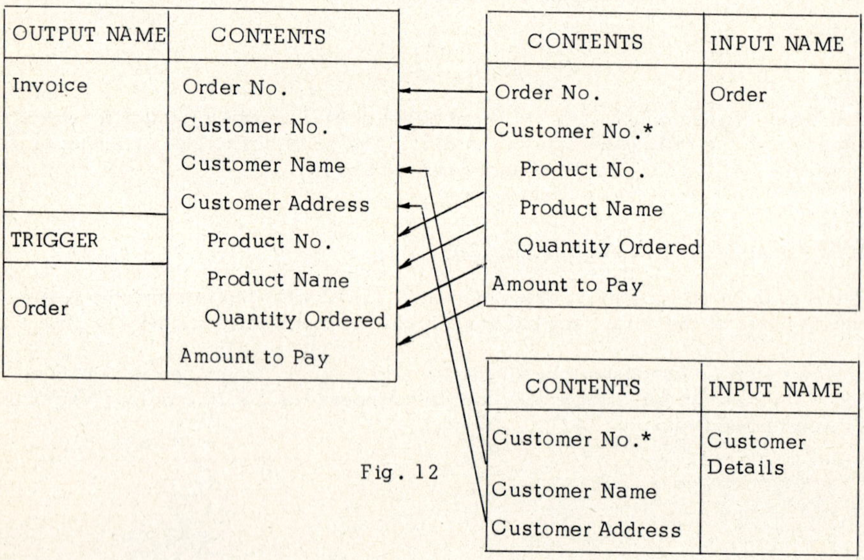

Fig. 12

Order no longer needs to show Customer Name and Address. Each time an Order triggers an Invoice these additional items can be joined to the Order through the Item they have in common, Customer No.*

We can input other constant items once only to the system. For example, Product Name can be input in a separate information set called Product Details. Fig. 13 illustrates this position.

OUTPUT NAME	CONTENTS
Invoice	Order No.
	Customer No.
	Customer Name
TRIGGER	Customer Address
Order	Product No.
	Product Name
	Quantity Ordered
	Amount to Pay

INPUT DICTIONARY

CONTENTS	Information Sets			
	1	2	3	
	Order	Customer Details	Product Details	
Order No.	✓			
Customer No.	✓	✓		
Customer Name		✓		
Customer Address		✓		
Product No.	✓		✓	
Product Name			✓	
Quantity Ordered	✓			
Amount to Pay	✓			

Fig. 13

To avoid drawing all the information sets separately, their contents are shown in an Input Dictionary. This dictionary illustrates the joining items more simply, i.e. these 'items in common' exist wherever there is more than one tick on the same row. The discipline is as follows :

- Every item on the output must be given in the trigger, i.e. have a tick in the trigger column,

  or

- be given previously.

Items to be given previously must have a tick in some other column - and this column must 'bridge' into the trigger column, i.e. it must contain at least one tick in common with the trigger column.

This discipline of tracing each output item back to its origins enables the analyst to construct the Input Dictionary. At this stage his main design criteria are :

1. To group together in separate columns the data sets whose new items are given at the same time.

2. To provide joins between the columns as required.

STEP 3 : Construct Derivations Dictionary

Our first model assumed every output item was given in the trigger (Fig. 11). Our second model allowed some items to be given before the trigger arrived (Fig. 13). We now allow for some output items to be derived by the system itself. For example, let us assume that Amount to Pay is not given to the system in the information set Order, but calculated by the system. Once again, the discipline is for the analyst to construct a complete chain back to the trigger. He does this in two stages. First he expresses the derived items in terms of a formula, all of whose components are given items. For example :

Amount to Pay	=	Quantity Ordered	x	Price
(derived)		(given)		(given)

Fig. 14 shows the derived item Amount to Pay expressed in the Output in terms of its given components.

OUTPUT NAME	CONTENTS
Invoice	Order No.
	Customer No.
	Customer Name
	Customer Address
	Product No.
TRIGGER	Product Name
Order	Quantity Ordered
	Amount to Pay i.e. Quantity Ordered x Price

Fig. 14

We observe, at this stage, that in designing a complex formula we may find it useful to express the formula in a series of levels. For example, we may design Amount to Pay as being equal to Quantity Ordered x Price. Price itself may be a derived item. If so, a further formula for Price must be designed, e.g. Price = 120% Cost + Postage. This process must be continued until, at a final level, all components are given items.

To save repeating formulae they may be written once only in a Derivations Dictionary and thereafter referred to by the name of the derived Data set only.

Fig. 15 shows the name of the data set Amount to Pay entered in the output, with its components shown in a Derivations Dictionary.

OUTPUT NAME	CONTENTS
Invoice	Order No.
	Customer No.
	Customer Name
TRIGGER	Customer Address
Order	Product No.
	Product Name
	Quantity Ordered
	Amount to Pay

DERIVATIONS DICTIONARY

DERIVED DATA SET	Op^n	COMPONENTS
Amount to Pay		Quantity Ordered
	x	Price
Price		1.2
	x	Cost
	+	Postage

Fig. 15

The second stage is to take each given component in the formulae and design its relationships with the trigger. This is done using the Input Dictionary as before. Every given component must be entered in the Input Dictionary, and receive a tick in the trigger column, or in some other column which is joined to the trigger column.

Fig. 16 shows the complete analysis of the system, with each output item related to the trigger.

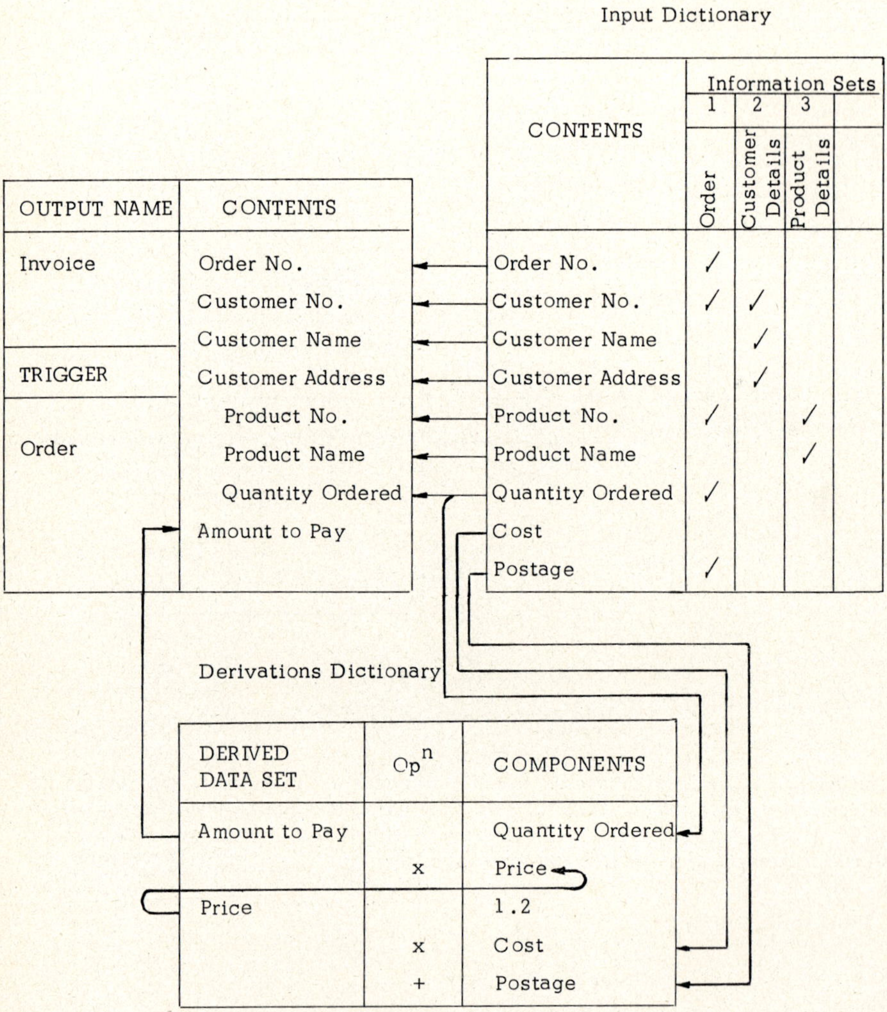

Fig. 16

We notice that the design discipline has forced us to add Cost and Postage to the Input Dictionary. This in turn forces us to consider how they are to be input. Postage we can add to the trigger column Order. Since we do not expect a fresh Cost every time a product is ordered, we do not enter a tick in the trigger column in this case. Instead we redesign the Product Details information set to include Cost. This set is already joined to the trigger through Product Number.

STEP 4 : Construct Main File Dictionary

In order to design the main files for the system we take each output in turn and compare it with its trigger. Every item on the output which is not contained in the trigger must be stored on a file. Figure 17 shows the first stage of constructing a Main File Dictionary.

FILE CONTENTS					
Customer Name					
Customer Address					
Product Name					
Cost					

Fig. 17

Working down the list of contents of Invoice (Fig. 16) we enter in the column File Contents each item not present in the trigger. Given items are straight-forward. The last item, Amount to Pay, is a derived item, however. In the case of derived items we have the choice of storing on file either the derived item or its components. Three factors govern the choice :

1. The time of receipt of the components.

   If one or more of the components is contained in the trigger, the remaining components should be stored on the file. The derived item itself cannot be stored since it cannot be calculated until the trigger arrives.

   This is the case with Amount to Pay in our example. The Derivations Dictionary shows us that :

   Amount to Pay = Quantity Ordered x 1.2 x Cost + Postage.

   Quantity Ordered and Postage are contained in the trigger, so Amount to Pay cannot be stored for Invoice. We therefore enter the remaining component 'Cost' in File Contents. (The constant 1.2 could also be stored in the Main File. A preferable strategy for this type of components is normally to store them as program parameters in a Table.)

2. The volume of components.

An economy in file size will usually be obtained if the derivative is stored rather than its components. For example, suppose Customer's Balance is an item on an output called Statement. If

$$\text{Balance} = \sum \text{Payments} - \sum \text{Amounts to Pay},$$

it will clearly be more economical in file space to store Balance rather than all the Amounts to Pay and all the Payments related to a particular customer.

3. The presence of the components in an output.

Any components which are required for an output must be stored. For example, suppose statement is as shown in Figure 18.

OUTPUT NAME	CONTENTS
Statement	Customer No.
	Customer Name
	Customer Address
	Date
	Prev. Balance*
	Invoice No. this period*
TRIGGER	Amount to Pay " "
	Payment No. " "
Statement	Payment " "
Request	Balance

Fig. 18

Some components of Balance must be stored on file, - namely those Amounts to Pay and Payments related to the current period*. These, together with Prev. Balance, are sufficient to calculate Balance when the trigger is received.

---

* The following conventions will be found useful :

Prev.	the state of a derived item after receiving the previous trigger of this type.
Old	the state of a derived item before receiving this trigger.
This Period	all items given to or derived by the system since the previous trigger of this type.

These three factors are each further illustrated in the final example at the end of this paper.

Having completed the File Contents column, the second stage of constructing the Main File Dictionary is performed by analysing the items according to their Primary Identifier, as shown in Fig. 19.

	PRIMARY IDENTIFIER	
FILE CONTENTS	Customer No.	Product No.
Customer No.	I	
Customer Name	✓	
Customer Address	✓	
Product No.		I
Product Name		✓
Cost		✓

Fig. 19

Primary Identifiers are those Data sets whose members are related to only one member of another set. For example :

> Product No. is the primary identifier of Price
> (if each product has only one price).

At the same time :

> Price is the secondary identifier of Product No.
> (if many products have the same price).

The third stage consists of a further classification according to trigger requirements, as shown in Fig. 20.

FILE CONTENTS	PRIMARY IDENTIFIER: Customer No.	PRIMARY IDENTIFIER: Product No.	TRIGGERS: Order	TRIGGERS:
Customer No.	I		J	
Customer Name	✓		✓	
Customer Address	✓		✓	
Product No.		I	J	
Product Name		✓	✓	
Cost		✓	✓	

Fig. 20

In this example we only have one trigger, namely 'Order'. We show that all the items in our Main File are required by Order in order to produce its outputs. The items which join the trigger to the files are shown with a 'J'.

The final stage is to construct the main files themselves, as shown in Fig. 21.

FILE CONTENTS	PRIMARY IDENTIFIER: Customer No.	PRIMARY IDENTIFIER: Product No.	TRIGGER: Order	MAIN FILES: Customer	MAIN FILES: Product
Customer No.	I		J	✓	
Customer Name	✓		✓	✓	
Customer Address	✓		✓	✓	
Product No.		I	J		✓
Product Name		✓	✓		✓
Cost		✓	✓		✓

Fig. 21

In this simple example, each primary identifier column becomes a main file. In other cases the primary identifier columns may be Partitioned, Combined or Replicated according to certain principles. These principles are given in the more complicated example in Fig. 22 below, which illustrates most of the circumstances encountered in practice. The example represents the specification of an Order Processing System which produces two outputs :

Invoices (to the customer for goods ordered which are in stock. Orders which are not in stock are held in the system until stock arrives).

Statements (to the customer at the end of a period).

OUTPUTS

OUTPUT NAME	CONTENTS
Invoice	Invoice No.
	Customer No.
TRIGGER	Customer Name
	Customer Address
Order	Product No.
or	Product Name
Production Advice	Quantity Ordered
	Amount to Pay
: Old Stock	
Quantity Ordered	

OUTPUT NAME	CONTENTS
Statement	Date
	Customer No.
	Customer Name
TRIGGER	Customer Address
	Prev. Balance
Statement Request	Invoice No.
	Amount to Pay
	Payment No.
	Payment
	Balance

DERIVATIONS DICTIONARY

DERIVED DATA SET	Op^n	DERIVATIONS
Invoice No.	=	Order No.
Amount to Pay	=	Quantity Ordered
	x	Price
Price	=	1.2
	x	Cost
	+	Postage
Stock	=	Receipts
	-	Quantity Ordered
Balance	=	Payments
	-	Amounts to Pay

INPUT DICTIONARY

CONTENTS	Information Sets					
	1	2	3	4	5	6
	Order	Payments	Production Advice	Customer Details	Product Details	Statement Request
Order No.	✓					
Customer No.	✓	✓		✓		All*
Customer Name				✓		
Customer Address				✓		
Product No.	✓		✓		✓	
Product Name					✓	
Quantity Ordered	✓					
Cost					✓	
Postage	✓					
Receipts			✓			
Payments		✓				
Payment No.		✓				
Date						✓

* When 'all' is specified there is no need to provide the actual values in the input.

MAIN FILE DICTIONARY

FILE CONTENTS	PRIMARY IDENTIFIERS					TRIGGERS			MAIN FILES: CUSTOMER			MAIN FILES: PRODUCT	
	Customer No.	Product No.	Order No.	Invoice No.	Payment No.	Order	Production Advice	Statement	Customer No.	Invoice No. (this period)	Payment No. (this Period)	Product No.	Order No. (not despatched)
Customer No.	I					J	✓	J	I				✓
Customer Name	✓					✓	✓	✓	✓				
Customer Address	✓					✓	✓	✓	✓				
Product No.		I				J	J					I	
Product Name		✓				✓	✓					✓	
Cost		✓				✓	✓					✓	
Stock		✓				✓	✓					✓	
Balance	✓							✓	✓				
Quantity Ordered		✓	✓				✓						✓
Postage		✓	✓				✓						✓
Invoice No.				I				✓		I			
Amount to Pay				✓				✓		✓			
Payment No.					I			✓			I		
Payment					✓			✓			✓		
Order No.			I				✓						I

Fig. 22

This more complex example makes it clear that the primary identifier analysis provides what might be termed 'Essential File Structures'*. The Main Files themselves are constructs of these essential structures, observing the following principles of Partitioning, Replication and Combination.

---

* or 'Normalized Relations' (Codd, 1970)

1. Partitioning

- Items required by less triggers than other items in the same structure are candidates for partitioning into separate files.

For example, Balance is not required by Order or Production Advice and need not be present in the Customer Main File used by them.

The decision to partition will be governed by the need to reduce Main File sizes to save space or run times and by physical location requirements in Distributed Processing systems.

2. Replication

- Items required by more than one trigger are candidates for replicating in other main files.

For example, Customer Name and Customer Address are required by Orders, Production Advices and Statement Requests. If these triggers are processed at different times, or in different places in distributed processing systems, these items might be replicated on further main files.

3. Combination

- Items in structures not joined to the trigger requiring them are candidates for being combined with structures which are.

For example, Production Advice requires Customer Name. It is not joined to the Customer Name structure, however. The only join between Production Advice and the Main File items is Product Number. Customer Name is therefore a candidate for combining with the Product Number's structure and could be held on the Product File for each unfulfilled order.

The decision to combine will be largely governed by whether the item is required by more than one trigger. In the example given in Fig. 22, Customer Name is also required by Order and Statement. If it were held in the Product File it would need to be replicated in the Customer File. The replication of such items can be avoided by replicating their primary identifiers only, thus providing a join between the two files.

This is the solution chosen in our example. Customer Number is replicated, and combined with the items in the Product File. This avoids the need to replicate and combine Customer Name and Customer Address as well.

If the items concerned are not required by other triggers they can be combined with items in the file joined to the trigger without involving replication. For example Invoice Number, Amount to Pay, Payment Number and Payment are all required by Statement Request but have no join with this trigger. The solution chosen in Fig. 22 is to combine them with the items in the Customer File which does have such a join. No replication is involved since these items are not required by any other trigger.

It should be noticed that any essential file structure having a Primary Identifier other than its Main File Primary Identifier will form a repeating sub-record within the main record. This can arise in two ways. The structure may be combined within another structure. For example, we combined Invoice Number and Amount to Pay with the items in the Customer File in Fig. 22. These two items form repeating sub-records for each Invoice for this period within a customer record. It can also arise if a structure has multiple primary identifiers. For example, Quantity Ordered and Postage in Fig. 22 have multiple primary identifiers. Product Number identifies many Quantities Ordered and Postages. So does Order Number. It is necessary to specify both Product Number and Order Number in order to identify a single Quantity Ordered and a single Postage. If Quantity Ordered and Postage are held in the Product File, as in our example, they will form repeating sub-records for each unfulfilled order within a product record.

CONCLUSION

Two stages in systems analysis and design can be identified (Langefors, 1978), the first concerned with identifying user needs - Infological problems, and the second concerned with designing and implementing solutions - Datalogical problems.

The first stage may be further broken down into two tasks :

Task 1 Defining organisational objectives and changes (the Object system).

Task 2 Defining the information required to support the achievement of the objectives (the supporting Information system).

A special case of precedence analysis may be identified, that of 'chaining outputs back to their triggers', which appears to be sufficient to complete task 2 of the Infological problem and also to design the main files needed to solve the Datalogical problem.

This analysis process may be illustrated as follows :

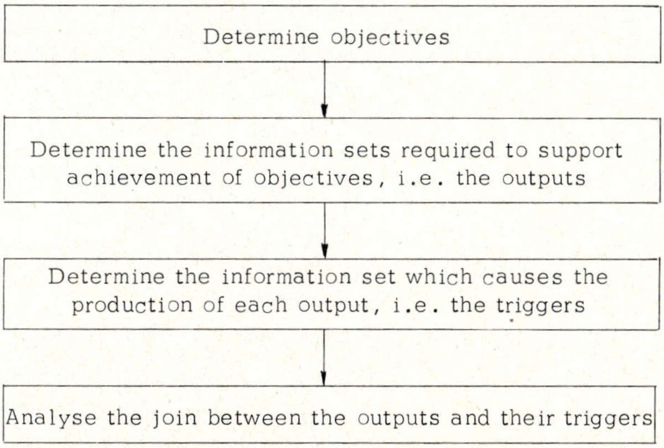

REFERENCES

(1) Bosak, R. et al., An Information Algebra, Comm. A.C.M. 5 (1962) 190-704.

(2) Codd, E.F., A Relational Model of Data for Large Shared Data Bases, Comm. A.C.M. 13 (1970) 377-387.

(3) Grindley, C.B.B., Systematics - A Non-Programming Language for Designing and Specifying Commercial Systems for Computers, Comp. Journ. 9 (1966) 124-128.

(4) Langefors, B., Theoretical Analysis of Information Systems, NCC Student Literature (1966).

(5) Langefors, B., Analysis of User Needs, 2nd Conference of European Co-operation in Informatics on Information Systems Methodology (Venice, 1978).

-0-0-0-0-0-

Formal Models and Practical Tools
for Information Systems Design
H.-J. Schneider, Editor
North-Holland Publishing Company

A MODEL AND A LANGUAGE FOR FUNCTIONAL SPECIFICATIONS AND EVALUATION OF INFORMATION SYSTEM DYNAMICS

François BODART and Yves PIGNEUR

Institut d'Informatique, F.N.D.P., Namur, Belgium

1. INTRODUCTION : OBJECTIVES, DEFINITIONS AND HYPOTHESES

1.1. The problem

An important discrepancy can exist between the representation that the users have of an information system when they give functional specifications and the behaviour of the implemented information system several months or some years later ! Such a discrepancy can generate a rejection by the users of the computerized information system and will generate software maintenance costs.
To reduce these discrepancies and their undesirable effects it is necessary to be able to evaluate in depth the functional specifications.

1.2. Objectives and hypotheses

Present problem specification languages contain very few constructs about dynamics such as synchronization between processes, dynamic allocation of resources, or timing of events that are useful for modelling dynamics. In particular, the constructs for dynamics are generally not adequate or complete enough to permit the generation of a simulation program of the information system.

The objectives of the research outlined in this paper are :
1. to define concepts and an associated language to describe functional specifications for an information system and store them in a data base, and
2. to derive, from the specification data base, a model of the information system that may be sufficient to evaluate the specifications by simulation with less time and effort than is required by present methods.

To accomplish these objectives it is assumed that the information system, whose functional behaviour is to be predicted, is the target information system. Processors and resources need only to be considered to the extent they constrain the functional system. The purpose is to design a target information system within the constraints of performances and availibility of the resources.

Specifically three hypotheses associated with this approach are :

1. Functional specifications are incomplete if the resource constraints are not taken into consideration because some functional specifications are dependent on resource limitations and performances.

2. A processor is considered as a black box : the design of the target system is independent of the (internal) design of the processors.

3. A priori performances of the processors are given.

To make these hypotheses more explicit, an analogy with the design of an urban transport system is suggested :

- functional specifications (flow network between shopping centers, business areas, suburbs, ...) will be based on present and planned transport resources (cars, busses, underground, ...);
- the design of the transport system is independent of the design of cars, busses or trains;

- designers know the performances (speed, capacity, cost, ...) of transport means, they do not have to wait until the implementation of the transport system to discover these performances.

The important part of the analogy between the design of an information system and the design of the urban transport system is the difficulty ot knowing a priori the performance characteristics of computer systems. This is not a reason to postpone the evaluation of an information system until its development and implementation but a reason to improve knowledge about computer system performances. We justify the performance hypothesis by another reason : computers are not the only processors in an information system and the utilization of those other processors, such as human processors, is frequently more critical than utilization of computers.

Given information system specifications that satisfy the above hypotheses, the evaluation may be accomplished at three levels :

1. Validation of the internal consistency. e.g. :
   - data requested by processes exist,
   - information flow is consistent,
   - activating schedules for processors and resources utilized by the processors are compatible.
2. Verification of the feasibility from the point of view of resource availability and performance characteristics of the processors.
3. Demonstration of the correctness : will the decision rule specified by a user procedure produce the results he wants it produces?

The first level of evaluation can be accomplish with current technics such as PSL-PSA. The research concerned in this paper is concerned with the second level of evaluation. The research does not cover the third level; one possibility that will be investigated in the futur is the use of (throw-away) code that could be produced from the data base.

1.3. Task of the research project

The main task of the research project is to obtain these evaluations by simulating the behaviour of the information system.
The basic elements of the software system are as shown in figure 1.1. :

- the specifications (1) described in a relational (PSL-like) form are stored by the analyser (2) in a data base (3);
- a simulation program (5) is generated by the simulation program generator (4) from the data base (3) by mapping of the "nested" specifications statements into simulation program statements;
- during the generation of the simulation program, the generator requests (6) data and simulation parameters from the designer (7);
- feedbacks are defined at two levels : modification of simulation and data parameters is the first one (8); modification of functional specifications is the second one (9);
- in addition to simulation reports (11), it would be possible to get others reports (10) such as syntax errors reports, consistency reports, information flow reports, analytically estimated reports related to process, and processor and resource activity reports.

The accomplish of the above task is based on the following :

1. The language is based on the ISDOS PSL language, developed at the University of Michigan [1]. The relation structure of PSL and its non-procedural aspect will be preserved in order to keep language flexibility and ease of use.

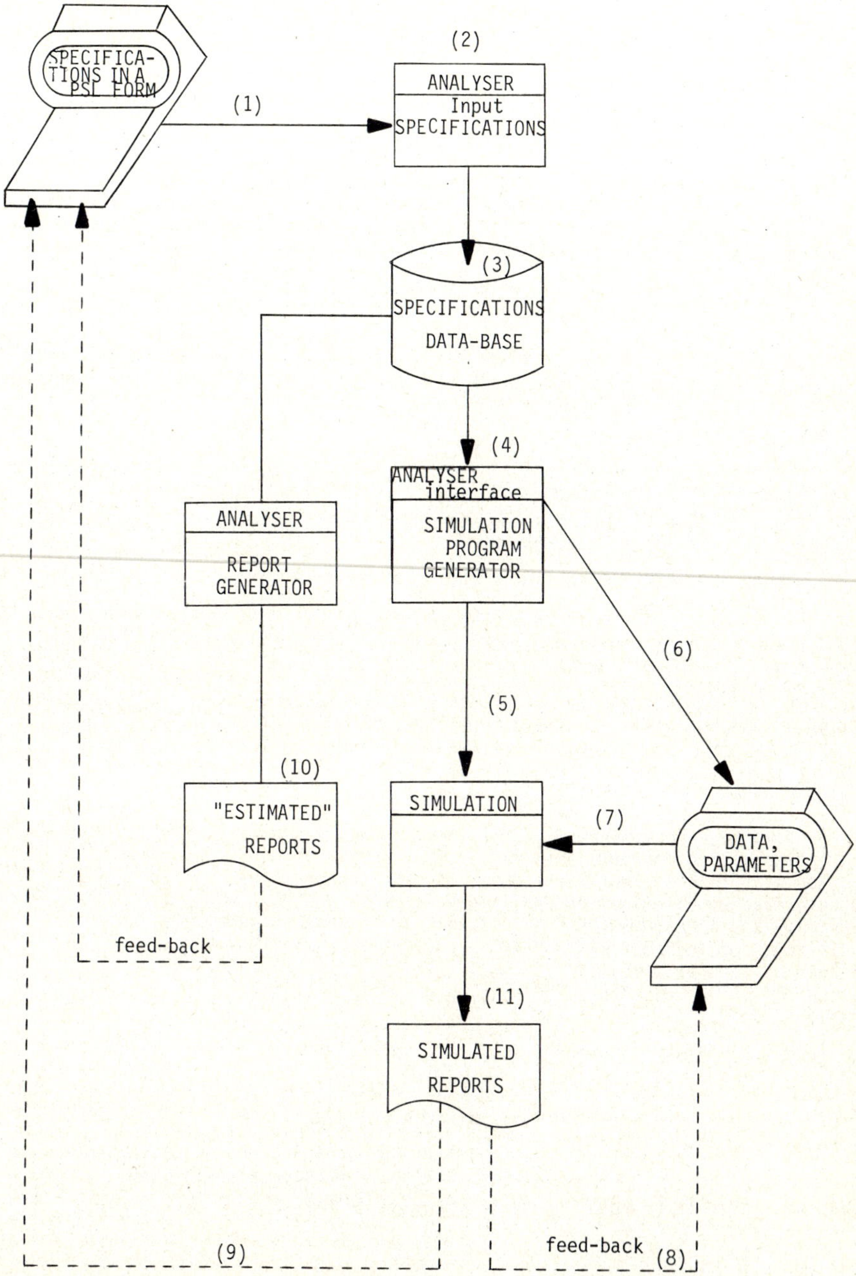

SPECIFICATIONS IN A PSL FORM
(1)
(2)
ANALYSER
Input SPECIFICATIONS
(3)
SPECIFICATIONS DATA-BASE
(4)
ANALYSER interface
SIMULATION PROGRAM GENERATOR
ANALYSER
REPORT GENERATOR
(6)
(5)
(10)
"ESTIMATED" REPORTS
SIMULATION
(7)
DATA, PARAMETERS
feed-back
(11)
SIMULATED REPORTS
(9)
feed-back
(8)

Fig. 1.1.

2. A modular and a team approach to the specification process. This suggests the following elements :
   - static specifications (environment, process, data messages);
   - dynamic specification for processes, i.e., dynamic properties the designer considers belong to the functional definition of the problem (for instance, after replenishment, backorders will be treated before normal orders);
   - processors and resources constraints.
3. Aggregation and decomposition both at the level of specification and the level of simulation by taking advantage of SUBPART clauses for processes and processors and by refining some dynamic relationships. For instance, to detail the dynamics of a data base, the USE relationships between process and data could be exploded in relationships such as DELETE, ADD, MODIFY, CREATE.
4. A single language to describe specifications both for documentation and for evaluation and simulation. The simulation program is to be generated automatically from the specification data base. To reach this objective, so as to realize the mapping from PSL Statements into the simulation program statements, we need to describe some comment entry (for instance for object types such as CONDITION (*), SYNCHRONIZATION-POINT (**), ...) in a formal "nested" syntax [6].

1.4. Content of this paper

This paper covers the analysis of concepts for an information system dynamics model and a language developed for this model. The structure of the paper is :

1. Brief description of concepts for static specifications as a background for dynamic specifications (section 2).
2. The concepts of quantification including a calendar to specify time (section 3).
3. Concepts for process dynamics independent of resource allocation (section 4).
4. Model extension for constraints of processors and resources on process dynamic (section 5).

The paper does not discuss the generation of the simulation program, the data estimation and validity for simulation, the evaluation of the proposed model for dynamics, the simulation, or the detailled syntax of the language (***).

2. STATIC MODEL FOR INFORMATION SYSTEMS SPECIFICATION

As stated above, the system specification language is a relational language like PSL. The modelling concepts are OBJECT types, RELATIONSHIPS between objects types and, for each object, PROPERTIES which may have PROPERTY VALUES. PSL model is characterized by allowing the use of only a limited number of predefined OBJECTS, PROPERTIES and RELATIONSHIPS. PSL A 4.2. [2,3] is concerned primarily with the static model of Information Processing System and the "static" model used here has been adapted from it. The concepts, however, do not constitute a simple subset or superset of it : some are left out, others added and some ones are differently defined or used.

2.1. Object types and properties

The basis object types used at the "static" level are :

PROCESS - objects describing information processing.

INTERFACE - objects describing some part of the organization or environment with which the target system interacts by message transmission.

MESSAGE - objects representing a transaction of information which, either, is

---

(*) See below 4.4.

(**) See below 4.3.

(***) The detailled syntax is described in an internal Working Paper - February 1979. Institut d'Informatique, F.N.D.P., Namur.

generated or received by the target system respectively to or from its environment, or, is transported inside the system, from a process to another one.

SET - objects to represent a collection (or "file) of information maintained internally in the system.

ENTITY - objects describing a type of information used by the target system to represent an "object type" or "concept" of the real world.

RELATION - objects representing an association of two or more entities.

ELEMENT - objects describing an atomic unit of information which cannot be be subdivided.

GROUP - objects describing a collection of logically related ELEMENTS and/or GROUPS

For each object, several properties may be defined :

SYNONYM - used to define alternative name(s) for a given object in the description of the system.

KEYWORD - used to logically relate objects together for retrieval and subsequent analysis purposes.

DESCRIPTION - used to specify information about an object in text format.

PROCEDURE - used to specify the operations of a PROCESS as text.

ATTRIBUTES - used to state specific characteristics which distinguish an object from other objects of the same type;
the ATTRIBUTE NAME designates the name of the characteristic and the ATTRIBUTE value, the value or range of this characteristic for a given object.

CARDINALITY - a predefined attribute used to specify either the maximum number in a SET of occurrences or the maximum number of occurrences of ENTITY, RELATION, GROUP or ELEMENT instances contained in a SET.

CONNECTIVITY - is another predefined attribute which allows to specify for a RELATION (A,B,C,D,...), the number of occurrences of (B,C,D,E,...) for an occurrence of A.

2.2. Relationships

The relationships may involve two or more objects. When two objects are involved the relationship may be stated in two "directions", active or passive.
(ex. active from : <process> RECEIVES <message> , passive form : <message> RECEIVED BY <process>).

The "static" relationships, illustrated in fig. 2.1., 2.2 and 2.3, are :

USES (USED BY)
- is a relationship specifying any use of a SET, ENTITY or RELATION by a PROCESS.

DERIVES (DERIVED BY)
- is an output relationship relating SET objects to the PROCESS objects which produce them.

GENERATES (GENERATED BY)
- is an output relationship relating MESSAGE objects to the PROCESS- or INTERFACE- objects which produce them.

RECEIVES (RECEIVED BY)
- is an input relationship relating MESSAGE objects to the PROCESS- or INTERFACE- objects which use them.

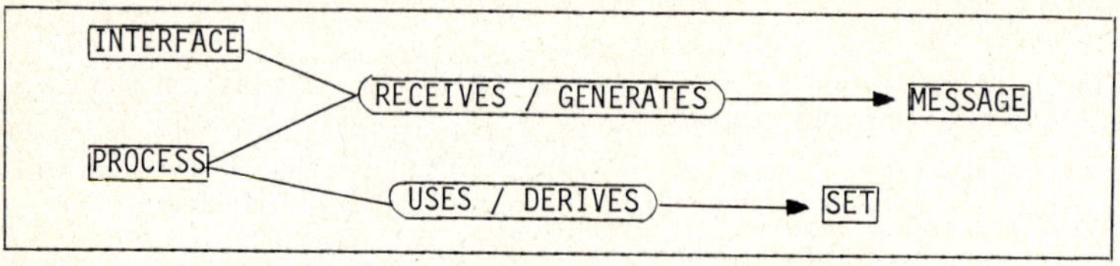

Fig. 2.1. Static flow relationships

SUBPARTS ARE (PART OF)
- used to show the hierarchical decomposition of processes.

CONSISTS OF (CONTAINED IN)
- relating information object to its components.

BETWEEN ... AND (RELATED TO ... AND ... VIA)
- used to define a RELATION between n ($\geqslant$2) ENTITIES.

IDENTIFIES (IDENTIFIED BY)
- giving the possible ELEMENT(S) or GROUP(S) which allow to uniquely (key) distinguish multiple instances of the same ENTITY or RELATION.

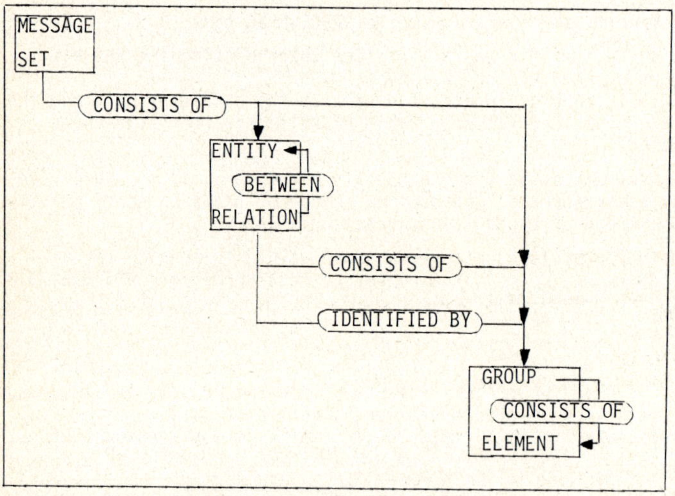

Fig. 2.2. Information structure relationships

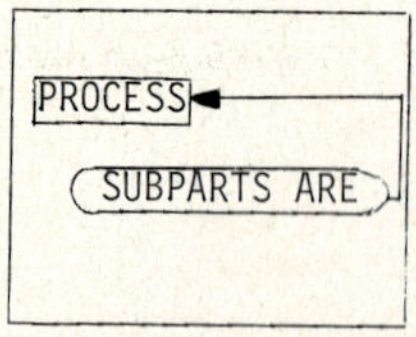

Fig. 2.3. Process structure relationship

In a GENERATES (GENERATED) relationship it is possible to specify the frequency of MESSAGE generation per time INTERVAL :

... GENERATES <message> AT FREQUENCY OF <parameter> TIMES PER <interval name>.

2.3. Example

Fig. 2.4. gives examples of static objects and relationships.

```
INTERFACE        customers-of-the-company;
   GENERATES A customer-order AT FREQUENCY OF as-many-orders TIMES PER day;

PROCESS          order-recording
   ATTRIBUTES ARE description-approved-by recording-service-manager,
                  complexity-level low ;
   SUBPARTS ARE  order-checking,order-coding;
   RECEIVES A   customer-order;
   GENERATES A  valid-order;
   USES WITH EXCLUSION customer-set;
   USES       product-set

   PROCEDURE;
              narrative description of the "ordering" task;

MESSAGE       valid-order;
   CONSISTS OF  order-line, customer-reference,
                order-heading;
   SYNONYMS ARE recorded-order, order-OK;

ENTITY      order-entity
   RELATED TO  customer VIA has-ordered-relat;
   CONSISTS OF order-number, order-date;
   IDENTIFIED BY order-number;
   SYNONYM IS order-heading;
```

Fig. 2.4.

3. QUANTITATIVE ASPECTS OF SPECIFICATION

In order to specify performance of information processing system it is necessary to declare not only the model of the system but also to give the quantitative information about it.

This section describes the object types SYSTEM PARAMETER, CALENDAR, UNIT and INTERVAL that allow quantifications and the relationships that are used to define them.

3.1. System-parameter

SYSTEM PARAMETER - an object used to represent a value relevant to characterizing system size (i.e. quantification).

Such an object has the following property : its value(s) need only be assigned when they are definitely needed :

```
DEFINE SYSTEM-PARAMETER system - parameter name ;
  VALUE IS ...
```

Whenever a specific value is needed, e.g. during simulation, the SYSTEM PARAMETER is replaced by a defined value. Such a value may be :

1. non deterministic by the use of a probability distribution function (DISTRIBUTED-VALUE ACCORDING TO ...);
2. dependent on time (... FOLLOWING a CALENDAR) ;
3. "computed" from another SYSTEM-PARAMETER (... MULTIPLIED BY).

Whenever a SYSTEM-PARAMETER name may appear, a value, which may be an INTEGER, a REAL number or a STRING, may appear instead.

3.2. CALENDAR object

The CALENDAR objects allows the specification of changes with respect to time in the system life :
- validity period for values of SYSTEM-PARAMETERS;
- occurrence of triggering EVENTS (section 4.2.);
- availability period for RESOURCES (section 5.2) and activity period for PROCESSORS (section 5.2.).

A CALENDAR may be specified by a combination of :

- actual point in time : ACTIVE AT TIME <event> ;
- intervals : ACTIVE FROM <event> TO <event> ;
- relative intervals : ACTIVE DURING <interval> AFTER <event>.

A period may be used to qualify these time location specifications :
- IN PERIOD FROM <event> TO <event> ;
- IN PERIOD DURING <interval> AFTER <event>.

3.3. INTERVAL and UNIT

UNIT and INTERVAL are units of measure. They are used to measure the quantity of RESOURCE or the activity of a PROCESSOR (see section 5.2.).
UNIT may be any unit of measure except unit of time.
INTERVAL is only a unit of time.

4. SYSTEMS DYNAMIC MODEL FOR INFORMATION PROCESSING SYSTEM

This section proposes a model for describing the dynamics of information flows, independent of processor and resource constraints, by expanding some what limited capability of PSL [4], which consists of :
- conditions and rules governing sequence of events and activities,
- environment operations characteristics and resources of the system, and
- changes with respect to time.

PROCESS and EVENT are the two basic concepts used to describe main aspects of dynamics of information system's activity. PROCESSES are defined in 4.1. and EVENTS in 4.2. The concept of SYNCHRONIZATION POINT, a special class of EVENT, is described in 4.3. and some standard dynamic structures in 4.4.

4.1. Concept of PROCESS

The declaration of a - type of - PROCESS in PSL establishes the characteristics of a task to be accomplished by the target system. The behaviour of the task is described by a PROCEDURE which is a set of logically related rules and activities.

From the system processing point of view, a PROCESS is a dynamic entity, an instance occurs at each execution of a PROCEDURE. At any point in time, several PROCESSES (occurrence) of the same type may coexist in the system, in varying stages of execution. Each of such PROCESSES may be possibly individualized among the other members of the same type by the attribute value of its ATTRIBUTES.

In this paper, when the context is clear enough, the word "PROCESS" will be used indifferently for representing a PROCESS type or an occurrence of PROCESS type.

It is important to note that the interest is in the external property (WHAT is made) of a PROCESS and not in the body of the PROCEDURE (HOW is made) which is considered, at this level of analysis, as a BLACK BOX (in PSL, as a narrative description or comment entry).

Consequently, a DURING construct(*) will be introduced, in section 5 to indicate the estimated execution time of a PROCESS since it cannot be derived from the PROCEDURE.

To illustrate the foregoing, a view of the life cycle of a PROCESS is developed by identifying the two observable transitions between two possible states ACTIVE and TERMINATED as illustrated in fig. 4.1. :

ACTIVE State :

- the PROCEDURE of a TRIGGERED PROCESS(**) is presently being executed.
  The state change, when PROCESS becomes ACTIVE, is called its "INCEPTION".

TERMINATED State

- after its estimated execution time, the PROCESS is supposed to have completed its activities.
  The state change, when a PROCESS ceases to be ACTIVE, is called its "TERMINATION".

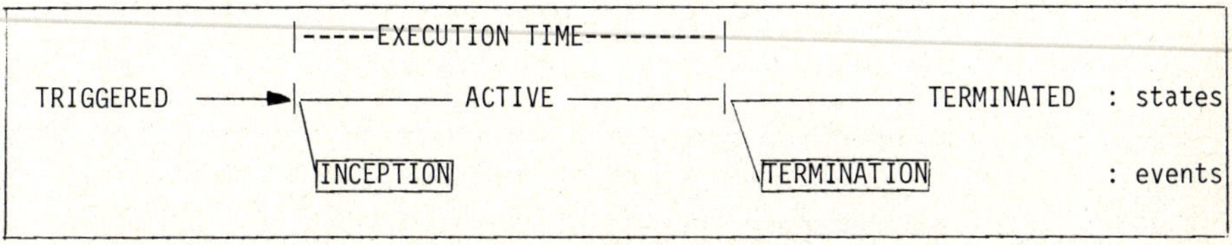

Fig. 4.1. Basic PROCESS state changes

The simple life cycle is enhanced, as shown in fig. 4.2., by the introduction of some refinements :

- the termination of a PROCESS may also be caused (or provoked) by an external mechanism : <process> ABORTED BY ... ;
- the PROCESS may also be temporary INTERRUPTED and RESUMED by a similar external mechanism :
  <process> [INTERRUPTED / RESUMED] BY ...

Since several occurrences of a PROCESS type may coexist in the system :

- either, there must be a mechanism to identify a particular occurrence among the members of the same type on the basis of the value of its ATTRIBUTES :
  ... ABORTS <process> WHERE <condition> , or
- precise semantics of the ABORTS, INTERRUPTS and RESUMES relationship must be given.

(*) See section 5.4.

(**) <process A> UTILIZES (UTILIZED BY) <process B> is a special case of TRIGGERS (TRIGGERED) relationship. Its meaning is : process A <u>creates</u> a <u>sub</u>process B

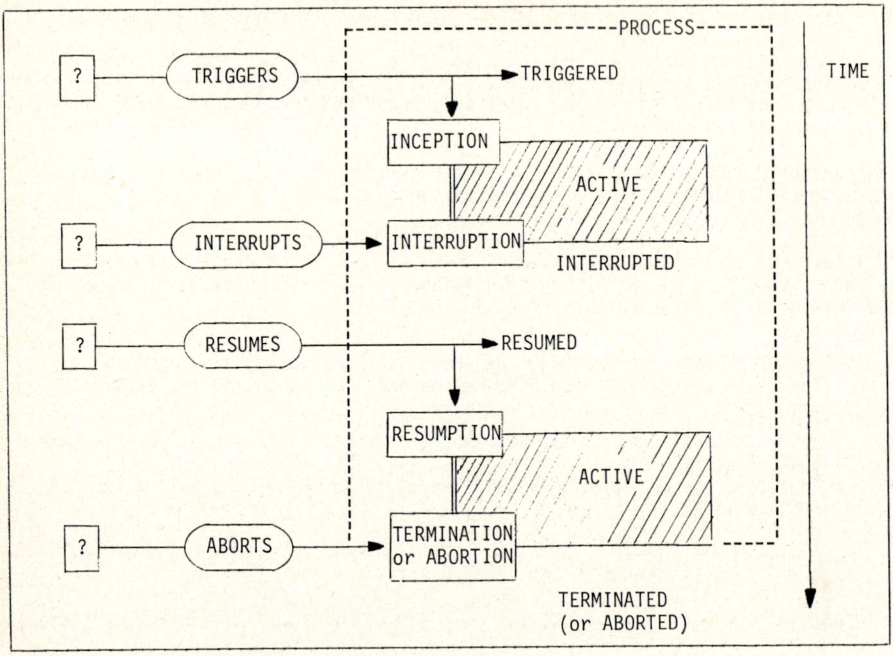

Fig. 4.2. PROCESS life cycle

If administrative and management informations systems are considered, the later solution appears to be more appropriate :

- the ABORTS and INTERRUPTS relationships mean that all the ACTIVE PROCESSES of the given type,existing in the system , have to be ABORTED or INTERRUPTED.
- the RESUMES relationships means that all the INTERRUPTED PROCESSES of the given type are to be RESUMED.

4.2. Concept of EVENT

Each PROCESS state change (INCEPTION, INTERRUPTION, ...) is caused by one and only one previous state change in the system. With each observable moment in the life of a PROCESS, peculiarly its INCEPTION, may be associated an object representing a certain state of the system. This state has to be reached in order to cause the corresponding state change of the PROCESS.

An "EVENT" is a system state change known by the intermediary of a MESSAGE. This MESSAGE includes attributes or characteristics of the corresponding event, such as, among others, event timing and location.

Depending on the kind of the system state change, we define the following typology of basic events.

4.2.1. EXTERNAL EVENTS

External EVENTS are stimuli generated by an INTERFACE to which the target system must react. The definition of the stimuli depends on whether information is associated with it or not.

- If a stimulus has associated information to be processed by the target system it corresponds to the GENERATION of an occurrence of a MESSAGE by an INTERFACE :

```
MESSAGE <message>
 GENERATED BY <interface> AT FREQUENCY OF <parameter> TIMES PER interval ;
 ON GENERATION TRIGGERS <process>... ;
 ON GENERATION [INTERRUPTS]  <process> ... ;
               [RESUMES   ]
               [ABORTS    ]
```

- If that stimulus in only a signal, without any other associated information it corresponds to an occurrence of an explicit EVENT object type :

```
EVENT <event>
  GENERATED BY <interface> AT FREQUENCY OF ... ;
  TRIGGERS <process> ... ;
  ...
```

Such explicit EVENT may be used to determine some specific points in time and be considered as GENERATED AT a given FREQUENCY BY an INTERFACE called "clock". Such a declaration may be useful to define an "ACTIVATION SCHEDULE" for a periodic task (*).

4.2.2. INTERNAL EVENTS

Internal EVENTS are those which occur inside the target system either as a state change of a PROCESS or as the GENERATION of an internal MESSAGE.

- A state change of a PROCESS is defined by :

```
PROCESS <process>
     [INCEPTION   ]
     [INTERRUPTION]
  ON [RESUMPTION  ]  TRIGGERS <process> ... ;
     [ABORTION    ]
     [TERMINATION ]
  ...
```

- The generation of an internal MESSAGE by a PROCESS :

```
MESSAGE <message>
   GENERATED BY <process> AT FREQUENCY OF ... ;
   ON GENERATION TRIGGERS <process> ... ;
   ...
```

Fig. 4.3. shows the basic object types and relationships for describing the EVENT/PROCESS flow of an information system.

(*) See CALENDAR and PARAMETER concepts, section 3.

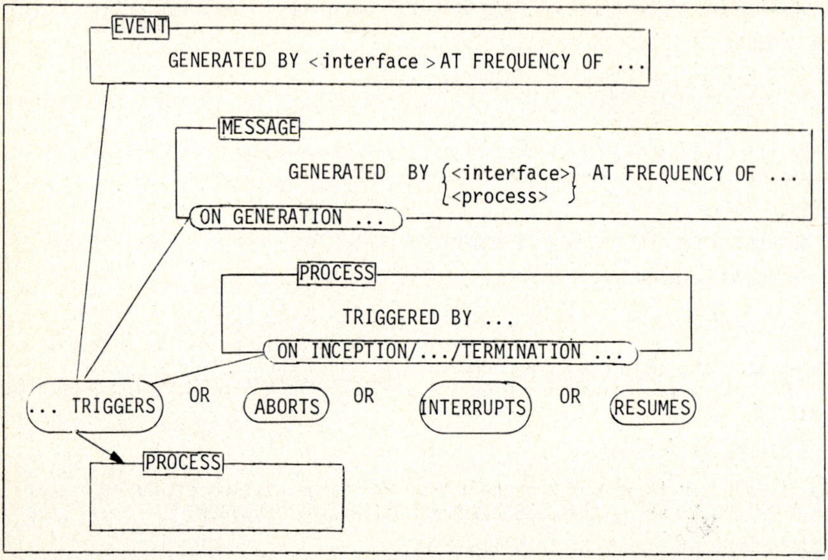

Fig. 4.3. Event/Process flow relationships

4.3. <u>Compound event : SYNCHRONIZATION POINT</u>

A system state change or EVENT occurs also when the system reaches a given state defined by a particular combination of basic events. A combination of basic EVENTS is called a SYNCHRONIZATION POINT (Fig. 4.4.).

The CONTRIBUTES/CONTRIBUTED relationship specify WHICH basic EVENT participate in the SYNCHRONIZATION POINT.

In the system life, a SYNCHRONIZATION POINT will be verified and the corresponding system state change (event) will occur ONLY when ALL the participating basic events will have occurred.

To indicate for a given SYNCHRONIZATION POINT how long the state generated by the occurrence of an EVENT contributing to that SYNCHRONIZATION POINT will last, the following statement is used :

<synchronization-point> CONTRIBUTED BY <event> UNTIL <event>.

In addition, it is possible to delay the participation of an EVENT in a SYNCHRONIZATION POINT by adding a construction "AFTER a given interval DELAY" to the CONTRIBUTES relationship :

```
SYNCHRONIZATION-POINT <name>
      CONTRIBUTED BY
     ┌ <event>                                    ┐
     │ ┌INCEPTION  ┐                              │ [UNTIL <event>]
    <  │    :      │ > OF <process>               > [AFTER <interval>]   ;
     │ └TERMINATION┘                              │
     └ GENERATION OF <message>                    ┘
```

A PREDICATE comment-entry is used to describe HOW basic EVENTS participate in the SYNCHRONIZATION POINT. To reach a higher formalization of this comment-entry so as to to allow an easy automatic generation of simulation language code, the PREDICATE will be described, as a boolean expression of basic EVENTS, using a simple - nested - syntax [6].

In this PREDICATE, it seems useful to introduce the capacity of choosing the contributing EVENTS on the basis of some of their ATTRIBUTES and SYSTEM-PARAMETERS. A "WHERE clause" could be used to qualify the EVENT. This WHERE clause would be another predicate, manipulating the ATTRIBUTES of the concerned EVENT and their attribute values in a boolean expression with its logical operators (AND/OR/NOT), relational operators (GREATER, EQUAL, LESS, ...) and constants.

Much convenience and flexibility could be achieved if the predicate could also base its behaviour :
- on ATTRIBUTES of other object-types, and
- on ATTRIBUTES of other occurrences.

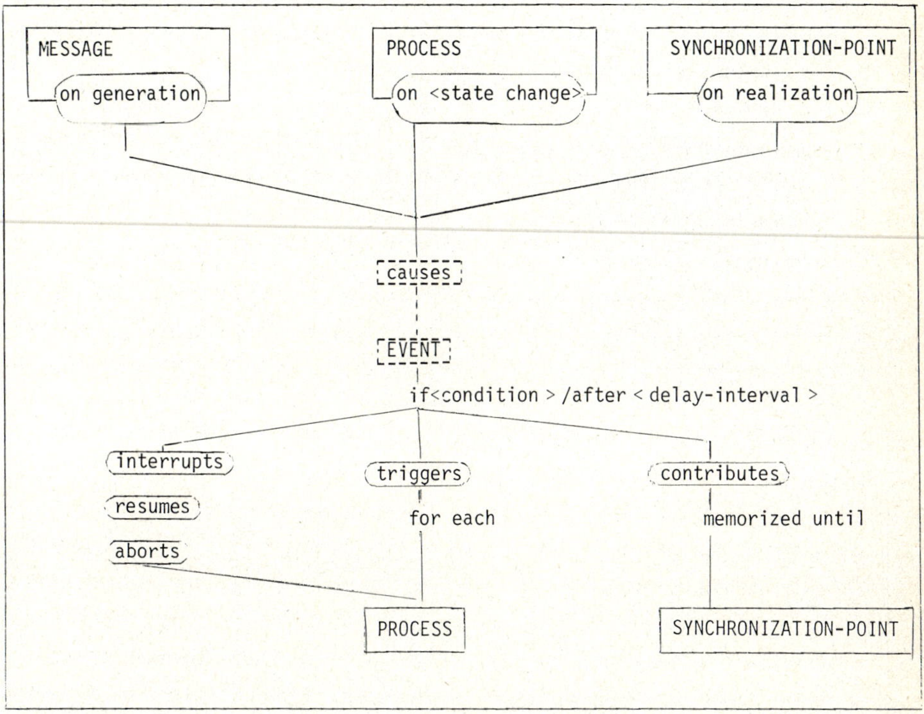

Fig. 4.4. Dynamical relationships

This capacity requires a special mechanism in order to connect :

- an ATTRIBUTE to a type : <attribute> OF <object-type>, and
- an ATTRIBUTE to an occurrence :
  <attribute> OF <object-type> WHERE clause.

4.4. Standard structures for dynamic information flows

The two basic object types (PROCESS and EVENT) may be linked, by using relationships described above, into arbitrary dynamic information flows. This section describes five structures which are frequently used as basic structures.

SEQUENTIAL STRUCTURES occur
when the termination of a PROCESS in the EVENT triggering the next PROCESS :
PROCESS first-process;
ON TERMINATION TRIGGERS second-process.

PARALLEL STRUCTURES occur
when an EVENT, such as a SYNCHRONIZATION POINT becoming true, triggers several PROCESSES of different types.
Subsequently, as shown in fig. 4.6., one of two situations may occur :

- either, the flow of each path will continue separately, (DIVERGENT parallel structure);
- or, the paths will converge to another SYNCHRONIZATION POINT, (CONVERGENT parallel structure).

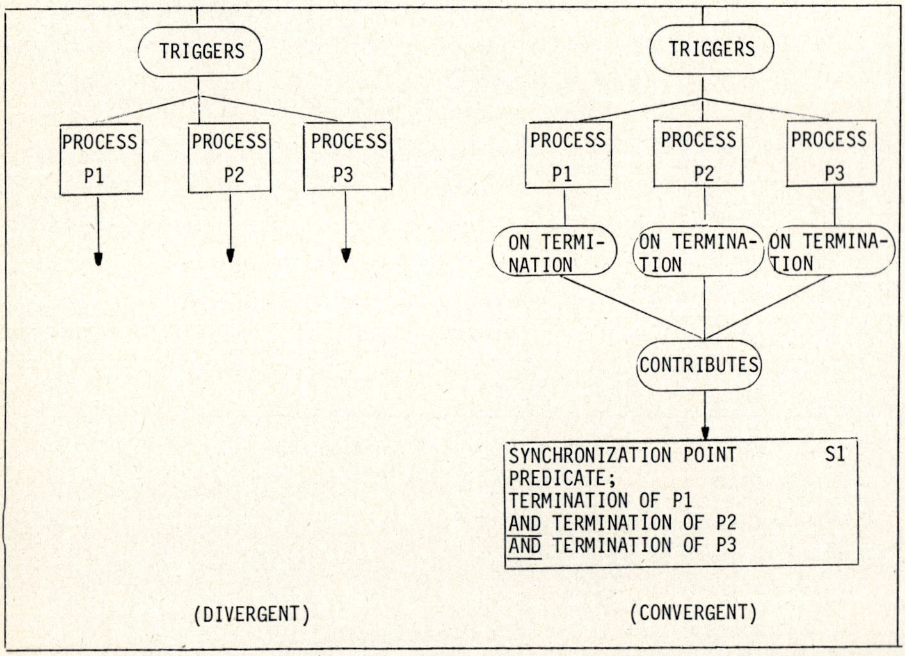

Fig. 4.6. Parallel dynamic information flows structures

DELAY STRUCTURE

It is possible to DELAY the dynamical effect (TRIGGERS, INTERRUPTS, RESUMES, ABORTS, CONTRIBUTES) of an EVENT by adding a clause "AFTER a given interval DELAY" to the dynamical statements :

```
{ <event >}   ( TRIGGERS ...          )
     :        (     :                 )   AFTER <interval >
     :        (     :                 )
     :        ( CONTRIBUTES TO ...    )
```

CONDITIONAL STRUCTURE occurs

when two paths are possible once the EVENT has occurred, but only one of these paths is to be choosen, depending on the state of a CONDITION, as illustrated in fig. 4.7.

To deal with this structure :

- a CONDITION OBJECT, naming a PREDICATE, is defined.
- this predicate (or CONDITION) is static, without any reference ot time since that aspect is localized in the SYNCHRONIZATION POINT.
- the current state of the CONDITION determines which path is to be followed
- the structure is specified by the following :
  <event >TRIGGERS <process(es)> [IF condition is TRUE] ;
  <event >TRIGGERS <process(es)> [IF condition is FALSE] ;

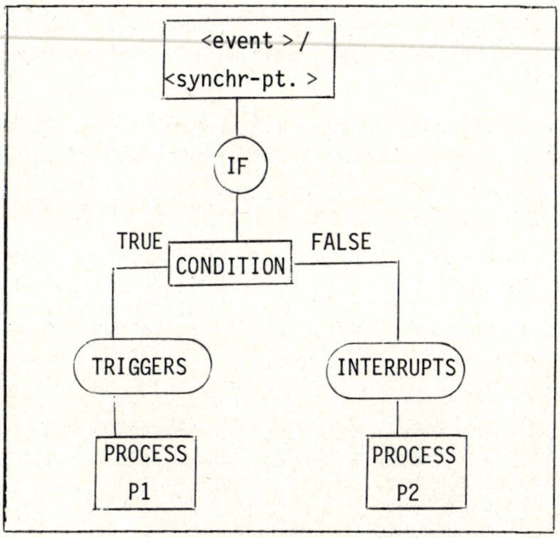

Fig. 4.7. Conditional structure

MULTIPLE OCCURRENCE TRIGGERING STRUCTURE occurs

when one EVENT triggers as many occurrences of a PROCESS type as there are elements in a SET or as specified by a SYSTEM-PARAMETER.

If we introduce that last refinement, the complete TRIGGERS relationships is defined by :

<event >TRIGGERS <process > [FOR EACH {<set > / <parameter >}][IF condition is {TRUE / FALSE}]

With this last structure may be associated a special case of synchronization-point to make clear the distinction between :

- a situation where the TERMINATION of each instance of the same PROCESS type CONTRIBUTES to different instances of the same SYNCHRONIZATION POINT object type,
- and a situation where the TERMINATION of ALL the instances of the same PROCESS type triggered by a common event, CONTRIBUTES TO the same occurrence of a SYNCHRONIZATION POINT object type.

5. SYSTEM ARCHITECTURE

As was stated in section 2, system dynamics is not fully specified until the resource requirements are not described; especially if the evaluation is to be performed by simulation analysis.

The system architecture topic deals with the description of the resources utilized in order to realize the logical functions of an information processing system. A system may be considered as a set of related processes and resources where a process may be any kind of work involved in the operation of the described system and a resource may be any kind of "available means" that the processes utilize in order to carry out their work.

Some new objects and relationships are added to provide a capability for describing this aspect of the information system similar to those defined in PSL 5.1. [13] .

5.1. System architecture objects

- PROCESS - dynamic entity corresponding to an execution (i.e. occurrence) of the PROCEDURE associated with a PROCESS type (see section 2 and 4).

The execution of a program, the recording of a customer order, an investment decision or an operation at a post office counter can be PROCESSES.

New object types are PROCESSOR, REUSABLE-RESOURCE and CONSUMABLE-RESOURCE.

- PROCESSOR - an object which can perform PROCESSES (i.e. execute the instructions of their PROCEDURE). This is to be used to model components of the system which use or consume resources in order to perform PROCESSES.

A computer, a customer service, a manager or a post office can be PROCESSORS.

- REUSABLE-RESOURCE - an object whose a part can be requested by a PROCESSOR when performing a PROCESS and, be at the system's disposal again once the PROCESS is terminated. "REUSABLE" resource cannot PERFORM PROCESSES or USE and CONSUME RESOURCES.

A central memory, terminals, micro-film viewers and desk-calculators can be REUSABLE-RESOURCES.

- CONSUMABLE-RESOURCE - an object which is irreplaceably consumed by PROCESSORS when performing PROCESSES and therefore the quantity consumed is no longer available when the PROCESS is terminated.

Computer paper, energy and money can be CONSUMABLE-RESOURCES.

5.2. System architecture object properties

The above defined objects may have some properties and each of these properties may have values. Most of those properties and their values are used to specify constraints on the resource availability.

- PRIORITY IS - a number may be assigned to each PROCESS competing for resources, to establish a procedence order among them.
- UNIT [OF MEASURE] - any UNIT of MEASURE (i.e. UNIT object) may be associated with a REUSABLE OF CONSUMABLE resource, while the activity of a PROCESSOR is only MEASURED in a unit of time (i.e. INTERVAL object). (*)
- {AVAILABLE / ACTIVE} FOLLOWING - a CALENDAR object may be associated with a RESOURCE or a PROCESSOR to specify the periods of availability of a RESOURCE or the active periods of a PROCESSOR

Sometimes, in addition to a global CALENDAR, it may be necessary to define specific CALENDARS of availability by PROCESS(ES).
For instance, a post office may not execute some operations during certain business hours :

```
DEFINE PROCESSOR post-office;
  ACTIVE FOLLOWING counter-business-hours-cal,
                   full-activity-calendar FOR cash-post-office-order;
```

- AVAILABILITY IS ... PER - during a given period of time (i.e. INTERVAL), the availability of a CONSUMABLE RESOURCE may be limited. For instance :

```
DEFINE CONSUMABLE-RESOURCE post-off-operational-expenditure;
  UNIT IS franc;
  AVAILABILITY IS exp-budget-estimate francs PER month;
```

- CAPACITY IS - often a REUSABLE RESOURCE - or a PROCESSOR - will have a limited CAPACITY

```
DEFINE REUSABLE-RESOURCE central-memory;
  UNIT IS K-byte;
  CAPACITY IS 512 K-bytes
```

Since the activity of a PROCESSOR, is always measured in UNIT of time, the CAPACITY-value gives the ACTIVITY level of the processor. For example :

```
DEFINE PROCESSOR post-office;
  UNIT IS minute;
  CAPACITY IS 5 ...
```

is understood to mean : 5 minutes of activity for each minute of elapsed time as if the post office was working during 5 minutes, in 1 minute, because there are 5 counters.

The CAPACITY-value of a resource may be varying in time, since the value of a SYSTEM-PARAMETER may change following a CALENDAR. (See section 3.1).

```
DEFINE PROCESSOR post-office
  CAPACITY IS number-of-working-counters ...

DEFINE SYSTEM PARAMETER number-of-working-counters;
  VALUE IS 6 FOLLOWING full-activity-calendar,
           4 FOLLOWING counter-business-hours-cal;
```

(*) See section 3.3.

• [CAPACITY] SHARABLE AMONG - the CAPACITY for a REUSABLE-RESOURCE - or a PROCESSOR - may be SHARABLE or not among several PROCESSES. The SHARABLE-value gives the number of "entry points" for a resource.

Different situations may be depicted using the combination of this value with the CAPACITY-value, as illustrated in the following examples :

DEFINE REUSABLE-RESOURCE computer memory;
  CAPACITY IS 512 K-bytes SHARABLE AMONG 10;
means that no more than 10 programs may simultaneously be in the computer's memory even if the memory is not fully saturated.

DEFINE PROCESSOR post-office;
  CAPACITY IS number-of-working-counters SHARABLE AMONG number-of-working-counters;
which models a post office as a set of interchangeable parallel processors.

The next example illustrates a situation where a logically no-sharable resource may be declared "time sharable" (*) i.e. where the SHARABLE-value is greater than the CAPACITY-value :

DEFINE PROCESSOR post-manager ;
  CAPACITY IS 1 SHARABLE AMONG 4;
which means that there is 1 post-manager who is able to perform, at the same time, 4 different activities.

5.3. System architecture relationships

The relationships between PROCESSES and RESOURCES may be of several kinds : a PROCESS may through the intermediary of a PROCESSOR :
- use a REUSABLE RESOURCE exclusively or share it with other processes for a certain period of time (**) or
- consume some quantity of a CONSUMABLE RESOURCE while it is running.

The objects and allowed relationships involved in describing system architecture are shown in fig. 5.1.

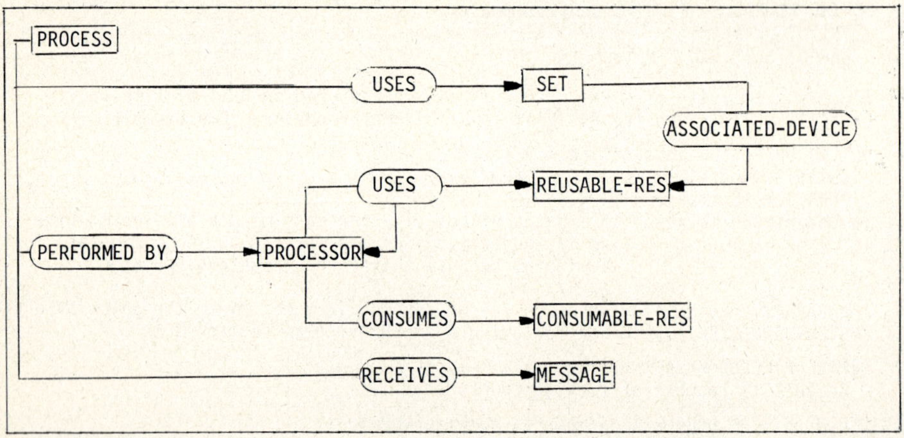

Fig. 5.1. System architecture relationships

(*) See below the statistical approach of the RATE clause in the USE relationship (5.4.)

(**) At a realization stage (i.e. simulation), since many PROCESSES are competing for use of the same limited RESOURCES, we will provide a capability for indicating some policy for their allocation (i.e. scheduling strategy).

- PERFORMS/PERFORMED - a PROCESSOR may PERFORM (i.e. carry out, do, realize) PROCESSES and every PROCESS (i.e. occurrence of the specified type) should be PERFORMED BY a PROCESSOR.

- PREEMPTS/PREEMPTED - when a PROCESS of higher priority is to be executed it may PREEMPT a (busy) PROCESSOR (i.e. one whose maximum CAPACITY has been reached), possibly interrupting other running PROCESSES.

- USES/USED - a PROCESSOR, when PERFORMING any PROCESS, may USE (i.e. require) REUSABLE-RESOURCES or, possibly, the activity of other PROCESSORS. These later PROCESSORS become "auxiliary" with respect ot the former PROCESSOR.

Example :

```
DEFINE PROCESSOR post-office-counters :
  PERFORMS postal-operations DURING ..., cash-post-office-order DURING ...
  USES postmen AT RATE OF ...
       franking-machine AT RATE OF
       post-manager AT RATE OF ...
```

This specifies that EACH postal-operations (i.e. each occurrence of that PROCESS type) requires a certain amount of the indicated RESOURCES during a certain period of time as described section 5.4.

- CONSUMES/CONSUMED - a PROCESSOR, to carry out a PROCESS, may CONSUME some amount of CONSUMABLE RESOURCES.

Once a quantity of CONSUMABLE RESOURCE is CONSUMED, it ceases to exist : the available CAPACITY continously falls until the next periodic supply.

Example :

```
DEFINE PROCESSOR post-office-counters;
  CONSUMES heating-expenses AT RATE OF ...
```

- [USE/CONSUME] TO PERFORM - since
  (a) a PROCESSOR may PERFORM PROCESSES of different types and
  (b) only a PROCESSOR may USE or CONSUME resources.
  then a capability is provided for describing USE or CONSUME relationships when a PROCESSOR performs specific named PROCESSES.

Example :

```
DEFINE PROCESSOR post-office-counters;
  USES postmen, franking-machine AT RATE OF ...
  USES desk-calculator AT RATE OF ... TO PERFORM cash-post-office-order;
```

This sate that, among all the postal operations, only the cash-post-office-order PROCESSES require the use of a desk-calculator in addition to the common requirements

The following relationships deal with the "information" resource :

- USES/USED - a PROCESS may share or USE exclusively one or several SETS.

• ASSOCIATED-DEVICE is - a SET is assigned to a physical device (i.e. ASSOCIATED-DEVICE). This relationship indicates the name and the amount of the REUSABLE-RESOURCE(S) that are indirectly used when the SET is manipulated (i.e. USED) by one or several PROCESSES sharing that SET.

Example :

```
DEFINE SET customer-file;
   USED BY record-customer-orders, list-customers, ...
   ASSOCIATED-DEVICES ARE 4000 index-cards OF manual-filing-system;
or ASSOCIATED-DEVICE is param-customer-sector tracks OF magnetic-disk;
```

• RECEIVES/RECEIVED - as indicated above, a PROCESS may RECEIVE MESSAGES which have previously been GENERATED by another PROCESS or by the system environment.

5.4. System architecture relationship properties

Most of the above mentioned relationships have clauses for specifying :
- How many RESOURCES are used or consumed : RATE-value,
- How long a REUSABLE RESOURCE is required for a process : DURING-value.

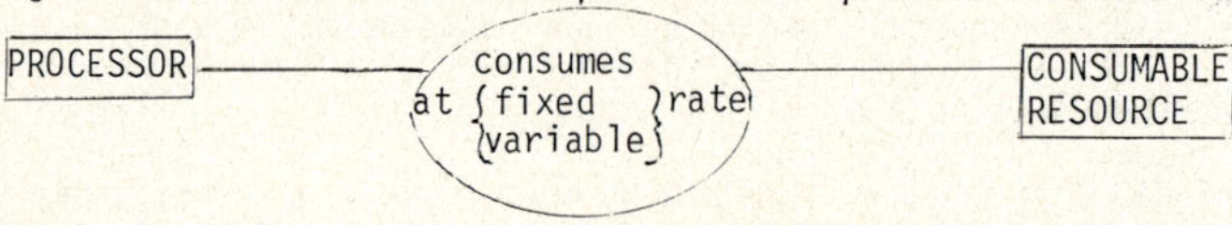

• AT {FIXED / VARIABLE} RATE OF - for a CONSUMES/CONSUMED relationship :
  • a FIXED rate gives the fixed amount of CONSUMABLE-RESOURCE consumed by the PROCESSOR, each time it starts to PERFORM a new PROCESS, whereas
  • a VARIABLE RATE indicates the portion of CONSUMABLE-RESOURCE consumed for each time UNIT of the PROCESSOR when performing a PROCESS.

The total amount of a CONSUMABLE-RESOURCE consumed by a PROCESS is evaluated by adding the FIXED-value to the VARIABLE-value multiplied with the DURING-value of the PERFORM relationship.

Example :

```
DEFINE PROCESSOR post-office-counters;
  CONSUMES overhead-expenses AT FIXED RATE OF 125 [ FRANCS]
           operational-expenditure AT VARIABLE RATE OF 25; [ understood : FRANCS
                                   per MINUTE of activity ]
  CONSUMES operational-expenditure AT VARIABLE RATE OF 50 TO PERFORM
                                   cash-post-office-order;
```

This later statement illustrates the use of a ternary relationship which allows to fixe, for a given named PROCESS, a new RATE-value in place of the standard one.

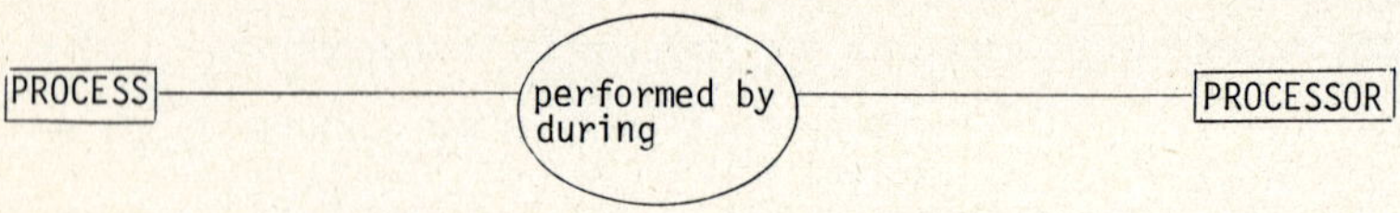

• DURING - Since the PROCEDURE of a PROCESS is considered as a black box, a delay construct is introduced to indicate the estimated execution time of a PROCESS occurrence.

By hypothesis, the DURING-value of a PERFORMS/PERFORMED relationship also represents the duration for which the specified PROCESSORS and REUSABLE-RESOURCES are required by the PROCESS.

Example :

```
DEFINE PROCESSOR post-office-counters
  UNIT IS minute;
  PERFORMS postal-operation DURING mean-exec-time,
           cash-post-office-order DURING 20 minutes;
```

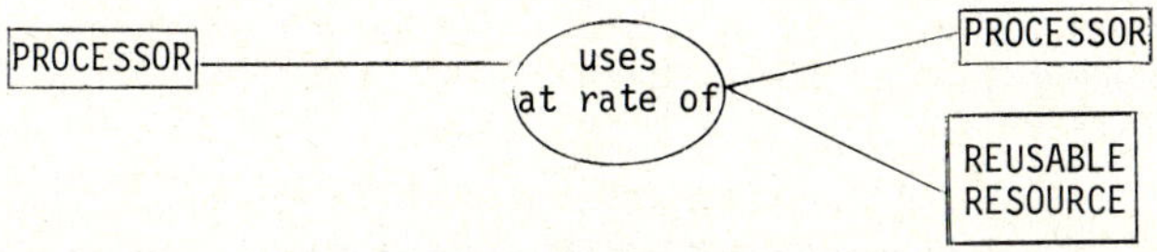

• AT RATE OF - for a REUSABLE-RESOURCE or an (auxiliary) PROCESSOR, the RATE-value of an USES/USED relationship gives the constant amount of the resource required when the PROCESSOR PERFORMS a PROCESS.

The RATE-value represents the average portion of the total CAPACITY of the resource that is used by each operating PROCESS.

In addition, when specifying a RATE-value, it is assumed that the resources required by a PROCESS, through the intermediary of a PROCESSOR, are :

1. completely allocated to the PROCESS in advance of its execution, and
2. required for its whole duration (see DURING-value).

The severity of these restrictions may be reduced by the use of :

1. an appropriate -statistical- RATE value, possibly allowing the (time-) sharing of a, strictly speaking, unsharable resource (see also SHARABLE-value)
2. an UTILIZES/UTILIZED (*) relationship that creates a subprocess with its own DURATION and its own resources consumption.

An example to illustrate this -statistical - view of the RATE-value is :

```
DEFINE PROCESSOR post-office-counters;
  USES postmen AT RATE OF 1 minute,
       franking-machine AT RATE OF 0.5,
       postmanager AT RATE OF 6 seconds;
  USES postmanager AT RATE OF 20 seconds, desk-calculator AT RATE OF 05
                 TO PERFORM cash-post-office-order;
```

Those statements model a situation :

- where each operation performed by the post-office requires, during the <u>whole</u> process execution time, (1) one postman, (2) one tenth of a post manager

(*) See section 4.1.

(i.e. 6 seconds of the post manager activity per minute of one "active" counter) and (3) one half franking-machine (in this later case, it may also be viewed as the use of a full franking-machine during the half of the process execution time).

- where each cash-post-office-order operation also requires - with the same interpretation -
  (1) the post-manager, but with another RATE,
  (2) and an additional resource, a desk-calculator.

A PERFORMS/PERFORMED relationship corresponds to an implicit USES/USED relationship which has an implicit RATE-value equivalent, by hypothesis, to the CAPACITY-value divided by the SHARABLE-value of the specified PROCESSOR.

Example :

```
DEFINE PROCESSOR post-manager;
  UNIT IS minute;
  CAPACITY IS 1 SHARABLE AMONG 5;
  PERFORMS managerial-function DURING 20 minutes; understood : AT RATE OF
           one fifth of his working CAPACITY.
```

- WITH EXCLUSION - this property of the USES/USED relationship indicates that a RESOURCE is USED EXCLUSIVELY by a PROCESS, independently of the specified RATE-, CAPACITY- and SHARABLE-values.
  In this case and even if the full CAPACITY IS not exceeded, no other PROCESSES may USE the mentioned resource during the former PROCESS operation.

6. SUMMARY AND CONCLUSION

This paper has outlined an information system description language. Its principle objective is to provide the capability to describe the system in sufficient detail so as to permit a simulation program to be derived automatically from it by the procedure shown in fig. 1.1. The next step in the project is to verify that the language meets this objective by applying it to one or more examples and to develop an algorithm to perform the translation automatically.

Another step in the project is to provide a metholology associated with the language which is both easy to use and sufficiently cost effective to persuade systems analysts and software engineer to use it in place of present system description and evaluation methods. Such a methodology should be tested by potential users.

AKNOWLEDGMENTS

The authors wishes to thank Professor D. Teichroew for his encouragement and specially for his detailed reading of the manuscript and his suggestions.

We thank also Mr. Hershey III E.A. for his comments and remarks.

Special acknowledgment is given to our colleagues Mrs. A.M. Hennebert and Mr. J.M. Leheureux for several and very helpful discussions.

References

|1| TEICHROEW D. and HERSHEY III. E.A.: PSL-PSA : a computer-aided technique for structured documentation and analysis of information processing systems, IEEE Transactions on Software engineering, vol. SE-3, n°1, January 1977

|2| ISDOS PROJECT : Problem Statement Language , (version 4.2.) - User's Manual, ISDOS Reference 7742-0142, University of Michigan, May 1977.

|3| ISDOS PROJECT : Problem statement Analyser, (version 4.2.) - User's Manual, ISDOS Reference 7742-0144, University of Michigan, May 1977.

|4| TEICHROEW D. and SPEWAK S. : Research in Simulation of Information System - guidelines for research by the ISDOS project, Manuscript, University of Michigan, February 1978.

|5| BODART F. : Logical specifications for system dynamics - An extension to PSL, ISDOS working paper n° 183, April 1977.

|6| KONSYNSKI B. : A model of computer-aided definition and analysis of information system requirements, Ph. D. Thesis, Purdue University, December 1975.

|7| HOLBAEK-HANSSEN, HANDLYKKEN and NYGAARD : Systems description and the DELTA language, DELTA Projekt report n°4, Norwegian computing Center, Oslo, February 1977.

|8| BELL, BIXLER and DYER : An extendable Approach to computer-aided software requirements Engineering, in IEEE Transactions on Software engineering, vol. SE-3, n°1, January 1977.

|9| DUFOURS J.F. : Modèle dynamique de système de traitement en organisation administrative, Centre de Recherches en Informatique de Nancy, N-76 R006, 1976.

|10| PECCOUD F. : MACSI, Méthode d'aide à la conception des systèmes d'information, Thèse d'Etat, Université de Grenoble, 1975.

|11| WILLIS R. : DAS - An Automated system to support design analysis, in Proceedings, 3de International Conference on Software engineering, May 1978, Atlanta.

|12| ROLLAND C. and FOUCAUT : Concepts for design of an information system conceptual schema and its utilization in Remora Project, Very Large Data Base, Berlin, 1978.

|13| ISDOS PROJECT : Problem Statement Language,(version 5.1.) - User's Manual, ISDOS Reference 79A51-0171, University of Michigan, February 1979.

|14| BODART F. and PIGNEUR Y. : Specifications dynamiques d'un système d'informations, Séminaire INFORSID, Cergy PONTOISE, Octobre 1978.

|15| PER AANSTAD CASCADE/2 FUNDAMENTALS, A user manual, The Computing Center at the University of Trondheim, 1976.

Formal Models and Practical Tools
for Information Systems Design
H.-J. Schneider, Editor
North-Holland Publishing Company

POSITION PAPERS FOR THE PANEL SESSION:

What is a Formal Requirements Specification? What does it Contain, How is it Structured and For What is it Useful?

Chairman: A. Sølvberg

Panel Members: J.K. Buckle, Börje Langefors, Heinrich C. Mayr

I. J.K. Buckle:

Requirements for System Requirements Definitions

The production of a definition of system requirements is the first step in a series of transformations from a vaguely expressed need for a system to an actual working manifestation. It is perhaps the most difficult and important transformation since its purpose is to specify the functional description of the final system and the boundary conditions for its realisation. It thus forms not only the basis for all further work but also the means by which the quality and applicability of the final system can be measured. There are three main problems concerned with the production of the definition: unlike all later transformations we have no firm base from which we can work; although much useful and interesting work is being done there is as yet no practically usable mathematics in which to express the functional description; and, because systems are, or should be, produced to satisfy human requirements, the needs will be expressed in ambiguous human fashion and the definition must be not just logically correct but easily understandable in human terms if its quality as an expression of the real needs is to be capable of being checked.

It should be noted that the lack of a mathematical functional description is not peculiar to computer or information systems. There is similarly no mathematics to describe the functions of a petrochemical complex, for example. However, in most other systems it is the boundary conditions which are more strict and easily expressible. The numbers of inputs to and outputs from the system, for example, are often fewer and almost better controlled than in information systems. We seem to be prepared to tackle in information systems much more complexity than other engineering disciplines - one wonders whether this optimism is justified by our success rate. Also, many of the boundary conditions in other fields have a physical manifestation which is inescapable. This is not true of information systems.

The need for the requirements definition to be easily understandable by the human potential users of the system (who will in general not be experts in system engineering) and at the same time to provide an unambiguous basis for the later transformations of the design and implementation stages, places severe constraints on the form of the functional specification. Experience with human understanding of complexity suggests a number of attributes that the specification should have. The following are perhaps some of the more important features.

1. A Hierarchic Format:

Trees seem to be a fundamental human approach to the structuring of complexity. It is certainly necessary to understand not only sub-functions of the system in isolation but also their relationship to each other, and this is best expressed as a hierarchy of specifictions with each level introducing a limited amount of extra detail. It should be noted that the modularity introduced by specifying the system in this way is not necessarily the modularity that must be adopted in the design and implementation. For example, it is normally easier to describe control functions in association with the process being controlled, while for implementation it is often more convenient to group all control functions together.

2. Transparency to design and implementation methodologies:

The process of requirements definition, that is, imposing a structure on vaguely expressed needs, is largely independent of the area of system application. To have a specification form which presupposes a particular implementation method is therefore unduly limited. Worse, such a form encourages consideration of 'how?' before 'why?' and 'what?' have been answered. A legitimate possible result of a good requirements definition should, after all, be a non-automated system, or even no system at all!

3. The ability to express viewpoints:

All information systems are in essence a model of some reality and it must be possible to describe the system from this viewpoint. Such a description must describe the real items in the external world with which the system is concerned and the actions which can take place on them. It must not confuse this with descriptions of the data structures which will represent them. We can call this viewpoint the external view. Equally important is the way in which a user will see the final system. He wishes to know how he interacts with the system, what he has to do and supply to it and what he can get from it. He must use this information to measure the fitness of the system described against his requirements. Finally, there is the viewpoint of the man who will use the specification as input to the next transformation process, whom we can call the implementor. We must express, in particular, boundary condition limitations on implementation, component parts of the system described and the interactions between them. The description must thus be capable of displaying these three viewpoints in isolation and also of relating them and allowing cross-checking for consistency. (It is interesting to note in passing that the same three viewpoints are equally applicable to the products of the later transformations - outline and detailed design, and implementation - although the people concerned with each viewpoint are different.)

4. Formalism:

The specification must be sufficiently formal to allow verification of consistency and completeness by logical proof, automatic checks, sampling techniques, simulation etc. This is not to say that is must resemble existing implementation languages. Indeed, since these are defined to allow the unabmiguous specification of algotithms and data structures they are by difinition unsuitable under the transparency requirement. Since human understanding is of paramount importance, by both looking at other branches of engineering and by remembering Confucius, a good case can be made out for a pictorial representation rather than a totally verbal or numerical one.

5. Maintainability:

Even if a system is implemented and forgotten, the requirements definition has the longest usefulness of all the system documentation since it is produced first but is used last to state the criteria for the measurement of system quality. In practice, of course, most systems last for much longer than their development period and during their lifetime they are changed and enhanced. It is of great value if the requirements documentation can be kept up to date with such changes since it should form the first object of sutdy when new features or other enhancements are proposed. This presupposes at least the availability of tools to allow easy maintenance of the definition and the ability to apply the same sort of checks to the revised document as were applied to the original one.

In considering any method of producing a requirements definition, these five points should be used as a first order checklist for determining whether the output of the method will meet the requirements of requirements definition itself.

II. Börje Langefors, University of Stockholm

My personal addition to the theme: How is the specification developed and constructed?

1. What is a formal requirement specification?

1.1. What is a requirement, in connection with system design?

Not all external (usage-focussed) properties are necessary. Some are more or less desirable. They call for a trade-off between desirability and consequences. When both the desires and the consequences have been estimated/developed/predicted, negotiations involving all the relevant people or interests have to result in decisions about the level at which desires can and shall be satisfied. This, then, defines what is to be required from the design.

1.2. A requirement statement is a goal statement.

Both state what is to be achieved and both call for a resource budget, but leave it to the implementors to decide how it is to be achieved. A requirement statement, like any other goal statement, must be clear and intelligible to both clients/users and to designers/implementors.

1.3. A formal requirements specification is an operational goal structure, essentially. It should be possible to assess the fulfilment (or not) of the specification. This should be done both in advance (correctness proof of design) and ex post (system evaluation/system audit). It should also be possible to assess/debate/negotiate the specification before design - a design can be proven correct in the sense of being consistent with the specification but the specification can not be proven - it can only be critically assessed from a number of aspects. The specification must be formal and stringent, to satisfy its functions, but it must be free from technical details and jargon. This is now known to be feasible.

2. For what is a formal specification useful?

- A requirements specification is a specification -

2.1. A specification is necessary (not merely useful) for any design to satisfy user needs or wants. To satisfy needs, designers must know then and the needs must be feasible.

As shown in [Langefors 1966, Theor. Analysis of I.S.] the design of a complex system to satisfy needs can only be achieved through a structured/iterative process in which subsystem specifications are defined such that they fulfil the system specification, and so forth. As was also shown there, the subspecifications ("subsystem structures") must be formalized (made "constructive") in order to allow the proving that one level is correct ("workable" = satisfies the spec) before proceeding to the next level. It was also shown that such formal subspecifications are necessary in order to enable communication, stringent enough, between distinct people concerned - without raising impossible requirements for sharing technical knowledge and organizational/managerial knowledge.

2.2. A structure of formal specifications is sufficient for workability proofs (correctness proofs) while "how questions" (implementation details) can be left open, without impairing the proof procedure.

2.3. A formal specification (structure) is a basis both for system usefulness evaluation and possibility and cost estimates.

2.4. A formal specification called for involves the system stakeholders in a pre-design assessment process and negotiations which helps users avoid being trapped into premature technology-dominated directions.

2.5. The formal specification usage allows managerial control of the design process (by whoever belong to the decision-making bodies).

2.6. The formal specification is the instrument for managing the changes. Regardless of the reasons for change (implementation difficulties or opportunities or new assessment of values) it has to be negotiated in the goal process before being authorized and implemented. Changes affecting the external system properties must be documented as a changed specification.

3. How is the formal specifiction structured?

The above discussion, [Langefors 1966] , clarifies some of the essential structure (2.1, 2.2). Details remain to be developed but it is important that agreements be obtained as soon as possible, if only in an incremental procedure, developing in the future.

4. What does the formal specification contain?

A lot has been said above about the content. However, detailed lists of spec. contents ought to be developed and agreed upon. Ideally, a system specification should state everything that the implementors need to know about the user needs and desires and the needs of the application. This includes trade-off decision rules when alternative levels or designs are available.

5. How is the specification developed and constructed?

The specification is the critical system design statement.

The development of the specification should be given at least the same effort and care as the techn. design. It must involve users/systemeers in a creative search-learning process. Activities must be undertaken/initiated/invented that involve the users actively and engagedly. It has to do with the future work of the users, primarily and only secondarily with technical means and implementation.

III. Heinrich C. Mayr, University of Karlsruhe

Some remarks in response to
"What is a formal requirement specification?..."

It is commonly agreed that "requirement analysis" is an important part of any system development process. In technical engineering this is a task of daily practice, supported by well-developed modelling and simulation methods. This task yields a set of physical reference values that are to be met by the future system within permissible limits.

In consequence, most authors discussing requirements propose a list of particular tasks that have to be fulfilled before approaching the system design. Others present a user interface to a program system for computer-aided requirement manipulation, and assume that most imaginable requirements could be formulated within this interface. Doubts as to the completeness of these approaches are wise, since the various proposed sets of concepts differ one from another. On the other hand, some kind of checklist will always be indispensable.

It is widely agreed that requirements refer to aspects that have to be studied before beginning with system design [4]. This seems to me a starting point to illustrate more clearly the notion of requirement and to separate it from others. For we can begin our considerations within the terminology of general system theory as will be outlined in the following.

An information system is a dynamic system that has to fulfil tasks by performing activities. The entirety of tasks is called the system function, that of the activities the system behaviour. Tasks are defined by the following characteristics:

- . a subject (performing the activity)
- . objects (affected by the activity)
- . location (spatial place of execution)
- . time (date of execution)
- . tools (supporting the execution)
- . type of activity

Evidently, if one considers an information system as a unit and speaks about its tasks, subject, location and tools can be disregarded. Furthermore, since in many applications time is defined in the sense of immediate task execution after a request, we distinguish between asynchronous and termporized tasks.

There exist several formal techniques for the specification of asynchronous tasks, among which the algebraic technique[1,2] seems to me the most promising one. It integrates the definition of objects and activities and their operands in a rather simple but precise formal fashion. However, an extension to the specification of temporized tasks still remains to be investigated.

Whereas the algebraic technique is a useful tool for the description of tasks, it offers no vehicle to find out <u>why</u> particular tasks have to be added to the system function. This will be the first important aspect of a "requirement analysis". I guess that we will never achieve an integrated formal tool for this purpose because of the close dependencies between the "necessity" of certain tasks and subjective opinions or decisions. However, formal techniques for the solution of particular subproblems are of great help in finding decisions, and can avoid decisions with unforeseen and undesired consequences. Such techniques imply the definition of formal concepts for reality modelling [5] and simulation, i.e., for describing the superordinate system in which the information system has to be integrated. Here I only want to mention two suitable approaches: the net theory [3], and the context analysis as discussed (with different terms) in [4,5,6].

Closely related with the question of "necessary" activities is the question, which indirect consequences and effects they will have, i.e. effects that are not explicitly stated as part of the respective tasks. An exact evaluation of this question may lead to further tasks handling the side effects.

The second essential point of requirement analysis concerns economical aspects like cost limits and optimal dates of task execution corresponding to marketing conditions. Obviously, this investigation can only be carried out in cooperation with specialists of industrial management and marketing. Formal modelling and evaluation techniques exist to some extent, e.g., in the area of operations research.

A third class of questions concern qualitative standards like reliability, flexibility, usability ("user friendliness"), availability etc. Among others they are influenced by economical aspects. Most of them cannot be quantified by measureable and calculable values and are, therefore, not accessible by formal methods.

Summing up, requirement analysis is a very heterogenous set of modelling, simulation, estimation, evaluation, and decision processes. It has to be carried out in a teamwork, i.e., by specialists of different problem areas, and it should lead to a complete statement of system tasks and related marginal conditions. It may partly be supported by specialized formal techniques, but there will be no selfcontained requirement analysis algorithm.

References

[1] Lockemann, P.Y.; Mayr, H.C.; Dittrich, K.R. (1979): A Pragmatic Approach to the Algebraic Specification of Software Modules. Int. Rep. 1/79, Univ. of Karlsruhe.

[2] Lockemann, P.C.; Mayr, H.C.; Weil, W.H.; Wohlleber, W.H. (1978): Data Abstractions for Database Systems. ACM Trans. on Database Systems Vol. 4,1,March 79.

[3] Petri, C.A. (1973): Concepts of Net Theory. Proc. Symp. on Mathematical Foundations of Comp. Science, High Tatras, pp. 137-146.

[4] Ross, D.T.; Schomann, K.E. (1977): Structured Analysis for Requirements Definition. IEEE Trans. on Software Engineering, Vol. SE3, No.1, Jan 77, pp. 6-15.

[5] Sundgren, B. (1978): Database Design and Practice - Towards an integrated methodology. Proc. 4th Conf. on Very Large Data Bases, Berlin 78, pp. 3-16.

[6] Teichroew, D.; Hershey, E.A. (1977): PSA/PSL: A Computer-Aided Technique for Structured Documentation and Analysis of Information Processing Systems. IEEE Trans. on Software Engineering, Vol. SE3, No.1, Jan 77, pp. 41-48.

LIST OF PARTICIPANTS

M. Alford
TRW
77o2 W. Governors Drive
Huntsville, Alabama 358o5
USA

F. Aschim
Sentralinstitutt for
Industriell Forskning
Forskningsveien 1
Oslo 3
Norway

F. van Assche
Control Data Belgium
46 Avenue des Arts
1o4o Bruxelles
Belgium

K. Augländ
Rogaland Distriktshøgskole
Ullandhaug
4ooo Stavanger
Norway

E. Bartezzaghi
Istitudo di Elettrotecnica
ed Elettronica
Politecnico di Milano
Piazza Leonardo da Vinci 32
2o133 Milano
Italy

Th.M.A. Bemelmans
Klaprooshof 12
5672 XC Nuenen
Netherlands

H. Biller
Siemens AG., DAPS DB2
Otto-Hahn-Ring 6
D-8ooo München 83
Germany

F. Bodart
Institut d'Informatique
Facultes Universitaires
N.D. de la Paix
rue Grandgagnage 21
B-5ooo Namur
Belgium

P.G. Bosch
Lid Nederlands Instituut
van Register Accountants
7491 CR Delden
Leeuwerikstraat 21
Nederland

A. Bosman
Faculteit der Economische Wetenschappen
Rijksuniversiteit
Afdeling Bedrijfshuishoudkunde
Groningen
Oude Boteringestraat 23
Holland

G. Bracchi
Istituto de Elettrotecnica
ed Elettronica
Politecnico di Milano
Piazza L. da Vinci 32
I-2o133 Milano
Italy

J. Buckle
83 Dukes Ride
Crowthorne, Berkshire
UK

J. Buxton
Dept. of Computer Science
University of Warwick
Coventry CV4 7AL
Warwickshire
UK

L. Capper
Hatfield Polytechnic
P.O. Box 1o9
Hatfield, Hertfordshire
UK

B. Cohen
Standard Telecommunications Laboratories
London Road
Harlow, Essex CM17 9NA
UK

S. Cool
The Legol Project
London School of Economics
& Political Science
Houghton Street
London WC2A 2AE
UK

S. Douglas
Dept. Systems Analysis
London School of Economics
& Political Science
Houghton Street
London WC2A 2AE
UK

J. Efstathiou
Durham University
Computer Science Laboratory
South Road
Durham DH1 3LE
UK

H. Ellis	ICL Computer House 292-298 High Street Slough, Berkshire UK
K. Grindley	London School of Economics & Political Science Houghton Street London WC2A 2AE UK
M. Hamilton	Higher Order Software, Inc. 8o6 Massachusetts Avenue Cambridge, Massachusetts o2139 USA
J. Hawgood	Durham University Science Laboratories South Road Durham DH1 3LE UK
H. Hackenroth	Ingénieur de Recherche au Centre d'Etude Technique de l'Equipement d'Aix-en-Provence (Minist. de l'Environnement - Zone Industrielle) 1329o - Les Milles France
T. Hoare	Oxford University Computing Lab. Programming Research Group 45 Banbury Road Oxford OX2 6PE UK
M. Jackson	1o1 Hamilton Terrace London NW8 UK
M. Janning	University of Stockholm Dept. Information Processing S-1o691 Stockholm Sweden
E. Jungert	Dept. Mathematics Informatics Laboratory Linkoping University S-58183 Linkoping Sweden
L. Kahn	University of Stockholm Dept. of Information Processing S-1o691 Stockholm Sweden

H. Kangassalo	University of Tampere Dept. of Computer Science Tampere Finland
P. Kerola	Oulun Yliopisto Inst. of DP Science (Tietojenkasittelyopin Laitos) Linnanmaa SF-9o57o Oulu 57 Finland
M. Klein	C.E.S.A. Dept. Informatique F-7835o Jouy-en-Josas France
Kouloumdjian	Montée du Carret o17oo Miribel France
P. Kovacs	National Bank of Hungary V Rosenberg Hazaspar U. 4 Budapest Hugary
F. Land	Dept. Systems Analysis London School of Economics & Political Science Houghton Street London WC2A 2AE UK
B. Langefors	University of Stockholm Fisktorpsvagen 16o/Fack S-1o691 Stockholm Sweden
T.J. Lincoln	IBM UK Ltd. 389 Chiswick High Road London W4 4AL UK
P. Lindgreen	Danish State Railways Organisation Office Kalvebod Brygge 3o.4 D-156o Copenhagen V Denmark
M. Lundeberg	Stockholm University Dept. Information Processing S-1o691 Stockholm Sweden
R. Lundquist	Infologigruppen AB Fiskargatan 14 S-11645 Stockholm Sweden

R. Maes
Katholieke University Leuven
Dept. voor Toegepaste
Economische Wetenschappen
Dekenstraat 2
B-3ooo Leuven
Belgium

A. de Maio
Istituto de Ricerca Intervento
sui Sistemi Organizzativi
Via Leopardi 1
I-2o123 Milano
Italy

C.P. Marks
Director of Systems Training
Civil Service College
11 Belgrave Road
London SW1
UK

P. Mason
The Legol Project
London School of Economics
& Political Science
Houghton Street
London WC2A 2AE
UK

A. Mayne
National Computing Centre Ltd.
Oxford Road
Manchester Ml 7ED
UK

H.C. Mayr
Universität Karlsruhe
Institut für Informatik II
Postfach 638o
D-75oo Karlsruhe 1
Germany

J.L. le Moigne
Grasce
Faculte d'Economie Appl.
3, Ave. R. Schuman
F-13621 Aix-en-Provence
France

B.E. Meyer
Institut für Angewandte Informatik
Technische Universität Berlin
Kurfürstendamm 2o2
D-1ooo Berlin 15
Germany

M. Newton
Faculty of Maths
Open University
Walton Hall
Milton Keynes MK7 6AA
UK

H. Oftedal	Division of Computing Science The Norwegian Institute of Technology N-7o34 Trondheim - NTH Norway
T.W. Olle	T. William Olle Associates, Ltd. 27 Blackwood Close West Byfleet, Surrey KT14 6PP UK
J.P. Paillard	IMAG BP 53 X 38o41 Grenoble-Cedex France
M.Ph. Pellaumail	Ingénieur à la Compagnie I.B.M. France Service 29o4 75 Avenue E. Vaillant Boite Postale 21o 921o8-Boulogne Billancourt Cedex France
Y. Pigneur	Institut d'Informatique Facultes Universitaires N.D. de la Paix Rue Grandgagnage 21 B-5ooo Namur Belgium
A. Pirotte	MBLE Research Laboratory Avenue em. van Becelaere 2 B-117o Brussels Belgium
J.A. van der Pool	IBM Nederland N.V.-HDK 8-C P.O. Box 9999 1oo6 CE Amsterdam Holland
P.H. Prowse	Esso Europe Inc. Controller's Dept. 5 Hanover Square London W1R OHQ UK
V. Rajkovic	University of Ljubfiann "I. Stefan" Institute Jarnova 39 Ljubcjana Yugoslavia
J. van Rees	Dept. of Mathematics Technical University P.O. Box 356 26oo AJ Delft Holland

W.E. Riddle
Dept. Computer Science
Campus Code No. 43o
University of Colorado
Boulder, Colorado 8o3o9
USA

C. Rolland
IRIA
Domaine de Voluceau
Rocquencourt
7815o le Chesnay
France

H.-J. Schneider
Institut für Angewandte Informatik
Technische Universität Berlin
Kurfürstendamm 2o2
D-1ooo Berlin 15
Fed.Rep.Germany

D. Seibt
Fachbereich Wirtschaftswissenschaften
Universität Essen/GHS
Universitätsstraße 2
D-43oo Essen L. FRG
Germany

A. Sernadas
Dept. Systems Analysis
London School of Economics
& Political Science
Houghton Street
London WC2A 2AE
UK

E. Shapiro
2o Neve Shaanan
Jerusalem
Israel

J.J.M.G. Snijders
Control Data Europe Inc.
46, Avenue des Arts
B-1o4o Bruxelles
Belgium

H.G. Sol
Dept. of Management Sciences
University of Groningen
P.O. Box 8oo
Groningen
Nederland

A. Sølvberg
Division of Computer Science
The Norwegian Institute of Technology
N-7o34 Trondheim-NTH
Norway

R. Stamper
The Legol Project
London School of Economics
& Political Science
Houghton Street
London WC2A 2AE
UK

P.M. Stocker	Computing Centre University of East Anglia Norwich NR4 7TJ UK
G. Stolker	DESISCO Nederland B.V. Elkenweg 48 Amsterdam Holland
E.K. Surboeck	Bunzl & Biach AG Postfach 161 A-1o2o Wien Österreich
J.M. Sykes	ICI Ltd. Central Managerial Services Fulshaw Hall Wilmslow Cheshire UK
R. Traunmüller	Institut für Statistik und Informatik Johannes Kepler Universität Linz A-4o45 Linz-Auhof Austria
C. Tully	University of York Heslington York Yo1 5DD UK
V. Uva	Corso Roma 2 Foggia Italy
A.A. Verrijn-Stuart	Institute of Applied Mathematics & Computer Science University of Leiden P.O. Box 9512 23oo Leiden Holland
K. Voss	Gesellschaft für Mathematik und Datenverarbeitung - GMD Schloß Birlinghoven D-52o5 St. Augustin Germany
A.I. Wasserman	Section on Medical Information Science University of California San Francisco, California 94143 USA

H. Wedekind
Betriebswirtschaftslehre
TH Darmstadt
Hochschulstraße 1
D-61oo Darmstadt
Germany

S. Zeldin
Higher Order Software, Inc.
8o6 Massachusetts Avenue
Cambridge, Massachusetts o2139
USA